GREAT CAKES, PIES, COOKIES, MUFFINS & *MORE*

SECRETS FOR SENSATIONAL SWEETS AND FABULOUS FAVORITE RECIPES

CAROLE WALTER

RODALE

Photograph and illustration credits are on page 385.

Book design by Patricia Field

Library of Congress Cataloging-in-Publication Data
Walter, Carole.
    Great cakes, pies, cookies, muffins & more : secrets for sensational sweets and fabulous favorite recipes / Carole Walter.
        p.   cm.
    Includes index.
    ISBN-13 978–1–60529–781–1   hardcover
    ISBN-10 1–60529–781–X   hardcover
  1. Baking. 2. Desserts. I. Title.
    TX765.W324 2009
    641.8'15—dc22   2009029758

2 4 6 8 10 9 7 5 3 1 hardcover

We inspire and enable people to improve their lives and the world around them

For more of our products visit **rodalestore.com** or call 800-848-4735

contents

everyday favorite cookies

carole's really great chocolate chip cookies

rocky road garganchewas

chocolate chip oatmeal cookies

oatmeal walnut crispies

oatmeal raisin cookies

nancy's nuthouse cookies

white chocolate chunk macadamia cookies

chock full of crunchies

peanut jumbles

honey-roasted peanut butter cookies

peanut butter balls

almondates

chocolate snowcaps

zach's chocolate coconut devils

black forest chews

joanna pruess's molasses spice cookies

crispy gingersnaps

crystallized ginger and macadamia wafers

snickerdoodles

crackly cinnamon wafers

sesame coins

poppy seed thumbprints

italian macaroons

rustic maple pecan cookies

golden almond amaretti

carole's really great chocolate chip cookies

MAKES ABOUT FORTY 2¾-INCH COOKIES

I love this recipe for chocolate chip cookies. It was truly a challenge to create one that was different because so many exist.

What I tried to zero in on was the most common complaint that bakers have about their cookies: the spreading of the cookie dough during baking. As a rule, cookies spread because of too much moisture in the dough. To overcome this problem, I created a recipe using very finely ground oatmeal to bind the dough and prevent it from spreading. The presence of the oatmeal is not detectable and the end result is delectable.

¾ cup lightly packed very fresh dark brown sugar

½ cup quick (1-minute) oatmeal

⅓ cup granulated sugar

1¾ cups all-purpose flour, spooned in and leveled

½ teaspoon baking soda

½ teaspoon salt

1 cup (2 sticks) unsalted butter, slightly firm

2 tablespoons light corn syrup

1 large egg

2 teaspoons pure vanilla extract

8 ounces fine-quality bittersweet or semisweet chocolate, such as Lindt Bittersweet, cut into ¼- to ½-inch pieces, or 1½ cups semisweet chocolate chips

1½ cups coarsely chopped walnuts (see page 356)

AT A GLANCE

PAN: Cookie sheets

PAN PREP: Ungreased

RACK LEVELS: Upper and lower thirds

OVEN TEMP: 375°F

BAKING TIME: 10–12 minutes

DIFFICULTY: 1

1. Position the racks in the upper and lower thirds of the oven. Heat the oven to 375°F.

2. Place the brown sugar, oatmeal, and granulated sugar in the work bowl of a food processor fitted with the steel blade and process 2½ to 3 minutes, stopping occasionally to pulse. The oatmeal must be very finely ground.

3. In a medium bowl, strain together the flour, baking soda, and salt. Set aside.

4. In the large bowl of an electric mixer fitted with the paddle attachment, mix the butter and corn syrup together on medium-low speed until smooth and creamy, about 1 minute. Add the oatmeal-sugar mixture in three additions and mix for 2 minutes. Add the egg and vanilla and mix for 1 minute longer, scraping down the bowl as needed. Reduce the mixer speed to low, add the dry ingredients one-half at a time, and mix *just* until blended. Using a large rubber spatula, fold in the chocolate pieces and walnuts.

5. Drop 1½-inch mounds of dough, about the size of a large walnut, from the tip of a tablespoon onto cookie sheets, about 3 inches apart. Scrape down the side of the bowl occasionally to ensure even distribution of the chocolate chips and nuts. Bake the cookies for 10 to 12 minutes, or until the edges *begin* to turn a golden brown. To ensure even browning, toward the end of baking time rotate the pans top to bottom and front to back. *Do not overbake.*

6. Remove the cookies from the oven and let stand for 2 minutes. Using a thin, metal spatula, carefully loosen. When firm enough to handle, transfer to cooling racks.

STORAGE: Store in an airtight container, layered between strips of wax paper, for up to 5 days. These cookies may be frozen.

rocky road garganchewas

MAKES TWENTY 4-INCH COOKIES

The tasty trio of ingredients that makes bumpy Rocky Roads so popular is miniature marshmallows, nuts, and chocolate. You've seen this flavor combination in a variety of sweets from candy, to pastries, to ice cream, and now—in a giant cookie! When the cookies are almost finished baking, invite your children to join you to stud the cookies with mini-marshmallows. Creating this cookie was a lot of fun—and eating it was even better!

2 cups all-purpose flour, spooned in and leveled

$\frac{2}{3}$ cup strained cocoa powder, spooned in and leveled

1 teaspoon baking powder

1 teaspoon salt

$\frac{1}{2}$ teaspoon baking soda

1 cup (2 sticks) unsalted butter, slightly firm

$1\frac{1}{2}$ cups sugar

2 large eggs

$\frac{2}{3}$ cup sour cream

2 teaspoons pure vanilla extract

$1\frac{1}{2}$ cups broken toasted pecans (see page 356)

2 cups semisweet chocolate chips, divided

2 to $2\frac{1}{2}$ cups mini-marshmallows

2 tablespoons unsalted butter

2 teaspoons boiling water

AT A GLANCE

PAN: Oversized (14- × 17-inch) cookie sheets

PAN PREP: Baking parchment

RACK LEVELS: Upper and lower thirds

OVEN TEMP: 350°F

BAKING TIME: 14–15 minutes

DIFFICULTY: 2

1. Position the racks in the upper and lower thirds of the oven. Heat the oven to 350°F. Dab the corners of the cookie sheets lightly with butter and line with baking parchment.

2. Strain together three times the flour, cocoa powder, baking powder, salt, and baking soda. Set aside.

3. Using an electric mixer fitted with the paddle attachment, beat the butter on medium speed until creamy and lightened in color, about 2 minutes. Add the sugar in a steady stream and beat 1 minute longer to combine well. Add the eggs one at a time, and beat 1 minute longer. Mix in the sour cream and vanilla.

4. Reduce the mixer speed to low and add the dry ingredients in two additions, mixing *just* until blended. Using a large rubber spatula, fold in the pecans and $1\frac{1}{2}$ cups of the chocolate chips.

5. Using a #16 ice cream scoop, portion six mounds of dough 3 inches apart onto each cookie sheet. Bake for 12 minutes, or until *just* starting to set on top. Remove from the oven and press nine or ten mini-marshmallows at random onto each top. Return the cookies to the oven and bake for another 2 minutes or just until the marshmallows start to soften. WATCH CARE-FULLY. Do not allow the marshmallows to become too hot or they will melt. These cookies are best slightly underbaked.

6. Let rest on the cookie sheets for 5 minutes or until firm enough to handle before loosening with a large metal spatula. Remove to a wire cooling rack set over a jelly roll pan or a sheet of wax paper.

7. Combine the remaining ½ cup chocolate chips and the butter in a medium bowl set over a pan of simmering water. Melt together, stirring occasionally. Add the boiling water, ½ teaspoon at a time, to thin to a pouring consistency. Using a spoon or a fork, drizzle the glaze over each cookie. Let stand on the cooling racks until the glaze sets.

STORAGE: Store in an airtight container, layered between strips of wax paper, for up to 5 days. These cookies may be frozen.

Secrets for Making Oversized Cookies

- Oversized cookies will have more interest if nuts, chocolate, and dried fruits are cut into larger pieces.

- Use your largest cookie sheets because only a few large cookies can be baked at a time.

- A #16 ice cream scoop, which is often used for portioning oversized cookies, has the same capacity as a ¼-cup dry measure. If a dry measure is used, pack it with the cookie dough and scrape out the dough with a small rubber spatula.

- For a more uniform appearance, reshape uneven edges on the mounds of dough with moistened fingertips.

- After baking, large cookies must stand longer on the cookie sheet before loosening because they take longer to set.

- To prevent oversized cookies from breaking when loosening from the cookie sheet, gently sweep a thin, long spatula underneath the baked cookie.

- Package oversized cookies in individual cellophane bags for party favors, gift giving, and/or mailing. Oversized cookies are great candidates for mailing because they are less fragile than normal-size cookies and are less likely to shift in the package.

chocolate chip oatmeal cookies

MAKES ABOUT 4½ DOZEN 2½-INCH COOKIES

Here is a variation of Carole's Really Great Chocolate Chip Cookie (page 2). The oatmeal imparts its own mellow flavor, which marries so well with the chocolate chips and nuts.

¾ cup lightly packed very fresh dark brown sugar

⅓ cup granulated sugar

2½ cups old-fashioned oatmeal, divided

1¼ cups all-purpose flour, spooned in and leveled

¾ teaspoon salt

½ teaspoon baking soda

1 cup (2 sticks) unsalted butter, slightly firm

2 tablespoons light corn syrup

1 large egg

2 teaspoons pure vanilla extract

2 cups semisweet chocolate chips

2 cups coarsely chopped walnuts (see page 356)

AT A GLANCE

PAN: Cookie sheets

PAN PREP: Lightly buttered

RACK LEVELS: Upper and lower thirds

OVEN TEMP: 375°F

BAKING TIME: 10–12 minutes

DIFFICULTY: 1

1. Position the racks in the upper and lower thirds of the oven. Heat the oven to 375°F. Lightly butter the cookie sheets.

2. Place the sugars and ½ cup of the oatmeal in the work bowl of a food processor fitted with the steel blade and process for 2½ to 3 minutes, or until the oatmeal is very finely ground and powdery.

3. In a medium bowl, strain together the flour, salt, and baking soda. Stir in the remaining 2 cups oatmeal and set aside.

4. In the bowl of an electric mixer fitted with the paddle attachment, mix the butter with the corn syrup on medium-low speed, mixing until smooth and lightened in color. Add the oatmeal-sugar mixture in three additions, mixing well after each addition. Add the egg and vanilla extract and mix for 1 minute longer. Scrape down the side of the bowl as needed. Reduce the mixer speed to low, then incorporate the dry ingredients in three additions, mixing *just* until blended. Fold in the chocolate chips and walnuts.

5. Drop golf ball–size mounds of dough from the tip of a tablespoon onto the cookie sheets, spacing them about 3 inches apart. If the dough begins to feel crumbly toward the bottom of the bowl, shape the balls with your fingers. Bake for 10 to 12 minutes, or until the edges *begin* to turn a golden brown. To ensure even baking, toward the end of baking time rotate the pans top to bottom and front to back. *Do not overbake.*

6. Remove the cookies from the oven and let stand for 2 minutes. Using a thin, metal spatula, carefully loosen and transfer to cooling racks.

STORAGE: Store in an airtight container, layered between strips of wax paper, for up to 2 weeks. These cookies may be frozen.

oatmeal walnut crispies

MAKES ABOUT 5 DOZEN 2½-INCH COOKIES

These wonderfully crunchy cookies receive their texture from flakes of oatmeal, chopped walnuts, and egg whites. The buttery batter is heightened with a hint of cinnamon, creating one heck of a delicious cookie.

1¾ cups all-purpose flour, spooned in and leveled

1 teaspoon baking soda

½ teaspoon salt

½ teaspoon ground cinnamon

1 cup (2 sticks) unsalted butter, at room temperature

1⅓ cups sugar

2 large egg whites

2 teaspoons pure vanilla extract

2 cups quick (1-minute) oatmeal

1¼ cups medium-chopped walnuts (see page 356)

1. Position the racks in the upper and lower thirds of the oven. Heat the oven to 375°F. Moderately butter the cookie sheets.

2. Strain together the flour, baking soda, salt, and cinnamon. Set aside.

3. In the large bowl of an electric mixer fitted with the paddle attachment, mix the butter on medium-low speed until smooth and lightened in color. Increase the speed to medium and gradually add the sugar over 2 to 3 minutes. Add the egg whites in two additions, beating well after each addition and scraping down the side of the bowl as needed. Blend in the vanilla.

AT A GLANCE

PAN: Cookie sheets

PAN PREP: Moderately buttered

RACK LEVELS: Upper and lower thirds

OVEN TEMP: 375°F

BAKING TIME: 13–15 minutes

DIFFICULTY: 1

4. Reduce the mixer speed to low. Add the dry ingredients in three additions, then blend in the oatmeal. Mix on low speed *just* until the ingredients are blended together. Using a large rubber spatula, fold in the nuts.

5. Using a teaspoon to portion the dough, make 1¼-inch walnut-size balls and place them 2 inches apart on the cookie sheets. Bake for 13 to 15 minutes, or until golden brown. Toward the end of baking time rotate the pans from top to bottom and front to back. Let stand for 2 or 3 minutes before loosening with a thin, metal spatula. Cool on wire racks.

STORAGE: Store in an airtight container, layered between strips of wax paper, for up to 2 weeks. These cookies may be frozen.

Chocolate Chip Oatmeal Crispies

Reduce walnuts to ½ cup. Blend in ¾ cup semisweet chocolate mini-morsels when you add the nuts. Proceed as directed above.

oatmeal raisin cookies

MAKES ABOUT 4 DOZEN 3-INCH COOKIES

Savor the flavors of this favorite comfort cookie made with old-fashioned oatmeal, brown sugar, molasses, cinnamon, raisins, and lots of toasted pecans. The orange zest really complements these ingredients.

2 cups all-purpose flour, spooned in and leveled

1½ teaspoons ground cinnamon

1 teaspoon baking soda

1 teaspoon salt

1 cup (2 sticks) unsalted butter, slightly firm

1 teaspoon grated navel orange zest

⅔ cup lightly packed dark brown sugar

½ cup granulated sugar

¼ cup dark unsulfured molasses

2 large eggs

2 teaspoons pure vanilla extract

2 cups old-fashioned oatmeal

1 cup broken, toasted pecans or walnuts (see page 356)

1 cup dark raisins, plumped (see page 358), drained, and patted dry on paper towels

AT A GLANCE

PAN: Cookie sheets

PAN PREP: Moderately buttered

RACK LEVELS: Upper and lower thirds

OVEN TEMP: 350°F

BAKING TIME: 15–17 minutes

DIFFICULTY: 1

1. Position the racks in the upper and lower thirds of the oven. Heat the oven to 350°F. Moderately butter the cookie sheets.

2. Strain together the flour, cinnamon, baking soda, and salt. Set aside.

3. In the large bowl of an electric mixer, using the paddle attachment, mix the butter with the orange zest on medium speed until smooth and creamy, about 1 minute. Add the brown sugar, then the granulated sugar, and mix until light in color, 2 to 3 minutes. Blend in the molasses and mix to combine. Add the eggs one at a time, then the vanilla, and mix for 1 minute longer.

4. Reduce the mixer speed to low and pour in the dry ingredients in two additions, mixing only to incorporate the flour, then blend in the oatmeal. Using a large rubber spatula, fold in the pecans and raisins.

5. Drop by rounded tablespoons 3 inches apart onto the cookie sheets. Bake for 15 to 17 minutes, or until the bottoms of the cookies are golden brown, rotating the pans top to bottom and front to back toward the end of baking time. Do not overbake or the cookies will be too crisp and difficult to remove from the pan. Let cookies stand for 2 minutes, then loosen with a thin, metal spatula. Transfer to cooling racks.

STORAGE: Store in an airtight container, layered between strips of wax paper, for up to 1 week. These cookies may be frozen.

nancy's nuthouse cookies

MAKES ABOUT 4 DOZEN 2½- TO 3-INCH COOKIES

One of the baking series that I teach at Kings Cooking Studio in New Jersey is "Mastery of American Cakes." One day I queried my class about chocolate chip cookies and asked each student to bring in his or her favorite recipe. The following week, Jeff Duffany brought in his candidate, which he aptly called Nancy's Nuthouse Cookies. If you are a fancier of nuts, as I am, nobody can outfancy Nancy!

1¼ cups all-purpose flour, spooned in and leveled

1 cup whole wheat flour, spooned in and leveled

1 teaspoon baking soda

½ teaspoon salt

1 cup (2 sticks) unsalted butter, slightly firm

1 cup lightly packed very fresh dark brown sugar

½ cup granulated sugar

2 teaspoons pure vanilla extract

2 large eggs

3 cups walnuts, halves or large pieces

1½ cups (8 ounces) fine-quality bittersweet or semisweet chocolate, such as Lindt Bittersweet, cut into ¾-inch chunks

1. Position the racks in the upper and lower thirds of the oven. Heat the oven to 375°F.

2. Whisk the all-purpose and whole wheat flours, baking soda, and salt thoroughly together in a large bowl. Set aside.

3. Using an electric mixer fitted with the paddle attachment, mix the butter, brown sugar, granulated sugar, and vanilla on medium-low speed until smooth and creamy, about 2 minutes. Add the eggs one at a time, mixing well after each addition and scraping the bowl as needed.

4. Reduce the mixer speed to low and add the flour mixture in three additions, mixing *just* until blended after each addition. Using a large rubber spatula, gently fold in the nuts and chocolate chunks.

5. Using your hands, roll rounded tablespoons of dough into 1½-inch balls, about the size of large walnuts. Place on ungreased cookie sheets 3 inches apart and flatten with the heel of your hand into disks ½ inch high and 2 inches wide. Scrape down the side of the bowl occasionally to ensure even distribution of the chocolate chunks and nuts. Bake the cookies for 9 to 11 minutes, or until golden and just set. To ensure even baking, rotate the pans from top to bottom and front to back toward the end of baking time. Let stand for 2 minutes, then loosen from the pan with a thin, metal spatula. Transfer to wire cooling racks.

STORAGE: Store in an airtight container, layered between strips of wax paper, for up to 5 days. These cookies may be frozen.

AT A GLANCE

PAN: Cookie sheets

PAN PREP: Ungreased

RACK LEVELS: Upper and lower thirds

OVEN TEMP: 375°F

BAKING TIME: 9–11 minutes

DIFFICULTY: 1

white chocolate chunk macadamia cookies

MAKES ABOUT FORTY 2¾-INCH COOKIES

When I make these cookies, I like to keep the chocolate and macadamia nuts in large pieces; I think it adds a lot of character to the cookie.

¾ cup lightly packed very fresh dark brown sugar

½ cup quick (1-minute) oatmeal

⅓ cup granulated sugar

1¾ cups all-purpose flour, spooned in and leveled

½ teaspoon baking soda

½ teaspoon salt

1 cup (2 sticks) unsalted butter, slightly firm

2 tablespoons light corn syrup

1 large egg

2 teaspoons pure vanilla extract

8 ounces fine-quality white chocolate, such as Lindt Swiss Classic White, cut into ¼- to ½-inch pieces

1½ cups coarsely chopped macadamia nuts (see page 356)

AT A GLANCE

PAN: Cookie sheets

PAN PREP: Ungreased

RACK LEVELS: Upper and lower thirds

OVEN TEMP: 375°F

BAKING TIME: 10–12 minutes

DIFFICULTY: 1

1. Position the racks in the upper and lower thirds of the oven. Heat the oven to 375°F.

2. Place the brown sugar, oatmeal, and granulated sugar in the work bowl of a food processor fitted with the steel blade and process 2½ to 3 minutes, stopping occasionally to pulse. The oatmeal must be very finely ground. Set aside.

3. In a medium bowl, strain together the flour, baking soda, and salt. Set aside.

4. In the large bowl of an electric mixer fitted with a paddle attachment, mix the butter and corn syrup together on medium-low speed, mixing until smooth and creamy, about 1 minute. Add the oatmeal-sugar mixture in three additions and beat for 2 minutes. Add the egg and vanilla and beat for 1 minute longer. Scrape down the bowl as needed. Reduce the mixer speed to low, add the flour mixture in two additions, and mix *just* until blended. Using a rubber spatula, fold in the chocolate and the nuts.

5. Drop 1½-inch mounds of dough onto the cookie sheets, about 3 inches apart. Bake the cookies for 10 to 12 minutes, or until the edges begin to turn a golden brown. To ensure even baking, toward the end of baking time rotate the pans top to bottom and front to back. *Do not overbake.*

6. Remove the cookies from the oven and let stand for 2 minutes. Using a thin, metal spatula, carefully loosen. When firm enough to handle, transfer to cooling racks.

STORAGE: Store in an airtight container, layered between strips of wax paper, for up to 5 days. These cookies may be frozen.

Secrets for Making Drop Cookies

- Butter that is too soft will result in a cookie that spreads.

- Overmixing the dough softens the butter, which causes the cookies to spread.

- If you like a thicker cookie, it will spread less if you chill the dough before portioning.

- To control the consistency of the cookie dough, it is essential that the flour be properly measured (see Measuring Flour and Dry Ingredients, page 352).

- If nuts are chopped more finely than indicated, the consistency of the cookie dough will be more firm.

- If you omit a chunky product from a recipe, substitute an equal amount of another chunky product. For example, if you omit raisins, substitute an equal amount of nuts or chocolate chips.

- If using a stand mixer, you can add chunky ingredients like chocolate, nuts, and fruit if the mixer has a paddle attachment. Otherwise, mix in with a large spatula.

- If you like more uniformly shaped cookies, chill the dough first and roll into balls before baking.

- If the dough becomes too soft to handle when portioning in warm or humid weather, or as it stands when batch baking, refrigerate it for a few minutes.

- Scrape down the side of the bowl frequently while portioning cookies to ensure even distribution of chocolate chips, nuts, and fruits.

- For a well-rounded cookie, drop the dough onto the cookie sheet from the tip, not the side, of the spoon.

- When dropping the dough from the tip of the spoon, hold the spoon with the tip pointing down, perpendicular to the cookie sheet.

- A #40 (1¼-inch) ice cream scoop is ideal to use for portioning drop cookies.

- Irregular mounds of cookie dough can be reshaped by gently rounding the dough with a moistened fingertip.

- You may change the size of the cookie by reducing or increasing the size of the mound of dough. Adjust the spacing of the mounds on the cookie sheet, and be sure to adjust the baking time accordingly.

- Since drop cookie dough is soft, allow enough space between the mounds of dough on the cookie sheets because this type of dough tends to spread.

- If you like softer cookies, remove them from the oven while still slightly underbaked.

chock full of crunchies

MAKES ABOUT 5 DOZEN 2½-INCH COOKIES

This is a crunch-lover's fantasy! The dough is made with oatmeal, coconut, and pecans and gets an added snap, crackle, and crunch from rice cereal! The combination of these wonderful textures and flavors makes this a cookie that will become a favorite!

2 cups all-purpose flour, spooned in and leveled

¾ teaspoon salt

½ teaspoon baking soda

½ teaspoon baking powder

1 cup (2 sticks) unsalted butter, slightly firm

¾ cup lightly packed light brown sugar

¾ cup granulated sugar

2 large eggs

1½ teaspoons pure vanilla extract

1 cup old-fashioned oatmeal

1 cup finely chopped sweetened, flaked coconut

1 cup crispy rice cereal

1 cup coarsely chopped toasted pecans (see page 356)

AT A GLANCE

PAN: Cookie sheets

PAN PREP: Moderately buttered

RACK LEVELS: Upper and lower thirds

OVEN TEMP: 375°F

BAKING TIME: 9–11 minutes

DIFFICULTY: 1

1. Position the racks in the upper and lower thirds of the oven. Heat the oven to 375°F. Moderately butter the cookie sheets.

2. Strain together the flour, salt, baking soda, and baking powder. Set aside.

3. Using an electric mixer fitted with the paddle attachment, mix the butter on medium-low speed until smooth and creamy. Add the brown sugar, then the granulated sugar, and mix until well blended, about 2 minutes. Add the eggs one at a time, then the vanilla, and mix for 1 minute longer. Reduce the mixer speed to low, then add the dry ingredients in three additions, mixing *just* until blended. Using a large rubber spatula, fold in the oatmeal, coconut, rice cereal, and pecans.

4. Drop walnut-size mounds from the tip of a tablespoon onto the cookie sheets, about 2 inches apart. Scrape down the side of the bowl frequently to maintain an even combination of dough to textured ingredients. Bake for 9 to 11 minutes, or until the edges begin to turn a golden brown, rotating the pans top to bottom and front to back toward the end of baking time. *Do not overbake.*

5. Remove the cookies from the oven and let stand for 2 minutes. Using a thin, metal spatula, carefully loosen and transfer to cooling racks.

STORAGE: Store in an airtight container, layered between strips of wax paper, for up to 2 weeks. These cookies may be frozen.

peanut jumbles

MAKES ABOUT 4 DOZEN 2¼-INCH COOKIES

Here is a play on the classic peanut butter cookie. It has a robust peanut butter flavor with lots of whole salted peanuts blended through the dough. Unlike the classic peanut butter cookie, the nuts in this recipe are left whole. If you are a peanut fan, don't wait for baseball season to get your peanut fix! With this cookie you can have it year-round!

2½ cups sifted cake flour, spooned in and leveled

½ teaspoon baking powder

½ teaspoon salt

¼ teaspoon baking soda

¾ cup (1½ sticks) unsalted butter, slightly firm

¾ cup creamy peanut butter

1 cup lightly packed dark brown sugar

½ cup granulated sugar

2 large eggs

2 teaspoons pure vanilla extract

2 cups whole salted peanuts

1. Position the racks in the upper and lower thirds of the oven. Heat the oven to 375°F. Line the cookie sheets with baking parchment.

2. Strain together the flour, baking powder, salt, and baking soda. Set aside.

3. In the large bowl of an electric mixer fitted with the paddle attachment, mix the butter on medium-low speed until smooth. Blend in the peanut butter. Gradually add the brown sugar, then the granulated sugar and beat until lightened in color, about 2 minutes. Blend in the eggs, one at a time, then the vanilla. Reduce the mixer speed to low. Add the dry ingredients in three additions and mix *just* until combined. Using a large, rubber spatula, fold in the peanuts.

AT A GLANCE

PAN: Cookie sheets

PAN PREP: Baking parchment

RACK LEVELS: Upper and lower thirds

OVEN TEMP: 375°F

BAKING TIME: 10–11 minutes

DIFFICULTY: 1

4. Drop golf ball–size mounds of dough from the tip of a tablespoon onto the cookie sheets, placing them 2 inches apart. Bake for 10 to 11 minutes, or until golden brown, rotating the pans top to bottom and front to back toward the end of the baking time. Let stand for 2 to 3 minutes before loosening with a thin, metal spatula. Transfer to wire cooling racks.

STORAGE: Store in an airtight container, layered between strips of wax paper, for up to 2 weeks. These cookies may be frozen.

honey-roasted peanut butter cookies

MAKES ABOUT FORTY 2½-INCH COOKIES

Peanut butter cookies, an all-American favorite, are also a favorite of mine. Since honey and peanut butter are a tasty flavor combination, I add honey-roasted peanuts to my cookie dough along with a touch of honey. The honey adds moistness to the cookie and contributes a lovely but subtle flavor.

1¼ cups all-purpose flour, spooned in and leveled

1 tablespoon wheat germ (optional)

½ teaspoon baking soda

½ teaspoon baking powder

½ teaspoon salt

1 cup crunchy peanut butter

¼ cup (½ stick) unsalted butter, softened

¼ cup vegetable shortening

2 tablespoons honey

½ cup granulated sugar

⅓ cup lightly packed light brown sugar

1 large egg

1 teaspoon pure vanilla extract

½ cup coarsely chopped honey-roasted peanuts (see page 356)

AT A GLANCE

PAN: Cookie sheets

PAN PREP: Ungreased

CHILLING TIME: 1 hour

RACK LEVELS: Upper and lower thirds

OVEN TEMP: 350°F

BAKING TIME: 11–13 minutes

DIFFICULTY: 1

MAKE THE DOUGH

1. In a large bowl, whisk together the flour, wheat germ if using, baking soda, baking powder, and salt. Set aside.

2. Using an electric mixer fitted with the paddle attachment, mix the peanut butter, butter, vegetable shortening, and honey until well blended. On medium speed, add the granulated sugar and then the brown sugar and mix for 1 minute, until combined. Add the egg and vanilla and mix for 1 to 2 minutes, or until the batter lightens in color.

3. Reduce the mixer speed to low and add the dry ingredients, mixing *just* until blended. Fold in the chopped peanuts and chill for 1 hour or until firm enough to handle.

BAKE THE COOKIES

4. Position the racks in the upper and lower thirds of the oven. Heat the oven to 350°F.

5. Roll the dough into 1¼-inch balls and place about 2 inches apart on the cookie sheets. Using a table fork that has been dipped in flour, slightly flatten the cookies while making a cross-hatch design across the tops. Bake for 11 to 13 minutes, or until lightly golden. Toward the end of the baking time rotate the pans from top to bottom and front to back. Let cookies stand for 1 minute before removing with a thin, metal spatula. Transfer to cooling racks.

STORAGE: Store in an airtight container, layered between strips of wax paper, for up to 2 weeks. These cookies may be frozen.

peanut butter balls

MAKES 5 DOZEN 1½-INCH COOKIES

One day, my assistant, Kathie, and I were comparing our grandmothers' recipe boxes (they happened to be identical!). Kathie's, like mine, was filled with hand-written recipes. They were gathered over the years by her mother, an avid baker. One of the recipes that caught my eye was from the kitchen of Noel Rozint, a dear friend of Kathie's mom.

It was a simple "no-bake" cookie made with the irresistible combination of peanut butter and chocolate. So, I decided to try it. I loved the results! If you have youngsters who enjoy "hands-on" baking, by all means, ask for their assistance when making these cookies. And don't forget to taste, I mean *test*, for quality while making them!

2⅓ cups strained confectioners' sugar, spooned in and leveled

1 cup graham cracker crumbs

½ cup (1 stick) unsalted butter, softened

¾ cup chunky peanut butter

10 ounces semisweet chocolate, coarsely chopped

2 teaspoons vegetable oil

2 cups salted peanuts, finely chopped (see page 356)

1. In a large bowl, stir together the confectioners' sugar and graham cracker crumbs. Add the butter and peanut butter and work with a wooden spoon or with your hands until thoroughly combined. Portion the dough into sixty 1-inch balls and place them on parchment-lined jelly roll pans.

AT A GLANCE

PAN: Jelly roll pans

PAN PREP: Baking parchment

DIFFICULTY: 1

2. Combine the chocolate and vegetable oil in a medium heat-proof bowl. Place the bowl over a medium saucepan filled with simmering water and slowly melt the chocolate, stirring occasionally. When the chocolate is melted, remove it from the heat, but keep the bowl over the pot of water. Place about ½ cup of the chopped peanuts in a low flat dish, such as a pie plate.

3. Using a chocolate dipping fork, or a 2-prong fork, dip one ball at a time in the melted chocolate. Tap the fork gently on the side of the bowl to help drain the chocolate from the cookie. The coating should be thin. Roll the dipped cookie in the chopped peanuts and coat it evenly. Remove the cookie with a 2-prong fork and place it back on the jelly roll pan to set. Repeat with the remaining cookies, adding peanuts as needed. (It is easier to roll the cookies in a small amount of peanuts.) If the chocolate begins to thicken, return the pan to the stove and heat until the chocolate thins. Let the cookies air-dry on the cookie sheets.

STORAGE: Store in an airtight container, layered between strips of wax paper, and refrigerate for up to 3 weeks. These cookies may be frozen.

almondates

I developed this easy no-bake cookie during my catering days to serve at outdoor parties. The combination of crunchy almonds and walnuts, chocolate chips, and chewy dates all rolled in coconut is irresistible.

½ cup coarsely chopped unblanched almonds (see page 356)

½ cup coarsely chopped walnuts (see page 356)

60 whole blanched almonds

1 cup (2 sticks) unsalted butter

¾ cup sugar

1 large egg, lightly beaten

1 pound pitted dates, chopped

2 cups crispy rice cereal

1 tablespoon amaretto liqueur

¾ cup semisweet chocolate mini-morsels, divided

2½ cups sweetened, flaked coconut

AT A GLANCE

PAN: Cooling racks and jelly roll pans

PAN PREP: None

DIFFICULTY: 1

1. Heat the oven to 325°F. Spread the chopped almonds and walnuts in a shallow baking pan. Bake for 8 to 10 minutes, or until lightly toasted. Empty them into a bowl. Then toast the whole blanched almonds for 12 to 15 minutes, or until lightly browned. Set aside.

2. In a heavy, medium saucepan over low heat, melt the butter, then add the sugar, egg, and dates. Bring to a slow boil and cook over low heat for 6 to 7 minutes, or until the mixture is slightly thickened and the dates are cooked. Be sure to stir frequently. Remove from the heat and pour the mixture into a large mixing bowl. Cool for 5 minutes.

3. Fold in the nuts, rice cereal, and amaretto. When the date mixture is tepid, fold in ½ cup of the mini-morsels. (If the mixture is too hot, the chocolate chips will melt.)

4. Take spoonfuls of the date mixture and form into about sixty 1¼-inch balls, moistening your hands with ice water as needed. (The batter will be sticky.)

5. Spread one-third of the coconut in a shallow dish, such as a pie plate. Shape the balls into logs 1 inch wide by 1½ inches long, then roll them in the coconut. Continue shaping the logs and rolling them in the coconut, replenishing the coconut as needed. *Do not spread all of the coconut in the shallow dish at once, as it tends to discolor with use.*

6. Have ready wire racks set over jelly roll pans. Place the remaining ¼ cup mini-morsels in a small, heat-proof custard cup and melt on medium setting in a microwave. Using a small offset spatula, spread a dab of the melted chocolate on one side of a toasted almond and press it firmly into a log. Repeat with the remaining almonds and logs. Place the logs on the wire racks to air-dry for 1 hour.

STORAGE: Refrigerate in an airtight container, layered between strips of wax paper, for up to 2 weeks. Freezing is not recommended.

chocolate snowcaps

MAKES ABOUT 4 DOZEN 2-INCH COOKIES

Nonpareil candies purchased from a specialty candy store will be well worth the investment.

1¾ cups all-purpose flour, spooned in and leveled

½ cup strained Dutch-processed cocoa powder, spooned in and leveled

¼ teaspoon salt

1 cup (2 sticks) unsalted butter, slightly firm

1 cup strained confectioners' sugar, spooned in and leveled

1 teaspoon pure vanilla extract

3 tablespoons granulated sugar

1½ teaspoons seedless raspberry preserves

48 semisweet chocolate nonpareil candies

MAKE THE DOUGH

1. Strain together the flour, cocoa, and salt. Set aside.

2. In the large bowl of an electric mixer fitted with the paddle attachment, mix the butter on low speed until smooth. Add the confectioners' sugar with the vanilla and mix just until blended.

3. Add half of the dry ingredients and mix briefly to incorporate. Using a wooden spoon, stir in the remaining dry ingredients by hand, working the mixture *just* until the dough is smooth. Do not overmix.

4. Scrape the dough onto a strip of plastic wrap, then shape it into a 6- × 8-inch rectangle. Wrap the dough in the plastic and refrigerate until firm, 45 to 60 minutes.

AT A GLANCE

PAN: Cookie sheets

PAN PREP: Well buttered

CHILLING TIME: 45–60 minutes

OVEN TEMP: 350°F

RACK LEVELS: Upper and lower thirds

BAKING TIME: 11–13 minutes

DIFFICULTY: 2

BAKE THE COOKIES

5. Position the racks in the lower and upper thirds of the oven. Heat the oven to 350°F. Butter the cookie sheets well.

6. Using a pastry scraper, divide the dough into forty-eight 1-inch squares. Roll each square into a ball and arrange about 2 inches apart on the cookie sheets. Place the granulated sugar in a shallow dish. Dip a flat-bottomed glass into the sugar, then press down on each ball to form a 2-inch disk. Using a small spatula, spread a *dab* of preserves on the bottom of a nonpareil and lightly press the candy, topside up, into the center of a disk. Repeat with the remaining disks.

7. Bake for 11 to 13 minutes, or until the cookies feel set on top. Rotate the pans from top to bottom and front to back toward the end of baking time. Let stand for 1 to 2 minutes before loosening with a metal spatula, then transfer to cooling racks.

STORAGE: Store in an airtight container, layered between strips of wax paper, for up to 3 weeks. These cookies may be frozen.

zach's chocolate coconut devils

MAKES ABOUT 4 DOZEN 2½-INCH COOKIES

My grandson Zach has had a sophisticated palate ever since he was a little boy. Coconut sweets were always his favorite, so when I wanted to create a cookie for him, choosing the right flavor was a cinch.

These cookies are intensely flavored with three kinds of chocolate and lots of chewy coconut. As the cookie bakes, the chocolates melt through the shards of sweet coconut, making one terrific-tasting cookie. Be sure to use high-quality chocolate here—it counts! And be careful not to overbake the cookies. The centers should be moist with coconut and fudgy with chocolate. Did Zach like the result? You bet! He gave me a wink and a "high five," and I knew I had scored.

2⅔ cups lightly packed sweetened, flaked coconut (1 7-ounce bag)

½ cup all-purpose flour, spooned in and leveled

¼ cup strained Dutch-processed cocoa powder, spooned in and leveled

¼ teaspoon baking soda

¼ teaspoon salt

½ cup (1 stick) unsalted butter

6 ounces fine-quality bittersweet or semisweet chocolate, such as Lindt Bittersweet, chopped

3 ounces unsweetened chocolate, chopped

3 large eggs

1⅓ cups superfine sugar

2 teaspoons pure vanilla extract

¼ teaspoon pure almond extract

AT A GLANCE

PAN: Cookie sheets

PAN PREP: Baking parchment

RACK LEVELS: Upper and lower thirds

OVEN TEMP: 350°F

BAKING TIME: 10–12 minutes

DIFFICULTY: 1

1. Position the racks in the upper and lower thirds of the oven. Heat the oven to 350°F. Dab the corners of the cookie sheets lightly with butter and line with baking parchment.

2. Place the flaked coconut in the work bowl of a food processor fitted with the steel blade and pulse 6 to 8 times, or until the coconut is medium chopped. Set aside.

3. Strain together the flour, cocoa, baking soda, and salt. Set aside.

4. In a medium bowl set over simmering water on low heat, melt the butter. Add the chopped bittersweet and unsweetened chocolates and *just* melt the chocolates, gently stirring occasionally. Remove from the heat and keep warm.

5. In the large bowl of an electric mixer using the whisk attachment, beat the eggs on medium speed until light. Gradually add the superfine sugar, taking about 2 minutes. Scrape down the side of the bowl as needed. Stop the mixer and pour in the warm melted chocolate mixture, then mix on medium speed just until combined. Add the vanilla and almond extracts.

6. Reduce the mixer speed to low and mix in the flour mixture. Remove the bowl from the mixer and let the batter rest for about 5 minutes, or until it begins to thicken. Then sprinkle handfuls of coconut over the batter, folding briefly with a large rubber spatula after each addition. Do not combine thoroughly. Some of the coconut flakes should still be visible.

7. Drop by heaping teaspoons onto the cookie sheets, about 2 inches apart. Bake for 10 to 12 minutes, or until the tops are *just* set but the cookies are still soft to the touch. The cookies will firm as they cool. To ensure even baking, rotate the pans top to bottom and front to back toward the end of baking time. Let stand for 1 to 2 minutes, then loosen with a thin, metal spatula. When cool enough to handle, transfer to cooling racks.

STORAGE: Store in an airtight container, layered between strips of wax paper, for up to 5 days. These cookies may be frozen.

Chocolate Coconut Pecan Devils

Fold in 1 cup toasted broken pecans with the coconut in step 6. Proceed as above.

black forest chews

MAKES ABOUT FORTY 2½-INCH COOKIES

These chewy chocolate cookies mirror the flavors of the renowned German Black Forest cake. They are chock full of dried cherries steeped in cherry liqueur, toasted almonds, and bittersweet chocolate chunks. The tops of these decadent cookies glisten with sparkling white sugar (available from The Baker's Catalogue, see page 381). They are as appetizing to look at as they are luscious to eat.

½ cup dried cherries

1 cup boiling water

2 tablespoons Cherry Heering liqueur

1¼ cups all-purpose flour, spooned in and leveled

½ teaspoon baking powder

¼ teaspoon baking soda

⅛ teaspoon salt

6 tablespoons (¾ stick) unsalted butter

3 ounces unsweetened chocolate, coarsely chopped

1 tablespoon light molasses

⅔ cup granulated sugar

½ cup lightly packed light brown sugar

1 large egg

2 tablespoons milk

1 teaspoon pure vanilla extract

1 (3.5-ounce) bar Lindt Bittersweet Chocolate, cut into ½-inch dice (or ⅔ cup bittersweet chocolate chunks)

1 cup well toasted unblanched almonds, coarsely chopped (see page 356), divided

1 tablespoon sparkling white sugar, for garnish

1 large egg white lightly beaten with 1 teaspoon water, for egg wash

AT A GLANCE

PAN: Cookie sheets

PAN PREP: Baking parchment

RACK LEVELS: Upper and lower thirds

OVEN TEMP: 350°F

BAKING TIME: 7–8 minutes

DIFFICULTY: 2

MAKE THE DOUGH

1. Place the cherries in a small bowl. Add the boiling water and let stand 1 or 2 minutes to soften. Drain and blot dry on paper towels. Return the cherries to the bowl, add the cherry liqueur, and let steep while preparing the cookie dough.

2. Position the oven racks in the upper and lower thirds of the oven. Heat the oven to 350°F. Dab the cookie sheets with butter and line with baking parchment.

3. Strain together the flour, baking powder, baking soda, and salt. Set aside.

4. Place the butter and unsweetened chocolate in a 3-quart saucepan and melt over low heat, stirring occasionally.

5. Off the heat, using a large wooden spoon or rubber spatula, stir in the molasses, then the granulated and brown sugars. Add the egg, milk, and vanilla and combine thoroughly. Stir in the macerated cherries with the liqueur, then stir in the dry ingredients, one half at a time, mixing *only* to combine. Stir in the chocolate chunks and ¼ cup of the almonds.

SHAPE THE DOUGH

6. Drop the dough from the tip of a teaspoon onto the cookie sheets, making 1¼-inch mounds about the size of walnuts, spaced 2 inches apart. The dough will firm as it stands. After the dough has been portioned, moisten your hands lightly with cold tap water and shape each mound into a ball, remoistening your hands as needed.

7. Place the remaining ¾ cup almonds and the sparkling white sugar in a large shallow dish (a pie plate works well).

8. Dip one side of a ball into the egg wash, then into the almond and sugar mixture, pressing to adhere the almonds and sugar to the dough. Place the ball back onto the cookie sheet, nut side up, and press the top gently with the heel of your hand to ½-inch thickness. Repeat with the remaining balls.

BAKE THE COOKIES

9. Bake the cookies for 7 minutes. Toward the end of baking time rotate the sheets top to bottom and front to back. Test for doneness by touching the tops of the cookies gently to see if they are set. If not, return to the oven for 1 minute and check again. *Do not overbake.* The cookies will be soft to the touch, but will firm upon cooling. Let the cookies stand about 5 minutes, then loosen them from the parchment with a thin, metal spatula and transfer to cooling racks to air-dry for about 1 hour.

STORAGE: Store in airtight containers, layered between sheets of wax paper, for up to 5 days. These cookies may be frozen.

joanna pruess's molasses spice cookies

MAKES ABOUT FORTY 2¾-INCH COOKIES

My friend, cookbook author and journalist Joanna Pruess, has the most extraordinary taste buds of anyone I know. When she offered her Molasses Spice Cookie recipe for my book, I knew it was going to be a winner. These cookies have everything a molasses spice cookie should: spectacular flavor, snappy crispness, and a crinkly, sugary surface. Thank you, Joanna, for your blue-ribbon recipe!

¾ cup (1½ sticks) unsalted butter

2 cups all-purpose flour, spooned in and leveled

2 teaspoons baking soda

1 teaspoon ground cinnamon

1 teaspoon ground ginger

¾ teaspoon salt

½ teaspoon ground cloves

2 cups sugar, divided

¼ cup dark molasses

1 large egg

AT A GLANCE

PAN: Cookie sheets

PAN PREP: Moderately buttered

CHILLING TIME: 30–45 minutes

RACK LEVELS: Upper and lower thirds

OVEN TEMP: 375°F

BAKING TIME: 8–10 minutes

DIFFICULTY: 1

MAKE THE DOUGH

1. Melt the butter in a 3-quart, heavy saucepan over low heat. (This cookie is mixed by hand in the pot.) Cool to tepid.

2. Strain together three times the flour, baking soda, cinnamon, ginger, salt, and cloves. Set aside.

3. Using a wooden spoon, stir 1½ cups of the sugar, the molasses, and egg into the butter, mixing until smooth. Add the dry ingredients, one-half at a time, and blend well. Cover with wax paper and chill for 30 to 45 minutes, until firm.

BAKE THE COOKIES

4. Position the racks in the upper and lower third of the oven. Heat the oven to 375°F. Moderately butter the cookie sheets.

5. Shape the dough into 1-inch balls between the palms of your hands. Place the remaining ½ cup of sugar in a shallow dish and roll the balls of dough in the sugar. Place the balls 2 inches apart on the cookie sheets.

6. Bake the cookies for 8 to 10 minutes, or until the tops begin to crack. Toward the end of baking time rotate the pans from top to bottom and front to back. Remove from the oven and let stand for 2 to 3 minutes. Loosen with a thin, metal spatula and transfer to cooling racks.

STORAGE: Store in an airtight container, layered between strips of wax paper, for up to 3 weeks. These cookies may be frozen.

Secrets for Making Hand-Formed Cookies

- Letting dough rest for a few minutes before shaping will reduce its stickiness.

- Scooping the dough with a spoon before hand-shaping helps ensure even-sized cookies.

- To divide cookie dough evenly, form into a square before chilling. When the dough is firm enough to handle, divide the square into cubes using a dough scraper. The size of the square is determined by the yield of the recipe. After the squares are cut, roll each into a ball.

- If cookie dough is too soft, chill it for approximately 30 minutes or until it is firm enough to handle. Always scrape down the side of the bowl before chilling the dough.

- Do not allow cookie dough to become too cold or it will crumble and be difficult to shape. Allow it to stand at room temperature until it is malleable.

- If the dough sticks to your hands, coat your hands with flour or sugar. Alternatively, if you have warm hands, periodically rinse them in very cold water, or put ice cubes in a metal bowl and hold the bowl to cool your hands. Washing your hands periodically will prevent the dough from sticking.

- When rolling dough into balls, only roll the ball three or four times between the palms of your hands. If the dough is overworked, it will become too soft. This will cause the dough to lose its shape during baking and will toughen the texture of the cookie.

- Hand-formed cookies lend themselves to coatings like sugar, finely chopped nuts, cocoa powder, decorative sugars, jimmies, nonpareils, and spice-flavored sugars. To make the coating adhere, the balls of dough are sometimes dipped in lightly beaten egg white.

- If the balls of dough are to be coated, let them air-dry a few minutes before trimming. They will be easier to handle.

- To apply the coatings neatly and evenly, place the coatings in a shallow pan or pie plate. Instead of using your hands to coat the dough, shimmy the pan back and forth, working with only a few balls at a time.

- Use only a portion of the coating at a time to guarantee a fresh appearance for the finished cookie.

crispy gingersnaps

MAKES ABOUT FORTY 2½-INCH COOKIES

What would a baking book be without a recipe for gingersnaps? Here we have a cookie that is power-packed with ginger flavor. I have added a contemporary touch with the addition of chopped, crystallized ginger. And unlike most gingersnaps, these are made without molasses, making them especially crispy. On a wintry day, with a hot cup of tea, this cookie really hits the spot.

2 cups all-purpose flour, spooned in and leveled

1 tablespoon ground ginger

1 teaspoon baking soda

1 teaspoon ground cinnamon

¼ teaspoon ground cloves

¼ teaspoon salt

⅔ cup (1⅓ sticks) unsalted butter, slightly firm

¾ cup granulated sugar

½ cup lightly packed dark brown sugar

1 large egg

1 teaspoon pure vanilla extract

1 teaspoon cider vinegar

3 tablespoons finely chopped crystallized ginger

AT A GLANCE

PAN: Cookie sheets

PAN PREP: Baking parchment

RACK LEVELS: Upper and lower thirds

OVEN TEMP: 375°F

BAKING TIME: 9–10 minutes

DIFFICULTY: 1

1. Position the racks in the upper and lower thirds of the oven. Heat the oven to 375°F. Line the cookie sheets with baking parchment.

2. Strain together the flour, ginger, baking soda, cinnamon, cloves, and salt. Set aside.

3. In the bowl of an electric mixer fitted with the paddle attachment, mix the butter with the granulated and brown sugars on medium-low speed until creamy and lightened in color, 2 to 3 minutes.

4. Add the egg and mix until well combined, about 1 minute. Scrape down the side of the bowl. Add the vanilla and the vinegar and mix for 1 minute longer. Reduce the mixer speed to low and add the dry ingredients in three additions, mixing *just* until combined. Using a large rubber spatula, blend in the crystallized ginger.

5. Break off walnut-size pieces of dough and roll into 1¼-inch balls. Place 2 inches apart on the cookie sheets. Bake for 9 to 11 minutes, or until golden brown. Toward the end of baking time, rotate the pans from top to bottom and front to back. Let rest on the cookie sheets for 2 minutes, then loosen with a thin, metal spatula and transfer to cooling racks.

STORAGE: Store in an airtight container, layered between strips of wax paper, for up to 3 weeks. These cookies may be frozen.

crystallized ginger and macadamia wafers

MAKES ABOUT 4 DOZEN 3-INCH COOKIES

These thin wafers are speckled with bits of crystallized ginger and chunks of macadamia nuts. The buttery nuts and the refreshing bite of candied ginger make a tantalizing combination.

1½ cups all-purpose flour, spooned in and leveled

1½ teaspoons ground ginger

¼ teaspoon salt

¾ cup (1½ sticks) unsalted butter, slightly firm

½ cup lightly packed light brown sugar

6 tablespoons granulated sugar

3 egg whites, at room temperature

1½ teaspoons pure vanilla extract

1 scant cup macadamia nuts, cut into quarters with a paring knife

1 (2.5-ounce) jar Australian crystallized ginger bits or ½ cup crystallized ginger chips

1. Position the racks in the upper and lower thirds of the oven. Heat the oven to 375°F. Moderately butter the cookie sheets.

2. Strain together the flour, ground ginger, and salt. Set aside.

3. In the large bowl of an electric mixer fitted with the paddle attachment, mix the butter on medium-low speed until lightened in color, about 1 minute. Add the brown sugar and then the granulated sugar, scraping down the side of the bowl as needed. Blend in the egg whites one at a time, then add the vanilla. (It is OK if the mixture appears to separate.)

4. Reduce the mixer speed to low and add the dry ingredients in three additions, mixing *just* until blended after each addition. Using a large rubber spatula, fold in the macadamia nuts and ginger bits. *Do not overmix.*

5. Drop 1¼-inch mounds from the tip of a teaspoon onto the cookie sheets, placing them about 3 inches apart (these cookies will spread). Dip your fingertips in ice water and gently flatten each mound.

6. Bake for 11 to 12 minutes, or until the edges are golden brown, rotating the pans top to bottom and front to back toward the end of the baking time. Remove from oven and let stand for 2 or 3 minutes or *just* until set. Using a thin, metal spatula, carefully loosen and transfer to cooling racks. If the cookies stick, return the pan to the oven and heat briefly.

STORAGE: Store in an airtight container, layered between strips of wax paper, for up to 3 weeks. Handle carefully; the cookies are fragile. These cookies may be frozen.

AT A GLANCE

PAN: Cookie sheets

PAN PREP: Moderately buttered

RACK LEVELS: Upper and lower thirds

OVEN TEMP: 375°F

BAKING TIME: 11–12 minutes

DIFFICULTY: 1

snickerdoodles

MAKES ABOUT 4 DOZEN 3-INCH COOKIES

One morning, my plumber, Bruce Robertshaw, walked in briskly to make a repair. Bruce, a no-nonsense man, said, "Hmmm . . . and what are we making today?" I recited my menu of cookies, one of which happened to be snickerdoodles. "Snickerdoodles," he said, "my wife makes the best! It was my grandmother's recipe and has been in my family for years." Needless to say, my curiosity was aroused and I had to try out the recipe for this book.

As Bruce left, he said with a gleam in his eye, "You know I timed this all wrong! I usually come at the end of the day so I can go home with a plateful of cookies!" For me, the timing was perfect. I put aside my own snickerdoodle recipe in anticipation of Grandma Robertshaw's. Grandma's snickerdoodles more than lived up to their reputation. Here is the Robertshaw family recipe. See if you don't agree!

2½ cups all-purpose flour, spooned in and leveled

2 teaspoons cream of tartar

1 teaspoon baking soda

½ teaspoon salt

½ cup (1 stick) unsalted butter, at room temperature

½ cup vegetable shortening

1¾ cups sugar, divided

2 large eggs

1 teaspoon pure vanilla extract

1 to 1½ teaspoons ground cinnamon

AT A GLANCE

PAN: Cookie sheets

PAN PREP: Lightly buttered

CHILLING TIME: 6–8 hours

RACK LEVELS: Upper and lower thirds

OVEN TEMP: 350°F

BAKING TIME: 10–12 minutes

DIFFICULTY: 1

MAKE THE DOUGH

1. Strain together the flour, cream of tartar, baking soda, and salt. Set aside.

2. In the large bowl of an electric mixer fitted with the paddle attachment, mix the butter and vegetable shortening on medium speed until lightened in color, about 2 minutes. Add 1½ cups of the sugar in a steady stream and mix for another 2 minutes. Reduce the mixer speed to low and add the eggs one at a time, mixing well after each addition and scraping down the side of the bowl as needed. Stir in the vanilla.

3. Add the dry ingredients in two additions, mixing *just* until blended after each addition. Scrape the dough into a clean bowl, cover with plastic wrap, and chill for 6 to 8 hours, or overnight.

BAKE THE COOKIES

4. Position the racks in the upper and lower thirds of the oven. Heat the oven to 350°F. Lightly butter the cookie sheets.

5. Divide the dough into quarters. With lightly floured hands, shape each quarter into a log. Slice each log into 12 equal pieces and roll into small, walnut-size balls.

6. Combine the remaining ¼ cup sugar with the cinnamon in a small mixing bowl. Working one piece at a time, place each ball in the mixture and briskly rotate the bowl in a circular motion to coat the dough evenly with the mixture.

7. Place the dough balls 3 inches apart on the cookie sheets. Bake for 10 to 12 minutes, or until lightly browned. Toward the end of baking time, rotate the pans from top to bottom and front to back. (A shorter baking time will make these cookies chewier, while longer baking results in crispiness.) Remove the cookies from the oven and let rest for 5 minutes. Transfer with a thin, metal spatula to wire racks to cool.

STORAGE: Store in an airtight container, layered between strips of wax paper, for up to 3 weeks. These cookies may be frozen.

crackly cinnamon wafers

MAKES ABOUT 7 DOZEN 2¾-INCH COOKIES

Here we have thin butter cookies with heady cinnamon flavor that are delicate and oh, so scrumptious! A light brushing of egg wash forms a whisper of a crust that twinkles with a sprinkling of sparkling coarse sugar. If these larger granules are difficult to obtain, granulated sugar may be substituted. The sparkly cookies are perfect to serve at teatime or on your best holiday table.

1¾ cups all-purpose flour, spooned in and leveled

1 tablespoon ground cinnamon

1 cup (2 sticks) unsalted butter, slightly firm

1 cup granulated sugar

1 large egg, separated

3 to 4 tablespoons sparkling white sugar (available from The Baker's Catalogue; see Sources, page 381), for garnish

AT A GLANCE

PAN: Cookie sheets

PAN PREP: Moderately buttered

CHILLING TIME: 1 hour

RACK LEVELS: Upper and lower thirds

OVEN TEMP: 350°F

BAKING TIME: 10–11 minutes

DIFFICULTY: 1

MAKE THE DOUGH

1. Strain together the flour and cinnamon. Set aside.

2. Using an electric mixer fitted with the paddle attachment on medium-low speed, mix the butter until smooth. Add the granulated sugar in a steady stream and beat until combined. Add the egg yolk and mix for 1 minute longer, scraping down the side of the bowl as needed. Reduce the mixer speed to low, then add the dry ingredients in three additions, mixing *just* until blended after each addition. Cover with plastic wrap and refrigerate for 1 hour.

BAKE THE COOKIES

3. Position the racks in the upper and lower thirds of the oven. Heat the oven to 350°F. Moderately butter the cookie sheets.

4. Roll dough into ¾-inch balls and place on the cookie sheets, about 2½ inches apart. Using the bottom of a flat-bottomed glass that has been covered with plastic wrap and dipped in flour, flatten the dough balls into 2½-inch disks.

5. In a shallow dish, lightly beat the egg white with 2 teaspoons cold water and brush the top of each cookie with the egg wash. Sprinkle each cookie with sparkling white sugar. Bake for 10 to 11 minutes, or until the edges are golden brown. Rotate the pans from top to bottom and front to back toward the end of baking time. Let stand for 1 minute, then loosen with a thin, metal spatula. Transfer to cooling racks.

STORAGE: Store in an airtight container, layered between strips of wax paper, for up to 3 weeks. These cookies may be frozen.

sesame coins

MAKES ABOUT 4 DOZEN 1¾-INCH COOKIES

What makes these tidbits so appealing is the crusty, sesame-seed coating combined with a melt-in-your-mouth, buttery crumb. If you can limit yourself to just one or two, you are better than I am!

1½ cups all-purpose flour, spooned in and leveled

½ teaspoon baking powder

¼ teaspoon salt

¾ cup (1½ sticks) unsalted butter, at room temperature

1¼ cups strained confectioners' sugar, spooned in and leveled

2 large egg whites, divided

1 teaspoon pure vanilla extract

1 teaspoon sesame oil

⅔ cup toasted sesame seeds (see page 356)

MAKE THE DOUGH

1. Strain together the flour, baking powder, and salt. Set aside.

2. In the large bowl of an electric mixer fitted with the paddle attachment, mix the butter on medium-low speed until creamy and lightened in color. Add the confectioners' sugar and beat for 1 to 2 minutes, until smooth. Blend in one egg white, then the vanilla and sesame oil.

3. Reduce the mixer speed to low and add the dry ingredients in three additions, mixing *just* until well combined after each addition. Loosely cover the dough with a sheet of wax paper and chill for at least 1 hour before shaping.

AT A GLANCE

PAN: Cookie sheets

PAN PREP: Moderately buttered or baking parchment

CHILLING TIME: 1 hour

RACK LEVELS: Upper and lower thirds

OVEN TEMP: 375°F

BAKING TIME: 9–10 minutes

DIFFICULTY: 2

BAKE THE COOKIES

4. Position the racks in the upper and lower thirds of the oven. Heat the oven to 375°F. Moderately butter cookie sheets, or alternatively, line with baking parchment.

5. Lightly beat the remaining egg white with 1 teaspoon of water in a low, flat dish. Place the sesame seeds in another low dish. Take small pieces of dough and roll between your palms into ¾-inch balls. Toss each ball of dough in egg white, then roll in sesame seeds. Place on the cookie sheets about 1½ inches apart and, using a flat-bottomed glass dipped in sugar, flatten to about 1½ inches in diameter.

6. Bake for 9 to 10 minutes, or until the edges are golden brown. Rotate the pans top to bottom and front to back toward the end of baking time. Remove from the oven and let stand for 2 or 3 minutes before loosening with a thin spatula. Cool on wire racks.

STORAGE: Store in an airtight container, layered between strips of wax paper, for up to 3 weeks. These cookies may be frozen.

poppy seed thumbprints

MAKES ABOUT FORTY 1¾-INCH COOKIES

Here is an easy cookie that will add pizzazz to any platter of sweets. The centers of the cookies are usually filled with colorful preserves, but sometimes I vary this selection with a bull's-eye of thickened Ganache Glaze (page 371). While I love the crunch that poppy seeds add, they can be omitted if you wish.

2 cups all-purpose flour, spooned in
    and leveled

¼ teaspoon salt

¼ cup poppy seeds

1 cup (2 sticks) unsalted butter, slightly firm

½ cup sugar

2 large egg yolks

1 teaspoon pure vanilla extract

Raspberry preserves

Apricot preserves

AT A GLANCE

PAN: Cookie sheets

PAN PREP: Ungreased

RACK LEVELS: Upper and
    lower thirds

OVEN TEMP: 350°F

BAKING TIME: 14–15 minutes

DIFFICULTY: 2

1. Position the racks in the upper and lower thirds of the oven. Heat the oven to 350°F.

2. Strain together the flour and salt in a large bowl. Whisk in the poppy seeds and set aside.

3. In the large bowl of an electric mixer fitted with the paddle attachment, mix the butter on medium-low speed until smooth. Pour in the sugar and mix *just* until incorporated. Add the egg yolks and vanilla, mixing only until blended. Using a wooden spoon, stir in the dry ingredients in two additions, mixing *just* to combine after each addition. *Note:* Do not overmix this dough or it will become oily.

4. Roll the dough into balls about the size of large walnuts and place 2 inches apart on the cookie sheets. Using a wooden spoon with a rounded handle no wider than ½ inch, make a deep indentation with the tip of the handle in the center of each cookie. If the dough sticks, dip the tip in flour before pressing.

5. Place the cookies in the oven. After 10 minutes, remove the cookies from the oven and re-press each indentation. Then fill the centers with preserves. To do this neatly, point the tip of the spoon down into the indentation and slide the preserves off with your fingertip. Do not overfill these or the preserves will run over.

6. Return the cookies to the oven, rotating the pans top to bottom and front to back. Bake for 4 to 5 minutes longer, or until the cookies are golden brown around the edges. Using a thin, metal spatula, loosen the cookies from the pans as soon as they are cool enough to handle. Cool on wire racks.

STORAGE: Store in an airtight container, layered between strips of wax paper, for up to 2 weeks. These cookies may be frozen.

italian macaroons

MAKES 3 DOZEN 2-INCH COOKIES

Here is a recipe for the classic Italian macaroon. Rich almond paste provides the cookie with a luxurious texture and flavor, while the combination of confectioners' sugar and granulated sugar creates a wonderfully crisp-chewy texture. Be sure the almond paste is very fresh. It does make a difference.

16 ounces almond paste (see page 355), at room temperature

¾ cup strained confectioners' sugar, spooned in and leveled

¾ cup granulated sugar, plus 2 tablespoons for sprinkling

¼ teaspoon salt

4 large egg whites, at room temperature

1. Position the racks in the upper and lower thirds of the oven. Heat the oven to 350°F. Dab the corners of the cookie sheets lightly with butter and line them with baking parchment. Butter the parchment.

2. In the bowl of an electric mixer fitted with the paddle attachment, mix the almond paste with the confectioners' sugar and ¾ cup of the granulated sugar on low speed until the mixture is the consistency of meal-size crumbs, 6 to 8 minutes.

3. Add the salt to the egg whites and whisk to blend. Add the egg whites to the almond paste mixture in four additions. Continue to mix until it starts to liquefy and stick to the bottom of the bowl. This will take 15 to 20 seconds. Let stand 10 minutes to thicken slightly.

4. Drop slightly full teaspoons of the batter from the tip of a teaspoon, forming 1½-inch mounds, onto the cookie sheets, spacing them about 2 inches apart. If the mounds are uneven, smooth with moistened fingertips. Sprinkle with the remaining granulated sugar.

5. Bake for 16 to 18 minutes, or until just lightly browned around the edges. To ensure even baking, rotate the sheets from top to bottom and front to back toward the end of baking time. Let rest on the cookie sheet for 5 minutes before transferring to cooling racks.

STORAGE: Store in an airtight container, layered between strips of wax paper, for up to 5 days. As the macaroons age, they develop flavor and become softer. These cookies may be frozen.

AT A GLANCE

PAN: Cookie sheets

PAN PREP: Buttered baking parchment

RACK LEVELS: Upper and lower thirds

OVEN TEMP: 350°F

BAKING TIME: 16–18 minutes

DIFFICULTY: 1

rustic maple pecan cookies

MAKES ABOUT 4 DOZEN 2¾-INCH COOKIES

This cookie is made with melted butter, to which maple syrup and orange juice are added. The melted butter gives the cookie its unique flavor and exceptionally crispy texture.

¾ cup (1½ sticks) unsalted butter

2 cups all-purpose flour, spooned in and leveled

½ teaspoon salt

¼ teaspoon baking soda

¼ cup pure maple syrup

1 large egg

2 tablespoons orange juice

1 teaspoon imitation maple extract

1 teaspoon pure vanilla extract

⅔ cup superfine sugar

½ cup very fresh lightly packed dark brown sugar

1½ cups coarsely chopped toasted pecans (see page 356)

AT A GLANCE

PAN: Cookie sheets

PAN PREP: Moderately buttered

RACK LEVELS: Upper and lower thirds

OVEN TEMP: 350°F

BAKING TIME: 12–14 minutes

DIFFICULTY: 1

1. Position the racks in the upper and lower thirds of the oven. Heat the oven to 350°F. Moderately butter the cookie sheets.

2. In a 3-quart, heavy-bottomed saucepan, melt the butter and set aside to *cool to tepid*.

3. Strain together the flour, salt, and baking soda. Set aside.

4. Using a wooden spoon, add the maple syrup to the melted butter, mixing well. Blend in the egg, orange juice, and the maple and vanilla extracts. Whisk in the superfine and brown sugars, stirring until well combined and free of lumps. Stir in the dry ingredients in three additions, then fold in the nuts with a large rubber spatula.

5. Using the tip of a teaspoon, drop mounds of dough the size of large walnuts onto the cookie sheets, placing them 2 inches apart. Bake for 12 to 14 minutes, or until the edges *just* begin to brown, rotating the pans top to bottom and front to back toward the end of the baking time. Remove from the oven and let stand for 2 to 3 minutes before loosening with a thin, metal spatula. Cool on wire racks.

STORAGE: Store in an airtight container, layered between strips of wax paper, for up to 3 weeks. These cookies may be frozen.

Rustic Maple Pecan Date Cookies

Reduce the chopped pecans to ¼ cup. Toss 1 teaspoon flour with 1 cup loosely packed, ¼-inch-diced dates to prevent them from sticking together. Mix the dates with the pecans and add to the dough in step 4, then proceed with step 5.

golden almond amaretti

MAKES THIRTY-TWO 2¼-INCH COOKIES

In order for the finished cookie to have a chewy texture, it is important that the almonds be very finely ground and the cookies not be overbaked.

2 cups sliced, unblanched almonds

1¼ cups sugar, divided

1½ teaspoons ground cinnamon

4 large egg yolks

½ teaspoon pure vanilla extract

½ teaspoon almond extract

2 large eggs

3 tablespoons amaretto liqueur

1 cup sliced, unblanched toasted, almonds (see page 356), crunched into small pieces with your hand

1. Position the racks in the upper and lower thirds of the oven. Heat the oven to 375°F. Dab the corners of the jelly roll pans lightly with butter and line with baking parchment. Lightly butter the parchment.

2. Place the sliced almonds, ¼ cup of the sugar, and the cinnamon in the work bowl of a food processor fitted with the steel blade. Process until the mixture begins to clump together, 45 to 60 seconds. Set aside.

3. In the bowl of an electric mixer fitted with the paddle attachment, beat the yolks on medium speed, then increase the speed to medium-high. Beat until thickened and lightened in color, 1½ to 2 minutes. Add ½ cup of the remaining sugar, taking about 1 minute, then mix for another 30 seconds. Beat in the vanilla and almond extracts.

4. Reduce the mixer speed to low and add the almond mixture in two additions.

5. Place the eggs and the amaretto in a low, flat dish, such as a pie plate, and whisk to blend. In another low, flat dish, combine the crushed almonds and the remaining ½ cup sugar.

6. Shape the dough into 1-inch balls. Roll each ball in the egg mixture, then in the almond-sugar mixture. Repeat the dipping procedure before placing the balls on the pans.

7. Bake the cookies for 10 to 11 minutes, or *just* until the bottoms are lightly browned. To ensure even browning, toward the end of baking time, rotate the pans from top to bottom and front to back. *Do not overbake.* Let rest on the pans for 4 to 5 minutes, then remove to cooling racks.

STORAGE: Store in an airtight container, layered between strips of wax paper, for up to 3 weeks. These cookies may be frozen.

AT A GLANCE

PAN: Jelly roll pans

PAN PREP: Buttered baking parchment

RACK LEVELS: Upper and lower thirds

OVEN TEMP: 375°F

BAKING TIME: 10–11 minutes

DIFFICULTY: 1

bake a batch of bar cookies

carole's best brownies

MAKES THIRTY-TWO 1½- × 2-INCH BROWNIES

Buttery, chewy, chocolatey brownies bursting with crunchy walnuts, along with a glass of ice-cold milk, send me over the top. When I get a midnight craving, I will bake brownies right then and there. The day I came home from the hospital after giving birth to each of my children, I made a beeline to the kitchen and immediately made a batch of brownies. They are my comfort food!!

---

1 cup (2 sticks) unsalted butter

5 ounces unsweetened chocolate, preferably Nestlé, coarsely chopped

4 large eggs, at room temperature

2 cups superfine sugar

2 teaspoons pure vanilla extract

¼ teaspoon salt

1 cup plus 2 tablespoons all-purpose flour, spooned in and leveled

2 cups coarsely chopped walnuts (see page 356)

AT A GLANCE

PAN: 9- × 13- × 2-inch baking pan

PAN PREP: Buttered heavy-duty aluminum foil

RACK LEVEL: Center

OVEN TEMP: 350°F

BAKING TIME: 28–30 minutes

DIFFICULTY: 1

1. Position the rack in the center of the oven. Heat the oven to 350°F. Invert the baking pan, then tear an 18- × 16-inch sheet of heavy-duty aluminum foil and center it over the top, smooth the surface, then press it down the sides. Carefully remove the foil shell, turn the pan right side up, and place the foil shell in the pan, shaping it smoothly across the bottom and snugly against the sides. Thoroughly butter the foil, taking care not to tear it.

2. Place the butter in a medium bowl and set it over a pot of simmering water. The bottom of the bowl should not touch the water. When the butter is almost melted, add the chocolate. After 1 minute, remove the pot from the heat. Let stand until the chocolate is completely melted, stirring occasionally.

3. In a large mixing bowl, whisk the eggs lightly, then stir in the sugar in a steady stream. Add the warm butter–chocolate mixture, and stir with the whisk to blend, taking care not to aerate. Mix in the vanilla and the salt.

4. Strain the flour over the chocolate mixture in three additions, folding gently each time with the whisk *just* until blended. Fold in the nuts with an oversize rubber spatula or a large wooden spoon. Immediately empty the batter into the pan, then spread evenly with the bottom of a large spoon. Bake for 28 to 30 minutes, or until a toothpick inserted into the center of the brownie bar comes out slightly moist. A few particles of the brownie should stick to the toothpick. *Do not overbake.*

5. Set the pan of brownies on a wire rack. Let stand at least 4 hours before cutting.

STORAGE: Store in an airtight container, layered between strips of wax paper, for up to 5 days. The brownies may be frozen.

chewy chocolate coco-nut bars

MAKES FORTY 1½- × 1¾-INCH BARS

This is a recipe that I created for the food processor when it was first introduced. It is a quick chocolate bar cookie with a brownie-like consistency and features one of my favorite combinations, coconut and walnuts. The result is a cookie that is moist and chewy, and impossible to resist!

1 cup walnuts, divided

½ cup (1 stick) unsalted butter

2 ounces unsweetened chocolate, coarsely chopped

1 cup sugar

⅔ cup all-purpose flour, spooned in and leveled

½ cup sweetened, flaked coconut

¼ teaspoon salt

2 large eggs

1 teaspoon pure vanilla extract

1. Position the rack in the center of the oven. Heat the oven to 350°F. Butter and flour the baking pan. Invert the pan and tap sharply over the sink to remove any excess flour.

2. Place ½ cup of the walnuts in the work bowl of a food processor fitted with the steel blade. Pulse three or four times, until medium chopped. Remove the nuts from the processor and set aside for the topping.

3. Place the butter in a medium bowl and set it over a pot of simmering water. The bottom of the bowl should not touch the water. When the butter is almost melted, add the chocolate. After 1 minute, remove the pot from the heat. Let stand until the chocolate is completely melted, stirring occasionally.

4. Place the sugar, flour, coconut, salt, and remaining ½ cup walnuts in the work bowl of the food processor. Pulse three or four times.

5. Stir the eggs and vanilla into the chocolate mixture, then pour into the food processor bowl. Pulse all of the ingredients together *just* until blended.

6. Pour the batter into the prepared pan and smooth the surface with the back of a tablespoon. Press the chopped nuts across the top. Bake for 15 to 18 minutes, or until set on top and the edges start to pull away from the sides of the pan. Place on a cooling rack. When cool, use a sharp knife to cut into 40 bars.

STORAGE: Store in an airtight container, layered between strips of wax paper, for up to 5 days. These squares may be frozen.

AT A GLANCE

PAN: 9- × 13- × 2-inch baking pan

PAN PREP: Buttered and floured

RACK LEVEL: Center

OVEN TEMP: 350°F

BAKING TIME: 15–18 minutes

DIFFICULTY: 1

sally's deep 'n dark frosted brownies

MAKES TWENTY-FIVE 1¾-INCH BROWNIES

This is a brownie for sophisticated palates, from an adventurous gal who knows a good thing when she tastes it! My friend and teaching compatriot Sally Kofke is known not only for her outstanding Italian cuisine but also for a dynamite brownie. This batter is richly flavored with premium chocolate, espresso powder, and freshly ground black pepper. After baking, Sally finishes her brownies with a satiny chocolate glaze. Take care not to overbake these brownies to retain their moist and chewy texture.

BROWNIES

8 ounces fine-quality bittersweet or semisweet chocolate, such as Lindt Bittersweet, coarsely chopped

½ cup plus 2 tablespoons (1¼ sticks) unsalted butter, slightly firm

¾ cup firmly packed light brown sugar

2 teaspoons instant espresso powder

1 teaspoon pure vanilla extract

½ teaspoon finely ground black pepper (if using preground pepper, increase to ¾ teaspoon)

⅛ teaspoon salt

3 large eggs

¾ cup all-purpose flour, spooned in and leveled

1 to 1½ cups coarsely chopped nuts (such as walnuts, pecans, or Brazil nuts; see page 356)

CHOCOLATE GLAZE

2 tablespoons water

¾ teaspoon instant espresso powder

2 ounces fine-quality bittersweet or semi-sweet chocolate, such as Lindt Bittersweet, finely chopped in a food processor

2 tablespoons (¼ stick) unsalted butter

AT A GLANCE

PAN: 9-inch square baking pan

PAN PREP: Buttered heavy-duty aluminum foil

RACK LEVEL: Center

OVEN TEMP: 325°F

BAKING TIME: 35 minutes

DIFFICULTY: 1

1. Position the rack in the center of the oven. Heat the oven to 325°F. Cut a 15-inch square of heavy-duty aluminum foil. Invert the pan and center the foil over the pan, pressing it across the bottom and down the sides. Remove the foil, turn the pan right side up, and place the foil shell into the pan, shaping it smoothly across the bottom and snugly against the sides of the pan. Thoroughly butter the foil, taking care not to tear it.

MAKE THE BROWNIES

2. Place the chocolate in a heat-proof bowl set over simmering water. Slowly melt the chocolate, stirring occasionally, then set aside to cool.

3. In the bowl of an electric mixer fitted with the paddle attachment, mix the butter on medium-low speed until smooth. Add the brown sugar, espresso powder, vanilla, black pepper, and salt, mixing until blended, about 1 minute. Add the eggs one at a time and mix 1 minute longer, scraping down the side of the bowl as needed. The mixture will look curdled.

4. With the machine off, add the melted chocolate, then mix on low speed for 15 to 20 seconds. Scrape down the bowl. Add the flour, mixing *just* until blended. Remove the bowl from the mixer and fold in the nuts with a rubber spatula. Scrape the batter into the prepared pan and smooth the top with the back of a tablespoon.

5. Bake for 35 minutes. A toothpick inserted in the center will still be wet. The brownies will set as they stand. While the brownies are baking, make the glaze.

MAKE THE GLAZE

6. Place the water in a microwave-safe custard cup and heat for 40 seconds or until steaming. Add the espresso powder and stir to dissolve. Place the dissolved espresso and the finely chopped chocolate in a small saucepan, add 1 tablespoon of the butter, and cook over low heat, stirring, until the chocolate is *almost* melted. This will only take a few seconds. Remove from the heat and add the remaining tablespoon of butter, stirring to incorporate.

7. Allow the glaze to stand for 5 to 10 minutes, or until slightly thickened, stirring occasionally. Do not allow the glaze to become too thick, or it will not spread.

8. While the brownies are still warm, pour the glaze over the top and spread it evenly using a small offset spatula. It is important not to overwork the glaze, or it will lose its shiny appearance. Allow to stand until the glaze is set. This could take a few hours, depending on the temperature of the room. When dry, using the foil as an aid, lift the brownies out of the pan and place on a cutting board. Smooth down the edges of the foil and cut the brownies with a long, sharp knife. Use an offset spatula to carefully remove the brownies from the foil and cut into 25 bars.

STORAGE: Store in an airtight container, layered between strips of wax paper, for up to 5 days. The brownies may be frozen.

Pointers for Better Brownies

- When melting better and chocolate over water, be sure that the water is at a *simmer*, not boiling.

- It's best to melt the butter first and then add the chopped chocolate. Stir occasionally and gently to ensure even melting and blending.

- When chocolate and butter are melted, do not allow the mixture to become too hot.

- The temperature of the chocolate/butter mixture determines the consistency of a better brownie. When it is cool, the batter will be thick; when warm, the batter will be thin.

- Always remember that brownies continue to bake even after being removed from the oven, so allow for this when testing for doneness.

- If nuts are omitted from a brownie recipe, the consistency will be entirely different. Not only can it affect baking time but the brownie will be dense. To replace the volume of the nuts, try substituting chocolate chips.

stephen schmidt's white chocolate macadamia bars

MAKES FORTY 1½- × 1¾-INCH BARS

One year, at a covered-dish supper held by the New York Association of Cooking Professionals, the buzz at dessert time was about a fantastic bar cookie brought by cookbook author and teacher Stephen Schmidt. The cookie was made with a mountain of salty macadamia nuts, lots of flaked, sweet coconut, and generous chunks of white chocolate, all bound with a mixture of heavy cream and sugar. This decadent bar cookie was so good that it's no wonder it was the hit of the evening. These bars will be the hit of your cookie platter, as well. Thanks, Stephen!

CRUST

2⅓ cups all-purpose flour, spooned in and leveled

⅔ cup strained confectioners' sugar, spooned in and leveled

½ teaspoon salt

¾ cup (1½ sticks) cold unsalted butter, cut into ½-inch dice

TOPPING

1 cup plus 2 tablespoons granulated sugar

1 cup heavy cream

¼ cup (½ stick) unsalted butter, melted

1 tablespoon strained fresh lemon juice

1½ teaspoons pure vanilla extract

½ teaspoon salt

3 cups (about 9 ounces) lightly packed sweetened, flaked coconut

2½ cups salted macadamia nuts, halved and toasted (see page 356)

8 to 9 ounces fine-quality white chocolate, such as Lindt Swiss Classic White, cut into ¼- to ½-inch chunks

AT A GLANCE

PAN: 9- × 13- × 2-inch metal baking pan

PAN PREP: Buttered heavy-duty aluminum foil

RACK LEVEL: Center

OVEN TEMP: 350°F, 325°F

BAKING TIME: 25 minutes, crust; 40–50 minutes, topping

DIFFICULTY: 1

1. Position the rack in the center of the oven. Heat the oven to 350°F. Lightly butter the baking pan. Tear an 18- × 16-inch sheet of heavy-duty aluminum foil. Invert the pan and center the foil over the pan, pressing it across the bottom and down the sides. Remove the foil, turn the pan right side up, and place the foil shell into the pan, shaping it smoothly across the bottom and snugly against the sides of the pan. Thoroughly butter the foil, taking care not to tear it.

MAKE THE CRUST

2. Combine the flour, confectioners' sugar, and salt in the work bowl of a food processor and pulse several times to blend. Add the cold butter and process until a smooth dough forms. Divide the dough into eight pieces and arrange them in two rows in the pan. Using a bâtarde or the bottom of a glass, press the dough evenly into the pan. Bake the crust until golden, about 25 minutes.

MAKE THE TOPPING

3. Combine the granulated sugar, heavy cream, melted butter, lemon juice, vanilla, and salt in a large bowl, mixing well. Add the coconut, nuts, and chocolate chunks, then stir until the ingredients are coated with the sugar-cream mixture. Empty the topping over the hot crust and smooth it with an offset spatula or the back of a spoon.

BAKE THE COOKIES

4. Reduce the oven temperature to 325°F. Place the pan in the oven and bake for 40 to 50 minutes, or until the topping has flattened, stopped bubbling, and is browned lightly. (Initially it will puff up.) Set the pan on a rack and cool to room temperature, then cover the pan with aluminum foil and refrigerate until cold. This will take several hours.

5. To release the bar from the pan, place the pan on top of the stove and over low heat, then rotate the pan until it is warm. Then, using the foil to grip the bar, lift it out of the pan. While the bar is still chilled, using a sharp, heavy knife, trim the hard edges, then cut the bar crosswise into eight strips. Divide each strip into five pieces to make 40 bars.

STORAGE: Refrigerate in an airtight container, layered between strips of wax paper, for up to 5 days.

chocolate cream cheese brownies

MAKES TWENTY-FIVE 1¾-INCH BROWNIES

Since brownies and cheesecakes are among our most favorite desserts, marrying the two is a sure winner. The dark chocolate batter is marbled with swirls of velvety cream cheese. For a contrast of texture, I added some toasted walnuts. When you marble the two batters together, be sure to keep your knife in the upper portion of the batters and do not overmix or the marble effect will be lost. Granted, these are sinfully rich, but once in a while a little indulgence is good for the soul.

CREAM CHEESE BATTER

6 ounces (2 3-ounce packages) cream cheese, at room temperature

¼ cup sugar

1 tablespoon all-purpose flour

1 large egg

2 tablespoons sour cream

½ teaspoon pure vanilla extract

2 teaspoons fresh lemon juice

BROWNIE BATTER

½ cup all-purpose flour, spooned in and leveled

¼ teaspoon baking powder

¼ teaspoon salt

6 tablespoons (¾ stick) unsalted butter

5 ounces fine-quality bittersweet or semisweet chocolate, such as Lindt Bittersweet, chopped

2 ounces unsweetened chocolate, chopped

3 large eggs

1¼ cups sugar

1½ teaspoons pure vanilla extract

¾ cup broken walnut pieces, toasted (see page 356)

AT A GLANCE

PAN: 9-inch square baking pan

PAN PREP: Buttered heavy-duty aluminum foil

RACK LEVEL: Center

OVEN TEMP: 350°F

BAKING TIME: 45–50 minutes

DIFFICULTY: 1

MAKE THE CREAM CHEESE BATTER

1. Place the cream cheese and sugar in a medium bowl and stir with a wooden spoon until smooth. Stir in the flour.

2. Whisk together the egg, sour cream, vanilla, and lemon juice and gradually add to the cream cheese mixture. Whisk until smooth. Set aside.

MAKE THE BROWNIE BATTER

3. Position the rack in the center of the oven. Heat the oven to 350°F. Cut a 15-inch square sheet of heavy-duty aluminum foil. Invert the baking pan and center the sheet of foil over the pan, pressing the foil across the bottom and down the sides. Remove the foil, invert the pan, and place the foil shell into the pan, shaping it smoothly across the bottom and snugly against the sides of the pan. Carefully and thoroughly butter the foil, taking care not to tear it. Set the pan aside.

4. Strain together the flour, baking powder, and salt. Set aside.

5. Place the butter in a medium bowl and set it over a pot of simmering water. The bottom of the bowl should not touch the water. When the butter is melted, add the chocolates, removing the pot from the heat after 1 minute. Let stand until the chocolates are melted, stirring occasionally.

6. Place the eggs in a large mixing bowl and whisk to blend. Using the whisk to stir, add the sugar in a steady stream, then pour in the chocolate mixture and whisk to blend. Stir in the vanilla.

7. Strain the flour mixture over the chocolate mixture in three additions, folding gently each time with a whisk just until blended. Fold in the walnuts with a rubber spatula. Remove 1 cup of the batter and set aside.

BAKE THE BROWNIES

8. Empty the remaining batter into the prepared pan and spread evenly with a spatula. Pour the cream cheese batter over the top and spread evenly. Drop the remaining batter by tablespoons randomly over the cream cheese mixture. Swirl the two layers together by inserting a sharp, thin-bladed knife about halfway in, then gently moving the knife back and forth to create a marbled effect with the batters. The knife should not go completely through to the bottom of the pan.

9. Bake the brownies for 45 to 50 minutes, or until the top is puffed and set. Remove from the oven and place on a cooling rack. Let the brownies stand for 3 to 4 hours before cutting into 25 squares.

STORAGE: Refrigerate in an airtight container, layered between strips of wax paper, for up to 5 days. These brownies may be frozen.

chocolate cappuccino cheesecake squares

MAKES TWENTY-FIVE 1¾-INCH SQUARES

These decadent bar cookies, a favorite of my son-in-law, Andy, have a chocolate crust topped with a chocolate cappuccino cream cheese filling and a light covering of sour cream. For ease of handling, I like to use decorative cupcake papers for holding the little squares.

CRUST

1 cup all-purpose flour, spooned in and leveled

½ cup sugar

⅓ cup strained Dutch-processed cocoa powder, spooned in and leveled

¼ teaspoon salt

½ cup (1 stick) butter, cut into ½-inch cubes and chilled

FILLING

12 ounces (1½ 8-ounce packages) cream cheese, at room temperature

½ cup sugar

1 large egg

¼ cup sour cream

2 ounces fine-quality bittersweet or semisweet chocolate, such as Lindt Bittersweet, melted and cooled to tepid

1 teaspoon instant espresso powder, dissolved in ½ teaspoon boiling water

½ teaspoon pure vanilla extract

TOPPING

1 cup sour cream

¼ cup sugar

½ teaspoon pure vanilla extract

AT A GLANCE

PAN: 9-inch square baking pan

PAN PREP: Buttered heavy-duty aluminum foil

RACK LEVEL: Center

OVEN TEMP: 325°F

BAKING TIME: 18–20 minutes, crust; 30 minutes, filling; 8–10 minutes, topping

DIFFICULTY: 2

1. Position the rack in the center of the oven. Heat the oven to 325°F. Cut a 15-inch square of heavy-duty aluminum foil. Invert the pan and center the foil over the pan, pressing it across the bottom and down the sides. Remove the foil, turn the pan right side up, and place the foil shell in the pan, shaping it smoothly across the bottom and snugly against the sides. Using a pastry brush, grease the bottom and sides with softened butter, taking care not to tear the foil. Set aside.

MAKE THE CRUST

2. Place the flour, sugar, cocoa, and salt in the work bowl of a food processor fitted with a steel blade and pulse to combine. Add the butter and process just until crumbs form. Pour the crumbs into the pan and press over the bottom. (See Spreading Batters and Doughs, page 366.) Straighten the edges of the dough by inserting a dough scraper or small spatula in between the dough and the foil. Bake for 18 to 20 minutes, or until set but still slightly soft. Allow the crust to stand for 5 minutes.

MAKE THE FILLING

3. Place the cream cheese and sugar in the work bowl of a food processor fitted with a steel blade and pulse just until smooth. Scrape down the processor bowl and process again for 5 seconds, but no longer. Add the egg, sour cream, chocolate, espresso powder, and vanilla and process for 5 seconds. Pour the filling over the *warm* crust. Bake for 30 minutes, or until set.

MAKE THE TOPPING

4. Mix the sour cream, sugar, and vanilla. Using a small offset spatula, spread smoothly over the warm filling and bake 8 to 10 minutes longer. Alternatively, for a decorative top, prepare half of the sour cream topping. Place in a plastic squeeze bottle and make five "stripes" about 1½ inches apart over the top of the warm filling. Using a small, offset spatula, spread the stripes to a width of about ¾ inch. Return to the oven and bake for 8 to 10 minutes, or until set.

5. Cool on a wire rack, then cover loosely with aluminum foil and refrigerate overnight. Using the foil as an aid, remove the bar from the pan and place on a cutting board or other flat surface. Have ready several damp paper towels. Using a long, thin knife, cut the bar into fifths, using the paper towel to clean the knife as needed. Give the bar a quarter turn and cut into fifths again, making twenty-five 1¾-inch squares.

STORAGE: Refrigerate, covered, for up to 5 days. These squares may be frozen.

triple chocolate peppermint bars

MAKES THIRTY-TWO 1½- × 2-INCH BARS

Variegated hues of chocolate from a chocolate shortbread crust, a brownielike center, and a ganache glaze make a bar cookie that will add an air of professionalism to any sweet table. The flavor of peppermint schnapps, a distilled liquor, gives this cookie its snappy peppermint taste.

CRUST

1½ cups all-purpose flour, spooned in and leveled

½ cup superfine sugar

6 tablespoons strained Dutch-processed cocoa powder, spooned in and leveled

¾ cup (1½ sticks) unsalted butter, slightly firm, cut into ½-inch slices

1 large egg yolk

CENTER LAYER

¼ cup (½ stick) unsalted butter

4 ounces fine-quality bittersweet or semisweet chocolate, such as Lindt Bittersweet, finely chopped

1½ ounces unsweetened chocolate, finely chopped

3 tablespoons peppermint schnapps

⅓ cup superfine sugar

2 large eggs, lightly beaten, at room temperature

1 teaspoon pure vanilla extract

½ cup all-purpose flour, spooned in and leveled

TOP LAYER

1 tablespoon peppermint schnapps

⅛ teaspoon peppermint extract

½ recipe Ganache Glaze (page 371)

AT A GLANCE

PAN: 9- × 13- × 2-inch baking pan

PAN PREP: Buttered heavy-duty aluminum foil

RACK LEVEL: Center

OVEN TEMP: 350°F

BAKING TIME: 14–15 minutes, crust; 10–11 minutes, center

DIFFICULTY: 2

1. Position the rack in the center of the oven. Heat the oven to 350°F. Invert the baking pan, then tear an 18- × 16-inch sheet of heavy-duty aluminum foil and center it over the top, smooth the surface, then press it down the sides. Carefully remove the foil shell, turn the pan right side up, and place the foil shell into the pan, shaping it smoothly across the bottom and snugly against the sides. Thoroughly butter the foil, taking care not to tear it.

MAKE THE CRUST

2. Strain together the flour, sugar, and cocoa. Place in the bowl of an electric mixer fitted with the paddle attachment. Add the butter and egg yolk and mix on low speed until a dough is formed.

3. Divide the dough into eight equal portions and distribute equally on the bottom of the pan. Press the dough until the bottom of the pan is evenly covered. (See Spreading Batters and Doughs, page 366.) Bake the dough for 14 to 15 minutes, or until firm to the touch. *Do not overbake.* Let the dough rest for 5 minutes.

MAKE THE CENTER LAYER

4. While the crust is baking, place the butter and chocolates in a large bowl (about 3-quart) set over a saucepan filled with 1 inch of simmering water. (The bottom of the bowl should not touch the water.) Melt the butter and the chocolates, stirring occasionally. When only a few pieces of chocolate remain, remove the bowl from the heat and let stand, stirring occasionally, until the chocolate is melted.

5. Using a large wooden spoon or rubber spatula, stir the peppermint schnapps and sugar into the warm chocolate mixture. Add the eggs one-third at a time. Then beat with a wooden spoon until shiny, taking approximately 25 to 30 strokes. Mix in the vanilla, then fold in the flour, stirring just until blended.

6. Pour the batter over the warm crust and, using a small offset spatula, spread it evenly. Bake for 10 to 11 minutes, or until just set on top. *Do not overbake.* A toothpick inserted should come out clean. Let stand for 15 to 20 minutes.

MAKE THE TOP LAYER

7. Gently stir the peppermint schnapps and extract into the ganache, stirring only to combine. Pour the ganache over the warm cake and spread it evenly with an offset spatula. To achieve a mirrorlike glaze, the ganache should be somewhat fluid. Let stand until the ganache is set before cutting into 32 bars.

STORAGE: Store in an airtight container, layered between strips of wax paper, for up to 5 days. These bars may be frozen, although the glaze will lose its gloss.

Secrets for Making Bar Cookies

- When melting butter for crusts, the butter must cool before adding the remaining ingredients. Otherwise, it will be too oily.

- If the bottom crust feels too oily, let it stand for 5 minutes. The flour will absorb the melted butter, making it easier to handle.

- To evenly distribute the dough for a bottom crust, divide it into eight balls and place in double rows down the pan. Flatten with a bâtarde, flat-bottomed glass, or floured heel of your hand.

- If the surface of the dough must be smoothed, a small offset spatula does the job.

- After the dough has been patted into the lined pan, run a dough scraper or spatula between the dough and the side of the pan. This gives the finished cookie a cleaner edge and aids in releasing the pan liner.

- Cool bar cookies thoroughly before cutting.

- For a neater edge, always wet the knife with hot water before cutting. Clean the knife as needed with damp paper towels.

ebony and ivory tiles

MAKES SIXTY-FOUR 1¼- × 1¾-INCH BARS

For these bar cookies, melted semisweet or bittersweet chocolate is sandwiched between a cookie dough crust and a nutty chocolate meringue top. Before baking, I sprinkle the meringue with sparkling white or granulated sugar, which creates a beautiful sparkle against the deep chocolate topping. Be sure to use a fine-quality chocolate here, as it really counts.

CRUST

1 cup (2 sticks) unsalted butter, softened

¾ cup granulated sugar

2 large egg yolks

1 teaspoon pure vanilla extract

2 cups all-purpose flour, spooned in and leveled

4 ounces fine-quality bittersweet or semisweet chocolate, such as Lindt Bittersweet, melted and kept warm

TOPPING

2 cups walnuts

¼ cup strained Dutch-processed cocoa powder

2 large egg whites, at room temperature

¼ teaspoon salt

⅔ cup granulated sugar

2 tablespoons unsalted butter, melted and cooled until tepid

1 teaspoon pure vanilla extract

2 tablespoons sparkling white sugar (available in The Baker's Catalogue; see page 381) or granulated sugar

AT A GLANCE

PAN: 10½- × 15½- × 1-inch jelly roll pan

PAN PREP: Buttered heavy-duty aluminum foil

RACK LEVEL: Center

OVEN TEMP: 350°F

BAKING TIME: 16–18 minutes, crust; 20–22 minutes, topping

DIFFICULTY: 2

1. Position the rack in the center of the oven. Heat the oven to 350°F. Tear a 15- × 18-inch sheet of heavy-duty aluminum foil. Invert the pan and center the foil over the pan, pressing it across the bottom and down the sides. Turn the pan right side up, and place the foil into the pan, shaping it smoothly. Using a pastry brush, grease the bottom and sides well with softened butter, taking care not to tear the foil.

MAKE THE CRUST

2. In the bowl of an electric mixer fitted with the paddle attachment, mix the butter with the granulated sugar on medium-low speed until smooth and lightened in color. Add the yolks one at a time, then the vanilla, mixing to blend. Scrape down the bowl as needed.

3. Reduce the mixer speed to low and mix in half of the flour. Remove the bowl from the machine and work in the remaining flour by hand, kneading to form a smooth dough. Shape into a 6- × 8-inch rectangle, then, using a dough scraper, divide the dough into 12 pieces.

4. Place the pieces of dough in the pan, making rows of four pieces across and three pieces down. Place a strip of plastic wrap over the pan. Using a bâtarde or the bottom of a glass, press the dough into the pan, making it as even and level as you can. (See Spreading Batters and Doughs, page 366.) Insert a dough scraper or spatula around the sides of the pan to clean and even the edges of the dough.

5. Bake for 16 to 18 minutes, or until the top is set and starting to brown. Remove from the oven, let stand 1 minute, then spread with the melted chocolate. Let stand for 20 minutes to cool, then refrigerate for 10 minutes, or until the chocolate is set.

MAKE THE TOPPING

6. Place the nuts and cocoa powder into the bowl of a food processor and pulse six to eight times, then process until very finely chopped. Stop the processor every 3 or 4 seconds and pulse, then return to processing. Set aside.

7. In the bowl of an electric mixer fitted with the whip attachment, beat the egg whites and salt on medium speed until frothy. Increase the speed to medium-high, add the granulated sugar 1 tablespoon at a time, and beat until stiff and shiny.

8. On low speed, add the cocoa–nut mixture, the tepid melted butter, and then the vanilla; mix 1 minute longer. Spread the meringue over the chocolate layer, smoothing with an offset spatula. Sprinkle evenly with sparkling white sugar.

BAKE THE COOKIES

9. Bake for 20 to 22 minutes, or until the top is set and starting to brown. Remove from the oven and cool completely. Using a thin-bladed knife, cut into sixty-four $1\frac{1}{4}$- × $1\frac{3}{4}$-inch bars, making eight strips down and eight strips across.

STORAGE: Store in an airtight container, layered between strips of wax paper, for up to 5 days. These cookies may be frozen.

blondies

MAKES 4 DOZEN 1¾- × 2½-INCH BARS

I suspect that blondies were born when a harried baker didn't have the patience to make individual chocolate chip cookies. Baking the batter as a bar cookie in this manner results in a thicker, moister, chewier cookie than its drop-cookie cousin.

2½ cups all-purpose flour, spooned in and leveled

½ teaspoon baking soda

½ teaspoon salt

1 cup (2 sticks) unsalted butter, divided

¾ cup lightly packed light brown sugar

¾ cup granulated sugar

2 large eggs

1½ teaspoons pure vanilla extract

1 cup walnuts, chopped (see page 356), divided

5 ounces high-quality bittersweet or semisweet chocolate, such as Lindt Bittersweet, cut into ¼-inch dice

AT A GLANCE

PAN: 10½- × 15½- × 1-inch jelly roll pan

PAN PREP: Well buttered

RACK LEVEL: Center

OVEN TEMP: 350°F

BAKING TIME: 28–30 minutes

DIFFICULTY: 1

1. Position the rack in the center of the oven. Heat the oven to 350°F. Butter the jelly roll pan well.

2. Strain together the flour, baking soda, and salt. Set aside. Cut ½ cup (1 stick) of the butter into pieces.

3. In a heavy-bottomed saucepan, warm the cut-up butter over medium-low heat until it is *almost* melted, but some solid pieces still remain. Remove from the heat and add the brown sugar, mixing well.

4. In the bowl of an electric mixer fitted with the paddle attachment, beat the remaining ½ cup (1 stick) of butter on medium speed. Add the granulated sugar in a steady stream and mix until lightened in color. Add the eggs one at a time, mixing well after each addition. Blend in the tepid melted butter–brown sugar mixture. (If the mixture has solidified, warm briefly over low heat to melt.) Beat on medium speed until thick and creamy, about 1 minute, scraping down the side of the bowl as needed. Beat in the vanilla.

5. Reduce the mixer speed to low and add the dry ingredients in two additions, mixing *only* to combine. Remove the bowl from the machine and, using a large wooden spoon or rubber spatula, fold in ¾ cup of the chopped walnuts and all of the diced chocolate. Scrape the batter into the pan, using the back of a large spoon to spread it evenly. Sprinkle with the remaining walnuts.

6. Bake for 28 to 30 minutes, or until the top is golden brown and the edges *just* begin to pull away from the sides of the pan. *Do not overbake.* Remove from the oven and place on a cooling rack. Let stand 1 hour, then cut into forty-eight 1¾- × 2½-inch bars.

STORAGE: Store in an airtight container, layered between strips of wax paper, for up to 5 days. These blondies may be frozen.

toffee nut bars

MAKES 5 DOZEN 1¼- × 2-INCH BARS

This recipe has been part of my baking repertoire for years. It was inspired by Blondies (opposite), but is a thinner version made only with brown sugar. Because I prefer to make these with light brown sugar, instead of dark brown, the cookie has a wonderful caramel flavor that complements the taste of the butter. It is essential that the brown sugar be very fresh, so this is the time to break open a new box. To retain the chewiness of the cookie, underbake them slightly.

2 cups all-purpose flour, spooned in and leveled

½ teaspoon baking soda

½ teaspoon salt

⅔ cup (1⅓ sticks) unsalted butter, slightly firm

2 cups lightly packed very fresh light brown sugar

2 large eggs

2 teaspoons pure vanilla extract

1 cup plus 2 tablespoons medium-fine chopped walnuts (see page 356), divided

1 cup semisweet chocolate chips

1. Position the rack in the center of the oven. Heat the oven to 350°F. Butter the jelly roll pan well.

2. Strain together the flour, baking soda, and salt. Set aside.

3. In the bowl of an electric mixer on medium speed, beat the butter until lightened in color. Add the brown sugar, about ¼ cup at a time, and beat well until light in color, about 2 minutes. Scrape down the side of the bowl as needed. Beat in the eggs one at a time, then the vanilla. Reduce the mixer speed to low and add the dry ingredients in three additions, mixing *just* to incorporate.

4. Remove the bowl from the mixer and, using a large rubber spatula, fold in 1 cup of the walnuts and the chocolate chips. Spread the mixture in the pan, smoothing the top with a small offset spatula. Sprinkle with the remaining 2 tablespoons of walnuts.

5. Bake for 16 to 18 minutes, or until the sides are lightly browned. *Do not overbake.* A toothpick inserted in the center should still show signs of moistness. Place on a cooling rack for 1 hour, then cut into sixty 1¾- × 2-inch bars.

STORAGE: Store in an airtight container, layered between strips of wax paper, for up to 5 days. These bars may be frozen.

AT A GLANCE
PAN: 10½- × 15½- × 1-inch jelly roll pan

PAN PREP: Well buttered

RACK LEVEL: Center

OVEN TEMP: 350°F

BAKING TIME: 16–18 minutes

DIFFICULTY: 1

mississippi bayou bars

MAKES SIXTY-FOUR 1¼- × 2-INCH BARS

These nutty bars bring back memories of my childhood in Tennessee. The flavor and textures of the coconut and pecans combined with brown sugar are the flavors I grew up with, so reminiscent of the Deep South. They make a chewy cookie that is irresistible and one that your family and friends are sure to love.

CRUST

1 cup (2 sticks) unsalted butter

3 cups all-purpose flour, spooned in and leveled

½ cup granulated sugar

½ cup firmly packed light brown sugar

TOPPING

1 (10-ounce) package sweetened, flaked coconut (3¾ cups)

2 tablespoons all-purpose flour

½ teaspoon baking soda

4 large eggs

½ cup dark corn syrup

1¼ cups firmly packed light brown sugar

2 tablespoons (¼ stick) unsalted butter, melted

2 teaspoons pure vanilla extract

1½ cups broken pecans, lightly toasted (see page 356)

AT A GLANCE

PAN: 10½- × 15½- × 1-inch jelly roll pan

PAN PREP: Buttered heavy-duty aluminum foil

RACK LEVEL: Center

OVEN TEMP: 350°F

BAKING TIME: 20 minutes, crust; 22–25 minutes, topping

DIFFICULTY: 2

1. Position the rack in the center of the oven. Heat the oven to 350°F. Tear a 15- × 18-inch sheet of heavy-duty aluminum foil. Invert the pan and center the foil over the pan, pressing it across the bottom and down the sides. Turn the pan right side up, and place the foil into the pan, shaping it smoothly. Using a pastry brush, grease the bottom and sides well with softened butter, taking care not to tear the foil.

MAKE THE CRUST

2. In a medium saucepan, melt the butter. Set aside to cool to tepid. Add the flour and sugars, blending with a fork until the mixture forms large crumbs.

3. Distribute the crumbs evenly over the bottom of the pan, pressing firmly. Lay a strip of plastic wrap over the surface, then smooth the crumbs with a flat-bottomed glass or a bâtarde. Remove the plastic wrap and use a small offset spatula to reach into the corners and even the surface. Test for evenness by inserting the tip of a knife or toothpick into the dough.

4. Bake the crust for 20 minutes, or until the top is set and the edges begin to brown. While the crust is baking, make the topping.

MAKE THE TOPPING

5. Place the coconut in the work bowl of a food processor fitted with a steel blade, then process for 10 to 15 seconds, or until finely chopped. Set aside.

6. Strain together the flour and baking soda. Set aside.

7. Place the eggs in a large mixing bowl and whisk to blend. Stir in the corn syrup, brown sugar, melted butter, and vanilla. Stir the dry ingredients into the egg mixture, then blend in the coconut. *Do not overmix,* or too many bubbles will form. Pour the mixture over the hot crust, then sprinkle the pecans over the top.

BAKE THE COOKIES

8. Bake for 22 to 25 minutes, or until the edges begin to brown and the top feels set. Place on a cooling rack and let stand for 15 minutes. Run a knife around the sides of the pan to loosen the crusty edges. Let stand for another 15 minutes.

9. Using a sharp knife, make seven cuts each way to cut into 64 bars. Let the bars air-dry on a cooling rack before storing.

STORAGE: Store in an airtight container, layered between strips of wax paper, for up to 3 weeks. These bars may be frozen.

apple pie bars

MAKES THIRTY-TWO 1½- × 2-INCH BARS

The recipe for these Apple Pie Bars was created by my talented assistant, Kathie Finn Redden. Kathie, one of my teaching peers at Kings Cooking Studio, has keen taste buds and a wonderful way with food. When testing recipes for an upcoming class, she told me of a terrific apple bar cookie that I might want to include in my book. And she was so right.

Kathie's cookies are made with sliced apples sautéed with brown sugar and honey. She places them on top of a buttery crust, then covers the apples with a cinnamon-scented pecan streusel. Not only am I lucky to have this spunky gal as my assistant, when it comes to creating great recipes, Kathie's a winner.

APPLES

6 Granny Smith or Golden Delicious apples, peeled, cored, and sliced ¼ inch thick (see Note)

⅓ cup firmly packed light brown sugar

2 tablespoons fresh lemon juice

1 tablespoon honey

CRUST

2¼ cups all-purpose flour, spooned in and leveled

½ teaspoon baking powder

½ teaspoon salt

1 cup (2 sticks) unsalted butter, slightly firm

½ cup lightly packed light brown sugar

1 large egg

STREUSEL TOPPING

1 cup all-purpose flour, spooned in and leveled

¼ cup granulated sugar

¼ cup lightly packed light brown sugar

1 teaspoon ground cinnamon

¼ teaspoon salt

½ cup (1 stick) cold unsalted butter, cubed

1 cup medium-chopped toasted pecans (see page 356)

AT A GLANCE

PAN: 9- × 13- × 2-inch baking pan

PAN PREP: Buttered heavy-duty aluminum foil

RACK LEVEL: Center

OVEN TEMP: 375°F, 350°F

BAKING TIME: 15–18 minutes, crust; 20–25 minutes, bar cookie

DIFFICULTY: 2

COOK THE APPLES

1. In a large skillet over medium heat, combine the apples with the brown sugar, lemon juice, and honey. Cover the pan for 2 to 3 minutes. Uncover when the apples have released their juices and cook, stirring occasionally, until the apples have turned a golden brown and there is no liquid left in the pan, about 15 minutes. Set aside to cool.

MAKE THE CRUST

2. Position the rack in the center of the oven. Heat the oven to 375°F. Tear an 18- × 16-inch sheet of heavy-duty aluminum foil. Invert the pan and center the foil over the pan, pressing it across the bottom and down the sides. Remove the foil, turn the pan right side up, and place the foil shell in the pan, shaping it smoothly across the bottom and snugly against the sides. Using a pastry brush, grease the bottom and sides with softened butter, taking care not to tear the foil.

3. Strain together the flour, baking powder, and salt. Set aside.

4. In the large bowl of an electric mixer fitted with the paddle attachment, mix the butter with the brown sugar on medium-low speed until smooth and creamy, about 2 minutes. Add the egg and mix to blend. On low speed, add the dry ingredients in two additions, mixing only to combine after each addition. Divide the mixture into eight parts and place them in two rows down the length of the pan. With lightly floured hands, press the mixture evenly into the pan. (See Spreading Batters and Doughs, page 366.) Bake for 15 to 18 minutes, or until the crust has turned golden brown and begins to release from the sides of the pan. While the crust is baking, prepare the streusel topping.

MAKE THE TOPPING

5. In the large bowl of an electric mixer fitted with the paddle attachment, combine the flour, granulated and brown sugars, cinnamon, and salt. Mix briefly on low speed. Add the butter and mix on medium-low speed until the mixture is crumbly and barely holds together when squeezed gently. Stir in the pecans with a large rubber spatula or a large wooden spoon. Set the topping aside.

BAKE THE COOKIES

6. When the crust is done, immediately spread the cooked apples evenly over the hot crust. Sprinkle the streusel topping over the apples, pressing gently to help it adhere.

7. Reduce the oven temperature to 350°F. Return the pan to the oven and bake for 20 to 25 minutes, or until the topping is lightly browned and crisp. Let rest in the pan for 2 to 3 hours before removing and slicing into 32 bars with a long, sharp knife. (Note: These slice better if they are chilled.)

NOTE: The apples can be sliced in a food processor using a #4 slicing disk.

STORAGE: Refrigerate the bars in a cookie tin, layered between strips of wax paper, for up to 5 days. Bring to room temperature before serving.

minna's apricot squares

MAKES TWENTY-FIVE 1¾-INCH SQUARES

A few years ago, I was visiting my friend Minna Berger, from Elizabeth, New Jersey, a gracious hostess and terrific baker. Minna had lots of practice baking because she had an audience of her husband and four sons, who not only appreciated fine food but also possessed a passion for fine sweets. On this occasion, she set a small platter of homemade cookies down for me to enjoy with my tea. My eye was instantly caught by a deep golden-brown bar cookie with pecans on top. Ooh! With my first bite, I thought, "Oh! I must have this recipe!" Minna generously shared it with me and now I happily share it with you.

4 ounces (⅔ cup packed) dried apricots

1½ cups water

CRUST

1 cup all-purpose flour, spooned in
   and leveled

¼ cup strained confectioners' sugar,
   spooned in and leveled

½ cup (1 stick) unsalted butter, slightly firm
   and cut in 1-inch pieces

TOPPING

⅓ cup all-purpose flour, spooned in
   and leveled

½ teaspoon baking powder

¼ teaspoon salt

2 large eggs

1 cup lightly packed dark brown sugar

½ teaspoon pure vanilla extract

¾ cup coarsely chopped walnuts (see page
   356), divided

AT A GLANCE

PAN: 9-inch square baking pan

PAN PREP: Buttered heavy-
   duty aluminum foil

RACK LEVEL: Lower third

OVEN TEMP: 350°F

BAKING TIME: 20 minutes,
   crust; 40 minutes, topping

DIFFICULTY: 1

1. Place the apricots and water in a small saucepan, cover, and bring to a boil. Reduce the heat to low and simmer for 20 minutes. Drain the apricots, rinse with cold water, then blot dry on paper toweling. When cool, place the apricots in the work bowl of a food processor fitted with the steel blade and pulse four or five times to coarsely chop. You should have about ¾ cup.

MAKE THE CRUST

2. Position the rack in the lower third of the oven. Heat the oven to 350°F. Tear a 15-inch square of heavy-duty aluminum foil. Invert the pan and center the foil over the pan, pressing it across the bottom and down the sides. Remove the foil, turn the pan right side up, and place the foil shell into the pan, shaping it smoothly across the bottom and snugly against the sides. Using a pastry brush, grease the bottom and sides with softened butter, taking care not to tear the foil.

3. Strain together the flour and confectioners' sugar. Place the dry ingredients in the bowl of an electric mixer fitted with the paddle attachment. Add the butter and mix on medium speed until the texture of coarse crumbs. Press the crumbs evenly into the pan, forming a smooth layer of dough. Bake for 20 minutes or until golden brown.

MAKE THE TOPPING

4. Strain together the flour, baking powder, and salt. Set aside.

5. In the bowl of an electric mixer fitted with the whip attachment, mix the eggs with the brown sugar on medium-low speed until lightened, about 2 minutes. Do not overbeat. Blend in the vanilla.

6. Reduce the mixer speed to low and add the dry ingredients. Stir in the chopped apricots and ½ cup of the walnuts. Pour the batter over the crust. Sprinkle with the remaining ¼ cup of chopped nuts.

BAKE THE COOKIES

7. Bake for 40 minutes, or until firm and just starting to pull away from the edges of the pan. Let cool in the pan before removing and cutting into 25 bars.

STORAGE: Store loosely covered in a container, layered between strips of wax paper, for up to 5 days. These squares may be frozen.

favorite lemon squares

MAKES FORTY 1½- × 1¾-INCH SQUARES

I suppose that lemon squares will forever be my daughter Pam's favorite cookies. I must admit, I am not far behind her!

Recipes for lemon squares may vary a bit, but for the most part the classic formula for the filling remains: eggs, sugar (lots of it!), lemon juice, and zest. It is similar to the classic lemon curd, without the butter.

For ease of cutting, make these bar cookies a day ahead. The filling requires standing time to set, and I promise that if you have the patience to wait, you will be well rewarded. For a neater appearance, the edges of the cookies can be trimmed and put aside for nibbling. In addition, after the cookies are cut, place them on a cooling rack to air-dry for several hours before storing.

CRUST

1 cup (2 sticks) unsalted butter

2 cups all-purpose flour, spooned in and leveled

½ cup strained confectioners' sugar, spooned in and leveled

TOPPING

4 large eggs

1¾ cups superfine sugar

1 tablespoon freshly grated lemon zest

⅓ cup fresh lemon juice

1 teaspoon baking powder

½ teaspoon salt

Strained confectioners' sugar, for dusting

AT A GLANCE

PAN: 9- × 13- × 2-inch baking pan

PAN PREP: Buttered heavy-duty aluminum foil

RACK LEVEL: Center

OVEN TEMP: 350°F

BAKING TIME: 20 minutes, crust; 25–28 minutes, topping

DIFFICULTY: 1

1. Position the rack in the center of the oven. Heat the oven to 350°F. Invert the baking pan, then tear an 18- × 16-inch sheet of heavy-duty aluminum foil and center it over the top, smooth the surface, then press it down the sides. Remove the foil, turn the pan right side up, and place the foil shell in the pan, shaping it smoothly across the bottom and snugly against the sides of the pan. Using a pastry brush, grease the bottom and sides with softened butter, taking care not to tear the foil.

MAKE THE CRUST

2. Place the butter in a medium saucepan and heat slowly until it is almost melted. Cool to tepid. Strain together the flour and confectioners' sugar. Using a fork, stir the dry ingredients into the tepid butter. Empty the mixture into the pan, dividing it into about eight portions. With the palm of your hand, press the dough evenly across the bottom. Then press the edges with a fork. Bake for 20 minutes, or until lightly browned around the edges.

MAKE THE TOPPING

3. Start 5 minutes before the crust is finished. In the bowl of an electric mixer fitted with the whisk attachment, beat the eggs on medium speed for about 1 minute. Increase the speed to medium-high and gradually add the superfine sugar over 2 minutes, beating the mixture until light and thickened. Add the lemon zest, juice, baking powder, and salt and beat for 1 minute longer.

BAKE THE COOKIES

4. Pour the filling over the top of the *hot* crust. Bake for 25 to 28 minutes or longer (the top will be brown, but it also must be *firm* to the touch). Remove from the oven and let cool 3 to 4 hours before cutting.

5. To divide into squares, lift the bar from the pan and place on a cutting board. Pull the aluminum foil down on all sides until it lies flat. Using a thin-bladed knife, cut into forty 1½- × 1¾-inch squares. Remove the lemon squares by lifting each with a small spatula and then place on a cooling rack to air-dry for several hours. When ready to serve, dust with confectioners' sugar.

STORAGE: Store in an airtight container, layered between sheets of wax paper, for up to 5 days. These squares may be frozen.

coconut-crusted key lime napoleons

MAKES TWENTY-FIVE 1¼-INCH SQUARES

If you like Key lime pie, here is an opportunity to savor a bite-size version of this oh-so-popular American favorite. Layers of crushed graham crackers and creamy Key lime filling are baked as a bar cookie, then sprinkled with crunchy toasted coconut before being cut into squares. For ease of handling, I place the cookies into petit-four cups and then either refrigerate or freeze them.

While you can make a tasty filling with fresh Persian limes, to be traditional I prefer to use the juice of the more tartly flavored Key limes. Because fresh Key limes are smaller in size, they yield very little juice. A great alternative is Nellie & Joe's Famous Key West Lime Juice, available bottled in many supermarkets.

CRUST

6 tablespoons (¾ stick) unsalted butter

1½ cups graham cracker crumbs
(7 to 8 whole graham crackers)

2½ tablespoons sugar

FILLING

3 large egg yolks

1 (14-ounce) can sweetened condensed milk

2 teaspoons freshly grated lime zest

½ cup Key lime juice (see headnote)

¾ cup lightly crushed toasted sweetened, flaked coconut, for garnish

AT A GLANCE

PAN: 8-inch square baking pan

PAN PREP: Buttered and floured heavy-duty aluminum foil

RACK LEVEL: Center

OVEN TEMP: 350°F

BAKING TIME: 7–8 minutes, crust; 27–29 minutes, filling

DIFFICULTY: 2

1. Position the rack in the center of the oven. Heat the oven to 350°F. Cut a 14-inch square of heavy-duty aluminum foil. Invert the pan and center the sheet of foil over the pan, pressing it across the bottom and down the sides. Remove the foil, turn the pan right side up, and place the foil shell in the pan, shaping it smoothly across the bottom and snugly against the sides of the pan. Butter the foil well, then dust with flour, shaking out the excess.

MAKE THE CRUST

2. Melt the butter in a 2-quart saucepan. Cool to tepid. Add the graham cracker crumbs and the sugar to the melted butter and stir with a fork to combine well.

3. Sprinkle half of the crumbs (approximately 1 cup) into the pan. Press the crumbs evenly, using a bâtarde or the bottom of a glass to tamp down the crumbs. Bake for 7 to 8 minutes, or until just set. While the crust is baking, prepare the filling.

MAKE THE FILLING

4. In the bowl of an electric mixer fitted with the whip attachment, beat the egg yolks on medium-high speed until slightly thickened and lightened in color, 3 to 4 minutes. Slowly add the condensed milk and beat 4 to 5 minutes longer. Reduce the mixer speed to medium-low and mix in the lime zest and juice.

5. Let the crust rest out of the oven for 2 or 3 minutes before pouring half of the filling (approximately 1 cup) over it, spreading with the back of a tablespoon. Give the pan several firm taps on a hard surface to spread the filling evenly. Return to the oven and bake for 9 to 10 minutes, or until set on top. (It's OK if a little sticks to your finger.)

6. Sprinkle the remaining crumbs over the warm filling, spreading them carefully. Press gently with the bottom of a glass to even the crumbs. Bake for 8 to 9 minutes, or until set. Let rest for 2 or 3 minutes.

7. Pour the remaining filling mixture over the crust, spreading evenly with the back of a tablespoon. Tap the pan on the counter to even the filling. Bake for 10 minutes, or until set.

8. Let stand for 2 or 3 minutes, then sprinkle with approximately half of the toasted coconut, pressing it in gently. Then top with the remaining coconut. Refrigerate for 4 to 5 hours before removing from the pan. Using a long, thin-bladed knife dipped in warm water as needed, cut into 25 squares.

STORAGE: Refrigerate in an airtight container, layered between strips of wax paper, for up to 5 days. These cookies may be frozen.

florentines

MAKES EIGHTY 1- × 1¾-INCH COOKIES

Festive Florentines have a thin nut crust topped with chewy, honey-flavored caramel. The golden caramel filling is chock full of sliced, unblanched almonds and colorful glacé fruits. The jewel-like filling sparkles through a web of chocolate zigzagged across the top.

CRUST

⅔ cup (1⅓ sticks) unsalted butter

1⅓ cups all-purpose flour, spooned in and leveled

⅓ cup confectioners' sugar

¼ teaspoon salt

½ cup sliced blanched almonds

FILLING

⅔ cup superfine sugar

⅓ cup (⅔ stick) unsalted butter, cut into ½-inch slices

⅓ cup heavy cream

¼ cup honey

⅛ teaspoon salt

¼ cup coarsely chopped glacé cherries

¼ cup coarsely chopped candied orange peel

¼ cup coarsely chopped candied lemon peel

1 teaspoon freshly grated orange zest

1 teaspoon freshly grated lemon zest

1 cup sliced unblanched almonds

TOPPING

2 ounces fine-quality bittersweet or semisweet chocolate, such as Lindt Bittersweet, coarsely chopped

½ teaspoon vegetable or canola oil

AT A GLANCE

PAN: 10½- × 15½- × 1-inch jelly roll pan

PAN PREP: Buttered heavy-duty aluminum foil

RACK LEVEL: Center

OVEN TEMP: 350°F

BAKING TIME: 15–16 minutes, crust; 13–15 minutes, filling

DIFFICULTY: 2

1. Position the rack in the center of the oven. Heat the oven to 350°F. Tear a 15- × 18-inch sheet of heavy-duty aluminum foil. Invert the pan and center the foil over the pan, pressing it across the bottom and down the sides. Remove the foil, turn the pan right side up, and place the foil shell into the pan, shaping it smoothly across the bottom and snugly against the sides. Using a pastry brush, grease the bottom and sides with softened butter, taking care not to tear the foil.

MAKE THE CRUST

2. Melt the butter in a medium saucepan. Cool to tepid.

3. Place the flour, confectioners' sugar, salt, and almonds in the work bowl of a food processor fitted with a steel blade. Pulse eight to ten times, then process for 60 seconds, until fine and cakey. Using a fork, stir the mixture into the tepid melted butter and mix thoroughly. Divide into eight portions and place in the pan, pressing it as evenly as you can. Insert a dough scraper or small spatula between the dough and the sides of the pan to clean and even the edges. Bake the crust for 15 to 16 minutes, or until lightly browned and set on top. Let stand for 8 to 10 minutes to firm.

MAKE THE FILLING

4. Place the sugar, butter, cream, honey, and salt in a heavy 2-quart saucepan. Bring to a boil, stirring gently but constantly. With a pastry brush, brush the insides of the pot with water to be sure the sugar has dissolved, then simmer for 1 minute longer.

5. Mix in the candied fruits, zests, and nuts, blending well. Cook the mixture over low heat for 6 to 8 minutes, or until it begins to thicken and the caramel starts to darken. The thickness of the pot will determine the cooking time. Watch the sides of the pot to see the first signs of thickening.

6. Immediately pour the filling onto the warm crust and spread evenly with a large *buttered* offset spatula, distributing the filling as best you can. Bake for 13 to 15 minutes, or until bubbly on top and the surface has begun to brown. *Do not overbake.* Cool on a wire rack.

TOP WITH THE CHOCOLATE

7. Melt the chocolate in a water bath (see page 353). When the chocolate is almost melted, stir in the vegetable oil. Do not let the chocolate mixture get too hot. Keep the chocolate warm while you unmold the cookies, gently stirring occasionally.

8. Lift the bar from the pan, using the foil as an aid, and place on a cutting board or flat surface. Before you web the bar with chocolate, cut the bar in half and slide each half off the foil.

9. Pour the warm chocolate into a plastic squeeze bottle or an 8-inch pastry bag fitted with a #2 standard writing tip. Starting at an upper corner of one of the cookie bars, make very fine lines at an angle, moving the pastry bag back and forth to the opposite corner until the entire surface is covered; if you wish, reverse the pattern, going in the opposite direction. Repeat with the remaining cookie bar. Let stand until the chocolate is set, then cut into eighty 1- × 1¾-inch bars.

STORAGE: Store in an airtight container, layered between strips of wax paper, for up to 5 days. These cookies may be frozen.

special occasion cookies

old-fashioned icebox cookies

chocolate fleck hubcaps

tutti-fruitti icebox cookies

rugelach

classic sugar cookies

sweethearts

chocolate-glazed pecan leaves

spritz cookies

chocolate espresso spritz cookies

almond spritz cookies

french lace what-nots

oatmeal almond jammies

pecan tassies

coconut lemon-lime tassies

scotch shortbread

chocolate shortbread nuggets

lemon poppy seed shortbread

old-fashioned icebox cookies

MAKES 12 DOZEN 1¾-INCH COOKIES

When you want to make cookies for gift-giving or when festive cookies are in order, this recipe for Old-Fashioned Icebox Cookies is a real bonanza. From the Master Recipe, you can make myriad flavors that are as visually appealing as they are palate-pleasing. Try colorful Confetti Cookies made with glacé cherries or Chocolate Icebox Cookies. These recipes are just a few of the many varieties you can create; experiment with your favorite flavors.

1½ cups (3 sticks) unsalted butter, slightly firm

¾ cup sugar

1 large egg

2 teaspoons pure vanilla extract

3 cups all-purpose flour, spooned in and leveled, divided

Coarse sugar, or other trimmings

1 large egg white, lightly beaten with 2 teaspoons water

AT A GLANCE

PAN: Cookie sheets

PAN PREP: Ungreased

CHILLING TIME: 2–3 hours

RACK LEVELS: Upper and lower thirds

OVEN TEMP: 375°F

BAKING TIME: 12–14 minutes

DIFFICULTY: 1

MAKE THE DOUGH

1. In the large bowl of an electric mixer fitted with the paddle attachment, mix the butter on medium-low speed until smooth and lightened in color. Add the sugar in a steady stream and mix until well blended, about 2 minutes. Mix in the egg and vanilla, scraping down the side of the bowl as needed.

2. Remove 1 cup of the flour and set aside. Reduce the mixer speed to low and add 2 cups of the flour, in three additions, mixing *just* until combined. Knead in the remaining 1 cup flour with your hands. Do not overwork the dough or it will become oily.

3. Divide the dough into sixths. Shape each piece into a cylinder measuring approximately 6 inches by 1¼ inches. Chill for 10 minutes.

4. Place the coarse sugar on a piece of wax paper. Working with one cylinder at a time, brush with the egg white mixture and then roll in the sugar, rotating back and forth until coated.

5. Wrap the log with plastic, twisting the ends tightly to secure. Repeat with the remaining cylinders, adding more sugar each time. Refrigerate for 2 to 3 hours, or until firm. (This dough will keep in the refrigerator for up to 3 days, or may be frozen for up to 1 month.)

BAKE THE COOKIES

6. Position the racks in the upper and lower thirds of the oven. Heat the oven to 375°F.

7. Using a thin, sharp knife, cut the dough into ¼-inch-thick slices, turning the dough every two or three cuts to maintain the shape. Do not make these cookies too thin. Place on the cookie sheets about 2 inches apart. Bake for 12 to 14 minutes, or until lightly golden brown around the edges. To ensure even browning, toward the end of baking time rotate the pans top to bottom and front to back. Remove from the oven and carefully loosen with a thin, metal spatula. Cool on wire racks.

STORAGE: Store in an airtight container, layered between strips of wax paper, for up to 3 weeks. These cookies may be frozen.

Confetti Cookies

MAKES ABOUT 2 DOZEN COOKIES

¾ cup Old-Fashioned Icebox Cookie dough
2 tablespoons chopped red glacé cherries

1 tablespoon chopped green glacé cherries

1. Using your hands, gently knead the chopped cherries into the dough. *Do not overwork.* Shape the dough into a cylinder measuring approximately 7 inches by 1¼ inches. Chill for 10 minutes. Garnish if desired (refer to step 4 of the Master Recipe).

2. Wrap the log with plastic, twisting the ends tightly to secure. Chill for 2 to 3 hours or until firm. (The dough may be frozen for up to 1 month.)

3. When ready to bake the cookies, proceed with step 6 of the Master Recipe.

Chocolate Icebox Cookies

MAKES ABOUT 2 DOZEN COOKIES

¾ cup Old-Fashioned Icebox Cookie dough
1 ounce unsweetened chocolate, melted and
  kept warm

1 tablespoon sugar

1. Place the cookie dough in a medium bowl. Blend in the warm chocolate and sugar with a spoon, being careful not to overwork the dough. Shape the dough into a cylinder, measuring approximately 6 inches by 1¼ inches. Chill for 10 minutes. Garnish if desired (refer to step 4 of the Master Recipe).

2. Wrap the log with plastic, twisting the ends tightly to secure. Chill for 2 to 3 hours or until firm. (The dough may be frozen for up to 1 month.)

3. When ready to bake the cookies, proceed with step 6 of the Master Recipe.

chocolate fleck hubcaps

MAKES ABOUT 4 DOZEN 1¾-INCH COOKIES

Here is a cookie that will absolutely make you look like a pro. It has a dark chocolate "hubcap" that is set off by a circle of vanilla cookie dough. The centers are made with a combination of ground chocolate and nuts heightened with a touch of cinnamon and cloves.

1 ounce semisweet chocolate, coarsely chopped

½ cup walnuts or pecans

5 tablespoons sugar, divided

½ teaspoon ground cinnamon

Pinch of ground cloves

1½ cups Old-Fashioned Icebox Cookie dough (page 66), divided

1 large egg white, lightly beaten with 2 teaspoons of water

AT A GLANCE

PAN: Cookie sheets

PAN PREP: Ungreased

CHILLING TIME: 2–3 hours

RACK LEVELS: Upper and lower thirds

OVEN TEMP: 375°F

BAKING TIME: 12–14 minutes

DIFFICULTY: 2

MAKE THE DOUGH

1. In the work bowl of a food processor fitted with the steel blade, finely grind the chocolate. Empty the ground chocolate onto a strip of wax paper.

2. Place the nuts, 3 tablespoons of sugar, the cinnamon, and cloves in the processor bowl and pulse until the nuts are finely chopped. Empty the mixture into a large bowl. Remove ¼ cup and set aside for trimming. Add the chocolate to the remaining nut mixture along with ½ cup of the cookie dough. Gently knead until the ingredients are just combined. *Do not overwork.* Form into two thin cylinders each about 6 inches long.

3. Roll the remaining 1 cup of dough into a rectangle measuring 10 inches wide by 6 inches long. Cut the rectangle in half, making two strips that are 5 inches wide and 6 inches long.

4. Brush each strip of dough with the beaten egg white. Place a chocolate-nut cylinder in the center of one rectangle, aligning it with the 6-inch side of the rectangle. Wrap the dough around the cylinder, forming a log. The two edges should only slightly overlap. If there is too much excess dough at the seam, remove it with a pastry scraper. Pinch the seam, then roll the cylinder back and forth to seal the seam well. Form another log with the remaining dough and cylinder. Chill the logs 10 minutes.

5. Place the reserved nut mixture on a piece of wax paper and combine with the remaining 2 tablespoons of sugar. Working with one log at a time, brush with the egg white mixture and then roll in the nut mixture, rotating back and forth until coated.

6. Wrap the logs with plastic, twisting the ends tightly to secure. Refrigerate for 2 to 3 hours, or until firm. (This dough will keep in the refrigerator for up to 3 days, or may be frozen for 1 month.)

BAKE THE COOKIES

7. Position the racks in the upper and lower thirds of the oven. Heat the oven to 375°F.

8. Using a thin, sharp knife, cut the dough into $\frac{1}{4}$-inch slices, turning the dough every two or three cuts to maintain the shape. Do not make these cookies too thin. Place on the cookie sheets about 2 inches apart. Bake for 12 to 14 minutes, or until lightly golden brown around the edges. To ensure even browning, toward the end of baking time, rotate the sheets top to bottom and front to back. Remove from the oven and carefully loosen with a thin, metal spatula. Transfer to cooling racks.

STORAGE: Store in an airtight container, layered between strips of wax paper, for up to 3 weeks. These cookies may be frozen.

tutti-frutti icebox cookies

MAKES 8 DOZEN 2½-INCH COOKIES

James Brackman, who hails from Austin, Texas, and is a graduate of the French Culinary Institute, passed this recipe for his grandmother's Christmas cookies on to me. The cookie dough is made with a jewel-like combination of candied or dried pineapple and glacé cherries with lots of chopped pecans mingled through the dough. Family recipes and grandmothers are true treasures—thank you, James, for sharing both with me.

2½ cups all-purpose flour, spooned in and leveled

1½ teaspoons baking soda

½ teaspoon salt

½ cup chopped dried or glacé pineapple

½ cup packed chopped glacé cherries

1 cup (2 sticks) unsalted butter, slightly firm

1 cup sugar

1 large egg

1 cup medium-chopped toasted pecans (see page 356)

AT A GLANCE

PAN: Cookie sheets

PAN PREP: Ungreased

CHILLING TIME: 3 hours

RACK LEVELS: Upper and lower thirds

OVEN TEMP: 375°F

BAKING TIME: 8–9 minutes

DIFFICULTY: 1

MAKE THE DOUGH

1. Strain together the flour, baking soda, and salt in a medium bowl. Combine the pineapple and cherries and toss with 3 tablespoons of the flour mixture, working the flour through the fruit with your fingers to separate the pieces. Set both aside.

2. In the large bowl of an electric mixer fitted with the paddle attachment, mix the butter on medium-low speed until creamy and lightened in color. Add the sugar in a steady stream and mix until well blended, about 2 minutes. Add the egg and mix 1 minute longer, scraping down the side of the bowl as needed.

3. Reduce the mixer speed to low and add the flour mixture in two additions, mixing *only* to blend after each addition. Using a large rubber spatula, fold in the fruits and the pecans.

4. Form the dough into a mound and divide into four equal pieces. Shape each piece into a 6- × 1½-inch log. Wrap each log with plastic, twisting the ends tightly to secure. Refrigerate for 3 hours or until firm. (This dough will keep in the refrigerator for up to 3 days, or may be frozen for 1 month.)

BAKE THE COOKIES

5. Position the racks in the upper and lower thirds of the oven. Heat the oven to 375°F.

6. Using a thin, sharp knife, cut the dough into ¼-inch slices, turning the roll every two or three cuts to maintain the shape. Place the slices 2 inches apart on the cookie sheets. Bake for

8 to 9 minutes, or until lightly browned. To ensure even browning, toward the end of baking time, rotate the pans top to bottom and front to back. Remove from the oven and let rest for 1 minute before loosening with a thin, metal spatula. Transfer to cooling racks.

STORAGE: Store in an airtight container, layered between strips of wax paper, for up to 3 weeks. These cookies may be frozen.

Secrets for Making Refrigerated Cookies

- When preparing the textured ingredients for the cookie dough, chop the pieces according to the thickness of the slices. Thinly sliced dough (up to $\frac{1}{4}$ inch) will require smaller pieces, while thicker slices (about $\frac{1}{2}$ inch) can accommodate larger pieces.

- When forming logs, make them shorter rather than longer. This makes them easier to handle.

- As you roll the log in plastic wrap, pull the dough toward you to ensure a more cylindrical shape. The tighter you twist the ends of the plastic wrap, the more cylindrical the log.

- To maintain the rounded shape of the logs of dough, turn them periodically while chilling.

- When shaping dark-colored doughs, use confectioners' sugar instead of flour for rolling. The sugar dissolves during baking and the color of the cookie is retained.

- Cookie logs trimmed with chopped nuts and colored sugars must be brushed with an egg wash before the garnish is applied.

- When brushing cookie logs with egg wash, place the log on a sheet of wax paper. Then lift the paper and roll the log directly into a shallow container filled with the trim.

- Many drop cookie doughs can be converted to refrigerated cookies by shaping the dough into logs and then wrapping, chilling, or freezing them.

- To retain the shape of refrigerated doughs, always slice them when they are well chilled and firm.

- Slicing refrigerator cookies is best done with a thin-bladed knife to avoid tearing the dough.

- Some refrigerator doughs can be sliced while frozen if you use a warm knife. Unused portions can be thoroughly rewrapped and refrozen for later use.

rugelach

MAKES 7 DOZEN 1¾-INCH COOKIES

Of all of the many "takes" on rugelach, this recipe remains my favorite. My pastry of choice is a simple cream cheese dough. The sweetness of the butter contrasted with the tang of the cheese imparts a pleasing flavor that is unique. I take extra care to avoid overworking the dough. When rolled in a mixture of confectioners' sugar and flour, the crust forms many delicate layers and becomes extra-special. I fill the dough with lots of chopped nuts, cinnamon, sugar, and moist, golden raisins.

CREAM CHEESE PASTRY

1 cup (2 sticks) unsalted butter, at room temperature

8 ounces cream cheese, at room temperature

2¼ cups all-purpose flour, spooned in and leveled, divided

¼ teaspoon salt

¼ cup strained confectioners' sugar, spooned and leveled

FILLING

¾ cup granulated sugar

1 tablespoon ground cinnamon

1½ cups finely chopped walnuts

1 cup golden raisins, plumped (see page 358)

Strained confectioners' sugar, for dusting

AT A GLANCE

PAN: Cookie sheets

PAN PREP: Ungreased

CHILLING TIME: 4 hours before shaping; ½ hour after shaping

RACK LEVELS: Upper and lower thirds

OVEN TEMP: 350°F (see Note)

BAKING TIME: 20–25 minutes (see Note)

DIFFICULTY: 2

MAKE THE PASTRY

1. In a large bowl, using a wooden spoon, mix together the butter and cream cheese until smooth and thoroughly blended.

2. Mix in 1 cup of the flour and the salt, working until almost incorporated. Cut in another ½ cup flour with the spoon, again working it until the flour is almost incorporated. Complete the process by kneading in another ½ cup flour. *Do not overwork.* (Note: The remaining ¼ cup of flour is used for rolling.)

3. With lightly floured hands, shape the dough into a mound, then divide in half and form two 5-inch disks. Dust the disks lightly with a little flour, score with the side of your hand to even the tops, and wrap with plastic. Chill for at least 4 hours or up to 3 days.

SHAPE AND FILL THE RUGELACH

This procedure will be used each time you roll a portion of the dough.

4. Remove the dough from the refrigerator and let stand at room temperature for 30 minutes before rolling. It is ready to roll when you can leave a slight imprint in the dough when you press it with your fingers. Combine the remaining ¼ cup flour and the confectioners' sugar. Dust a pastry board or other flat surface with this mixture. Have cookie sheets ready.

5. Divide 1 disk of the dough into thirds, coat each third lightly with the flour-sugar mixture, and form into cylinders. Working with one cylinder at a time, tap it about six times with a rolling pin to flatten. Then roll the cylinder into a long rectangle approximately 5 inches wide and 18 inches long, about $\frac{1}{16}$ inch thick.

6. Combine the granulated sugar and cinnamon. Sprinkle the strip of dough with 2 tablespoons of this mixture, along with $\frac{1}{4}$ cup of the chopped walnuts. Run the rolling pin gently over the walnuts to press them into the dough.

7. With a fluted pastry wheel, cut triangles at 2-inch intervals. Place six or seven raisins on the widest side of each triangle. Starting with the wide side, roll up loosely, tucking the end underneath. It's okay if some of the filling falls out; just sprinkle it back on. Place on the cookie sheets. Repeat with the remaining dough. Chill for $\frac{1}{2}$ hour before baking. (The rugelach may be frozen at this point for up to 1 month.)

BAKE THE RUGELACH

8. Position the racks in the upper and lower thirds of the oven. Heat the oven to 350°F.

9. Bake the rugelach for 20 to 25 minutes, or until golden brown. To ensure even browning, toward the end of baking time rotate the sheets top to bottom and front to back. Remove from the oven and let rest for 1 minute, then loosen with a thin, metal spatula. Transfer to cooling racks. When cool, sprinkle with confectioners' sugar.

NOTE: If the rugelach are frozen, do not defrost them before baking. Reduce the oven temperature to 325°F and add 4 or 5 minutes to the baking time.

STORAGE: Store in an airtight container, layered between strips of wax paper, for up to 1 week. These cookies may be frozen.

Chocolate Chip Rugelach

Follow the directions through step 5 of the Master Recipe. In a medium bowl, whisk together $\frac{3}{4}$ cup granulated sugar, 2 tablespoons strained unsweetened cocoa powder, and $\frac{1}{2}$ to 1 teaspoon cinnamon. Sprinkle each strip of pastry generously with this mixture. Top the strips with finely chopped walnuts, using $1\frac{1}{2}$ cups. Press the rolling pin lightly over the surface to press the topping into the dough.

With a pastry wheel, cut triangles at 2-inch intervals. Place about $\frac{1}{2}$ teaspoon of chocolate mini-morsels on the wide end of the triangles. Roll up and bake as recipe directs and dust with confectioners' sugar before serving.

classic sugar cookies

MAKES ABOUT 4 DOZEN 2-INCH COOKIES

For a delicious variety on the cookie plate, divide the dough into quarters and make classic sugar, nutty sugar, cinnamon swirl sugar, and chocolate fleck sugar flavors.

3 cups sifted cake flour, spooned in
    and leveled

¼ teaspoon baking powder

½ teaspoon salt

1 cup (2 sticks) unsalted butter, slightly firm

¾ cup superfine sugar

1 large egg

1½ teaspoons pure vanilla extract

1 large egg white lightly beaten with
    2 teaspoons of water, for egg wash

Sparkling white sugar, pearl sugar, or
    sanding sugar, for sprinkling (available
    from The Baker's Catalogue; see page 381)

AT A GLANCE

PAN: Cookie sheets

PAN PREP: Ungreased

CHILLING TIME: 15 minutes

RACK LEVELS: Upper and
    lower thirds

OVEN TEMP: 350°F

BAKING TIME: 12–14 minutes

DIFFICULTY: 1

1. Strain together the flour, baking powder, and salt. Set aside.

2. In the large bowl of an electric mixer fitted with the paddle attachment, mix the butter and sugar on medium-low speed.

3. Using a fork, beat the egg and vanilla together and mix into the butter-sugar mixture. Add the dry ingredients one-half at a time, mixing *only* until mixture begins to form a mass. Empty the dough onto a lightly floured surface and knead four or five times, or just until smooth. Divide the dough into quarters. Using lightly floured hands, shape the dough into four disks. Dust lightly with flour and wrap each with plastic. Chill for at least 15 minutes.

4. Position the racks in the upper and lower thirds of the oven. Heat the oven to 350°F.

5. On a lightly floured pastry cloth or board, working with one-fourth of the dough, roll the dough to a ³⁄₁₆-inch thickness. Cut into desired shapes with cookie cutters. After cutting, transfer the cookies to a sheet of wax paper. Brush the tops lightly with egg wash and sprinkle evenly with sparkling white sugar, pearl sugar, or sanding sugar. Carefully place on cookie sheets. Mix the three variation flavors and repeat step 5.

6. Bake the cookies for 12 to 14 minutes, or until the edges begin to brown. To ensure even browning, toward the end of baking time rotate the sheets from top to bottom and front to back. Let stand on pans for 1 or 2 minutes. With a thin, metal spatula, remove to cooling racks. Let cool before decorating.

STORAGE: Store in an airtight container, layered between strips of wax paper, for up to 3 weeks. These cookies may be frozen.

Nutty Sugar Cookies

Using one-fourth of the dough, knead in ¼ cup finely chopped pecans before chilling. Do not overwork.

Cinnamon Swirl Sugar Cookies

Combine ¾ teaspoon ground cinnamon with 2 teaspoons sugar. Add to one-fourth of the dough. Lightly knead the mixture three or four times into the dough to create a marbled effect. Do not overwork.

Chocolate Fleck Sugar Cookies

Using one-fourth of the dough, knead in ¼ cup finely shaved semisweet or bittersweet chocolate before chilling. Do not overwork.

Secrets for Making Rolled Cookies

- Dough that is too cold will crack and be difficult to roll. It should yield to the touch, but should not be "squishy soft."

- For ease of rolling, use a well-floured pastry cloth and rolling pin cover.

- It is best to roll one small piece of chilled dough at a time because it is easier to handle and less likely to become too soft. Keep the remaining dough refrigerated.

- When using a cookie cutter, always insert it into the rolled dough close to the previous cut to minimize waste.

- To prevent dough from sticking to the cookie cutter, dip the cutter frequently into a shallow bowl filled with flour, tapping the cutter on the side of the bowl to remove the excess flour.

- Before brushing cookies with egg wash and decorating with sprinkles, nuts, or sugars, transfer the cut-out cookies to a sheet of wax paper. This will keep the rolling area clean.

- To distribute granulated or colored decorating sugars evenly over the tops of cookies, hold the container 8 to 10 inches above the cookies and rapidly move it back and forth. For larger decorations like pearl or sparkling white sugars, sprinkles, and chopped nuts, take a handful of the garnish and make a fist. Hold your fist perpendicular to the pan at a height of 8 to 10 inches, then rapidly move it back and forth over the cookies, releasing a small amount of the garnish from the bottom of your fist.

- Choose flat cookie sheets instead of jelly roll pans for baking larger rolled cookies, such as Gingerbread People, or intricate shapes such as snowflakes; it will be easier to slide a spatula underneath the baked cookies to release them.

- The baking time of rolled cookies will vary according to the size of the cookie cutter used. For this reason, it is best to group cookies of similar sizes together on the pans.

sweethearts

MAKES ABOUT EIGHTEEN 2½-INCH SANDWICHES

Here is the ideal two-layer fruit-filled sandwich cookie. It has a delicate golden crumb, and its buttery flavor is complemented by the tang of raspberry preserves, perfect for romantic occasions. This cookie will keep longer if refrigerated. If you like, vary the filling with apricot or blackberry preserves. A variety of all three flavors makes a statement to seduce (or weaken!) any heart.

1¾ cups all-purpose flour, spooned in and leveled

¾ cup strained confectioners' sugar, spooned in and leveled

⅔ cup (1⅓ sticks) cold unsalted butter, cut into ½-inch cubes

3 large egg yolks

1 teaspoon pure vanilla extract

1 large egg white lightly beaten with 2 teaspoons water, for egg wash

2 tablespoons raspberry preserves

AT A GLANCE

PAN: Cookie sheets

PAN PREP: Lightly buttered

EQUIPMENT: 2½-inch and 1½-inch heart cookie cutters

CHILLING TIME: 1 hour (dough); 15 minutes (cookies)

RACK LEVELS: Upper and lower thirds

OVEN TEMP: 350°F

BAKING TIME: 10–12 minutes

DIFFICULTY: 2

MAKE THE DOUGH

1. Place the flour, confectioners' sugar, and butter in the bowl of a food processor fitted with a steel blade. Pulse four or five times to combine, then process for 10 seconds, or until the mixture is the texture of fine meal.

2. Combine the yolks and vanilla and add, with the processor off, to the work bowl. Pulse two or three times, then process for 8 to 10 seconds, or *just* until a mass forms. Empty the dough out onto a lightly floured surface. With lightly floured hands, shape into a 6-inch disk. Wrap in plastic and refrigerate for 1 hour or up to 3 days. (The dough may be frozen at this point for up to 1 month.)

SHAPE THE COOKIES

3. Lightly butter the cookie sheets.

4. On a lightly floured pastry cloth or rolling surface, working with only one-fourth of the dough at a time so it doesn't dry out, roll to a ⅛-inch thickness. Cut hearts using a 2½-inch, heart-shaped cookie cutter, positioning the cutter as close as possible to the last cut. Place half of these hearts on the cookie sheets and brush with the egg wash.

5. Use the remaining rolled-and-cut-out hearts for the top layer. Using a 1½-inch, heart-shaped cutter, cut the centers out of the remaining hearts to create a hole. Position the cut-out hearts on top of the solid hearts. Fill the cavity of each cookie with ¼ teaspoon of raspberry preserves. Do not overfill the cavity. Seal the edges with the tines of a fork. Before baking, chill the sandwiched cookies for at least 15 minutes. This will help to retain their shape. (*Note:* If the dough begins to stick to the fork, chill before pressing with the fork.)

BAKE THE COOKIES

6. Position the racks in the upper and lower thirds of the oven. Heat the oven to 350°F.

7. Bake the cookies for 10 to 12 minutes, or until golden brown. To ensure even browning, toward the end of baking time rotate the pans from top to bottom and front to back. Let cool for 2 minutes before loosening with a thin, metal spatula. Transfer to cooling racks. If desired, dust with confectioners' sugar before serving. To brighten the preserves before serving, use the opposite end or tip of a slim teaspoon to dip into the preserves and add a bit to touch up the center of each cookie.

STORAGE: Refrigerate in an airtight container, layered between strips of wax paper sprayed with nonstick cooking spray, for up to 2 weeks. These cookies may be frozen.

chocolate-glazed pecan leaves

MAKES 5 DOZEN 3-INCH OVAL COOKIES

These buttery cookies are glazed with a thin layer of chocolate ganache and then dipped in chopped, toasted pecans. The tender crumb of the cookie, the crunch of the pecans, and the mellow chocolate is a combination that I adore.

3 cups sifted cake flour, spooned in
   and leveled

¼ teaspoon baking powder

½ teaspoon salt

1 cup (2 sticks) unsalted butter, slightly firm

¾ cup superfine sugar

1 large egg

1½ teaspoons pure vanilla extract

Ganache Glaze

1 cup chopped, toasted pecans (see page 356),
   in ⅛-inch pieces, preferably hand-chopped

AT A GLANCE

PAN: Cookie sheets

PAN PREP: Ungreased

EQUIPMENT: 3-inch
   fluted-edge oval cookie
   cutter

CHILLING TIME: 15 minutes

RACK LEVELS: Upper and
   lower thirds

OVEN TEMP: 350°F

BAKING TIME: 12–14 minutes

DIFFICULTY: 1

MAKE THE CREAM CHEESE DOUGH

1. Strain together the flour, baking powder, and salt. Set aside.

2. In the large bowl of an electric mixer fitted with the paddle attachment, mix the butter and sugar on medium-low speed.

3. Using a fork, beat the egg and vanilla together and mix into the butter-sugar mixture. Add the dry ingredients, one-half at a time, mixing *only* until mixture begins to form a mass. Turn the dough out onto a lightly floured surface and knead four or five times, or just until smooth. Divide the dough into quarters. Using lightly floured hands, shape the dough into four disks. Dust lightly with flour and wrap each with plastic. Chill for at least 15 minutes.

BAKE THE COOKIES

4. Position the racks in the upper and lower thirds of the oven. Heat the oven to 350°F.

5. On a lightly floured pastry cloth or board, roll out the dough to a ³⁄₁₆-inch thickness. Cut into leaf shapes using a 3-inch oval cookie cutter with a fluted edge.

6. Place on the cookie sheets and bake for 12 to 14 minutes, or until the edges begin to brown. To ensure even browning, toward the end of baking time rotate the sheets from top to bottom and front to back. Let stand on the pans for 1 minute, then remove to wire racks using a thin, metal spatula.

7. When the cookies are cool, using a small offset spatula, spread a thin layer of ganache over the tops. Dip each cookie, top side down, into the chopped pecans. Set on wire racks until the ganache has hardened.

STORAGE: Store in an airtight container, layered between strips of wax paper, for up to 1 week. These cookies may be frozen.

ganache glaze

MAKES 1 GENEROUS CUP

The versatility of ganache is a gift to a sweet kitchen. It makes a mirror-like glaze when pourable. When chilled, it thickens to a consistency suitable for filling cookies, or it can be piped into rosettes, lines, or other beautiful ornamentations.

6 ounces fine-quality semisweet or bittersweet chocolate, such as Lindt Bittersweet, cut into 1-inch chunks

¾ cup heavy cream

1 tablespoon light corn syrup

¾ teaspoon pure vanilla extract

½ to 1 teaspoon hot water, if needed

1. Place the chocolate in the work bowl of a food processor fitted with the steel blade and process until finely chopped.

2. In a small saucepan, over low heat, heat the heavy cream and corn syrup together until it comes to a simmer. *Immediately* pour the hot cream over the chocolate in the processor bowl. Let stand for 1 minute so that the chocolate begins to melt. Pulse three or four times, then let rest 1 additional minute. Add the vanilla and pulse three or four more times.

3. Empty into a container. If the ganache's surface appears oily, add the hot water, a few drops at a time, stirring well after each addition. The ganache will thicken as it stands, but should remain pourable. If the sauce fails to thicken, refrigerate it for 4 to 5 minutes.

STORAGE: Ganache may be left at room temperature for several hours, but should be reheated over low heat if being used as a glaze. When ganache is used as a filling for a drop or sandwich cookie, it is best chilled to spreading consistency. It may also be made ahead and stored in the refrigerator in an airtight container for up to 2 weeks or frozen for up to 9 months. To thaw frozen ganache, heat slowly in a water bath (see "Using a Water Bath," page 355) or a double boiler or place entire container in a pan of hot water.

spritz cookies

MAKES 4 DOZEN 2-INCH COOKIES

Almost everyone who has eaten a cookie has, at some time, tasted a Scandinavian spritz cookie. Named for the German word spritzen, meaning to squirt, these delightful little cookies are made from dough that is either pressed from a cookie gun or piped from a pastry bag. They typically have a pronounced buttery flavor enhanced with a hint of almond extract, and an extremely tender texture. Because the dough is so versatile, I like to make it in several flavors. You can let your imagination really go to work. To create eye appeal and enhance the taste, I dip the edges of the cookies into Chocolate Candy Glaze (page 371). After dipping, I garnish them with chocolate or colorful sprinkles, chopped nuts or coconut, or colored sugars.

2¼ cups all-purpose flour, spooned in and leveled

⅛ teaspoon salt

1 cup (2 sticks) unsalted butter, slightly firm

⅔ cup sugar

3 large egg yolks

1½ teaspoons pure vanilla extract

½ teaspoon almond extract

AT A GLANCE

PAN: Cookie sheets

PAN PREP: Ungreased

EQUIPMENT: Cookie press

RACK LEVELS: Upper and lower thirds

OVEN TEMP: 350°F

BAKING TIME: 12–14 minutes

DIFFICULTY: 1

1. Position the racks in the upper and lower thirds of the oven. Heat the oven to 350°F.

2. Strain together the flour and salt. Set aside.

3. In the large bowl of an electric mixer fitted with the paddle attachment, mix the butter on medium-low speed until creamy and lightened in color, about 2 minutes. Add the sugar in a steady stream, and continue mixing until well blended, about 2 minutes. Blend in the egg yolks and the vanilla and almond extracts, scraping down the side of the bowl as needed.

4. Reduce the mixer speed to low and add the dry ingredients in three additions, mixing *only* to combine after each addition.

5. Choose a forming plate for the cookie press. Following the manufacturer's instructions, fill the press with the dough and press the cookies onto the cookie sheets, spacing them about 1½ inches apart. Bake the cookies for 12 to 14 minutes, or until the bottoms are very lightly browned. Toward the end of baking time, rotate the sheets top to bottom and front to back. Let rest for 2 or 3 minutes before loosening with a thin, metal spatula. Cool on wire racks.

STORAGE: Store in an airtight container, layered between strips of wax paper, for up to 3 weeks. These cookies may be frozen.

Chocolate Spritz Cookies

Place 1 cup of the cookie dough in a medium bowl. Blend in 1 ounce warm, melted chocolate and 1 tablespoon sugar with a spoon, until the chocolate dough is similar in consistency to the original dough. Proceed with step 5 of the Master Recipe. Makes about 1 dozen cookies.

Cinnamon-Orange Spritz Cookies

Place 1 cup of the cookie dough in a medium bowl. Using a large rubber spatula, stir 1 tablespoon ground cinnamon and 1 tablespoon freshly grated Valencia or navel orange zest into the dough. Proceed with step 5 of the Master Recipe. Makes about 1 dozen cookies.

Marble Spritz Cookies

Use 1 cup each of the Spritz Cookie Dough and the Chocolate Spritz Cookie Dough. When filling the cookie press, alternately place tablespoons of the regular dough with the chocolate dough, pressing gently but firmly to achieve a marbled dough. Bake as directed in step 5 of the Master Recipe. Makes about 2 dozen cookies.

Secrets for Making Pipe and Press Cookies

- Nuts or other textured ingredients must be finely chopped to avoid clogging the cookie plates and to achieve a clean design.

- Tinting portions of the cookie dough with vegetable coloring and arranging it inside of the cookie gun can create multicolored cookies. This can also be done with flavorings like chocolate and vanilla.

- Cookies will adhere to a cookie sheet better if the sheet is not buttered.

- Before baking, pay attention to the consistency of the dough. If it is too soft, chill it briefly to retain the pattern of the cookie.

- If the dough sticks to the gun while piping the cookies, it is too stiff. Thin it with a small amount of milk or orange juice.

- Load the cookie gun cylinder from the front end where the plate will be inserted, and smooth the edge with a spatula. This will avoid air pockets.

chocolate espresso spritz cookies

MAKES 4 DOZEN 2-INCH COOKIES

Here is a recipe for chocolate spritz cookies that is a sure winner. The deep-chocolate dough is richly flavored with cocoa powder, espresso, and lots of butter. What could be bad?

2 cups all-purpose flour, spooned in and leveled

½ cup strained Dutch-processed cocoa powder, spooned in and leveled

1½ teaspoons instant espresso powder

½ teaspoon boiling water

1 cup (2 sticks) unsalted butter, slightly firm

1 cup sugar

1 large egg

2 teaspoons pure vanilla extract

Chocolate Candy Glaze (page 371)

AT A GLANCE

PAN: Cookie sheets

PAN PREP: Ungreased

EQUIPMENT: Cookie press

RACK LEVELS: Upper and lower thirds

OVEN TEMP: 375°F

BAKING TIME: 12–14 minutes

DIFFICULTY: 1

1. Position the racks in the upper and lower thirds of the oven. Heat the oven to 375°F.

2. Strain together the flour and cocoa three times. Set aside. Dissolve the espresso powder in the boiling water. Set aside.

3. Place the butter in the large bowl of an electric mixer fitted with the paddle attachment and mix on medium-low speed until creamy and lightened in color, about 2 minutes. Add the sugar in a steady stream and continue mixing until well blended, about 2 minutes. Blend in the egg, vanilla, and espresso liquid, scraping the bowl as needed.

4. Reduce the mixer speed to low and add the dry ingredients in three additions, mixing *just* until blended.

5. Place the forming plate of your choice into the cookie press. Following the manufacturer's instructions, fill the cylinder with the dough and press the cookies onto the cookie sheets, spacing them about 1½ inches apart. Bake the cookies for 12 to 14 minutes, or until the tops are set. To ensure even baking, toward the end of baking time rotate the sheets top to bottom and front to back. Let rest for 2 or 3 minutes before loosening with a thin, metal spatula. Transfer to cooling racks. Glaze the cookies as desired.

STORAGE: Store in an airtight container, layered between strips of wax paper, for up to 3 weeks. These cookies may be frozen.

almond spritz cookies

MAKES 4 DOZEN 2-INCH COOKIES

Traditional spritz cookies are made with ground almonds, and that's what we have here. The toasted almonds add terrific flavor and texture to the delicate, buttery cookies. If you want the cookie to have a beautiful, golden hue, be sure to use blanched almonds.

1 cup toasted blanched almonds (see page 356)

2 cups all-purpose flour, spooned in and leveled

¼ teaspoon salt

1 cup (2 sticks) unsalted butter, slightly firm

4 ounces almond paste (see page 356), finely shredded, at room temperature

⅔ cup sugar

2 large egg yolks

1½ teaspoons pure vanilla extract

½ teaspoon almond extract

1. Position the racks in the upper and lower thirds of the oven. Heat the oven to 375°F.

2. In the work bowl of a food processor fitted with a steel blade, pulse the almonds five or six times until they are coarsely chopped. Add ½ cup of the flour and process until the mixture develops a sandy texture and holds together when pressed gently in your hand, about 30 seconds. Add the remaining flour and salt and pulse to combine. Set aside.

3. In the standing bowl of an electric mixer fitted with the paddle attachment, mix the butter on medium-low speed until creamy and lightened in color, about 2 minutes. Add the almond paste and mix 30 seconds to combine. Pour in the sugar in a steady stream, then add the egg yolks one at a time, scraping down the side of the bowl as needed. Beat in the vanilla and almond extracts.

4. Reduce the mixer speed to low and add the dry ingredients in three additions, mixing *only* to combine after each addition.

5. Place the desired forming plate into the cookie press. Following the manufacturer's instructions, fill the press with the dough and press the cookies onto the cookie sheets, spacing them about 1 inch apart.

6. Bake the cookies for 9 to 11 minutes, or until the bottoms are very lightly browned. To ensure even browning toward the end of baking time, rotate the cookie sheets top to bottom and front to back. Let rest for 2 or 3 minutes before loosening with a thin, metal spatula. Cool on wire racks.

STORAGE: Store in an airtight container, layered between strips of wax paper, for up to 3 weeks. These cookies may be frozen.

AT A GLANCE

PAN: Cookie sheets

PAN PREP: Ungreased

EQUIPMENT: Cookie press

RACK LEVELS: Upper and lower thirds

OVEN TEMP: 375°F

BAKING TIME: 9–11 minutes

DIFFICULTY: 1

french lace what-nots

MAKES ABOUT 4 DOZEN 3-INCH COOKIES

Wait until you hear the raves when you serve these charming French Lace What-Nots! These buttery lace cookies literally melt in your mouth. Instead of molding the cookies into uniform shapes, I push the edges of the hot cookies toward their centers to make a variety of whimsical shapes. For a finishing touch, I web the tops with thin lines of melted chocolate.

COOKIES

1/2 cup cake flour, spooned in and leveled

3 ounces (about 1/2 cup) whole, blanched almonds

Pinch of salt

1/2 cup (1 stick) unsalted butter

1/3 cup lightly packed light brown sugar

1/4 cup light corn syrup

1/2 teaspoon pure vanilla extract

GLAZE

2 ounces fine-quality bittersweet or semisweet chocolate, such as Lindt Bittersweet, chopped

1/2 teaspoon vegetable oil

AT A GLANCE

PAN: Cookie sheet

PAN PREP: Silpat or other nonstick baking mat or well-buttered and floured cookie sheet

RACK LEVEL: Center

OVEN TEMP: 350°F

STANDING TIME: 1 hour

BAKING TIME: 5–7 minutes

DIFFICULTY: 2

MAKE THE BATTER

1. Combine the flour, almonds, and salt in the work bowl of a food processor fitted with the steel blade. Pulse five or six times, then process for 40 to 50 seconds, until the mixture has a fine, meal-like consistency. Stop occasionally to scrape around the side of the work bowl. Set aside.

2. Combine the butter, brown sugar, and corn syrup in a small, heavy saucepan. Bring to a slow boil over low heat and simmer for 20 to 30 seconds. Remove from the heat and stir in the vanilla and the flour-nut mixture. Scrape the batter into a bowl and let stand for about 1 hour. The batter will thicken as it cools and will be somewhat oily.

BAKE THE COOKIES

3. Position the rack in the center of the oven. Heat the oven to 350°F. Line a cookie sheet with a Silpat or other nonstick baking mat. Alternatively, generously butter the cookie sheet and, using a flour shaker, dust evenly with flour. Tap firmly over the sink to remove any excess flour.

4. Shape the batter into marble-size 1/2- to 3/4-inch balls, placing no more than six on the cookie sheet at a time, spacing them evenly apart. *Do not crowd.* The batter will spread. Bake the cookies for 5 to 7 minutes, or until they are golden brown and no longer bubbling. Watch carefully! They overbake quickly.

5. Remove from the oven and let cool 1 minute. Loosen one cookie at a time from the sheet and place top side up on a double sheet of paper towels. While still soft and pliable, push the edge of the cookie to the center, first pushing in from the right and left sides, then from the top and bottom. Use another piece of paper towel or more as needed to *protect your fingers while molding the hot cookie.* Repeat with the remaining cookies. If the cookies become too brittle to shape, return them to the oven for a few seconds to soften. Place the formed cookies on a cooling rack set over a sheet of wax paper.

GLAZE THE COOKIES

6. When all the cookies are baked, melt the chocolate over a water bath (see page 353). When the chocolate is almost melted, stir in the vegetable oil. Do not let the chocolate mixture get too hot; the chocolate is ready when it is warm and runny. Dip the tines of a fork into the melted chocolate and zigzag the glaze over the tops of the cookies. Let the cookies rest at room temperature until the chocolate is set. This could take several hours, depending on the humidity and the season of the year.

STORAGE: The cookies may be stored in an airtight container, carefully layered between strips of wax paper, for up to 3 weeks.

oatmeal almond jammies

MAKES ABOUT 5 DOZEN 2-INCH COOKIES

Oatmeal, almond paste, toasted almonds, and a touch of cinnamon make an exciting kaleidoscope of flavors for Oatmeal Almond Jammies. The center of this thumbprint-style cookie is chewy with almond paste, while the crust is crunchy with toasted almonds. While some recipes for thumbprint cookies have their cavities filled before baking, I think you achieve a prettier end result if the depression is made twice: once before the cookies are baked and again midway through baking. Although I love these cookies filled with blackberry preserves, you may use any flavor of preserves you wish.

1½ cups all-purpose flour, spooned in and leveled

¾ cup old-fashioned oatmeal

1½ teaspoons baking powder

¾ teaspoon ground cinnamon

½ teaspoon salt

¾ cup (1½ sticks) unsalted butter, at room temperature

3 ounces almond paste, shredded (see page 355)

1¼ cups sugar

1 large egg

2 large egg yolks

1½ teaspoons pure vanilla extract

½ teaspoon pure almond extract

1½ cups sliced unblanched almonds, toasted (see page 356)

2 large egg whites, lightly beaten with 2 teaspoons water

½ cup blackberry preserves

AT A GLANCE

PAN: Jelly roll pans

PAN PREP: Baking parchment

CHILLING TIME: 30–45 minutes

RACK LEVELS: Upper and lower thirds

OVEN TEMP: 350°F

BAKING TIME: 20–24 minutes

DIFFICULTY: 2

MAKE THE DOUGH

1. Place the flour, oatmeal, baking powder, cinnamon, and salt in the bowl of a food processor fitted with a steel blade and process for 15 seconds. Pulse four times, then process for another 25 seconds. The mixture will be cakey in texture. Set aside.

2. In the large bowl of an electric mixer fitted with the paddle attachment, mix the butter on medium-low speed until smooth and lightened in color. Add the almond paste and mix until completely smooth, 3 to 4 minutes. Add the sugar in three additions, scraping the bowl after the final addition. Add the egg, egg yolks, and vanilla and almond extracts and mix until well blended, scraping the side of the bowl as needed.

3. Reduce the mixer speed to low and add the dry ingredients in two additions, mixing *just* until blended after each addition. Cover the bowl with plastic wrap and chill for 30 to 45 minutes, until firm enough to handle.

BAKE THE COOKIES

4. Position the racks in the upper and lower thirds of the oven. Heat the oven to 350°F. Line the pans with baking parchment.

5. Place the almonds in a large, shallow dish, such as a pie plate, then break them up coarsely with your fingers.

6. Roll the dough into 1-inch balls. Roll each ball in the egg whites, then roll in the crumbled almonds to coat. Place 2 inches apart on the cookie sheets. Using the handle of a wooden spoon, poke an indentation in the center of each. (If dough sticks, dip the end of the spoon in flour.)

7. Bake for 12 to 14 minutes, remove from the oven, and re-press each indentation. Fill each with a scant $\frac{1}{2}$ teaspoon jam and return to oven. (Do *not* overfill.) Bake for an additional 8 to 10 minutes, or until the edges are golden brown. Toward the end of the baking time, rotate the pans from top to bottom and front to back. Remove from the oven and let stand for 2 or 3 minutes before loosening with a thin, metal spatula. Cool on a wire rack.

STORAGE: Store in an airtight container, layered between strips of wax paper, for up to 2 weeks. These cookies may be frozen.

pecan tassies

MAKES 4 DOZEN 1¾-INCH TASSIES

When I grew up down South, one of my favorite sweet treats was Pecan Tassies. These miniature cookie-like tartlets are reminiscent of the ultimate Southern favorite, pecan pie. The Tassies have a flaky cream cheese pastry with an addictive brown sugar and butter filling with lots of chopped pecans.

Admittedly, Tassies are a time-consuming project—but they can be made ahead and they will freeze beautifully. I guarantee that when you serve them, the oohs and ahhs will more than compensate you for your efforts! As a matter of fact, I wish I had one right now!

Cream Cheese Pastry (page 72, rugelach), formed into 2 4- x 6-inch rectangles, wrapped in plastic, and chilled

FILLING

2 large eggs

2 cups lightly packed very fresh dark brown sugar

2 tablespoons unsalted butter, melted and cooled

¼ teaspoon salt

2 teaspoons pure vanilla extract

2 cups coarsely chopped, lightly toasted pecans (see page 356), divided

AT A GLANCE

PAN: Mini-muffin tins

PAN PREP: Ungreased

CHILLING TIME: Pastry: 4 hours

RACK LEVELS: Upper and lower thirds

OVEN TEMP: 325°F

BAKING TIME: 20–25 minutes

DIFFICULTY: 3

1. Divide each rectangle of pastry into twenty-four 1-inch squares. Roll each square into a ball and place into mini-muffin tins. Mold the dough into each hole, pressing it up the sides. Chill while preparing the filling.

2. Position the racks in the upper and lower thirds of the oven. Heat the oven to 325°F.

3. Place the eggs, brown sugar, butter, salt, and vanilla in a large bowl. Whisk together until smooth.

4. Distribute 1 cup of the pecans among the pastry-lined muffin cups. Empty the filling into a measuring cup with a spout and pour the mixture into the tins, *filling them no more than two-thirds full.* Sprinkle the tops with the remaining 1 cup nuts.

5. Bake for 20 to 25 minutes or until the pastry is golden brown around the edges. Rotate the pans from top to bottom and front to back toward the end of baking time. Let stand 5 minutes. Using the tip of a paring knife, run the blade carefully around the edges of the muffin cups to loosen the Tassies. When the Tassies are cool enough to handle, remove them from the pan and set on cooling racks. (*Note:* The Tassies can either be eased out with the tip of the knife or inverted onto the cooling rack.)

STORAGE: Store in an airtight container, layered between strips of wax paper, for up to 5 days. These cookies may be frozen.

coconut lemon-lime tassies

MAKES 4 DOZEN 1¾-INCH TASSIES

Here is a citrusy twist on the classic Tassie recipe. A tangy, lemon-lime filling is nestled between layers of flaky coconut. The flavor of the buttery pastry along with the tang of the cream cheese makes the perfect background for these tartlets.

Cream Cheese Pastry (page 72), formed into
  2 4- × 6-inch rectangles

FILLING

3 tablespoons all-purpose flour

½ teaspoon baking powder

¼ teaspoon salt

4 large egg yolks

1¼ cups sugar

2 teaspoons freshly grated lemon zest

2 teaspoons freshly grated lime zest

3 tablespoons fresh lemon juice

3 tablespoons fresh lime juice

1 cup chopped sweetened, flaked coconut,
  divided

Vanilla Glaze (page 368)

1. Divide each rectangle of pastry into twenty-four 1-inch squares. Roll each into a ball and place into mini-muffin tins. Mold the dough into each hole, pressing it up the sides. Chill while preparing the filling.

2. Position the racks in the upper and lower thirds of the oven. Heat the oven to 350°F.

3. Strain together the flour, baking powder, and salt. Set aside.

4. In a large bowl of an electric mixer fitted with the whip attachment, beat the egg yolks on medium speed until lightened in color. Add the sugar in a steady stream, beating until thickened. On low speed, blend in the zests and juices. Remove the bowl from the machine and fold in the dry ingredients and ½ cup of the coconut.

AT A GLANCE

PAN: Mini-muffin tins

PAN PREP: Ungreased

CHILLING TIME: Pastry:
  4 hours

RACK LEVELS: Upper and
  lower thirds

OVEN TEMP: 350°F

BAKING TIME: 30–32 minutes

DIFFICULTY: 3

5. Sprinkle the remaining coconut into the pastry-lined muffin cups. Using a measuring cup with a spout, pour the mixture into the tins, *filling them no more than two-thirds full.*

6. Bake for 30 to 32 minutes, or until the pastry is golden brown around the edges. Toward the end of baking time, rotate the pans top to bottom and front to back. Let stand 5 minutes. Using the tip of a paring knife, run the blade carefully around the edges of the muffin cups to loosen the Tassies. When the cups are cool enough to handle, remove them from the pan and set on cooling racks. While they are slightly warm, apply a small amount of Vanilla Glaze to the top of each Tassie, spreading it with the bottom of a teaspoon.

STORAGE: Refrigerate in an airtight container, layered between strips of wax paper, for up to 5 days. These cookies may be frozen.

scotch shortbread

MAKES TWENTY-FIVE 1¾-INCH SQUARES

Scotch shortbread, a thick butter cookie famous for its velvety texture, is a memorable treat. Traditionally made by hand, it has but three ingredients: butter, sugar, and flour (plus a little salt). Although it may seem like a "Plain Jane," the freshness of the ingredients and how they are put together make the difference between an ordinary cookie and one that is extraordinary.

Start with the freshest butter and mix it with superfine sugar, which dissolves more readily than ordinary granulated sugar. The velvety texture comes from a combination of all-purpose flour blended with rice flour, which can be purchased in health food stores or Asian markets. Because the dough is so rich with butter, it should never be overworked, lest the butter begin to melt and impair the beautiful, fine layers of delicate crumbs.

Scots who take their shortbread very seriously bake their cookies in round, wooden, patterned molds, which today have become prized among collectors of antique bakeware.

1¾ cups all-purpose flour, spooned in and leveled

½ cup rice flour, spooned in and leveled

¼ teaspoon salt

1 cup (2 sticks) unsalted butter, slightly softened

½ cup superfine sugar

1 tablespoon sparkling white sugar (available in The Baker's Catalogue; page 381)

AT A GLANCE

PAN: 9-inch square baking pan and cookie sheet

PAN PREP: Heavy-duty aluminum foil

RACK LEVEL: Center

OVEN TEMP: 300°F

BAKING TIME: 1 hour, 10 minutes, baking; 10 minutes, crisping

DIFFICULTY: 1

1. Position the rack in the center of the oven. Heat the oven to 300°F. Cut a 15-inch square of heavy-duty aluminum foil. Invert the pan and center the foil over the pan, pressing it across the bottom and down the sides. Remove the foil, turn the pan right side up, and place the foil shell in the pan, shaping it smoothly across the bottom and snugly against the sides.

2. Strain the flour, rice flour, and salt together three times and set aside.

3. Place the butter in the bowl of an electric mixer fitted with the paddle attachment. Mix on medium-low speed until smooth and creamy, about 1 minute. Add the sugar gradually, taking about 1 minute, then mix for 1 minute longer, scraping the side of the bowl as needed.

4. Remove the bowl from the machine and transfer the mixture to a large, wide bowl for ease of mixing. Using a wooden spoon, cut half of the dry ingredients into the butter mixture until it is almost incorporated. Work in the remaining flour by hand, adding it in five or six additions. Gently knead the mixture just until a smooth dough is formed. Be careful not to overwork the dough, as this will result in a tough cookie.

5. Press the dough evenly into the pan using a bâtarde or flat-bottomed glass wrapped in plastic. Be sure the dough is pushed into the corners of the pan. Test for evenness by inserting a toothpick or the point of a knife randomly into the dough. Clean the edges of the pan by inserting a dough scraper or a small spatula in between the dough and the side of the pan.

6. Bake the shortbread for 55 to 60 minutes, or until the top feels set. Remove from the oven and let stand for 5 minutes. Using a pastry scraper, cut straight down through the dough at 1¾-inch intervals, making five strips. Give the pan a quarter turn and repeat, cutting 25 squares. Sprinkle with sparkling white sugar, return to the oven, and bake for another 10 minutes or until lightly brown.

7. Remove from the oven and let rest for 10 minutes. Have a cookie sheet without sides ready. Using the foil as an aid, lift the shortbread from the pan and place it on the cookie sheet. Gently pull the aluminum foil so it releases from the sides of the shortbread, wrapping longer sides of the foil under the pan and smoothing the foil as best you can to prevent it from sliding. Cut through the shortbread again, and using a thin, metal spatula, spread the cookies slightly apart. Return to the oven for 10 more minutes to dry and crisp the cookies. Remove from the oven and let cool for 5 to 10 minutes before transferring to a cooling rack.

STORAGE: Store in an airtight container, layered between strips of wax paper, for up to 3 weeks. These cookies may be frozen.

chocolate shortbread nuggets

MAKES THIRTY-TWO 1- × 2-INCH COOKIES

Here is a shortbread recipe for the chocolate lovers in the house! The rich, chocolatey cookie is cut into bite-sized nuggets, then dipped in melted chocolate. Whenever I serve these, they are the first to go, and they meet with rave reviews.

1¼ cups all-purpose flour, spooned in and leveled

½ cup rice flour, spooned in and leveled

½ cup strained, Dutch-processed cocoa powder, spooned in and leveled

¼ teaspoon salt

1 cup (2 sticks) unsalted butter, slightly softened

⅔ cup superfine sugar

1 teaspoon pure vanilla extract

1 tablespoon sparkling white sugar (available in The Baker's Catalogue; see page 381)

GARNISH

4 ounces fine-quality bittersweet or semi-sweet chocolate, such as Lindt Bittersweet, melted

1 teaspoon vegetable or canola oil

AT A GLANCE

PAN: 9-inch square baking pan and cookie sheet

PAN PREP: Heavy-duty aluminum foil

RACK LEVEL: Center

OVEN TEMP: 300°F

BAKING TIME: 50–55 minutes, baking; 10 minutes, crisping

DIFFICULTY: 2

1. Position the rack in the center of the oven. Heat the oven to 300°F. Cut a 15-inch square of heavy-duty aluminum foil. Invert the pan and center the foil over the pan, pressing it across the bottom and down the sides. Remove the foil, turn the pan right side up, and place the foil shell in the pan, shaping it smoothly across the bottom and snugly against the sides.

2. Strain the flour, rice flour, cocoa, and salt together three times. Set aside.

3. Place the butter in the bowl of an electric mixer fitted with the paddle attachment and mix on medium-low speed until smooth and creamy, about 1 minute. Add the sugar gradually, taking about 1 minute, then mix for 1 minute longer, scraping the side of the bowl as needed. Add the vanilla and mix to combine.

4. Remove the bowl from the machine and transfer the mixture to a large, wide bowl for ease of mixing. Using a wooden spoon, cut half of the dry ingredients into the butter mixture until it is almost incorporated. Work in the remaining dry ingredients by hand, adding in five or six additions. All of the flour does not have to be incorporated after each addition. Gently knead the mixture just until a smooth dough is formed. Be careful not to overwork the dough, as this will result in a tough cookie.

5. Press the dough evenly into the pan, using a bâtarde or flat-bottomed glass wrapped in plastic. Be sure the dough is pushed into the corners. Test for evenness by inserting a toothpick or the point of a knife randomly into the dough. Clean the sides of the pan by inserting the flat side of a dough scraper or a small metal spatula in between the dough and the sides of the pan.

6. Bake for 50 to 55 minutes, or until set on top. Take out and let rest for 5 minutes. Using a dough scraper, cut straight down through the dough at about 1-inch intervals, making eight strips. Give the pan a quarter-turn and cut four more strips at 2-inch intervals. Sprinkle with the sparkling white sugar. Return to the oven and bake for another 10 minutes.

7. Remove from the oven and let rest for 10 minutes. Have a cookie sheet without sides ready. Using the foil as an aid, lift the shortbread from the pan and place it on the cookie sheet. Pull the aluminum foil so it releases from the sides of the shortbread, wrapping the larger sides of the foil under the pan to prevent it from sliding and smoothing the foil as best you can. Cut through the shortbread again, and using a spatula, spread them slightly apart. Return to the oven for 10 more minutes to crisp and dry the cookies. Remove from the oven and let cool for 5 to 10 minutes before transferring to a cooling rack.

GARNISH THE SHORTBREAD

8. Stir together the melted chocolate and vegetable oil. While the cookies are still tepid, dip each cookie into the chocolate mixture to a depth of ¾ inch. Place on a cooling rack and allow to stand until the chocolate sets.

STORAGE: Store in an airtight container, layered between strips of wax paper, for up to 3 weeks. These cookies may be frozen.

lemon poppy seed shortbread

MAKES TWENTY-FIVE 1¾-INCH SQUARES

This pretty shortbread cookie is flecked with poppy seeds and generously flavored with grated lemon zest, along with lemon oil. The top has a filigree of white chocolate, giving the cookie a more elegant finish.

1¾ cups all-purpose flour, spooned in and leveled

½ cup rice flour, spooned in and leveled

¼ teaspoon salt

3 tablespoons poppy seeds

1 cup (2 sticks) unsalted butter, slightly softened

2 tablespoons freshly grated lemon zest

½ teaspoon lemon oil (see page 351)

½ cup superfine sugar

2 ounces fine-quality white chocolate, such as Lindt Classic Swiss White), melted

AT A GLANCE

PAN: 9-inch square baking pan and cookie sheet

PAN PREP: Heavy-duty aluminum foil

RACK LEVEL: Center

OVEN TEMP: 300°F

BAKING TIME: 50–55 minutes, baking; 10 minutes, crisping

DIFFICULTY: 2

1. Position the rack in the center of the oven. Heat the oven to 300°F. Cut a 15-inch square of heavy-duty aluminum foil. Invert the pan and center the foil over the pan, pressing it across the bottom and down the sides. Remove the foil, turn the pan right side up, and place the foil shell in the pan, shaping it smoothly across the bottom and snugly against the sides.

2. Strain the flour, rice flour, and salt together three times. Stir in the poppy seeds and set aside.

3. Place the butter in the bowl of an electric mixer fitted with the paddle attachment. Mix on medium-low speed until smooth and creamy. Add the lemon zest and lemon oil and mix for 1 minute. Add the sugar gradually, then mix for 1 minute longer, scraping the bowl as needed.

4. Remove the bowl from the machine, and transfer the mixture to a large, wide bowl. Using a wooden spoon, cut half of the dry ingredients into the butter mixture until almost incorporated. Work in the remaining flour by hand, adding it in five or six additions. Gently knead the mixture just until a smooth dough is formed. Be careful not to overwork the dough, as this will result in a tough cookie.

5. Press the dough evenly into the pan, using a bâtarde or flat-bottomed glass wrapped in plastic to spread it. Be sure the dough is pushed into the corners. Test for evenness by inserting a toothpick or the point of a knife randomly into the dough. Clean the edges of the pan by inserting a dough scraper or a small spatula in between the dough and the sides of the pan.

6. Bake the shortbread for 55 to 60 minutes. Remove from the oven and let rest for 10 minutes. Have a cookie sheet without sides ready. Using the foil as an aid, lift the shortbread from the pan and place it on the cookie sheet. Pull the aluminum foil so it releases from the sides of the shortbread. To prevent the foil from sliding, wrap the longer sides under the cookie sheet and smooth it as best you can. Using a long, serrated knife, cut five 1¾-inch strips. Give the cookie sheet a quarter turn and cut five more strips, forming 25 squares. Using a spatula, spread the cookies apart. Return to the oven for 10 more minutes to dry and crisp the cookies. Remove from the oven and let cool for 5 to 10 minutes before transferring to a cooling rack.

7. Pour the tepid melted white chocolate into a small plastic squeeze bottle and move it back and forth over the cookies to create squiggly lines of chocolate. For alternatives, you can use a small pastry bag fitted with a #2 decorating tube, or you can also dip a fork into the melted chocolate and let it drip from the tines while moving the fork back and forth over the cookies. Let the cookies stand at room temperature until the chocolate has set.

STORAGE: Store in an airtight container, layered between strips of wax paper, for up to 3 weeks. These cookies may be frozen.

best biscuits, scones, biscotti, and muffins

old-fashioned buttermilk biscuits

cinnamon pull-apart biscuits

cornmeal buttermilk biscuits

naughty sweet cream biscuits

angel biscuits

a dilly of a cheese scone

sedona cream scones

cranberry-pecan cream scones

country cherry honey scones

toasted pecan mandelbrot

chocolate chocolate chocolate biscotti

jeweled almond biscotti

shaved chocolate and pistachio biscotti

glazed lemon–pine nut biscotti

favorite vanilla muffins

cape cod cranberry muffins

oatmeal raisin muffins

ultra-rich corn muffins

blueberry corn muffins

sam's oodles of apple muffins with country crunch topping

peanut butter banana muffins

jeff's chocolate-glazed midnight muffins

zach's blueberry buttermilk muffins with streusel topping

old-fashioned buttermilk biscuits

MAKES 12 BISCUITS

What is more welcome at breakfast time than a basket of freshly baked biscuits, warm from the oven and slathered with butter and your favorite fruit preserves? These biscuits are made the classical way, a method whereby the butter is rubbed into flake-like particles by hand. This gives the biscuits an especially tender crumb. With your first bite, I am sure you will agree that the extra effort is well worth the reward.

When do-ahead planning is needed, I make a batch of the crumb mixture, pack it in an airtight resealable plastic bag, and store it in the refrigerator or freezer. The crumbs will keep up to 5 days in the refrigerator and about 1 month in the freezer. When I'm ready to bake a batch of biscuits, I empty the contents into a large bowl and let them stand until the buttery flakes begin to soften. Add the buttermilk, and, *voilà!* Mix, roll, bake, and enjoy!

$3\frac{1}{3}$ cups all-purpose flour, spooned in and leveled, plus additional for kneading and rolling

$4\frac{1}{2}$ teaspoons baking powder

1 teaspoon baking soda

$1\frac{1}{4}$ teaspoons salt

$\frac{3}{4}$ cup ($1\frac{1}{2}$ sticks) cold unsalted butter, plus 2 tablespoons melted

$1\frac{2}{3}$ cups buttermilk

AT A GLANCE

PAN: Large cookie sheet

PAN PREP: Ungreased

RACK LEVEL: Center

OVEN TEMP: 400°F

BAKING TIME: 18–20 minutes

DIFFICULTY: 1

1. Position the rack in the center of the oven. Heat the oven to 400°F.

2. In a large bowl, thoroughly whisk together the flour, baking powder, baking soda, and salt.

3. Shave the chilled butter into $\frac{1}{8}$-inch slices using a dough scraper or a sharp knife. Add the butter to the dry ingredients, one-third at a time, rubbing it between your fingertips to form flake-like pieces. Work gently and quickly so the butter does not become too warm. You should have both large and small pieces.

4. Add the buttermilk, pouring it around the edge of the bowl. Using a rubber spatula, push the mixture toward the center, working your way around the bowl to blend the buttermilk with the flakes. The mixture will be soft and resemble large curds of cottage cheese. Let stand for 2 or 3 minutes while you prepare the rolling surface.

5. Sprinkle a pastry board or other flat surface generously with flour, about 2 tablespoons. Empty the dough onto the board. *The dough will be sticky.* With the help of a dough scraper, lift the dough four or five times to coat it with flour. With floured hands, gently knead the dough six or eight times, or *just* until it forms a "skin" (see Forming a Skin, page 107). It's OK if larger particles of butter are visible. Do not overwork the dough or your biscuits will not be tender. When the dough is ready, slide it aside and clean the work surface.

6. Lay a pastry cloth on the surface and fit a rolling pin with a pastry sleeve or rolling pin cover. Rub an additional 2 to 3 tablespoons of flour into the pastry cloth and sleeve.

7. Place the dough on the cloth and pat it lightly with floured hands, shaping it into a rectangle. Roll the dough into a 10- × 14-inch rectangle, with the 10-inch side parallel to the edge of the counter. Fold the dough into thirds, like a business letter. To do this, lift the far side of the pastry cloth up and fold the top third of the dough over on itself. Press the dough to align the edges as best you can. Lift the lower edge of the pastry cloth and flip the bottom third of the dough over on itself, keeping the edges as best you can. You will now have three layers of dough. Press the top gently with your hands, then roll the dough into a 5- × 15-inch strip, with a thickness of a generous $\frac{1}{2}$ inch.

8. Using a $2\frac{1}{4}$-inch straight-sided cookie cutter dipped in flour, cut straight down into the dough, without twisting the cutter, cutting two rows of six biscuits. Be sure to dip the cutter in flour before each cut and cut as close to the previous biscuit as possible. Place on the cookie sheet, *inverting* each biscuit and spacing them about $1\frac{1}{2}$ inches apart. (See What to Do with Bits and Pieces of Dough, page 109.)

9. Brush the tops with the melted butter and bake for 18 to 20 minutes, or until golden brown. Remove the biscuits from the oven and let cool for about 5 minutes before loosening with a thin metal spatula. Serve the biscuits warm. If baking ahead, warm the biscuits for a few minutes in a 300°F oven.

STORAGE: Store in an airtight plastic bag for up to 3 days. These biscuits may be frozen.

cinnamon pull-apart biscuits

MAKES 1 LARGE CAKE, 12 SERVINGS

Here is an interesting way to serve biscuits. The rounds of dough are baked in a springform pan, forming a cake. The biscuit dough is filled with lots of cinnamon and sugar, along with, if you would like, pieces of toasted pecans. After placing the rounds of dough in the pan, they are sprinkled with more cinnamon and sugar. This cake is a lot of fun to serve at a Sunday brunch or other festive occasions. There's no need to slice; your guests simply pull off a round. Serve these with Orange Honey Butter (page 113).

2⅔ cups all-purpose flour, spooned in and leveled, plus additional for rolling

4 tablespoons sugar, divided

4 teaspoons baking powder

¾ teaspoon baking soda

¾ teaspoon salt

⅔ cup (1⅓ sticks) unsalted butter, cubed and chilled, plus 2 tablespoons melted

1¼ cups buttermilk, chilled

½ cup broken, toasted pecans (see page 356; optional)

1 teaspoon ground cinnamon

AT A GLANCE

PAN: 10-inch springform pan

PAN PREP: Buttered

CHILLING TIME: 30 minutes

RACK LEVEL: Center

OVEN TEMP: 400°F

BAKING TIME: 24–26 minutes

DIFFICULTY: 1

1. Position the rack in the center of the oven. Heat the oven to 400°F. Butter a 10-inch springform pan and set aside.

2. Combine the flour, 2 tablespoons of the sugar, the baking powder, baking soda, and salt in the work bowl of a food processor fitted with a steel blade. Chill for at least 30 minutes.

3. Pulse the dough three or four times to blend. Add one-half of the chilled butter and pulse six times, then process for 10 seconds. Add the remaining chilled butter and pulse six or seven times to form coarse crumbs.

4. Transfer the mixture to a large bowl and run your fingers through it to break any large pieces of butter into flakes. Add the buttermilk, pouring it around the edge of the bowl. Using a rubber spatula, push the mixture toward the center, working your way around the bowl to blend the buttermilk with the crumbs. Add the optional pecans, and work them gently into the dough.

5. Combine the remaining 2 tablespoons sugar and the cinnamon and set aside.

6. Empty the mixture onto a well-floured surface and, with the aid of a dough scraper, knead the dough six or eight times. It will not be smooth.

7. Cover a pastry board or other flat surface with a pastry cloth and rub a generous amount of flour into it. Pat the dough out lightly with your hands.

8. Fit a pastry sleeve onto the rolling pin, flour the pin, and roll the dough into a 12- × 9-inch rectangle with the 9-inch side parallel to the counter. Brush with half of the melted butter and sprinkle with 4 teaspoons of the sugar/cinnamon mixture. Fold the rectangle into thirds as if you were folding a letter. Press the top gently with your hands, then roll the dough into a 5- × 15-inch strip.

9. Using a $2\frac{1}{4}$-inch straight-sided cookie cutter dipped in flour, cut straight down into the dough, without twisting the cutter, forming 12 rounds. Be sure to dip the cutter in flour before cutting each biscuit. The biscuits should be inverted before being placed in the pan. Place 10 rounds around the perimeter of the pan and set the remaining two rounds aside. Gather the scraps of dough together and knead gently two or three times. Pat the dough into a $\frac{3}{4}$-inch-thick rectangle. Fold it in half and roll it into a $\frac{1}{2}$-inch-thick rectangle. Cut two more biscuits. Fill in the center of the pan with the four cut biscuits, alternating the rounds from first and second roll. The rounds should barely touch each other. Discard the scraps.

10. Brush the tops with the remaining melted butter and sprinkle with the remaining sugar/cinnamon mixture. Place the pan in the oven on a square of aluminum foil to catch any leakage. Bake the biscuits for 24 to 26 minutes, or until golden brown.

11. Remove the pan from the oven, place on a wire rack, and let the biscuits cool in the pan for about 10 minutes before removing the side of the pan. Invert the biscuits on the rack and carefully remove the bottom of the pan. Then invert on a napkin-lined serving platter. Serve the biscuits warm. If baking ahead, warm the cake in a 300°F oven.

STORAGE: Store in an airtight plastic bag for up to 3 days. These biscuits may be frozen.

cornmeal buttermilk biscuits

MAKES 12 BISCUITS

I am a big fan of mixing cornmeal with my biscuit dough. It adds an interesting crunch, which I love.

2⅓ cups all-purpose flour, spooned in and leveled, plus additional for kneading and rolling

⅔ cup stone-ground cornmeal, spooned in and leveled, plus 1 tablespoon for topping

4 teaspoons baking powder

½ teaspoon baking soda

½ teaspoon salt

¾ cup (1½ sticks) unsalted butter, cubed and chilled, plus 2 tablespoons melted

1½ cups buttermilk, chilled

AT A GLANCE

PAN: Large cookie sheet

PAN PREP: Ungreased

RACK LEVEL: Center

OVEN TEMP: 400°F

BAKING TIME: 18–20 minutes

DIFFICULTY: 1

1. Position the rack in the center of the oven. Heat the oven to 400°F.

2. Place the flour, cornmeal, baking powder, baking soda, and salt in the bowl of a processor fitted with the steel blade. Process for 15 seconds.

3. Add one-half of the cubed butter to the bowl; pulse five times, then process for 5 seconds. Add the remaining butter; pulse five times, then process for 5 seconds. You should have both large and small pieces of butter.

4. Empty the crumb mixture into a large bowl and add the buttermilk, pouring it around the edge of the bowl. Using a rubber spatula, push the mixture toward the center, working your way around the bowl to blend the buttermilk with the crumbs. The mixture will be soft and resemble large curds of cottage cheese.

5. Sprinkle a pastry board or other flat surface generously with 2 tablespoons flour. Empty the dough onto the board with the help of a palm-size plastic bowl scraper or rubber spatula. With floured hands, gently knead the dough six or eight times, or just until it forms a "skin" (see Forming a Skin, page 107). The dough will not be smooth. Use a dough scraper to help lift the dough as needed. Do not overwork the dough or your biscuits will not be tender. When the dough is ready, move it aside and clean the work surface.

6. Lay a pastry cloth on the surface and fit a rolling pin with a pastry sleeve. Rub another 2 tablespoons of flour into the pastry cloth and sleeve.

7. Place the dough on the cloth and pat it lightly with floured hands, shaping it into an 8-inch square. Roll it into a 10- × 14-inch rectangle, with the 10-inch side parallel to the edge of the counter. Fold the dough into thirds like a business letter. To do this, lift the far side of the pastry cloth up and fold the top third of the dough over on itself. Lift the lower edge of the pastry cloth and flip the bottom third of the dough over on itself, evening the edges and creating three layers of dough. Press the top gently with your hands, then roll it into a 5- × 15-inch strip.

8. Using a 2¼-inch straight-sided cookie cutter dipped in flour, cut straight down into the dough, without twisting the cutter, cutting two rows of six biscuits. Be sure to dip the cutter in flour before each cut and cut as close to the previous biscuit as possible. Place on the cookie sheet, *inverting* each biscuit and spacing them about 1½ inches apart. (See What to Do with Bits and Pieces of Dough, page 109.)

9. Brush the tops with the melted butter, sprinkle with the 1 tablespoon cornmeal, and bake for 18 to 20 minutes, or until golden brown. Remove the biscuits from the oven and let cool for about 5 minutes before loosening with a thin metal spatula. Serve the biscuits warm. If baking ahead, warm the biscuits for a few minutes in a 300°F oven.

STORAGE: Store in an airtight plastic bag for up to 3 days. These biscuits may be frozen.

About Biscuits and Scones

Every baker should have a good biscuit and scone recipe in his or her repertoire. Take care to follow recipe directions carefully to incorporate the fats into the flour.

- Choose a large bowl for blending the fats into the flour.

- Always chill butter and vegetable shortening before using. This makes it easier to form crumbs and prevents the mixture from becoming oily.

- Before working the butter and vegetable shortening into the flour, toss the pieces with flour to coat them.

- When working the fats into the flour, be sure to use only your fingertips.

- It's OK to have pea-size pieces of fat. This will create more tender pastries.

- Work with the side of the fork around the perimeter of the bowl toward the center when incorporating the liquid.

- Chilling the dough before rolling makes it easier to handle.

- Use a palm-size plastic bowl scraper or oversize rubber spatula to help remove the dough from the bowl.

- Biscuit dough should be wet, so a well-floured surface (about 2 tablespoons of flour) will prevent it from sticking when kneading.

- Replace the flour on the kneading surface as it becomes too coarse (bits of dough will fall off into the flour as you knead and should not be reincorporated into the dough).

naughty sweet cream biscuits

MAKES 12 BISCUITS

If you're looking for a sweet biscuit to use for a traditional strawberry shortcake, you can stop right here. These are perfect! The sweet biscuit dough is enriched with butter and bound with heavy cream. After baking, split the biscuit in half and fill the bottom with juicy macerated berries and a spoonful of whipped cream. Cover with the top of the biscuit and finish it off with, yes, more whipped cream. Yum!

2¾ cups all-purpose flour, spooned in and leveled, plus additional for kneading and rolling

6 tablespoons granulated sugar

1 tablespoon baking powder

1 teaspoon salt

½ cup (1 stick) unsalted butter, cut into ½-inch cubes and chilled

1½ cups heavy cream

1 teaspoon pure vanilla extract

3 to 4 teaspoons sparkling sugar (available in The Baker's Catalogue; see page 381), for sprinkling

AT A GLANCE

PAN: Large cookie sheet

PAN PREP: Ungreased

RACK LEVEL: Center

OVEN TEMP: 375°F

BAKING TIME: 18–20 minutes

DIFFICULTY: 1

1. Position the rack in the center of the oven. Heat the oven to 375°F.

2. Place the flour, granulated sugar, baking powder, and salt in the work bowl of a food processor fitted with the steel blade. Pulse three or four times to blend.

3. Add one-half of the butter and pulse five times, then process for 8 seconds. Add the remaining butter, pulse three times, then process for 5 seconds. Empty the mixture into a large bowl. Rub the mixture between your fingertips to reduce any large pieces of butter into flakes.

4. Remove 2 tablespoons of heavy cream and set aside. Stir the vanilla into the remaining cream. Pour the liquid around the edge of the bowl. Using a rubber spatula, push the mixture toward the center, working your way around the bowl to blend the cream with the flour/butter mixture. The mixture will be soft and resemble large curds of cottage cheese.

5. Sprinkle a pastry board or other flat surface generously with flour, about 2 tablespoons. Empty the dough onto the board with the help of a palm-size plastic bowl scraper or a rubber spatula. *The dough will be sticky.* With floured hands, gently knead the dough five or six times, or until it *just* forms a "skin" (see Forming a Skin, page 107). The dough will not be smooth. Use a dough scraper to help lift the dough as needed. Do not overwork the dough or your biscuits will not be tender. When the dough is ready, move it aside and clean the work surface.

6. Lay a pastry cloth on the surface and fit a rolling pin with a pastry sleeve. Rub another 2 tablespoons of flour into the pastry cloth and sleeve.

7. Place the dough on the cloth, and with floured hands, pat it lightly, shaping it into an 8-inch square. Roll the dough into a 10- × 14-inch rectangle with the 10-inch side parallel to the counter. Fold the dough into thirds like a business letter. To do this, lift the far side of the pastry cloth up and fold the top third of the dough over on itself. Press the dough to line up the edges as best you can. Lift the lower edge of the pastry cloth and flip the bottom third of the dough over on itself. You will now have three layers of dough. Press the top gently with your hands, then roll into a 5- × 15-inch strip.

8. Using a 2¼-inch straight-sided cookie cutter dipped in flour, cut straight down into the dough, without twisting the cutter, cutting two rows of six biscuits. Be sure to dip the cutter in flour before each cut and cut as close to the previous biscuit as possible. Place on the cookie sheet, *inverting* each biscuit and spacing them about 1½ inches apart. (See What to Do with Bits and Pieces of Dough, page 109.)

9. Brush the top of each biscuit with some of the reserved cream and sprinkle with ¼ teaspoon of sparkling sugar. Bake for 18 to 20 minutes, or until golden brown. Remove the biscuits from the oven and let cool for about 5 minutes before loosening with a thin metal spatula. Serve the biscuits warm. If baking ahead, warm the biscuits for a few minutes in a 300°F oven.

STORAGE: Store in an airtight plastic bag for up to 3 days. These biscuits may be frozen.

angel biscuits

MAKES 12 BISCUITS

Angel biscuits are traditionally made with yeast, which gives them an especially delicate texture. If you have never baked with yeast, try this easy recipe (see Working with Yeast, page 197). Instead of baking these biscuits free-form, they are arranged in a pan. To serve, separate the biscuits and place them in a napkin-lined basket.

2 tablespoons plus 1 teaspoon sugar

2 tablespoons warm water (110° to 115°F)

½ package active dry yeast

2¼ cups all-purpose flour, spooned in and leveled, plus additional for kneading and shaping

1 teaspoon salt

¼ teaspoon baking soda

½ cup (1 stick) unsalted butter, cut into ½-inch cubes and chilled, plus 2 tablespoons melted

1 cup buttermilk

AT A GLANCE

PAN: 9-inch square baking pan

PAN PREP: Buttered

RACK LEVEL: Center

OVEN TEMP: 400°F

BAKING TIME: 25–30 minutes

DIFFICULTY: 2

1. Rinse a small bowl in hot water to warm it. Add 1 teaspoon of the sugar and the water. Sprinkle the yeast over the water. *Do not stir.* Cover the bowl with a saucer and let the mixture stand for 5 minutes. Stir it briefly with a fork, cover again, and let it stand for 2 to 3 minutes, or until bubbly.

2. Place the flour, remaining 2 tablespoons sugar, the salt, and baking soda in the work bowl of a food processor fitted with the steel blade. Pulse two or three times to blend. Add the chilled butter and pulse until the mixture forms crumbs the size of small peas. Empty into a large bowl.

3. Combine the buttermilk with the yeast mixture and pour it around the edge of the bowl containing the crumbs. Using a rubber spatula, push the mixture toward the center, working your way around the bowl to blend the mixture with the crumbs.

4. Sprinkle a pastry board or other flat surface *generously* with flour. Empty the dough onto the board with the help of a palm-size plastic bowl scraper or a rubber spatula. *The dough will be sticky and soft.* With floured hands, gently knead the dough six to eight times, or just until it forms a "skin" (see Forming a Skin, opposite). Use a dough scraper to help lift the dough as needed. Do not overwork the dough or your biscuits will not be tender.

5. Using a dough scraper or a sharp knife, divide the dough into quarters, then divide each quarter into thirds, making a total of 12 pieces.

6. Butter a 9-inch square pan.

7. Place about ¼ cup of flour in a shallow dish, such as a pie plate. Working with one piece of dough at a time, roll it in the flour, coating it well on all sides. Gently shape it into an oval and place it in the prepared pan. Repeat with the remaining pieces of dough, making three rows across and four down. The ovals of dough do not have to touch each other, and it's OK if they are well coated with flour. Cover with a tea towel and set in a warmish place to rise until almost doubled, about 1 hour.

8. Fifteen minutes before baking, position the rack in the center of the oven. Heat the oven to 400°F. Brush the tops of the biscuits generously with the melted butter and bake for 25 to 30 minutes, or until golden brown. Remove from the oven and let cool in the pan for 10 minutes. Serve the biscuits warm. If baking ahead, warm the biscuits for a few minutes in a 300°F oven.

STORAGE: Store in an airtight plastic bag for up to 3 days. These biscuits may be frozen.

Forming a Skin

When dough is prepared, it usually has a tacky surface. In order to bring it to a state where you can easily handle it, you must form a "skin" on the surface. To do this, place the dough on a floured surface. Most dough requires a lightly floured surface—that is, about 2 tablespoons of flour sprinkled over a wide area, about 16 inches round. For a well-floured surface, 4 tablespoons of flour should be used for the same area.

Empty the dough onto the floured surface, and with floured hands, knead it as many times as the recipe directs. A dough scraper is a very helpful tool to have on hand. The object in kneading is to form a thin layer of flour on the surface. This layer of flour, referred to as a "skin," will prevent the dough from sticking.

When the dough has to be divided, whether into large pieces or small, each time it is cut, the skin is broken. The cut surface will be sticky and the dough must be kneaded again to form another skin.

a dilly of a cheese scone

MAKES 12 SCONES

Here is a delicious, savory scone made with shredded Jarlsberg cheese and lots of finely chopped fresh dill. These are shaped into triangles, and are wonderful to serve for a brunch or lunch with chicken or fish. Be sure to use only fresh dill, not dried; it makes a vast difference. For buffet service, it's OK if you wish to divide the dough into smaller portions.

1¾ cups all-purpose flour, spooned in and leveled, plus additional for kneading and rolling

2 tablespoons sugar

1 tablespoon baking powder

½ teaspoon salt

Pinch of nutmeg

⅓ cup (⅔ stick) unsalted butter, cut into ½-inch cubes and chilled

¾ cup (about 3 ounces) shredded Jarlsberg cheese

3 tablespoons chopped, fresh dill

1 large egg

¾ cup heavy cream, plus 1 tablespoon for brushing

AT A GLANCE

PAN: Large cookie sheet

PAN PREP: Buttered

RACK LEVEL: Center

OVEN TEMP: 400°F

BAKING TIME: 18–20 minutes

DIFFICULTY: 1

1. Position the rack in the center of the oven. Heat the oven to 400°F. Butter a large cookie sheet and set aside.

2. Place the flour, sugar, baking powder, salt, and nutmeg in the work bowl of a food processor fitted with a steel blade. Pulse two or three times to combine. Add the butter and pulse five times, then process for 8 seconds. Add the cheese and dill, pulsing twice to blend. Empty into a large mixing bowl.

3. In a small bowl, whisk together the egg and ¾ cup cream. Make a well in the center of the dry ingredients and pour in the liquid. Using a rubber spatula, push the crumb mixture into the well, working your way around the bowl to form a rough dough. With lightly floured hands, knead the dough three or four times in the bowl. Divide the dough in half.

4. Lay a pastry cloth on a pastry board or other flat surface and fit a rolling pin with a pastry sleeve. Rub about 2 tablespoons of flour into the pastry cloth and sleeve.

5. Place one piece of dough on the cloth and, with floured hands, shape into a ball. Flatten the ball into a disk and roll into a 7-inch circle about ½ inch thick. Cut into six wedges using a bench scraper or sharp knife. Place on the prepared cookie sheet. Repeat with the remaining dough.

7. Brush with 1 tablespoon heavy cream and bake for 18 to 20 minutes, or until lightly browned. Remove from the oven and cool slightly on the cookie sheet before loosening with a thin-bladed metal spatula. Serve warm. If baking ahead, reheat the scones in a 300°F oven.

STORAGE: Store in an airtight plastic bag for up to 3 days. These scones may be frozen.

What to Do with Bits and Pieces of Dough

Most of the recipes in this chapter specify a yield of 12 biscuits or scones. That amount is based on the first cut of the dough. Since these types of doughs should be handled with a deft touch, the first cut gives the best rise. However, the leftover bits and pieces can be rerolled.

To do this, clean and reflour your pastry cloth or work surface. Gather the bits and pieces and lightly press them together into a rectangle. Roll the dough to a ¼-inch thickness and fold it in thirds. Give the dough a quarter turn and gently roll it again into a long strip, approximately ½ inch thick and 2½ to 3 inches wide. Dip the cutter into flour, then cut the rounds as close together as possible. Invert the rounds on the cookie sheet, and finish according to the recipe. Discard the remaining dough. These types of doughs should not be worked beyond the second cut.

sedona cream scones

MAKES 12 SCONES

A few years ago, on a visit to Sedona, Arizona, I stopped for lunch at the well-known Shugrue's Hillside Grill. To my delight, a basket of scones was offered, and I can tell you, these were not ordinary scones. They had a golden crust and a crumb that melted in your mouth.

The baker's name was Ruth Titus, and I asked her if she would be kind enough to share her recipe with me. And that she did! She told me that the recipe was her grandmother's, who originally lived in Scotland. Here is my improvisation on Ruth's recipe.

2 cups sifted cake flour, spooned in and leveled

1⅓ cups all-purpose flour, spooned in and leveled, plus additional for kneading and rolling

6 tablespoons granulated sugar

4½ teaspoons baking powder

¾ teaspoon salt

½ cup (1 stick) unsalted butter, cut into ½-inch cubes and chilled

1 cup plus 2 tablespoons heavy cream

1 large egg

1 large egg yolk (reserve white for egg wash)

1 egg white beaten with 1 teaspoon cold water, for egg wash

1 tablespoon sparkling sugar (available in The Baker's Catalogue; see page 381)

AT A GLANCE

PAN: Large cookie sheet

PAN PREP: Ungreased

RACK LEVEL: Center

OVEN TEMP: 375°F

BAKING TIME: 16–18 minutes

DIFFICULTY: 1

1. Position the rack in the center of the oven. Heat the oven to 375°F.

2. Combine the cake and all-purpose flours, granulated sugar, baking powder, and salt in the bowl of an electric mixer fitted with the paddle attachment. Add the butter and mix for 2 to 2½ minutes, or until the mixture forms pea-size bits.

3. Whisk together the cream, egg, and egg yolk. Remove the paddle attachment and replace with the dough hook. With the machine off, add the cream/egg mixture to the flour mixture, then blend on low speed *only* until a dough is formed.

4. Sprinkle a pastry board or other flat surface with about 2 tablespoons of all-purpose flour. Empty the dough onto the board with the aid of a palm-size plastic bowl scraper or a rubber spatula. With floured hands, knead five or six times to form a "skin" (see Forming a Skin, page 107), then press into a square about 8 inches. With the aid of a dough scraper, move the dough aside and clean the work surface.

5. Lay a pastry cloth on the surface and fit a rolling pin with a pastry sleeve. Rub an additional 2 tablespoons of flour into the pastry cloth and sleeve.

6. Place the dough on the cloth and roll into a 9- × 12-inch rectangle, with the 9-inch side parallel to the edge of the counter. Fold the dough into thirds like a business letter. To do this, lift the far side of the pastry cloth and fold the top third of the dough over onto itself. Press the dough to align the edges as best you can. Lift the lower edge of the pastry cloth and flip the bottom third of the dough over on itself. You will now have three layers of dough. Press the top gently with your hands, then roll into a 15- × 5-inch strip.

7. Using a 2¼-inch straight-sided cookie cutter dipped in flour, cut straight down into the dough, without twisting the cutter, making six rounds across and two down. Be sure to dip the cutter in flour before cutting each round. Place on the cookie sheet, *inverting* each scone and spacing them about 1½ inches apart. Brush the tops with the egg wash and sprinkle with sparkling sugar. (See What to Do with Bits and Pieces of Dough, page 109.)

8. Bake for 16 to 18 minutes, or until firm to the touch. Remove from the oven and let cool on the cookie sheet for about 5 minutes before loosening with a thin, metal spatula. Serve the scones warm. If baking ahead, warm the scones in a 300°F oven.

STORAGE: Store in an airtight plastic bag for up to 3 days. These scones may be frozen.

Chocolate Chip Scones

In step 2, blend ½ cup chocolate mini-morsels into the flour/butter mixture. Prepare and cut the dough as directed in the recipe. Before baking, brush the tops of the scones with egg wash and sprinkle with sparkling sugar. Bake and store as directed.

cranberry-pecan cream scones

MAKES 14 SCONES

This recipe is based on Sedona Cream Scones (page 110). The sweet-tart cranberries and crunchy pecans add just the right amount of flavor and texture. I like to serve these with Orange Honey Butter. The flavors of the scones and the butter make for a happy marriage.

2 cups cake flour, spooned in and leveled

$1\frac{1}{3}$ cups all-purpose flour, spooned in and leveled, plus additional for kneading and rolling

6 tablespoons sugar

$4\frac{1}{2}$ teaspoons baking powder

$\frac{3}{4}$ teaspoon salt

$\frac{1}{2}$ cup (1 stick) unsalted butter, cut into $\frac{1}{2}$-inch cubes and chilled

1 teaspoon freshly grated navel orange zest

$\frac{1}{2}$ cup sweetened dried cranberries (not organic), plumped (see page 358), patted dry

$\frac{1}{2}$ cup toasted broken pecans

1 cup plus 2 tablespoons heavy cream

1 large egg

1 large egg yolk (reserve white for egg wash)

1 teaspoon pure vanilla extract

1 egg white mixed with 1 teaspoon cold water, for egg wash

AT A GLANCE

PAN: Cookie sheet

PAN PREP: Ungreased

RACK LEVEL: Center

OVEN TEMP: 375°F

BAKING TIME: 16–18 minutes

DIFFICULTY: 1

1. Position the rack in the center of the oven. Heat the oven to 375°F.

2. Combine the cake and all-purpose flours, the sugar, baking powder, and salt in the bowl of an electric mixer fitted with the paddle attachment and mix for 5 seconds. Add the butter and orange zest and mix on low speed for 2 to $2\frac{1}{2}$ minutes, or until the mixture forms pea-size bits. Add the cranberries and mix for 5 seconds. Add the pecans and mix for 5 seconds more.

3. In a small bowl, whisk together the cream, egg, egg yolk, and vanilla. Remove the paddle attachment and replace with the dough hook. With the mixer off, add the liquid to the flour mixture. Then mix on low speed, scraping down the side of the bowl as needed. Mix until a rough dough is formed. *Note:* Discard any small particles remaining at the bottom of the bowl.

4. Sprinkle a pastry board or other flat surface with about 2 tablespoons of flour. Empty the dough onto the board with the aid of a palm-size plastic bowl scraper or rubber spatula. With floured hands, knead the dough five or six times to form a skin (see Forming a Skin, page 107), then press it into a square. With the aid of a dough scraper, move the dough aside and clean the work surface.

5. Lay a pastry cloth on the surface and fit a rolling pin with a pastry sleeve. Rub an additional 2 tablespoons of flour into the pastry cloth and sleeve.

6. Place the dough on the cloth and roll into a 12-inch square. Fold the dough into thirds like a business letter. To do this, lift the far side of the pastry cloth and fold the top third of the dough over on itself. Press the dough to align the edges as best you can. Lift the lower edge of the pastry cloth and flip the bottom third of the dough over on itself. You will now have three layers of dough. Press the top gently with your hands, then roll into an 18- × 5-inch strip.

7. Using a straight-sided 2¼-inch cookie cutter dipped in flour, cut straight down into the dough, without twisting the cutter, making seven rounds across and two down. Be sure to dip the cutter in flour before cutting each round. Place on the cookie sheet, *inverting* each scone and spacing them about 1½ inches apart. Brush the tops with the egg wash. (See What to Do with Bits and Pieces of Dough, page 109.)

8. Bake for 16 to 18 minutes, or until firm to the touch. Remove from the oven and let cool on the cookie sheet for about 5 minutes before loosening with a thin, metal spatula. Serve the scones warm. If baking ahead, warm the scones for a few minutes in a 300°F oven.

STORAGE: Store in an airtight plastic bag for up to 2 days. Freezing is not recommended.

orange honey butter

MAKES ⅔ CUP

This spread is perfect with a fresh-from-the-oven biscuit or scone. I must admit to indulging in a dollop (or two) on a croissant, as well!

½ cup (1 stick) unsalted butter, softened
3 tablespoons honey

½ teaspoon freshly grated navel orange zest

Combine the butter, honey, and zest in a medium bowl. Stir with a spoon until well blended. Place in a ramekin or a small bowl and refrigerate. Let soften to spreading consistency before serving.

STORAGE: Refrigerate, tightly covered with plastic wrap, for up to 1 week. This butter may be frozen.

country cherry honey scones

MAKES 12 SCONES

If you want to make a pretty scone, this is the recipe to choose. The dough is flavored with honey and orange zest, and has chopped dried cherries throughout. When you chop the cherries, make sure they are free of pits. The scones are cut into triangles and the tops are trimmed with sparkling sugar. If you have a long basket, these are beautiful served with the tips of the triangles angled in different directions.

2½ cups all-purpose flour, spooned in and leveled, plus additional for kneading and rolling

2 tablespoons very fresh light brown sugar

1 tablespoon baking powder

½ teaspoon salt

¼ teaspoon baking soda

1 teaspoon freshly grated navel orange zest

½ cup (1 stick) cold unsalted butter

½ cup (about 2½ ounces) dried cherries (not organic), plumped (see page 358) and coarsely chopped

1 large egg

¼ cup honey

½ cup half-and-half

1 large egg lightly beaten with 1 teaspoon water, for egg wash

1 tablespoon sparkling sugar (available in The Baker's Catalogue; see page 381)

AT A GLANCE

PAN: Large cookie sheet

PAN PREP: Buttered

RACK LEVEL: Center

OVEN TEMP: 400°F

BAKING TIME: 14–16 minutes

DIFFICULTY: 1

1. Position the rack in the center of the oven. Heat the oven to 400°F. Butter a large cookie sheet and set aside.

2. In a large bowl, thoroughly whisk together the flour, brown sugar, baking powder, salt, and baking soda. Add the orange zest and work it into the dry ingredients with your hands.

3. Shave the butter into ⅛-inch slices using a dough scraper or sharp knife. Add the butter to the dry ingredients, rubbing it between your fingertips until the mixture resembles coarse meal. It's OK if some larger flakes of butter are visible. Add the cherries and toss to coat with the crumbs.

4. In a small bowl, combine the egg, honey, and half-and-half. Make a well in the center of the dry ingredients and add the liquid. Using a rubber spatula, draw the crumbs into the center, working your way around the side of the bowl until a soft dough is formed. With floured hands, knead the dough gently five or six times to form a "skin" (see Forming a Skin, page 107). Divide the dough in half and form a skin on the cut side, and set aside.

5. Lay a pastry cloth on a pastry board or other flat surface and fit a rolling pin with a pastry sleeve. Rub about 2 tablespoons of flour into the pastry cloth and sleeve.

6. Place 1 piece of dough on the cloth and, with floured hands, turn the dough two or three times to coat it with the flour. Pat the dough into a disk, then roll it into a 7-inch circle about $\frac{1}{2}$ inch thick. Cut into six wedges using a dough scraper or sharp knife. Place on the cookie sheet. Repeat with the remaining dough.

7. Brush with the egg wash and sprinkle each scone with $\frac{1}{4}$ teaspoon sparkling sugar. Bake for 14 to 16 minutes, or until lightly browned. Remove from the oven and cool slightly on the cookie sheet before loosening with a thin-bladed, metal spatula. Serve warm. If baking ahead, reheat the scones in a 300°F oven.

STORAGE: Store in an airtight plastic bag for up to 3 days. These scones may be frozen.

toasted pecan mandelbrot

MAKES ABOUT 4 DOZEN 4-INCH MANDELBROT

My students often ask me what cookie is my husband, Gene's, favorite. Without hesitation, I always reply, "Toasted Pecan Mandelbrot!" This recipe, which originated with Rita Hirsch, from Greensboro, North Carolina, has been in my repertoire for years. Because my husband liked them so much, his mother asked for the recipe.

Whenever we visited her, she always made the mandelbrot. The only problem for me was that hers were better than mine! I repeatedly asked her, "Mom, what did you do differently with the recipe?" And she repeatedly said, "Nothing!" Years later, after she had passed away, I saw her recipe lying on the counter in my sister-in-law's kitchen. As my eyes glanced at it, the mystery was solved. Instead of the 1 teaspoon of baking powder that I used, Mom used 1 tablespoon! And what a difference that made! The cookie was lighter and crispier than the original. This was one mistake that we all benefited from!

2½ cups less 2 tablespoons all-purpose flour, spooned in and leveled

1 tablespoon baking powder

3 large eggs

1 cup plus 2 teaspoons sugar, divided

2 teaspoons pure vanilla extract

½ cup canola or safflower oil

1 cup broken pecans, lightly toasted

½ teaspoon ground cinnamon

AT A GLANCE

PAN: Jelly roll pans

PAN PREP: Buttered

RACK LEVELS: Upper and lower thirds

OVEN TEMP: 350°/325°F

CHILLING TIME: 1 hour

BAKING TIME: 20 minutes, baking; 15–18 minutes, toasting

DIFFICULTY: 1

MAKE THE DOUGH

1. Strain together the flour and baking powder three times. Set aside.

2. In the large bowl of an electric mixer fitted with the whip attachment, beat the eggs on medium speed until lightened in color, about 2 minutes. Gradually add 1 cup of the sugar, taking about 2 minutes, then beat in the vanilla. Pour the oil down the side of the bowl and beat 30 seconds longer.

3. Reduce the mixer speed to low and add the dry ingredients in two additions, mixing only to combine. Using an oversize rubber spatula, fold in the pecans. Cover with plastic and refrigerate for 1 hour or longer.

BAKE THE DOUGH

4. Position the racks in the upper and lower thirds of the oven. Heat the oven to 350°F. Butter the jelly roll pans.

5. Spoon the chilled batter onto the prepared pans, forming three 16-inch logs. Using your hands, even the sides of the logs as best you can. If the mixture is too sticky, moisten your hands with a little water.

6. Combine the remaining 2 teaspoons sugar and the cinnamon and sprinkle *lightly* over the surface of the logs. (A sugar shaker is best for this) Bake for 20 minutes or until set on top and just beginning to brown. To ensure even browning, toward the end of baking time, rotate the pans top to bottom and front to back. Cool in the pans for 5 minutes.

TOAST THE SLICES

7. Reduce the oven temperature to 325°F. Using a serrated knife, cut the logs on the diagonal into ½-inch-thick slices. Turn the pieces on their sides. Sprinkle the cut side *lightly* with cinnamon and sugar and toast for 8 to 10 minutes. Turn the mandelbrot over and sprinkle the second side *lightly* with cinnamon and sugar and toast for 6 to 8 minutes longer, or until very crisp and the edges show signs of browning. To ensure even browning, rotate the pans top to bottom and front to back towards the end of baking time. Let cool in the pans.

STORAGE: Store in an airtight container, layered between strips of wax paper, for up to 3 weeks. These cookies may be frozen.

chocolate chocolate chocolate biscotti

MAKES 6 DOZEN 3½-INCH BISCOTTI

Here is a recipe for Chocolate Biscotti from my former assistant, Judie Levenberg. Judie, an excellent baker, was the owner of Bake My Day, and much to her clients' delight, one of her specialties was biscotti. Her father recently told me that his favorite cookie of Judie's was Chocolate Chocolate Chocolate Biscotti. I asked him if he would give me the recipe, and when he did, there was a certain familiarity to it. Eventually, I came to discover that Judie adapted it from a recipe by Nick Malgieri, who in turn had adapted it from my recipe for Toasted Pecan Mandelbrot (page 116)! The old adage, "What goes around, comes around," certainly did come true!

Nibbling on these rich, chocolaty bars brought back many happy memories of the hours Judie and I spent baking together. Once you try them, I know they will create wonderful memories for you as well.

2 cups all-purpose flour, spooned in and leveled

⅓ cup strained Dutch-processed cocoa powder, spooned in and leveled

1 tablespoon baking powder

3 large eggs

Pinch of salt

1 cup sugar

1 teaspoon pure vanilla extract

½ cup (1 stick) unsalted butter, melted and cooled to tepid

1 cup coarsely chopped walnuts

1 (12-ounce) bag semisweet chocolate chips

CHOCOLATE GLAZE

⅓ cup water

⅓ cup light corn syrup

1 cup sugar

8 ounces fine-quality bittersweet or semisweet chocolate, such as Lindt Bittersweet, chopped

AT A GLANCE

PAN: Jelly roll pans

PAN PREP: Baking parchment

RACK LEVELS: Upper and lower thirds

OVEN TEMP: 350°/325°F

BAKING TIME: 20–25 minutes, baking; 19 minutes, toasting

DIFFICULTY: 1

1. Position the racks in the upper and lower thirds of the oven. Heat the oven to 350°F. Lightly dab the corners of the jelly roll pans with butter and line them with baking parchment. Set aside.

2. Whisk together the flour, cocoa, and baking powder. Set aside.

3. In the bowl of an electric mixer fitted with the whip attachment, beat the eggs and salt on medium speed until lightened in color, about 2 minutes. Gradually add the sugar, taking about 2 minutes, then beat in the vanilla. Pour the *tepid* butter down the side of the bowl and beat for 30 seconds longer.

4. Remove the bowl from the mixer and, using an oversize rubber spatula, stir in the walnuts and chocolate chips, then fold in the dry ingredients in three additions, mixing only until combined. The dough will be very soft. For ease of handling, let the dough rest for 10 minutes to thicken.

5. Drop the dough by heaping spoonfuls onto the pans and form four logs, measuring about 12 inches long and 2 inches wide. Flour your hands lightly and even the sides as best you can. It's OK if the logs are somewhat irregular.

6. Bake for 20 to 25 minutes, or until set on top. To ensure even baking, rotate the pans top to bottom and front to back toward the end of baking time. Remove from the oven and let cool for at least 20 minutes.

7. Lower the oven temperature to 325°F. Using a serrated knife, cut the logs on the diagonal into $\frac{1}{2}$-inch-thick slices. Turn the slices cut side up and return to the oven for 12 minutes. Turn the biscotti over and bake for 7 minutes longer or until crisp.

8. While the biscotti are toasting, make the glaze. Place the water, corn syrup, and sugar in a heavy 2-quart saucepan. Bring to a boil over low heat, stirring occasionally. Remove from the heat and add the chocolate. Let stand for 2 to 3 minutes, then whisk to smooth. While the biscotti are still warm, dip the ends into the glaze and set on parchment-lined pans to dry.

STORAGE: Store in an airtight container, layered between strips of wax paper, for up to 3 weeks. These cookies may be frozen, but the glaze may dull.

jeweled almond biscotti

MAKES FORTY 3-INCH BISCOTTI

Here are biscotti that are as pretty to look at as they are delicious to eat. They are flecked with dried apricots and cranberries that have been steeped in amaretto liqueur. Crushed anise, lemon zest, and chopped almonds round off these wonderful flavors.

½ cup dried apricots, packed

¼ cup dried cranberries

2 tablespoons amaretto liqueur

2 tablespoons water

2½ cups all-purpose flour, spooned in and leveled

2 teaspoons baking powder

¼ teaspoon salt

1 teaspoon crushed anise seed

¾ cup (1½ sticks) unsalted butter, slightly firm

1 teaspoon freshly grated lemon zest

1 cup sugar

2 eggs

1 teaspoon pure vanilla extract

½ cup coarsely chopped toasted unblanched almonds

AT A GLANCE

PAN: Jelly roll pan

PAN PREP: Buttered

RACK LEVEL: Center

OVEN TEMP: 350°/300°F

BAKING TIME: 20–25 minutes, baking; 24 minutes, toasting

DIFFICULTY: 1

1. Place the apricots, cranberries, amaretto, and water in a small, heavy-bottomed saucepan. Cover with a tight-fitting lid and simmer over low heat for 3 to 4 minutes, or until the liquid evaporates. Watch carefully: the fruit should be tender, but not mushy. Set the fruit aside to cool, then place in a single layer on a cutting board and cut into ¼-inch dice.

2. Position the rack in the center of the oven. Heat the oven to 350°F. Butter the jelly roll pan and set aside.

3. Strain the flour, baking powder, and salt together three times. Stir in the anise seed and set aside.

4. In the bowl of an electric mixer fitted with the paddle attachment, beat the butter and the lemon zest on medium speed until smooth. Gradually add the sugar, taking about 2 minutes, then beat for 2 minutes longer. Add the eggs one at a time, then the vanilla, and beat for 2 more minutes.

5. Reduce the mixer speed to low and add the dry ingredients in three additions, mixing only to blend. Remove the bowl from the machine and gently fold in the fruits and almonds, using an oversize rubber spatula.

6. Drop the dough by tablespoons onto the pan, forming two 16-inch logs. With floured hands gently even the sides and pat the logs into loaf shapes. Bake for 20 to 25 minutes, or until the bottom of each loaf is lightly browned.

7. Remove from the oven and reduce the oven temperature to 300°F. Let the loaves rest on the pan for 15 minutes, then use a long serrated knife or dough scraper to angle-cut each loaf into ½-inch-thick slices. Place the slices on their sides in the pan and return to the oven for 12 minutes. Turn the slices over and bake for another 12 minutes, or until lightly browned. Remove from the oven and let cool on the pan.

STORAGE: Store in an airtight container, layered between strips of wax paper, for up to 3 weeks. These cookies may be frozen.

Secrets to Making Biscotti and Such

- If the dough sticks to your hands when shaping the loaves, you can either wet the palms of your hands with cold water, flour your palms, or rub them lightly with bland salad oil.

- When shaping biscotti loaves, it's okay if the sides are somewhat irregular.

- Before baking the biscotti loaves, the tops can be finished with sugar, nuts, or both.

- Sugar will adhere to biscotti dough, but an egg wash must be used to attach the nuts.

- Baking biscotti on buttered pans encourages browning when toasting.

- While necessary at times, a pan lined with baking parchment is more awkward to use because the paper slides. Anchoring it with dabs of butter to hold it in place is helpful.

- Jelly roll pans or pans with rimmed sides are the easiest to use for toasting because the biscotti slices are less likely to fall off.

- Since biscotti and mandelbrot are twice-baked, do not overbake the logs during the first baking. They should show signs of light browning on the bottom and the top should be firm to the touch.

- Biscotti should rest at least 10 minutes before slicing. Biscotti containing chunky pieces of nuts and/or fruit should rest longer.

- A serrated bread knife usually works best for smooth or less textured biscotti. Avoid moving the knife back and forth. Just cut down while drawing the knife toward you.

- Cut straight down with a dough scraper to slice coarse-textured, fruity biscotti that a knife would tear (for example, Jeweled Almond Biscotti or Shaved Chocolate and Pistachio Biscotti).

- Cutting biscotti on the diagonal will give larger slices; cutting straight across the loaves makes them smaller.

- Biscotti made without fat are usually hard, and therefore are best sliced in thin pieces, about ¼ inch.

- Biscotti made with fat will be more delicate and are best sliced in thicker pieces, about ⅜ to ½ inch.

- To give the cookies extra crunch, when the oven cools down to warm, return the biscotti and mandelbrot to the oven to crisp further.

shaved chocolate and pistachio biscotti

MAKES 5 DOZEN 4-INCH BISCOTTI

Pistachio and chocolate is a flavor combination that was a favorite of my mother's, and I fell for its charm, too. These special biscotti are made with lots of toasted green pistachios and streaks of shaved chocolate. The dough is highlighted with the tang of orange and lemon zests. These are habit forming!

2½ cups all-purpose flour, spooned in and leveled

1 teaspoon baking powder

¼ teaspoon baking soda

½ teaspoon salt

¾ cup (1½ sticks) unsalted butter, slightly firm

2 teaspoons freshly grated navel orange zest

2 teaspoons freshly grated lemon zest

1 cup plus 1 tablespoon sugar, divided

2 large eggs

1 teaspoon pure vanilla extract

1 cup plus 2 tablespoons (about 5 ounces) coarsely chopped unsalted, unskinned, toasted pistachios, divided

1 (3.5-ounce) bar Lindt Bittersweet chocolate, shaved (about ¼ cup)

1 large egg beaten with 2 teaspoons water, for egg wash

AT A GLANCE

PAN: Jelly roll pans

PAN PREP: Buttered

CHILLING TIME: 1 hour

RACK LEVELS: Upper and lower thirds

OVEN TEMP: 350°/300°F

BAKING TIME: 25 minutes, baking; 22–25 minutes, toasting

DIFFICULTY: 1

MAKE THE DOUGH

1. Strain the flour, baking powder, baking soda, and salt together three times. Set aside.

2. In the bowl of an electric mixer fitted with the paddle attachment, mix the butter with the zests on medium-high speed until smooth, about 1 minute. Slowly add 1 cup of sugar and beat for 1 minute longer.

3. Add the eggs one at a time, then beat again for 1 minute more, scraping down the bowl as needed. Beat in the vanilla. Reduce the mixer speed to low and add the dry ingredients in three additions, mixing *just* until combined.

4. Remove the bowl from the machine and, using a large rubber spatula, fold in 1 cup of the pistachios and the shaved chocolate. Cover the bowl with plastic wrap and chill for 1 hour.

BAKE THE COOKIES

5. Position the racks in the upper and lower thirds of the oven. Heat the oven to 350°F. Butter the jelly roll pans and set aside.

6. Divide the dough into thirds, and on a lightly floured surface, roll each piece into a 14-inch log and place on the pans. Brush each log with the egg wash, then sprinkle the tops with the remaining 2 tablespoons pistachios and 1 tablespoon sugar.

7. Bake the logs for 25 minutes or until just lightly browned. To ensure even browning, toward the end of baking time rotate the pans from top to bottom and front to back. Remove from the oven and let rest on the pan for 5 minutes.

8. Reduce the oven temperature to 300F°. Using a dough scraper, cut the logs into $\frac{1}{2}$-inch-thick slices. Lay the slices on their sides and return to the oven for 15 minutes, or until they just start to brown. Remove from the oven, turn the slices over, and bake for another 7 to 10 minutes. Let rest on the pan for 5 minutes before transferring to cooling racks.

STORAGE: Store in an airtight container, layered between strips of wax paper, for up to 3 weeks. These cookies may be frozen.

glazed lemon–pine nut biscotti

MAKES ABOUT FORTY 3-INCH BISCOTTI

Once in a while a recipe comes together almost effortlessly—the texture is perfect, the flavors blend (almost magically!), and the appearance of the finished cookie is just what I had hoped it would be. Zesty lemon and toasted pine nuts combine with a background hint of cardamom to make a buttery, not-too-sweet cookie that is finished with a drizzled lemon glaze. Not only were these cookies a joy to develop, they are a joy to devour as well!

2 cups all-purpose flour, spooned in and leveled

1 teaspoon baking powder

¾ teaspoon ground cardamom, preferably freshly ground

½ teaspoon salt

½ cup (1 stick) unsalted butter, slightly firm

1 tablespoon plus 1 teaspoon freshly grated lemon zest, divided

¾ cup sugar

1 large egg

2 large egg yolks

1 teaspoon pure vanilla extract

1 cup toasted pine nuts, divided

1 large egg white, lightly beaten with 2 teaspoons water

1½ cups strained confectioners' sugar, spooned in and leveled

1 tablespoon fresh lemon juice

1 tablespoon corn syrup

About 1 tablespoon hot water

AT A GLANCE

PAN: Jelly roll pans

PAN PREP: Buttered

RACK LEVELS: Upper and lower thirds

OVEN TEMP: 350°/325°F

BAKING TIME: 18–20 minutes, baking; 18 minutes, toasting

DIFFICULTY: 1

1. Position the racks in the upper and lower thirds of the oven. Heat the oven to 350°F. Butter the jelly roll pans.

2. Strain together the flour, baking powder, cardamom, and salt. Set aside.

3. In the bowl of an electric mixer fitted with the paddle attachment, mix the butter and 1 tablespoon of the zest together on medium-low speed. Increase the speed to medium and add the sugar in a steady stream. Beat for 1 minute longer.

4. Beat in the egg, then the yolks and vanilla and beat for 1 minute. Reduce the mixer speed to low and add the dry ingredients in two additions, mixing just until incorporated. Remove the bowl from the machine and fold in ¾ cup of the pine nuts, using a large rubber spatula. Spoon the dough onto the jelly roll pans. With floured hands, form into two 2- × 14-inch logs and place one on each pan.

5. Brush the logs with the egg wash. Sprinkle the remaining ¼ cup pine nuts on top and press gently into the dough to adhere.

6. Bake for 18 to 20 minutes, or until set on top and lightly browned, rotating the pans front to back and top to bottom toward the end of the baking. Remove from the oven and let rest for 10 to 15 minutes.

7. Lower the oven temperature to 325°F. Working with one log at a time, carefully lift it onto a cutting board with a large spatula. Using a serrated knife, cut each log into ½-inch-thick slices and lay them flat side down on the jelly roll pans. Return to the oven for 10 minutes. Turn the biscotti over and bake for another 8 minutes or until lightly browned.

8. While the biscotti are toasting, combine the confectioners' sugar, lemon juice, corn syrup, remaining 1 teaspoon zest, and enough water to make a pourable glaze. Use the water sparingly—a little goes a long way. While the biscotti are still warm, drizzle them with the glaze. To do this, place the biscotti very close together on one jelly roll pan, then dip a fork into the glaze and quickly move it back and forth over the biscotti. Let the biscotti rest at room temperature until the glaze has thoroughly dried.

STORAGE: Store in an airtight container, layered between strips of wax paper, for up to 3 weeks. These cookies may be frozen.

favorite vanilla muffins

MAKES 12 MUFFINS

Here is a vanilla muffin that children will surely love. This tender, textured muffin has a top that glistens with crunchy sugar crystals. Those of you who favor chocolate should not overlook the chocolate chunk variation—fine-quality chocolate is cut into ¼-inch chunks and folded throughout the batter. Whether you like your muffins plain or with chocolate or almond crunch, these are bound to become a family favorite.

1½ cups all-purpose flour, spooned in and leveled

¾ teaspoon baking powder

½ teaspoon salt

¼ teaspoon baking soda

½ cup (1 stick) unsalted butter, slightly firm

2 teaspoons pure vanilla extract

1 cup granulated sugar

2 large eggs

½ cup sour cream

3 to 4 teaspoons sparkling sugar (available in The Baker's Catalogue; see page 381)

AT A GLANCE

PAN: Standard muffin pan

PAN PREP: Paper or foil cupcake liners

RACK LEVEL: Lower third

OVEN TEMP: 375°F

BAKING TIME: 23–25 minutes

DIFFICULTY: 1

1. Position the rack in the lower third of the oven. Heat the oven to 375°F. Line a muffin pan with paper or foil cupcake liners.

2. In a large bowl, thoroughly whisk together the flour, baking powder, salt, and baking soda. Set aside.

3. Cut the butter into 1-inch pieces and place in the bowl of an electric mixer fitted with the paddle attachment. Add the vanilla and mix on medium speed until smooth and lightened in color, about 1 minute.

4. Add the granulated sugar in four additions and mix for 1 minute longer. Scrape down the side of the bowl. Blend in the eggs, one at a time, and mix for another minute.

5. Reduce the mixer speed to low and add the flour mixture alternately with the sour cream, dividing the dry ingredients into two parts, starting and ending with the flour. Mix just until blended after each addition.

6. Portion the batter into the prepared pan using a #16 ice cream scoop ($\frac{1}{4}$-cup capacity). Sprinkle the top of each muffin with about $\frac{1}{4}$ teaspoon of the sparkling sugar.

7. Bake for 23 to 25 minutes, or until the muffins are golden brown and the tops are springy to the touch. To ensure even baking, toward the end of baking time, rotate the pans top to bottom and front to back. Remove from the oven and place on a rack to cool.

STORAGE: Store at room temperature, tightly wrapped in aluminum foil, for up to 3 days. These muffins may be frozen.

Chocolate Chunk Vanilla Muffins

Cut 1 (3.5-ounce) bar fine-quality bittersweet chocolate, such as Lindt, into $\frac{1}{4}$-inch dice. In step 5, when the bowl is removed from the mixer, fold in the chocolate chunks using an oversize rubber spatula. Proceed with step 6 of the recipe.

Almond Crunch Muffins

In step 5, when the bowl is removed from the mixer, sprinkle half of Almond Crunch Streusel (page 379) over the top of the batter, but do not mix through. Proceed with step 6 of the recipe and brush the tops of the muffins with 1 large egg mixed with 1 teaspoon water. Distribute 1 tablespoon of the remaining streusel over each muffin, pressing lightly with your fingertips.

cape cod cranberry muffins

MAKES 14 MUFFINS

Several years ago, I took cooking lessons at a bed-and-breakfast in New England. Dave, my cooking partner and a chef from Cape Cod, shared with me his marvelous cranberry muffin recipe.

5 ounces (1¼ cups) fresh or frozen cranberries

2¼ cups all-purpose flour, spooned in and leveled

1½ teaspoons baking powder

½ teaspoon baking soda

½ teaspoon salt

3 tablespoons unsalted butter

3 tablespoons canola oil

¾ cup sugar

2 large eggs, lightly beaten

⅔ cup orange juice

¾ cup coarsely chopped toasted walnuts (see page 356)

AT A GLANCE

PANS: Two standard muffin pans

PAN PREP: Paper or foil cupcake liners

RACK LEVELS: Upper and lower thirds

OVEN TEMP: 375°F

BAKING TIME: 18–20 minutes

DIFFICULTY: 1

1. Position the racks in the upper and lower thirds of the oven. Heat the oven to 375°F. Line 14 muffin cups with paper or foil cupcake liners.

2. Coarsely chop the berries in the food processor using the steel blade.

3. In a large bowl, whisk together the flour, baking powder, baking soda, and salt.

4. Heat the butter and oil in a small saucepan until the butter melts. Remove from the heat and blend in the sugar. The sugar will not dissolve.

5. Using a wooden spoon, stir together the eggs and orange juice in a large bowl. Blend in the warm sugar mixture. Add the dry ingredients and stir *just* until moistened. When the flour is *almost* incorporated, gently fold in the nuts and cranberries.

6. Portion the batter into the prepared pans using a #16 ice cream scoop (¼-cup capacity). Fill the cups until *almost* full. Bake for 18 to 20 minutes, or until the muffins are golden brown and the tops are springy to the touch. To ensure even baking, toward the end of baking time, rotate the pans top to bottom and front to back. Remove from the oven and place on a rack to cool.

STORAGE: Store at room temperature, tightly wrapped in aluminum foil, for up to 3 days. These muffins may be frozen.

oatmeal raisin muffins

MAKES 12 MUFFINS

Oatmeal raisin muffins are among the most popular of all varieties, and for good reason, since they are one of the more healthful muffins. If you wish to skip the nuts, simply increase the raisins.

1¼ cups all-purpose flour, spooned in and leveled

1¼ cups old-fashioned oats, divided

1 teaspoon baking powder

1 teaspoon baking soda

¾ teaspoon salt

1½ teaspoons ground cinnamon

½ teaspoon ground nutmeg

¼ teaspoon ground allspice

2 large eggs

¾ cup lightly packed dark brown sugar

1 cup buttermilk

½ cup canola oil

1 teaspoon pure vanilla extract

½ cup dark raisins, plumped, drained, and patted dry (see page 358)

½ cup coarsely chopped, toasted walnuts (see page 356)

1. Position the rack in the lower third of the oven. Heat the oven to 375°F. Line a muffin pan with paper or foil cupcake liners.

2. Combine the flour, ¼ cup of the oats, the baking powder, baking soda, salt, cinnamon, nutmeg, and allspice in the bowl of a food processor fitted with the steel blade. Pulse ten times. Empty into a large bowl and add the remaining ½ cup oats. Make a well in the center.

3. In a medium bowl, whisk together the eggs and brown sugar, then add the buttermilk, oil, and vanilla and pour the mixture into the well. Using an oversize rubber spatula, incorporate the mixtures by pushing them from the side of the bowl toward the center. Fold in the raisins and nuts. Let stand for 5 minutes.

4. Portion the batter into the prepared pan using a #16 ice cream scoop (¼-cup capacity). The batter should be filled to slightly below the top of the paper liner (about three-fourths full). Bake for 23 to 25 minutes, or until the muffins are golden brown and the tops are springy to the touch. To ensure even baking, toward the end of baking time, rotate the pans top to bottom and front to back. Remove from the oven and place on a rack to cool.

STORAGE: Store at room temperature, tightly wrapped in aluminum foil, for up to 5 days. These muffins may be frozen.

AT A GLANCE

PAN: Standard muffin pan

PAN PREP: Paper or foil cupcake liners

RACK LEVELS: Lower third

OVEN TEMP: 375°F

BAKING TIME: 23–25 minutes

DIFFICULTY: 1

ultra-rich corn muffins

MAKES 12 MUFFINS

The velvety crumb of this corn muffin comes from the addition of cream-style corn and sour cream and is contrasted by the crunch of stone-ground cornmeal.

⅓ cup (⅔ stick) unsalted butter

¼ cup canola oil

1¼ cups stone-ground cornmeal, spooned in and leveled

¾ cup all-purpose flour, spooned in and leveled

⅓ cup sugar

1 tablespoon baking powder

¾ teaspoon salt

¼ teaspoon baking soda

1 cup canned yellow cream-style corn

½ cup sour cream

3 large eggs

2 tablespoons milk

1 teaspoon pure vanilla extract

AT A GLANCE

PAN: Standard muffin pan

PAN PREP: Buttered/oiled

RACK LEVEL: Lower third

OVEN TEMP: 400°F

BAKING TIME: 20–22 minutes

DIFFICULTY: 1

1. Position the rack in the lower third of the oven. Heat the oven to 400°F.

2. Place the butter in a heavy 2-quart saucepan and melt over low heat. Continue to simmer, skimming the foam from the top as it forms. The butter is ready when it is a rich golden brown and has a nutty fragrance. This will take 5 to 7 minutes or more, depending on the weight of the pan. *Watch carefully to avoid burning.* Pour the browned butter into a glass measuring cup and add the oil. Spoon a scant 1 teaspoon of the tepid butter/oil mixture into each cup of a muffin pan.

3. In a large bowl, whisk together the cornmeal, flour, sugar, baking powder, salt, and baking soda.

4. In a medium bowl, combine the corn, sour cream, eggs, milk, and vanilla.

5. Make a well in the center of the dry ingredients and add the liquid, along with the remaining butter/oil mixture. Using an oversize rubber spatula, incorporate the dry ingredients into the liquid by pushing them from the side of the bowl toward the center. *Do not overmix.*

6. Portion level scoops of the batter into the muffin cups using a #16 ice cream scoop (¼-cup capacity).

7. Bake for 20 to 22 minutes, or until the muffins are golden brown and the tops are springy to the touch. To ensure even baking, toward the end of baking time, rotate the pans top to bottom and front to back. Remove from the oven and place on a rack to cool.

STORAGE: Store at room temperature, tightly covered with plastic wrap, for up to 3 days. These muffins may be frozen.

blueberry corn muffins

MAKES 16 MUFFINS

It's midsummer and guests are coming for the weekend. I can't think of a nicer treat for Sunday brunch than warm corn muffins filled with blueberries. Because blueberries are so plump, I like to chop some of the berries just enough to break them up, and add them to the batter along with the whole berries. This way I can incorporate more berries in the batter.

Batter for Ultra-Rich Corn Muffins, but increase the canola oil to ⅓ cup when preparing the pans

1¼ cups fresh blueberries, washed and dried (see page 357)

1. Position the racks in the upper and lower thirds of the oven. Heat the oven to 400°F. Follow the pan preparation instructions for Ultra-Rich Corn Muffins (opposite), using 16 cups in two pans.

2. Prepare the muffin batter with the change noted above.

3. Place ¾ cup of the blueberries in the work bowl of a food processor fitted with a steel blade. Pulse three or four times, until very coarsely chopped. *Immediately* fold the chopped and remaining whole berries into the batter using an oversize rubber spatula.

4. Portion level scoops of the batter into the muffin cups using a #16 ice cream scoop (¼-cup capacity).

5. Bake for 20 to 25 minutes, or until the muffins are golden brown and the tops are springy to the touch. To ensure even baking, toward the end of baking time, rotate the pans top to bottom and front to back. Remove from the oven and place on a rack to cool.

STORAGE: Store at room temperature, tightly wrapped in aluminum foil, for up to 3 days. These muffins may be frozen.

AT A GLANCE

PANS: Two standard muffin pans

PAN PREP: Buttered/oiled

RACK LEVELS: Upper and lower thirds

OVEN TEMP: 400°F

BAKING TIME: 20–25 minutes

DIFFICULTY: 1

sam's oodles of apple muffins with country crumb topping

MAKES 16 MUFFINS

My granddaughter Samantha, a terrific baker in her own right, loves apples. When creating recipes for this book, what better muffin to make for Sam than one loaded with all the flavors that she loves. The batter is filled with chopped apples, brown sugar, honey, and spices, and accented with raisins and pecans. The crumb topping is made with a buttery mixture of white and whole wheat flours, along with oatmeal, brown sugar, and cinnamon. When Sam took her first bite, the twinkle in her eye told me that this muffin was a winner.

3 medium McIntosh apples (about 1 pound), peeled, cored, and cut into eighths

1¾ cups all-purpose flour, spooned in and leveled

1 teaspoon baking powder

1 teaspoon ground cinnamon

½ teaspoon ground nutmeg

½ teaspoon baking soda

½ teaspoon salt

2 large eggs

1 cup lightly packed very fresh dark brown sugar

2 tablespoons honey

1 teaspoon pure vanilla extract

¼ cup (½ stick) unsalted butter, melted and cooled

2 tablespoons canola oil

½ cup dark raisins, plumped (see page 358)

½ cup medium-chopped toasted pecans (see page 356)

Country Crumb Topping

AT A GLANCE

PANS: Two standard muffin pans

PAN PREP: Paper or foil cupcake liners

RACK LEVELS: Upper and lower thirds

OVEN TEMP: 375°F

BAKING TIME: 20–25 minutes

DIFFICULTY: 1

1. Position the racks in the upper and lower thirds of the oven. Heat the oven to 375°F. Line 16 muffin cups with paper or foil cupcake liners.

2. Place the apples in the work bowl of a food processor fitted with a steel blade and pulse eight to ten times, or until the apples are chopped into ¼-inch pieces.

3. In a medium bowl, thoroughly whisk together the flour, baking powder, cinnamon, nutmeg, baking soda, and salt. Set aside.

4. In the bowl of an electric mixer fitted with the whip attachment, beat the eggs on medium-high speed until lightened in color, about 2 minutes. Add the brown sugar, 1 to 2 tablespoons at a time, taking about 2 minutes, and beat the mixture for 1 minute longer.

5. *Stop the machine* and add the honey and vanilla. Turn the mixer on to medium speed and mix to combine. In a small bowl, whisk together the melted butter and oil and pour it into the egg mixture in a steady stream, taking about 1 minute. Add the apples and blend well.

6. Reduce the mixer speed to medium-low and add the dry ingredients all at once, blending *just* until incorporated. Remove the bowl from the mixer, and using an oversize rubber spatula, fold in the raisins and pecans.

7. Portion the batter into the prepared pans using a #16 ice cream scoop ($\frac{1}{4}$-cup capacity). Top each muffin with a few tablespoons of the crumb topping, pressing it gently into the batter.

8. Bake for 20 to 25 minutes, or until the streusel is golden brown. To ensure even baking, toward the end of baking time, rotate the pans top to bottom and front to back. Remove from the oven and place on a rack to cool.

STORAGE: Store at room temperature, tightly wrapped in aluminum foil, for up to 5 days. These muffins may be frozen.

country crumb topping

MAKES ENOUGH FOR ONE 10-INCH ROUND OR 9- × 13- × 2-INCH COFFEE CAKE, OR 16 TO 18 MUFFINS

This topping is loaded with old-fashioned farmhouse textures and flavors. Chopped walnuts and oatmeal combined with nutty whole wheat flour blend with dark brown sugar and cinnamon to form the perfect topping for fruit muffins or coffee cakes.

$\frac{3}{4}$ cup all-purpose flour, spooned in and leveled

$\frac{1}{2}$ cup medium-chopped walnuts or pecans (see page 356)

$\frac{1}{4}$ cup whole wheat flour

$\frac{1}{4}$ cup lightly packed very fresh dark brown sugar

$\frac{1}{4}$ cup granulated sugar

$\frac{1}{4}$ cup old-fashioned oatmeal

$\frac{3}{4}$ teaspoon ground cinnamon

$\frac{1}{2}$ teaspoon baking powder

$\frac{1}{4}$ teaspoon salt

7 tablespoons unsalted butter, softened

1. Combine the all-purpose flour, nuts, whole wheat flour, brown and granulated sugars, oatmeal, cinnamon, baking powder, and salt in a large mixing bowl.

2. Add the softened butter and work through with your fingertips until the mixture begins to form coarse crumbs. Gently squeeze the mixture with your hand to form larger lumps, then break them apart with your fingertips. Before using, let the streusel stand for 10 to 15 minutes.

peanut butter banana muffins

MAKES 14 MUFFINS

Here we have a muffin featuring that dynamic duo—peanut butter and banana—accented with mini chocolate chips and chopped Spanish peanuts. Be sure to seek out the little, oval Spanish peanuts; their thin red skins add marvelous flavor and a touch of color to the muffins.

When you make the muffin batter, the butter should be very soft so it will blend smoothly with the peanut butter. I don't recommend using "natural-style" peanut butter, as the finished muffin will have a drier texture.

1½ cups all-purpose flour, spooned in and leveled

1 teaspoon baking powder

½ teaspoon salt

¼ teaspoon baking soda

⅓ cup (⅔ stick) unsalted butter, very soft

⅓ cup smooth peanut butter

½ cup lightly packed very fresh dark brown sugar

⅓ cup granulated sugar

1 large egg

1 teaspoon pure vanilla extract

½ cup plain yogurt

½ cup mashed bananas (about 1½ medium, very ripe bananas)

⅓ cup medium-chopped salted Spanish peanuts

½ cup chocolate mini-morsels

4 teaspoons sparkling sugar (available in The Baker's Catalogue; see page 381)

AT A GLANCE

PANS: Two standard muffin pans

PAN PREP: Paper or foil cupcake liners

RACK LEVELS: Upper and lower thirds

OVEN TEMP: 375°F

BAKING TIME: 25–27 minutes

DIFFICULTY: 1

1. Position the racks in the upper and lower thirds of the oven. Heat the oven to 375°F. Line 14 muffin cups with paper or foil cupcake liners.

2. In a medium bowl, thoroughly whisk together the flour, baking powder, salt, and baking soda.

3. Combine the butter and peanut butter in the bowl of an electric mixer fitted with the paddle attachment. Mix on medium speed until smooth, about 1 minute.

4. Add the brown sugar, then the granulated sugar, and mix on medium speed for 2 minutes, scraping down the side of the bowl as needed. Add the egg and vanilla and mix for about 1 minute.

5. Combine the yogurt with the bananas. Reduce the mixer speed to low and add the dry ingredients alternately with the yogurt/banana mixture, dividing the flour into three parts and the yogurt mixture into two parts, starting and ending with the flour. Do not overmix.

6. Set aside 2 tablespoons of the peanuts for garnishing. Remove the bowl from the mixer. Using a rubber spatula, fold the remaining peanuts and the chocolate morsels into the batter.

7. Portion level scoops of the batter into the prepared pans using a #16 ice cream scoop ($\frac{1}{4}$-cup capacity). Sprinkle the top of each muffin with a scant $\frac{1}{2}$ teaspoon of chopped peanuts and about $\frac{1}{4}$ teaspoon of sparkling sugar.

8. Bake for 25 to 27 minutes, or until the muffins are golden brown and the tops are springy to the touch. To ensure even baking, toward the end of baking time, rotate the pans top to bottom and front to back. Remove from the oven and place on a rack to cool.

STORAGE: Store at room temperature, tightly wrapped in aluminum foil, for up to 3 days. These muffins may be frozen.

jeff's chocolate-glazed midnight muffins

MAKES 12 MUFFINS

Ever since my grandson Jeffrey was a little boy his love of chocolate has never waned, and that was quite evident when he tasted these muffins. Since chocolate is my weakness as well, I guess Jeffrey is a chocolate chip off the old block.

If you wish, these deep, dark chocolate muffins can be studded with toasted walnuts that add a marvelous crunch. Be sure to add the nuts in two additions. This will ensure that the nuts will be evenly distributed when the batter is portioned.

$\frac{2}{3}$ cup strained cocoa powder, spooned in and leveled

6 tablespoons hot water

$\frac{1}{2}$ cup sour cream

$\frac{1}{2}$ cup canola oil

2 large eggs

1 teaspoon pure vanilla extract

$1\frac{3}{4}$ cups all-purpose flour, spooned in and leveled

$1\frac{1}{4}$ cups sugar

$\frac{1}{2}$ teaspoon baking soda

$\frac{1}{2}$ teaspoon baking powder

$\frac{1}{4}$ teaspoon salt

$\frac{3}{4}$ cup broken toasted walnuts (see page 356; optional)

Midnight Chocolate Glaze (page 370)

AT A GLANCE

PAN: Standard muffin pan

PAN PREP: Paper or foil cupcake liners

RACK LEVEL: Lower third

OVEN TEMP: 350°F

BAKING TIME: 20–25 minutes

DIFFICULTY: 1

1. Position the rack in the lower third of the oven. Heat the oven to 350°F. Line a muffin pan with paper or foil cupcake liners.

2. In a medium bowl, blend the cocoa powder and hot water to form a smooth paste. Stir in the sour cream. Whisk in the oil in four additions, then add the eggs and vanilla, whisking until smooth.

3. In a large bowl, thoroughly whisk together the flour, sugar, baking soda, baking powder, and salt.

4. Make a well in the center of the dry ingredients. Add the chocolate mixture and, using an oversize rubber spatula, incorporate the dry ingredients into the liquid by pushing them from the side of the bowl toward the center. If using walnuts, blend in $\frac{1}{2}$ cup as you fold.

5. Portion level scoops of the batter into the prepared pan using a #16 ice cream scoop ($\frac{1}{4}$-cup capacity). As you reach the batter in the bottom of the bowl, fold in the remaining optional walnuts (see headnote).

6. Bake for 20 to 25 minutes, or until the tops of the muffins are springy to the touch. To ensure even baking, toward the end of baking time, rotate the pans top to bottom and front to back. Remove from the oven and place on a rack. While the muffins are slightly warm, drizzle with Midnight Chocolate Glaze. Leftover glaze may be refrigerated for up to several weeks, or frozen.

STORAGE: Store at room temperature, tightly wrapped in aluminum foil, for up to 3 days. These muffins may be frozen before glazing.

Muffins in Minutes

Muffin batters refrigerate beautifully, so the batter may be made ahead and the muffins, baked as needed. In fact, I have found that muffin batter that has been refrigerated often produces muffins with a better dome on top.

After you make the batter, you may either keep it in a bowl to scoop out as needed or, alternatively, portion it into muffin tins ready for baking. The batter will keep for up to 3 days, well covered with plastic wrap. If portioning into muffin tins in advance, I like to use aluminum foil liners because they are stronger and the batter does not seep through the bottom as it does with paper liners.

Muffin batters that have been made ahead can go from refrigerator to oven. Simply add a few additional minutes to the baking time.

zach's blueberry buttermilk muffins with streusel topping

MAKES 14 MUFFINS

Until I created this chapter, I never realized that blueberry muffins were so popular. When I announced to my grandson Zach that I was writing a book that contained a chapter on muffins, he said, "You are putting in a recipe for blueberry, aren't you? It's my favorite!" Zach is not alone. Blueberry muffins are at the top of many people's list.

These blueberry muffins are absolutely heavenly. They are flavored with a hint of lemon zest and are topped with a thick layer of buttery streusel crumbs. To overcome the problem of the berries sinking to the bottom of the muffins, instead of folding the berries through the batter, I top the batter with a handful of berries. Then I cover the berries with a generous handful of streusel. The blueberry muffin lovers in your life are in for a real treat.

1¾ cups all-purpose flour, spooned in and leveled

½ teaspoon baking powder

½ teaspoon salt

¼ teaspoon baking soda

⅔ cup (1⅓ sticks) unsalted butter, slightly firm

2 teaspoons finely grated lemon zest

¾ cup sugar

1 large egg

1 teaspoon pure vanilla extract

½ cup buttermilk

1½ cups fresh blueberries, washed and well dried (see page 357)

Carole's Favorite Streusel (see page 187)

AT A GLANCE

PANS: Two standard muffin pans

PAN PREP: Paper or foil cupcake liners

RACK LEVELS: Upper and lower thirds

OVEN TEMP: 375°F

BAKING TIME: 25–30 minutes

DIFFICULTY: 1

1. Position the racks in the upper and lower thirds of the oven. Heat the oven to 375°F. Line 14 muffin cups with paper or foil cupcake liners.

2. In a large bowl, thoroughly whisk together the flour, baking powder, salt, and baking soda. Set aside.

3. Cut the butter into 1-inch pieces and place in the bowl of an electric mixer fitted with the paddle attachment. Add the lemon zest and mix on medium speed until smooth and lightened in color, about 1 minute. Add the sugar in a steady stream, then blend in the egg and vanilla, scraping down the side of the bowl as needed.

4. Reduce the mixer speed to low and add the flour mixture alternately with the buttermilk, dividing the flour into three parts and the buttermilk into two, starting and ending with the flour. Mix *just* until blended after each addition.

5. Portion *half* scoops of the batter into the prepared pans using a #16 ice cream scoop (¼-cup capacity). Place a layer of blueberries evenly over the batter, then place a dollop of batter on top of the blueberries. It's okay for the berries to show. Take a handful of the streusel topping and crumble it over the batter and berries, completely covering the tops of the muffins with the crumbs. Press gently to adhere. Brush any stray crumbs from the top of the muffin pans using a small pastry brush.

6. Bake for 25 to 30 minutes, or until the streusel topping is golden brown. To ensure even baking, toward the end of baking time, rotate the pans top to bottom and front to back. Remove from the oven and place on a rack to cool.

STORAGE: Store at room temperature, tightly wrapped in aluminum foil, for up to 3 days. These muffins may be frozen.

Raspberry Buttermilk Muffins with Streusel Topping

Replace the blueberries in step 6 with 2 (6-ounce) packages fresh raspberries, washed and well dried (see page 357). Proceed with the recipe as written.

creative crisps, cobblers, pies, and tarts

three-berry crisp with butter-nut crumb topping

maple pecan apple crisp

peachy peach cobbler

double-crust blackberry cobbler

double-header pear cobbler

autumn fruit crumble with oatmeal crunch topping

flaky pie pastry

old-fashioned american apple pie

blueberry crumb pie with warm blueberry sauce

pear and apricot strudel pie

black and blue mango pie

strawberry rhubarb pie with lattice crust

tropical pineapple pie

terry ford's green tomato pie

main attraction chocolate chip cookie pie

southern pecan pie

lemon meringue pie

the "real" tavern toasted coconut cream pie

banana cream pie with pecan brittle

fruity viennese linzer tart

fluted cream cheese flan with fresh berries

three-berry crisp
with butter-nut crumb topping

MAKES 6 TO 8 SERVINGS

This crisp made from raspberries, blackberries, and blueberries is a treat. Walnuts add a crunchy contrast to the melt-in-your-mouth texture of the topping.

FRUIT FILLING

3 cups raspberries (two 6-ounce baskets), washed and dried (see page 357)

1½ cups blackberries (6-ounce basket), washed and dried (see page 357)

2 cups blueberries (pint basket), washed and dried (see page 357)

½ cup granulated sugar

2 tablespoons cornstarch

2 teaspoons fresh lemon juice

BUTTER-NUT CRUMB TOPPING

1¾ cups unsifted all-purpose flour

½ teaspoon baking powder

½ cup granulated sugar

¼ cup strained confectioners' sugar

½ teaspoon ground cinnamon

1 cup broken walnuts

⅔ cup (1⅓ sticks) unsalted butter, melted and cooled

AT A GLANCE

PAN: 7- × 11- × 1½-inch oven-proof glass baking dish

PAN PREP: Buttered

RACK LEVEL: Lower third

OVEN TEMP: 375°F

BAKING TIME: 30–35 minutes

DIFFICULTY: 1

1. Position the rack in the lower third of the oven. Heat the oven to 375°F. Butter the baking dish.

MAKE THE FILLING

2. Place the berries in the baking dish. Strain the sugar and cornstarch together. Sprinkle the mixture over the berries along with the lemon juice. Toss the berries gently in the pan, but *do not stir*.

MAKE THE CRUMB TOPPING

3. Strain the flour, baking powder, granulated and confectioners' sugars, and cinnamon together into a large bowl. Add the walnuts.

4. Pour in the butter and toss with a fork to form crumbs. Take clumps of the crumb mixture in your hands and squeeze gently to form a larger clump. Break the larger clump apart over the fruit. Repeat, using all of the crumb mixture. *Do not press the crumbs into the berries.*

BAKE THE CRISP

5. Bake for 30 to 35 minutes, or until the crumbs begin to brown and the fruit juices are bubbling. Serve warm with ice cream or frozen yogurt.

STORAGE: Refrigerate, lightly covered with a sheet of wax paper then aluminum foil, for up to 2 days. Reheat before serving. This crisp can be frozen.

maple pecan apple crisp

MAKES 6 TO 8 SERVINGS

This apple crisp scored especially high with my team of recipe testers. The captivating flavor comes from the sweetness of maple. When combined with apples, pecans, and browned butter, it's a real winner. I originally tested this recipe with maple sugar that I purchased while visiting the Taftsville Country Store in Taftsville, Vermont. Maple sugar is available through their mail-order catalog and www.Taftsville.com, but imitation maple flavor blended with granulated sugar in a food processor is an acceptable alternative.

2½ pounds Granny Smith apples (about 6 apples), peeled, cored, and cut into ¼-inch slices

1 tablespoon fresh lemon juice

¼ cup plus 2 tablespoons maple syrup, divided

⅓ cup (⅔ stick) unsalted butter

⅓ cup sugar

¾ teaspoon imitation maple flavor

1⅓ cups unsifted all-purpose flour

½ teaspoon baking powder

⅛ teaspoon salt

¾ cup broken pecans, divided

1. Position the rack in the lower third of the oven. Heat the oven to 350°F. Butter the baking dish.

2. Place the sliced apples in the pan, then drizzle with the lemon juice and ¼ cup of the maple syrup.

3. Melt the butter in a medium-size heavy saucepan. When it starts to brown, remove it from the heat and cool until tepid. Stir in the remaining 2 tablespoons maple syrup.

4. Place the sugar in a medium-size bowl and stir in the maple flavor, mixing until thoroughly blended. Add the flour, baking powder, and salt and mix well to combine. Empty the mixture into the butter-syrup mixture in the saucepan along with ¼ cup of the broken pecans. Toss with a fork to form crumbs. Take clumps of the crumb mixture in your hand and squeeze gently to form a larger clump. Break the larger clump apart over the apples. Repeat, using all of the crumb mixture. Sprinkle the remaining ½ cup pecans over the top.
Do not press the surface.

5. Bake for 40 to 45 minutes, or until the fruit juices are bubbling. If the nuts are browning too quickly, cover loosely with a sheet of aluminum foil for the final 5 to 10 minutes of baking. Serve warm.

STORAGE: Refrigerate, covered with a sheet of wax paper then aluminum foil, for up to 2 days. Reheat before serving. This crisp can be frozen.

AT A GLANCE

PAN: 7- × 11- × 1½-inch oven-proof glass baking dish

PAN PREP: Buttered

RACK LEVEL: Lower third

OVEN TEMP: 350°F

BAKING TIME: 40–45 minutes

DIFFICULTY: 1

peachy peach cobbler

MAKES 6 TO 8 SERVINGS

I can't think of a better dessert to savor at the end of a warm summer evening's meal than a home-made peach cobbler. The thickly cut slices of golden orange fruit with their succulent sweet juices are surely one of the gastronomical treasures of the season. While excessively juicy fruits like peaches can be challenging to use in pies, the juices work in your favor in cobblers. Since I always eat my cobblers à la mode, I like to spoon these juices over the top of the ice cream and fruit. What could be better?

8 to 9 cups fresh peaches (about 3½ pounds), wiped

¾ cup plus 1 teaspoon sugar, divided

¼ cup cornstarch

½ teaspoon ground cinnamon

1 tablespoon fresh lemon juice

2 tablespoons unsalted butter, cut into pieces

Short Pastry Dough for Cobblers, shaped into a rectangle for rolling

AT A GLANCE

PAN: 7- × 11- × 1½-inch oven-proof glass baking dish

PAN PREP: Buttered

PASTRY PREP: Unbaked

RACK LEVEL: Lower third

OVEN TEMP: 425°F

BAKING TIME: 40–45 minutes

DIFFICULTY: 1

1. Position the rack in the lower third of the oven. Heat the oven to 425°F. Butter the baking dish.

2. Cut the peaches into 1-inch slices and place in a large bowl.

3. Combine ¾ cup of the sugar, the cornstarch, and cinnamon. Add to the peaches, then toss gently to coat with the sugar mixture. Empty the mixture into the baking dish, spreading the fruit evenly. Sprinkle with the lemon juice and dot with the butter.

4. On a floured pastry cloth, roll the pastry into a rectangle measuring 8 × 12 inches. Place the pastry loosely over the fruit. Turn the edges under and press the dough against the side of the baking dish with a fork. Prick the top in several places with a fork to make steam vents. Sprinkle the top with the remaining 1 teaspoon sugar.

5. Make an aluminum foil drip pan to place on the rack below the cobbler halfway through the baking: Cut an 18-inch square of heavy-duty aluminum foil. Fold each edge twice (about 1 inch per fold) standing the folded edges upright to form a 4-sided pan.

6. Bake the cobbler for 40 to 45 minutes, or until the juices begin to bubble and the top is golden brown. (Halfway through baking, place the drip pan on the rack below.) Serve the cobbler warm with ice cream or whipped cream.

STORAGE: Refrigerate, covered with a sheet of wax paper then aluminum foil, for up to 4 days. Reheat before serving. This cobbler can be frozen.

Peach and Blueberry Cobbler

Add 1½ cups blueberries, washed and well dried (see page 357), to the peaches. Proceed with the recipe.

short pastry dough for cobblers

MAKES 1 CRUST FOR A 7- × 11-INCH COBBLER

Pastry referred to as "short" is one that usually has a high ratio of fat to flour. For easier handling, the manner in which the liquid is added to the crumbs here is slightly different from other doughs. I like to use this dough for cobblers because it is especially flaky.

1½ cups strained all-purpose flour, plus additional for dusting

½ teaspoon salt

¼ teaspoon baking powder

½ cup well-chilled vegetable shortening, cut into small pieces

3 tablespoons well-chilled unsalted butter, cut into small pieces

3 tablespoons ice water

1. Strain the flour, salt, and baking powder together into a large bowl. Add the shortening and butter, and toss to coat the pieces of fat with flour. With a pastry blender, cut the fats into the flour until the mixture resembles coarse meal. Scrape the blender clean every so often.

2. Place the ice water in a small bowl. Stir in ¼ cup of the crumb mixture with a fork. Then sprinkle the water mixture over all of the remaining crumbs and toss with a fork. *Do not mash—toss.* Gradually the crumbs will form into clumps.

3. With floured hands, form the dough into a mass by pressing the mixture against the side of the bowl. All of the crumbs should adhere to the dough and clean the bowl. If not, add a few more drops of water. Form the dough into a flat rectangle (if you are using an oblong dish) or shape into a flat disk. Dust the dough generously with flour, score with the side of your hand, and cover with plastic wrap. Chill in the refrigerator for 1 hour or longer. Roll as directed in recipe.

double-crust blackberry cobbler

MAKES 6 TO 8 SERVINGS

This recipe comes from a Southern friend, Carolyn Beck, who is an outstanding cook and baker. She was raised in Mississippi, where her family owned a fruit orchard. Her mother made cobblers in a most unusual manner: she layered the fruits and pastry, baking one layer at a time. The berries are cooked first with lots of butter, creating a flavor that is memorable and a syrup with a gorgeous deep, indigo color. While Carolyn makes her cobbler without thickening, I prefer to add a bit of cornstarch to bind the juices.

This cobbler is richer than most, but well worth the treat. If you can't get blackberries, try substituting raspberries, black raspberries, or blueberries. Be sure to sample the berries for sweetness and adjust the sugar according to your own taste.

PASTRY

2¾ cups strained all-purpose flour, plus additional for dusting

¾ teaspoon salt

¾ cup well-chilled vegetable shortening, cut into ½-inch pieces

6 to 8 tablespoons ice water

FILLING

5 to 6 cups fresh blackberries (four or five 6-ounce baskets)

¾ cup (1½ sticks) unsalted butter, divided

1¼ cups sugar, divided

4 teaspoons cornstarch (optional)

1 teaspoon fresh lemon juice

AT A GLANCE

PAN: 7- × 11- × 1½-inch oven-proof glass baking dish

PAN PREP: Sprayed with nonstick coating

PASTRY PREP: Unbaked

RACK LEVEL: Lower third

OVEN TEMP: 350°F

BAKING TIME: 60–70 minutes

DIFFICULTY: 2

MAKE THE PASTRY

1. Strain the flour and salt into a large bowl. Add the shortening and shake the bowl to coat the fat with flour. Using a pastry blender, cut the fat into the flour until the mixture resembles coarse meal.

2. Add the ice water, 1 tablespoon at a time, using a fork to blend. The dough has enough water when it will form a mass when pressed against the side of the bowl. If it fails to adhere, add more water sparingly.

3. With floured hands, form the dough into two flat rectangles. Dust with flour and wrap in plastic wrap. Chill 1 hour or longer. (The dough will keep for 3 days in the refrigerator or up to 6 months in the freezer. To thaw, transfer from the freezer to the refrigerator. Thaw overnight or for at least 12 hours.)

MAKE THE FILLING

4. Wash and thoroughly dry the blackberries (see page 357).

5. Place $\frac{1}{2}$ cup of the butter in a large skillet. Combine 1 cup of the sugar and the cornstarch (if using) in a small bowl. Add to the skillet and melt over low heat. Add the berries and heat over low heat until the berries release their juices and the mixture comes to a gentle boil and thickens. Remove from the heat, and stir in the lemon juice. Set aside.

6. Position the rack in the lower third of the oven. Heat the oven to 350°F. Spray the baking dish with nonstick coating.

ASSEMBLE AND BAKE THE COBBLER

7. Using a slotted spoon, place half the berries in the pan. Ladle in about $\frac{1}{2}$ cup of the berry juice. Do not add all of the juice.

8. On a lightly floured surface, roll one piece of pastry into a rectangle measuring about 8 × 12 inches. Lay the pastry loosely over the berries and prick the surface 10 to 12 times with a fork to allow the steam to escape. Dot the top of the pastry with 2 tablespoons of the remaining butter and sprinkle with 2 tablespoons of the remaining sugar. Bake for 30 to 35 minutes, or until the top is golden brown. Remove from the oven.

9. With a slotted spoon, place the remaining berries on top of the baked pastry. Empty the remaining berry juice into a small, heavy saucepan.

10. Roll the remaining pastry into a rectangle measuring 8 × 12 inches and place it on top of the second layer of berries. Prick the surface with a fork. Dot the top of the dough with the remaining 2 tablespoon butter and sprinkle with the remaining 2 tablespoon sugar.

11. Return the cobbler to the oven and bake for 30 to 35 minutes, or until the top is golden brown and the juices bubble at the sides. Remove from the oven and cool 1 hour or longer before serving.

12. Bring the reserved syrup to a boil over medium heat. Reduce the heat and simmer until it reduces slightly. Cut the cobbler into squares and serve while still warm in bowls with the heated sauce and vanilla ice cream or with whipped cream.

STORAGE: Refrigerate, covered with a sheet of wax paper then aluminum foil, for up to 3 days. Reheat before serving. This cobbler can be frozen.

double-header pear cobbler

MAKES 6 TO 8 SERVINGS

Jeffrey and Neil, my twin grandsons, have opposite likes and dislikes. Jeff is the chocolate kid, while Neil loves the taste of butterscotch. This double-header recipe covers both bases. Jeff's cobbler has pears baked in a fudge sauce, nestled under delicate flaky pastry. Neil's is made with pears in a pool of butterscotch, covered with a biscuit topping. Mix or match the crusts, however you choose. I guarantee that spoons will be licked clean, especially when the cobbler is served with a scoop of vanilla ice cream, topped with warm fudge or butterscotch sauce.

1 tablespoon unsalted butter

9 to 10 Anjou pears (about 4 pounds), peeled, cored, and cut into sixths

⅔ cup plus 2 teaspoons sugar

1½ tablespoons cornstarch

1½ tablespoons fresh lemon juice

1 teaspoon grated navel or Valencia orange zest

Warm Fudge Sauce (page 375) or Butterscotch Sauce (page 376)

Short Pastry Dough for Cobblers (page 145), shaped into a rectangle for rolling; or 1 small recipe Sweet Cream Biscuit Dough (page 104)

1 large egg white

AT A GLANCE

PAN: 7- × 11- × 1½-inch oven-proof glass baking dish

PAN PREP: Buttered

PASTRY PREP: Unbaked

RACK LEVEL: Lower third

OVEN TEMP: 400°F

BAKING TIME: 35–40 minutes with short pastry; 25–30 minutes with biscuit dough

DIFFICULTY: 2

MAKE THE PEAR FILLING

1. Melt the butter in a large, heavy sauté pan. Add the pears, cover, and cook over medium-high heat for 5 minutes. Drain in a colander. Discard the juices.

2. In a small bowl, combine ⅔ cup of the sugar and the cornstarch.

3. Return the pears to the sauté pan and stir in the sugar mixture, lemon juice, and orange zest. Bring to a boil, then reduce the heat to medium-low and cook, stirring occasionally, until the juices come to a boil and thicken. Remove from the heat and set aside.

4. Position the rack in the lower third of the oven. Heat the oven to 400°F. Butter the baking dish.

ASSEMBLE THE COBBLER

5. Spoon half of the fudge sauce or butterscotch sauce into the baking dish. Use a slotted spoon to transfer the pears to the dish. Discard excess liquid. Press the fruit gently into the sauce, making an even surface. Cool to tepid.

6. For short cobbler pastry: On a floured surface, roll out the pastry into an 8- × 12-inch rectangle. Cover the cobbler with the pastry, tucking the edges under. Prick the top in several places with a fork. **For sweet cream biscuit dough:** On a floured surface, roll out the dough into an 8- × 12-inch rectangle. Cut the pastry into 15 rectangular pieces with a scraper or knife. Arrange the dough over the fruit, five pieces across and three down. They should not touch.

7. Using a fork, lightly beat the egg white with 1 teaspoon of the remaining sugar. Brush lightly on the top of the short pastry or biscuit dough, and sprinkle with the remaining 1 teaspoon sugar.

BAKE THE COBBLER

8. Make an aluminum foil drip pan to place on the rack below the pie halfway through the baking: Cut an 18-inch square of heavy-duty aluminum foil. Fold each edge twice (about 1 inch per fold) standing the folded edges upright to form a 4-sided pan.

9. For the short pastry, bake the cobbler for 35 to 40 minutes. For the biscuit dough, bake for 25 to 30 minutes. (Halfway through baking, place the drip pan on the rack below.) The cobbler is done when the fruit juices begin to bubble and the top is golden brown. Let stand at least 30 minutes before serving. Serve in bowls with vanilla ice cream and the remaining fudge or butterscotch sauce spooned over the top.

STORAGE: Refrigerate, covered loosely with wax paper then aluminum foil, for up to 3 days. Reheat before serving. This cobbler can be frozen.

autumn fruit crumble with oatmeal crunch topping

MAKES 6 TO 8 SERVINGS

Make the most of autumn's bounty with this fruit crumble made of apples, pears, and cranberries. This dessert is quick to make, do-aheadable, and a perfect choice for a homestyle family supper.

TOPPING

¾ cup unsifted all-purpose flour

¾ cup whole wheat pastry flour

½ cup quick rolled oats

½ cup walnuts

¼ cup granulated sugar

¼ cup lightly packed light brown sugar

¼ teaspoon baking powder

¼ teaspoon salt

¼ teaspoon ground cinnamon

⅔ to ¾ cup (1⅓ to 1½ sticks) unsalted butter, melted and cooled

FILLING

3 Cortland apples (or Empire, Macoun, or Granny Smith)

4 firm Red Bartlett or Anjou pears

1½ cups fresh cranberries, washed and dried (see page 357)

2 teaspoons fresh lemon juice

½ cup granulated sugar

1½ tablespoons cornstarch

½ teaspoon ground cinnamon

1 teaspoon grated navel or Valencia orange zest

AT A GLANCE

PAN: 7- × 11- × 1½-inch oven-proof glass baking dish

PAN PREP: Generously buttered

RACK LEVEL: Lower third

OVEN TEMP: 350°F

BAKING TIME: 50–55 minutes

DIFFICULTY: 1

1. Position the rack in the lower third of the oven. Heat the oven to 350°F. Generously butter the baking dish.

MAKE THE TOPPING

2. Place the all-purpose and whole wheat flours, oats, walnuts, granulated and brown sugars, baking powder, salt, and cinnamon in the bowl of a food processor fitted with the steel blade. Pulse until blended and the nuts are finely chopped. Empty the contents into a large bowl.

3. Pour the melted butter over the flour mixture and toss with a fork to form crumbs. Set aside.

MAKE THE FILLING

4. Cut the apples into quarters, core, and peel. Cut Cortland apples into ¾-inch pieces. If using apples other than Cortlands, cut into ½-inch-thick pieces.

5. Cut the pears in half, core, peel, and cut into chunks.

6. Place the apples, pears, and cranberries in a large bowl. Drizzle with the lemon juice. Combine the granulated sugar, cornstarch, cinnamon, and orange zest. Sprinkle over the fruit, then shake the bowl to distribute. Empty the mixture into the baking dish. Sprinkle the topping over the fruit. Do not press.

BAKE THE CRUMBLE

7. Bake for 50 to 55 minutes, or until the top is golden brown and the juices are bubbly. Serve warm with ice cream, frozen yogurt, or whipped cream.

STORAGE: Refrigerate, loosely covered with a sheet of wax paper then aluminum foil, for up to 2 days. Reheat before serving. This crumble can be frozen.

Making Great Cobblers, Crisps, and Crumbles

- Soft-fleshed fruits (like kiwis and bananas) and citrus fruits are not the best candidates for a cobbler. Use them only in small amounts as an accent ingredient.

- A small amount of dried fruits—such as dried cherries, cranberries, currants, or raisins—can be added to any cobbler or crisp. Always plump the dried fruits before using.

- Both fresh and dried fruits or berries can be macerated in liqueur before using. The steeping liquid can be added along with the fruit or reserved and used to flavor a topping.

- It's okay to add extra fruit to these desserts, but take care not to overload the baking dish. The juices will bubble up and overflow into the oven. To be safe, place an aluminum foil drip pan on the rack below when baking.

- Rolled oats can be substituted for part of the flour in most crumb toppings.

- For a crumb topping, never use hot melted butter. It should be *tepid*. Otherwise the crumbs will be oily and will not form as well.

- Crumb toppings will be crispier if the crumbs are not pressed into the fruit. Sprinkle them over the fruit instead.

- Crumb toppings are best if allowed to stand for 10 to 15 minutes after the melted butter has been added. This gives them time to absorb the fat. The surface of the crumb will be less oily and will form better crumbs.

- Never cover a crumb topping with plastic wrap because the crumbs will become soggy. A loose covering of aluminum foil works best.

- Because cobblers are single-crusted, the top crust can be rolled slightly thicker than you would for a pie.

- Always serve crisps, cobblers, and similar desserts warm.

flaky pie pastry

MAKES 1 DOUBLE CRUST FOR A 9-INCH PIE

This is a wonderful, all-purpose, American-style pastry for all manner of pies.

2½ cups sifted all-purpose flour

1 tablespoons sugar

¾ teaspoon salt

½ cup firm, unsalted butter, cut into ½-inch cubes

½ cup chilled vegetable shortening, cut into small pieces

5 to 6 tablespoons ice water, or more as needed

1. Sift together the flour, sugar, and salt in a large mixing bowl. Add the butter and shortening and toss to coat the fats with flour.

2. Using a pastry blender, cut the fats into the flour until the mixture resembles coarse meal with some pea-size particles. Position your hand at the far side of the bowl. Draw the blender toward the center while scraping it along the bottom of the bowl. Rotate the bowl with your free hand to keep the pastry blender in the same position. *Do not turn or twist your wrist,* or the crumbs will become too sticky. Scrape the blender clean every so often. Break up larger particles of fat by pressing the blender straight down on them.

3. Add the ice water, *1 tablespoon at a time,* drizzling it around the rim of the bowl. Use a kitchen fork to push the mixture toward the center with each addition. Do this around the entire bowl. As more water is added, clumps of dough will form. They will become larger with each addition. Add the final tablespoon of water, a teaspoon at a time. Now feel the dough with your hand; it should feel cool and slightly moist.

To determine if the mixture has enough water, gather some in your hand and press it against the bowl to see if it will hold together. If not, add more water *sparingly,* about 1 teaspoon at a time, adding only enough for it to form a mass. *Too much liquid and/or overworking the dough will toughen it.*

4. With floured hands, press the dough against the side of the bowl, forming two balls. All of the crumbs should adhere to the balls and clean the bowl. If not, add a few drops of water. Flatten the balls into two 4- to 5-inch disks.

5. Dust the disks generously with flour, then score with the side of your hand to relax the gluten. Cover with plastic wrap. Chill 30 minutes or longer before using.

STORAGE: The dough will keep for up to 3 days in the refrigerator or 6 months in the freezer. To thaw; transfer from the freezer to refrigerator. Thaw overnight or at least 12 hours.

old-fashioned american apple pie

MAKES 6 TO 8 SERVINGS

There is no better time to get started than now. Read the recipe through, then organize your ingredients in the order they are listed. Remember, apple pies are a cinch to make once you have a little know-how.

Flaky Pie Pastry (page 152)

FILLING

1½ to 2 pounds Cortland or Rome apples (about 4 large)

1 pound Granny Smith apples (about 3 medium)

2 teaspoons fresh lemon juice

¾ cup lightly packed light brown sugar

¼ cup granulated sugar

3 tablespoons cornstarch

1 teaspoon ground cinnamon

⅛ teaspoon grated nutmeg (optional)

1 tablespoon unsalted butter

EGG WASH AND GARNISH

1 large egg white beaten with 1 teaspoon water, for egg wash

1 teaspoon granulated sugar

⅛ teaspoon ground cinnamon (optional)

AT A GLANCE

PAN: 9-inch ovenproof glass pie plate

PAN PREP: Buttered

PASTRY PREP: Unbaked

RACK LEVEL: Lower third

OVEN TEMP: 400°F

BAKING TIME: 50–60 minutes

DIFFICULTY: 2

MAKE THE FILLING

1. Cut the apples into quarters. Remove the cores and peels. Cut the Cortland or Rome apples into ¾-inch slices and the Granny Smith apples into ¼-inch slices. Place in a large bowl, sprinkle with the lemon juice, and toss.

2. Combine the brown and granulated sugars, cornstarch, cinnamon, and nutmeg in a small bowl. Set aside. *Do not add to the fruit; the sugar draws moisture from the apples and will make the filling too watery.*

ASSEMBLE THE PIE

3. Position the rack in the lower third of the oven. Heat the oven to 400°F. Butter the pie plate.

4. Roll one pastry disk into a 13-inch circle. Line the pie plate with the dough. Brush a thin layer of egg wash onto the bottom and side of the dough.

5. Toss the sugar mixture with the apples. Empty the filling into the pie shell, forming the apples into a snug mound with your hands. Fill in spaces with apple wedges. Dot the pie with the butter. Trim the edge with scissors, leaving a ¼-inch overhang.

6. Roll out the other pastry disk into a 13-inch circle and place it on top of the apples. With your hands, push the dough gently toward the center to allow the dough to drop during baking. Then press the top and bottom layers of pastry together with your fingers.

7. With a small knife, trim the dough flush against the rim of the pie plate. To seal the edge, dip a 4-prong fork into flour, and press the fork gently into the edge of the dough, going completely around the rim of the pie.

8. Prick the top of the pastry in several places with a fork to allow steam to escape during baking. Lightly brush the top of the pie with the egg wash. To garnish, sprinkle with the sugar and cinnamon.

BAKE THE PIE

9. To prevent the edge from burning, make aluminum foil bands: Cut two 3-inch-wide strips of 18-inch heavy-duty aluminum foil: Fold 1 inch of each strip to the center, making a double thickness of foil on one side. Cover the edge of the pie with the bands, keeping the double fold on top of the dough. Be careful not to mash the edge of the pastry. Seal the bands together with tape.

10. Make an aluminum foil drip pan to place on the oven rack below the pie to catch any juices that may overflow during baking: Cut an 18-inch square of heavy-duty aluminum foil. Double-fold each edge (about 1-inch per fold), turning the foil up at the second fold, forming a rim.

11. Bake the pie for 45 to 50 minutes. (Halfway through baking, place the drip pan on the rack below.) Remove the foil bands from the edge, and continue to bake 5 to 10 minutes longer. The pie is done when the juices begin to bubble through the top crust and the edge and bottom crust are golden brown. Cool at least 4 hours before serving.

STORAGE: This pie will keep for 1 day at room temperature. For longer storage, refrigerate, covered with aluminum foil, for up to 5 days. Before serving, warm in a 350°F oven for 15 to 20 minutes. This pie can be frozen.

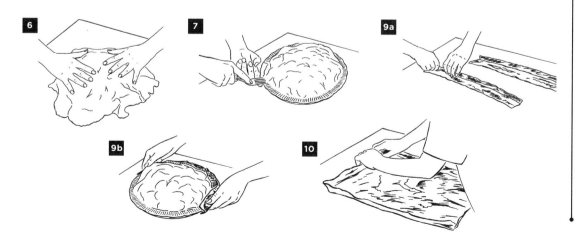

blueberry crumb pie with warm blueberry sauce

MAKES 6 TO 8 SERVINGS

It's no surprise that blueberry pie is a Fourth of July favorite. This sweet, succulent berry—native to our country—is in its prime at that time of year, and it makes sensational pies. When I make blueberry pie, I always parcook the filling first, removing some of the juice before filling the pie shell. This helps prevent the bottom crust from becoming soggy.

½ recipe Flaky Pie Pastry (page 152)

1 large egg white beaten with 1 teaspoon water, for egg wash

FILLING

¾ cup granulated sugar

2 tablespoons cornstarch

½ teaspoon ground cinnamon

¼ cup water

6 to 7 cups blueberries (3 pint baskets), washed and dried (see page 357)

1 tablespoon instant tapioca

1 tablespoon unsalted butter

1½ to 2 teaspoons fresh lemon juice

STREUSEL CRUMB TOPPING

1 cup unsifted all-purpose flour

¼ cup finely chopped walnuts (see page 356)

¼ cup granulated sugar

¼ cup lightly packed light brown sugar

1 teaspoon ground cinnamon

¼ teaspoon baking powder

⅛ teaspoon salt

⅓ cup (⅔ stick) unsalted butter, melted and cooled to tepid

WARM BLUEBERRY SYRUP

Reserved syrup from filling

½ cup water

1 to 2 tablespoons crème de cassis or kirschwasser

1 teaspoon fresh lemon juice

AT A GLANCE

PAN: 9-inch ovenproof glass pie plate

PAN PREP: Buttered

PASTRY PREP: Unbaked

RACK LEVEL: Lower third

OVEN TEMP: 400°F

BAKING TIME: 50–55 minutes

DIFFICULTY: 2

1. Position the rack in the lower third of the oven. Heat the oven to 400°F. Butter the pie plate.

2. On a floured pastry cloth, roll the pastry into a circle measuring approximately 13 inches. Fit loosely into the pie plate. Trim the edge with scissors, leaving a 1-inch overhang. Fold over and flute or crimp the edge (see pages 363–364). Brush the dough with a thin layer of the egg wash to seal the surface.

MAKE THE FILLING

3. Whisk together the granulated sugar, cornstarch, and cinnamon in a large skillet. Stir in the water. Add the blueberries and stir gently. Bring to a slow boil, then cook over low heat, stirring occasionally with a rubber spatula, for about 5 minutes, or *just* until the mixture thickens. *Avoid mashing the blueberries.* Be careful not to overcook the blueberries.

4. Using a slotted spoon, transfer the blueberries to a large, shallow container about one-third at a time, sprinkling each layer with tapioca. Let stand for 15 minutes to soften the tapioca. Reserve the syrup for the blueberry sauce. Empty the filling into the pie shell. Dot with the butter and sprinkle with the lemon juice.

MAKE THE TOPPING

5. Combine the flour, walnuts, granulated and brown sugars, cinnamon, baking powder, and salt in a medium bowl. Add the cooled, melted butter and toss with a fork to make crumbs. Take clumps of the crumb mixture in your hand and squeeze gently to form a larger clump. Then break the large clump apart over the blueberry filling. Repeat using all of the crumbs. Do not press the crumbs into the filling.

BAKE THE PIE

6. To prevent the edge of the pie from burning, make aluminum foil bands: Cut two 3-inch-wide strips of 18-inch heavy-duty aluminum foil. Fold 1 inch of each strip to the center, making a double thickness of foil. Mold the foil around the edge of the pie, keeping the double fold on top of the dough. Be careful not to crush the edge of the pastry. Secure the bands with tape.

7. Make an aluminum foil drip pan to place on the rack below the pie halfway through the baking: Cut an 18-inch square of heavy-duty aluminum foil. Fold each edge twice (about 1 inch per fold) standing the folded edges upright to form a 4-sided pan.

8. To prevent the crumbs from overbrowning, cover the pie loosely with a sheet of aluminum foil. Bake for 40 minutes. (Halfway through baking, place the drip pan on the rack below.) Remove the foil bands and the foil from the top and continue baking for 10 to 15 minutes, or until the bottom crust and crumbs are golden brown. Cool on a rack for 4 hours before cutting.

MAKE THE WARM BLUEBERRY SYRUP

9. Place the reserved blueberry syrup and water in a medium, heavy saucepan. Bring to a slow boil, stirring constantly. Off the heat, stir in the cassis, then return to the boil and cook for 30 seconds longer. If the sauce is too thick, add a little more water. Stir in the lemon juice and empty into a container. This sauce can be made ahead and reheated as needed.

10. Serve the pie with vanilla ice cream or frozen yogurt and the blueberry sauce.

STORAGE: Refrigerate, loosely covered with a sheet of wax paper then aluminum foil, for up to 2 days. This pie can be frozen.

pear and apricot strudel pie

MAKES 6 TO 8 SERVINGS

This pastry is reminiscent of a huge fruit strudel. Layers of crisp phyllo encase chunks of sautéed pears and dried apricots, all baked in a pie plate. The tissue-thin strips of dough are brushed with butter, then sprinkled with sweetened chopped almonds. The top is finished with a confetti of shredded phyllo that is heavily dusted with confectioners' sugar. A word of caution: this pie is good only when served warm, as it loses its crispness when cold.

½ cup plus 2 tablespoons (1¼ sticks) unsalted butter, divided

¾ cup unblanched almonds, lightly toasted (see page 356)

2 tablespoons plain, dry bread crumbs

6 tablespoons granulated sugar, divided

½ teaspoon ground cinnamon

3 pounds ripe but firm Red Bartlett or Anjou pears

6 ounces dried apricots, halved (about 1 cup)

1 teaspoon grated lemon zest

6 tablespoons lightly packed dark brown sugar

2 tablespoons cornstarch

⅛ teaspoon ground allspice

7 sheets phyllo pastry, preferably not frozen

1 tablespoon fresh lemon juice

2 tablespoons confectioners' sugar, for garnish

AT A GLANCE

PAN: 9-inch ovenproof glass pie plate

PAN PREP: Buttered

RACK LEVEL: Lower third

OVEN TEMP: 375°F

BAKING TIME: 40–45 minutes

DIFFICULTY: 1

MAKE THE FILLING

1. Place ½ cup of the butter in a heavy, medium saucepan. Melt over low heat. Remove the white foam as it forms on the surface (see Clarifying Butter, page 359). Continue to skim the surface until no more foam is present. Cook the butter slowly until a brown sediment begins to form on the bottom of the pot, about 10 minutes. Remove from the heat. Let stand until ready to use.

2. Place the almonds, bread crumbs, 2 tablespoons of the granulated sugar, and the cinnamon in the bowl of a food processor. Process until the nuts are finely chopped. Add 2 tablespoons of the clarified butter. Pulse 3 or 4 times to combine. Set aside.

PREPARE THE FRUIT

3. Peel and core the pears, then cut them lengthwise into $\frac{1}{2}$-inch slices.

4. Melt the remaining 2 tablespoons butter in a 12-inch skillet. Add the pears, apricots, lemon zest, and remaining 4 tablespoons granulated sugar. Turn the fruit with a large spatula to coat with sugar. Over medium-high heat, sauté for 8 to 10 minutes, turning occasionally with the spatula. Drain the mixture in a large colander and discard the juices.

5. Mix the brown sugar, cornstarch, and allspice in a small bowl.

ASSEMBLE THE PIE

6. Position the rack in the lower third of the oven. Heat the oven to 375°F. Butter the pie plate.

7. Arrange 6 phyllo sheets in the pie plate in the following manner: Center a double sheet of phyllo over the pie plate and press it in. Brush the phyllo with clarified butter and sprinkle with 2 tablespoons of the ground nut mixture. Repeat the above procedure, crisscrossing 1 sheet at a time until a total of 6 sheets are used.

8. Fill the pie shell by layering the pears in 3 additions alternating with the brown sugar mixture in 2 additions, starting and ending with the fruit. Drizzle the lemon juice over the top. Finish the pie by folding the edges of the phyllo over the filling, brushing each layer with butter, and sprinkling each layer again with the nut mixture. Reserve 2 tablespoons of the nut mixture to garnish the top.

9. Brush the top of the pie with more butter. Roll the remaining sheet of phyllo into a cylinder. Using a sharp knife, shred the phyllo into $\frac{1}{4}$-inch slices. Sprinkle the shredded phyllo over the pie. Drizzle with any remaining butter. Scatter the reserved nut mixture over the top.

BAKE THE PIE

10. Bake for 40 to 45 minutes, or until the pie is well browned. Let stand at least 30 minutes before cutting. Put confectioners' sugar in a strainer and sprinkle it over the top. This pie must be served warm.

STORAGE: Refrigerate, covered with a sheet of wax paper then aluminum foil, for up to 4 days. Reheat before serving. This pie can be frozen before or after baking.

black and blue mango pie

MAKES 6 TO 8 SERVINGS

The luscious combination of blackberries, blueberries, and mangoes is one that came about by chance. After days of testing recipes, I had some leftover berries and mango in the refrigerator. Rather than waste them, I put the fruit together for a pie. It turned out to be one of my favorite recipes in this book. Try this, and see if you don't agree.

2 large or 3 medium mangoes	⅔ cup plus 1 teaspoon sugar, divided
2 cups (1 pint basket) blueberries	3 tablespoons cornstarch
1½ cups (6-ounce basket) blackberries	2 teaspoons fresh lemon juice
Flaky Pie Pastry (page 152)	2 tablespoons unsalted butter

AT A GLANCE

PAN: 9-inch ovenproof glass pie plate

PAN PREP: Buttered

PASTRY PREP: Unbaked

RACK LEVEL: Lower third

OVEN TEMP: 400°F

BAKING TIME: 55–60 minutes

DIFFICULTY: 2

PREPARE THE FRUIT

1. Remove the cheeks from the mangoes. Score the flesh into ¾-inch squares and remove from the skin. Trim the flesh from the pit area and dice (see pages 357–358).

2. Wash and thoroughly dry the blueberries and blackberries (see page 357). Cut the larger blackberries in half.

ASSEMBLE THE PIE

3. Position the rack in the lower third of the oven. Heat the oven to 400°F. Butter the pie plate.

4. Roll half the pastry into a 13-inch circle. Line the pie plate with the pastry. Trim the edge, leaving a ½-inch overhang.

5. Place the diced mangoes and berries in a large bowl. Combine ⅔ cup of the sugar and the cornstarch in a small bowl. Sprinkle 2 tablespoons of this mixture on the bottom of the pie shell. Add the remaining sugar mixture to the fruit and shake the bowl to distribute. *Do not stir;* you will crush the fruit.

6. Empty the fruit mixture into the pie shell, mounding the fruit in the center. Sprinkle with the lemon juice and dot with the butter.

7. Make a lattice top with the remaining pastry as follows: Roll the pastry into a 13-inch circle. Using a pastry wheel, divide pastry into twelve ¾-inch strips. Evenly space the pastry, starting with 2 longer strips placed to the left and right of the center, about ¾ inch apart. Continue, using 2 more strips on either side, keeping the shortest strips toward the outer edge. Rotate the pie 90 degrees and repeat the process, weaving new strips over and under the initial 6 strips (see Making Lattice Crusts, pages 361–362). Trim, leaving a 1-inch overhang.

8. Seal the edge by folding the pastry strips under the bottom layer of dough. Flute the edge of the pastry (see pages 363–364). Sprinkle the lattice with the remaining 1 teaspoon sugar.

BAKE THE PIE

9. To prevent the edge from burning, make aluminum foil bands: Cut two 3-inch-wide strips of 18-inch heavy-duty aluminum foil. Fold 1 inch of each strip to the center, making a double thickness of foil. Mold the foil around the edge of the pie, keeping the double fold on top of the dough. Be careful not to crush the edge of the pastry. Secure the bands with tape.

10. Make an aluminum foil drip pan to place on the rack below the pie halfway through the baking: Cut an 18-inch square of heavy-duty aluminum foil. Fold each edge twice (about 1 inch per fold) standing the folded edges upright to form a 4-sided pan.

11. Bake the pie for 45 minutes. (Halfway through baking, place the drip pan on the rack below.) Remove the aluminum foil bands. Continue baking for 10 minutes longer, or until the crust is golden brown and the juices begin to bubble. Remove the pie from the oven and cool on a rack. Let stand at least 4 hours before serving.

STORAGE: Refrigerate, covered with a sheet of wax paper then aluminum foil, for up to 4 days. This pie can be frozen.

strawberry rhubarb pie with lattice crust

MAKES 6 TO 8 SERVINGS

Tart rhubarb complements sweet berries in this pie, making a favorite fruit combination. To retain the character of the strawberries, keep them in large chunks because if cut too small, the delicate berries become mushy when baked. Don't forget to remove the leafy parts of the rhubarb; the stalks are perfectly safe, but the leaves are toxic.

Flaky Pie Pastry (page 152)

¾ cup plus 2 teaspoons sugar, divided

3 tablespoons cornstarch

½ teaspoon ground cinnamon

½ teaspoon grated navel or Valencia orange zest

3 cups (1½ pints) fresh strawberries, cleaned, hulled, and cut into 1½-inch chunks

3 cups fresh rhubarb (about 1 pound), cleaned and sliced into pieces

1 teaspoon fresh lemon juice

2 tablespoons unsalted butter

2 tablespoons milk

AT A GLANCE

PAN: 9-inch ovenproof glass pie plate

PAN PREP: Buttered

PASTRY PREP: Unbaked

RACK LEVEL: Lower third

OVEN TEMP: 400°F

BAKING TIME: 45 minutes

DIFFICULTY: 2

1. Position the rack in the lower third of the oven. Heat the oven to 400°F. Butter the pie plate.

2. On a floured pastry cloth, roll half the pastry into a 13-inch circle. Line the pie plate with the pastry. Trim the edge, leaving a ½-inch overhang.

3. Combine ¾ cup of the sugar, the cornstarch, cinnamon, and orange zest in a small bowl, using a whisk to combine well. Sprinkle 2 tablespoons of this mixture over the pie shell.

4. Place the strawberries and rhubarb in a large bowl. Pour the remaining sugar-cornstarch mixture over the fruit. Shake the bowl briskly to distribute the dry ingredients through the fruit.

5. Empty the fruit into the pie shell, making sure it is evenly spread. Sprinkle with the lemon juice and dot with the butter.

6. Make a diagonal lattice top with the remaining pastry (see Making Diagonal Lattice Crusts, page 363). Trim, leaving a 1-inch overhang.

7. Seal the edges by folding the pastry strips under the bottom layer of dough. Flute the edge of the pastry (see pages 363–364). Brush the lattice lightly with the milk and sprinkle with the remaining 2 teaspoons sugar.

8. To prevent the edge from burning, make aluminum foil bands: Cut two strips of 3-inch heavy-duty aluminum foil. Fold 1 inch of each strip to the center, making a double thickness of foil. Mold the foil around the edge of the pie, keeping the double fold on top of the dough. Be careful not to crush the edge of the pastry. Secure the bands with tape.

9. Make an aluminum foil drip pan to place on the rack below the pie halfway through the baking: Cut an 18-inch square of heavy-duty aluminum foil. Fold each edge twice (about 1 inch per fold) standing the folded edges upright to form a 4-sided pan.

10. Bake the pie for 35 minutes. (Halfway through baking, place the drip pan on the rack below.) Remove the aluminum foil bands. Continue baking for 10 minutes longer or until the crust is golden brown and the juices begin to bubble. Remove the pie from the oven and cool on a rack. Let stand at least 3 hours before serving.

STORAGE: Refrigerate, covered with a sheet of wax paper then aluminum foil, for up to 3 days. Reheat before serving. This pie can be frozen.

tropical pineapple pie

MAKES 6 TO 8 SERVINGS

Some years ago, whenever I ran out of ideas as to what kind of dessert to make, my husband would say, "pineapple pie." The truth is, this was a pie that I had never made, nor ever eaten, because quite frankly it didn't appeal to me. One day I broke down, pulled cans of crushed pineapple off the shelf, and went to work. Much to my surprise, the pie turned out great. I more than liked it—I loved it.

Don't bother making this with fresh pineapple. Canned crushed pineapple packed in unsweetened juice works just fine. If you can handle the calories, keep the amount of the butter as is. The flavors of pineapple and butter are extremely complementary.

Flaky Pie Pastry (page 152)

1 large egg white beaten with 1 teaspoon water, for egg wash

1 (1-pound 4-ounce) can plus 1 (8-ounce) can crushed pineapple packed in unsweetened pineapple juice

½ cup plus 1 teaspoon sugar, divided

3 tablespoons cornstarch

¼ teaspoon salt

3 to 4 tablespoons unsalted butter, cut into pieces

1½ teaspoons grated lemon zest

¾ teaspoon grated navel or Valencia orange zest

1 tablespoon fresh lemon juice

AT A GLANCE

PAN: 9-inch ovenproof glass pie plate

PAN PREP: Buttered

PASTRY PREP: Unbaked

RACK LEVEL: Lower third

OVEN TEMP: 400°F

BAKING TIME: 40–50 minutes

DIFFICULTY: 1

1. Position the rack in the lower third of the oven. Heat the oven to 400°F. Butter the pie plate.

PREPARE THE CRUST

2. On a floured pastry cloth, roll 1 disk of pastry into a circle measuring approximately 13 inches. Fit loosely into the pie plate. Trim the edge with scissors, leaving a ½-inch overhang. Brush the dough with the egg wash. Reserve the remaining egg wash for glazing the top of the pie. Chill the shell while preparing the filling.

MAKE THE FILLING

3. Drain the pineapple well in a strainer placed over a bowl. Reserve 1⅓ cups of the pineapple juice.

4. Whisk together ½ cup of the sugar, the cornstarch, and salt in a 3-quart saucepan. Slowly whisk in the reserved pineapple juice, mixing until smooth. Bring the mixture to a slow boil over medium-low heat, stirring constantly with a wooden spoon, until it is smooth and thickened. Simmer for 1 minute longer. Remove from the heat and add the crushed pineapple, butter, lemon and orange zests, and lemon juice. Stir gently until the butter is melted. Let cool before filling the pie shell.

ASSEMBLE THE PIE

5. Empty the filling into the pie shell, smoothing the top with the back of a tablespoon. Roll the second half of the pastry into a 13-inch circle. Place the dough on top of the filling. Trim excess with scissors, leaving a 1-inch overhang. Tuck the top edge of the dough under the bottom, pressing the two layers together to form a wall. Crimp or flute the edge (see pages 363–364). Make steam vents on top of the pastry. Brush the top with the remaining egg wash and sprinkle with the remaining 1 teaspoon sugar.

BAKE THE PIE

6. To prevent the edge from burning, make aluminum foil bands: Cut two 3-inch-wide strips of 18-inch heavy-duty aluminum foil. Fold 1 inch of each strip to the center, making a double thickness of foil. Mold the foil around the edge of the pie, keeping the double fold on top of the dough. Be careful not to crush the edge of the pastry. Secure the bands with tape.

7. Make an aluminum foil drip pan to place on the rack below the pie halfway through the baking: Cut an 18-inch square of heavy-duty aluminum foil. Fold each edge twice (about 1 inch per fold) standing the folded edges upright to form a 4-sided pan.

8. Bake the pie for 35 minutes. (Halfway through baking, place the drip pan on the rack below.) Remove the foil bands, and bake for 5 to 10 minutes longer, or until the crust is golden brown on the top and bottom. Cool on a rack. Let stand 3 to 4 hours before serving.

STORAGE: Refrigerate, loosely covered with wax paper and then aluminum foil, for up to 4 days. Reheat before serving. This pie may be frozen.

terry ford's green tomato pie

MAKES 6 TO 8 SERVINGS

Ripley, Tennessee, is the home of Terry Ford, owner of *The Lauderdale County Enterprise,* a local newspaper his family started in 1885. Imagine my surprise when I learned that Terry has one of the largest private cookbook collections in the United States. Terry loves to cook and bake. Through his media contacts, he has amassed an incredible amount of culinary knowledge. So who better to ask when I needed a recipe for a green tomato pie? Of course, he had one!

His version of this Pennsylvania Dutch pie is made with chopped green tomatoes, golden raisins, and pecans and is flavored with balsamic vinegar, sugar, and spices. The mixture is bound with lots of tapioca and has a texture similar to mincemeat. If you prefer a looser filling, reduce the tapioca to 2 to 3 tablespoons.

4 cups diced green tomatoes, in ⅜-inch pieces (do not remove the skins or seeds)

4 to 6 tablespoons instant tapioca

1 cup golden raisins

1 cup pecans, coarsely chopped

1 cup granulated sugar

¼ cup firmly packed dark brown sugar

2 tablespoons unsalted butter, softened

2 tablespoons balsamic vinegar

1 teaspoon ground cinnamon

½ teaspoon freshly grated nutmeg

¼ teaspoon ground allspice

½ recipe Flaky Pie Pastry, rolled out, fitted into the pie plate, and baked (page 152)

AT A GLANCE

PAN: 9-inch ovenproof glass pie plate

PAN PREP: Buttered

PASTRY PREP: Baked

RACK LEVEL: Lower third

OVEN TEMP: 350°F

BAKING TIME: 45–55 minutes

DIFFICULTY: 1

1. Layer the tomatoes and tapioca in a large, nonreactive bowl. Toss with your hands to distribute the tapioca. Let stand for 15 minutes.

2. Position the rack in the lower third of the oven. Heat the oven to 350°F. Lightly butter a 2-quart casserole dish.

3. Add the raisins, pecans, granulated and brown sugars, butter, vinegar, cinnamon, nutmeg, and allspice to the tomatoes. Empty the mixture into the casserole. Bake the mixture, uncovered, for 45 to 55 minutes. Stir 2 or 3 times as it bakes. The filling is cooked when it is very bubbly and all the tapioca seems dissolved.

4. Remove the casserole from the oven and let stand about 15 minutes. It will become very thick. Empty the filling into the baked pie shell. Smooth the top, and let stand at room temperature for several hours, until set. Serve the pie with dollops of lightly whipped cream or vanilla ice cream.

STORAGE: Store at room temperature, covered with wax paper then aluminum foil, for up to 1 week. Freezing is not recommended.

main attraction chocolate chip cookie pie

MAKES 6 TO 8 SERVINGS

On a trip to Vermont, my husband and I stopped for lunch in Bennington at a restaurant called the Main Attraction. I thought I was in heaven when I took a bite of my dessert: a pie so special that I had to include the recipe for it in my book. The waitress was kind enough to get me a copy from the kitchen staff.

When you prepare the pie shell, be sure to make a fluted edge (see pages 363–364) so the filling will have enough room to rise in the pan. The pie should not be cut when it is fresh out of the oven, as the center will be too wet. The filling needs at least 4 hours to set, but be sure to reheat the pie before serving. Lovers of warm and chewy chocolate chip cookies will find this pie absolutely scrumptious.

1¼ cups strained all-purpose flour

½ teaspoon salt

¼ teaspoon baking soda

½ cup (1 stick) unsalted butter, melted and cooled

½ cup lightly packed light brown sugar

⅓ cup granulated sugar

2 large eggs, lightly beaten

1 teaspoon pure vanilla extract

1 cup (one 6-ounce package) semisweet chocolate chips

¾ cup walnuts, coarsely chopped (see page 356), divided

½ recipe Flaky Pie Pastry, rolled out, fitted into the pie plate, edge fluted, and baked (page 152)

Vanilla ice cream or Warm Fudge Sauce (page 375) for serving

1. Position the rack in the lower third of the oven. Heat the oven to 350°F.

2. Strain together the flour, salt, and baking soda. Set aside.

3. Place the melted butter in a large bowl. Using a wire whisk, gradually blend in the brown and granulated sugars. Stir in the eggs, then the vanilla. Stir in the dry ingredients, ½ cup at a time. Add the chocolate chips and ½ cup of the walnuts.

4. Pour the batter into the baked pie shell. Sprinkle the remaining ¼ cup walnuts over the top. Bake for 35 to 37 minutes, or until top of the pie is lightly browned and the center is *just* set—a toothpick inserted into the center should remain slightly moist. *Do not overbake.* The filling will set as it cools. Cool for at least 4 hours.

5. Before slicing, reheat the pie in a 325°F oven for 8 to 10 minutes. Serve with vanilla ice cream or fudge sauce.

STORAGE: Refrigerate, covered with aluminum foil, for up to 5 days. Reheat for a few minutes before serving. This pie can be frozen.

AT A GLANCE

PAN: 9-inch ovenproof glass pie plate

PAN PREP: Buttered

PASTRY PREP: Baked

RACK LEVEL: Lower third

OVEN TEMP: 350°F

BAKING TIME: 35-37 minutes

DIFFICULTY: 1

southern pecan pie

MAKES 6 TO 8 SERVINGS

When I was a teenager growing up in the South, I used to wonder what people loved about pecan pies. They held absolutely no appeal for me, as most of those I had eaten were either store-bought or poorly made. Years later, on a visit to Memphis, I sampled one made by a former schoolmate, Shirley Roberts, and instantly changed my opinion. Shirley shared her recipe with me, and since then pecan pie has become one of my favorites. I love to eat it warm, topped with a glob of bourbon-flavored whipped cream. It's so sinful and so good!

½ recipe Flaky Pie Pastry (page 152)

4 large eggs, slightly beaten

2 tablespoons heavy cream

½ cup granulated sugar

½ cup lightly packed light brown sugar

4 teaspoons unsifted all-purpose flour

⅛ teaspoon salt

1⅓ cups light corn syrup

5 tablespoons unsalted butter, melted, divided

1½ teaspoons pure vanilla extract

1 tablespoon bourbon (optional)

1½ cups broken pecans, lightly toasted (see page 356)

AT A GLANCE

PAN: 9-inch ovenproof glass pie plate

PAN PREP: Sprayed with nonstick coating

PASTRY PREP: Unbaked

RACK LEVEL: Lower third

OVEN TEMP: 325°F

BAKING TIME: 75–90 minutes

DIFFICULTY: 1

1. Position the rack in the lower third of the oven. Heat the oven to 325°F. Spray the pie plate with nonstick coating.

2. On a floured pastry cloth, roll out the pastry into a circle measuring approximately 13 inches. Fit loosely into the pie plate. Trim the edge with scissors, leaving a 1-inch overhang. Roll the edges of the dough under, forming a wall around the outer rim of the pie plate. Flute the edges (see pages 363–364). Chill the pastry while preparing the filling.

3. Blend the eggs and cream in a medium bowl. Combine the granulated and brown sugars, flour, and salt. Stir the flour mixture into the eggs along with the corn syrup and 3 tablespoons of the melted butter. *Do not overmix.* Blend in the vanilla, and bourbon if using.

4. Pour the mixture into the pastry shell. Sprinkle the pecans over the top, then drizzle with the remaining 2 tablespoons melted butter.

5. To prevent the edge of the pie crust from burning, make aluminum foil bands: Cut two 3-inch strips of 18-inch heavy-duty aluminum foil. Fold 1 inch of each strip to the center, making a double thickness of foil. Mold the foil around the edge of the pie, keeping the double fold on top of the dough. Be careful not to crush the edge of the pastry. Secure the bands with tape.

6. Make an aluminum foil drip pan to place on the rack below the pie halfway through the baking: Cut an 18-inch square of heavy-duty aluminum foil. Fold each edge twice (about 1 inch per fold) standing the folded edges upright to form a 4-sided pan.

7. Bake the pie for 75 to 90 minutes. (Halfway through baking, place the drip pan on the rack below.) Remove the foil bands during the last 10 minutes of baking. If the top is browning too quickly, lay a piece of aluminum foil loosely over the surface. The pie is done when the bottom crust is golden brown. The center of the pie should quiver slightly when the pie is moved. It will firm as it cools. The pie should stand at least 3 hours before cutting. Serve slightly warm with bourbon-flavored whipped cream or vanilla ice cream.

STORAGE: Refrigerate, covered with aluminum foil, for up to 3 days. This pie can be frozen.

Chocolate Pecan Pie

Blend 6 tablespoons of strained nonalkaline cocoa powder, such as Hershey's, into the egg mixture. Reduce the vanilla to 1 teaspoon and increase the bourbon to 2 tablespoons.

lemon meringue pie

MAKES 6 TO 8 SERVINGS

This is a pie that I made for my children, Frank and Pam, when they were growing up. It was their favorite then, and still is today. The pastry remains dry and flaky, the sweet and tart lemon filling will cut like a charm, and the velvety meringue will not weep. The pie is impossible to resist, especially when freshly made. It's a slice of heaven!

FILLING

1¼ cups granulated sugar

6 tablespoons cornstarch

¼ teaspoon salt

1½ cups cold water

5 large egg yolks

2 tablespoons unsalted butter

1 tablespoon grated lemon zest

⅓ cup fresh lemon juice

MERINGUE

7 tablespoons sugar, preferably superfine

3 tablespoons strained confectioners' sugar

Pinch of salt

5 large egg whites, at room temperature

½ teaspoon cream of tartar

½ teaspoon pure vanilla extract

3 gingersnaps, finely crushed

½ recipe Flaky Pie Pastry, rolled out, fitted into the pie plate, and baked (page 152)

AT A GLANCE

PAN: 9-inch ovenproof glass pie plate

PAN PREP: Buttered

RACK LEVEL: Lower third

PASTRY PREP: Baked

OVEN TEMP: 325°F

BAKING TIME: 15–18 minutes

DIFFICULTY: 2

MAKE THE FILLING

1. Combine the granulated sugar, cornstarch, and salt in a medium, heavy, nonreactive saucepan. Stir in about ¼ cup of the water, mixing until smooth. Blend in the remaining water.

2. Cook over medium-low heat, stirring constantly, until the mixture comes to a boil, 4 to 5 minutes. Reduce the heat to low and cook for 1 minute longer, stirring occasionally to prevent scorching on the bottom of the pan.

3. Lightly beat the eggs yolks in a small bowl. Off the heat, stir a small amount of filling into the egg yolks to temper, or warm, them. Pour the yolk mixture into the pot. Gently mix with a whisk.

4. Cook the filling over low heat until it comes to a slow boil. Continue to simmer for a minute longer to thicken the filling and cook the yolks. Stir slowly to prevent scorching, but *do not overmix*. Remove the pan from the heat, blend in the butter, lemon zest, and juice, and set aside.

5. Position the rack to the lower third of the oven. Heat the oven to 325°F.

MAKE THE MERINGUE

6. Whisk together the superfine and confectioners' sugars and salt in a small bowl until thoroughly combined.

7. In the large bowl of an electric mixer fitted with beaters or the whip attachment, beat the egg whites on medium speed until frothy. Add the cream of tartar and increase the mixer speed to medium-high. Beat the egg whites until they form firm peaks but are not dry. Add the sugar mixture, 1 tablespoon at a time, taking about 1 minute. Add the vanilla and beat the whites until thick and glossy, 30 to 45 seconds longer.

ASSEMBLE AND BAKE THE PIE

8. Sprinkle the gingersnap crumbs over the baked pie shell. Warm the filling briefly over very low heat. Again, *do not overmix*. Immediately pour the filling into the pie shell.

9. With a tablespoon, drop mounds of meringue in a ring around the edge of the filling, then fill in the center. With the back of a tablespoon, spread the meringue to cover the filling *completely*. Swirl the meringue with the back of the tablespoon to form peaks.

10. Bake the pie for 15 to 18 minutes, or until golden brown. Cool the pie on a rack away from drafts to prevent the meringue from weeping. When cool, serve at once, or refrigerate until ready to use.

STORAGE: Refrigerate, loosely covered with an aluminum foil tent, for up to 3 days. *Never* cover with plastic wrap; too much condensation will form under the wrapping. Freezing is not recommended.

Hints for Making "Weep-Proof" Meringue

- It is essential that the baked pie shell have no cracks or holes in it.

- Blend the superfine and confectioners' sugars thoroughly.

- Beat the sugars into the whipped egg whites slowly.

- Spread the meringue onto the filling while the filling is hot.

- Use a large tablespoon to drop mounds of meringue around the outer part of the pie filling first, then cover the center. Gently press down on the meringue to fill in any air pockets.

- Be sure that the filling is *completely* covered. The meringue must touch the edge of the pie crust.

- Cool away from drafts.

the "real" tavern toasted coconut cream pie

MAKES 6 TO 8 SERVINGS

In looking through my recipe files, I came across an index card written in childish script with a recipe for "The Tavern Toasted Coconut Cream Pie." The handwriting was mine. I could not have been more than twelve years old when I wrote it. When I was nine, my family moved from Elizabeth, New Jersey, to Memphis, Tennessee, but my summer vacations were spent visiting our family in the suburbs of Newark, New Jersey.

Desserts were my passion for as long as I can remember. A meal at the Tavern, a landmark restaurant in Newark, was quite a treat, especially since the restaurant was known for its heavenly desserts. At one particular dinner, I asked our waiter if I could have the recipe for my favorite pie, a Bavarian-style coconut cream topped with a thick layer of crunchy toasted coconut. Eager to please the young visitor from down South, he returned from the kitchen with recipe in hand.

Years later, after the restaurant had closed, the Bauman brothers, owners of the Weequahic Diner in Newark, opened the showy Claremont Diner in Verona, New Jersey, and supposedly hired the former pastry chef of the Tavern. Hence, the Claremont Diner became renowned for its desserts, the most popular being, you guessed it, "The Tavern's Coconut Cream Pie." Having tasted the pie in both restaurants, my childhood memories of the original from the Tavern remain the most unforgettable. To this day, I believe this recipe to be the real McCoy.

1½ cups sweetened flaked coconut

1 tablespoon water

1½ teaspoons unflavored gelatin

3 large eggs, separated

½ cup sugar

1 cup hot milk

1 teaspoon pure vanilla extract

1 cup well chilled heavy cream

½ recipe Flaky Pie Pastry, rolled out, fitted into the pie plate, and baked (page 152)

AT A GLANCE

PAN: 9-inch ovenproof glass pie plate

PAN PREP: Buttered

PASTRY PREP: Baked

DIFFICULTY: 1

1. Position the rack in the lower third of the oven. Heat the oven to 325°F.

2. Sprinkle the coconut in a large, shallow baking pan and toast in the oven for 8 to 10 minutes, or until golden brown. Watch carefully. Since the coconut browns around the edges of the pan first, occasionally stir it with a fork. When evenly brown, remove from the oven. The coconut will crisp as it cools.

3. Place the water in a small heatproof container and sprinkle the gelatin over the surface. Let stand 3 to 5 minutes to soften. Do not stir. Place the container in a small skillet filled with ½ inch simmering water. Heat in the water bath (see page 355) until the gelatin is clear and dissolved. Set aside to cool to *tepid.*

4. Put the egg yolks in a large bowl and whisk until light in color. Gradually whisk in the sugar and beat until thickened. Pour about a quarter of the hot milk into the yolks to temper them. Stir in the remaining milk, then pour the mixture into a heavy medium saucepan.

5. Cook over low heat, stirring constantly, until the mixture forms a thin custard the consistency of heavy cream, 3 to 5 minutes. Do *not* boil or it will curdle. Immediately pour the custard into a large, stainless steel bowl. Stir in the dissolved gelatin and the vanilla extract. Set the bowl in a sink filled with 2 inches of ice-cold water. Cool to tepid, stirring frequently to keep the consistency smooth. Do not beat. When the custard begins to gel, remove the bowl from the ice water to prevent the mixture from becoming too firm.

6. In a chilled bowl with chilled beaters or whisk, whip the cream until it forms soft peaks and set aside.

7. Place the egg whites in the large bowl of an electric mixer. Using beaters or whip attachment, whip the whites on medium speed until frothy. Increase speed to medium-high and whip until the whites form soft peaks. *Do not overbeat.*

8. Using a balloon whisk, stir about a third of the whites into the custard. With an oversize rubber spatula, fold in the remaining whites, then immediately fold in the whipped cream.

9. Spoon the filling into the baked pie shell, mounding it in the center. Sprinkle the top with half of the toasted coconut. Refrigerate the pie for at least 4 hours before cutting. When ready to serve, garnish with the remaining toasted coconut.

STORAGE: Refrigerate, covered loosely with an aluminum foil tent, for up to 3 days. Freezing is not recommended.

banana cream pie with pecan brittle

MAKES 6 TO 8 SERVINGS

This sophisticated banana cream pie features rum-flavored pastry cream that's topped with mirror-like bits of crunchy, caramelized pecans. If you prefer a more traditional banana cream pie, omit the rum, the rum extract, and the caramelized pecans.

2½ cups milk

½ cup granulated sugar, divided

4 large egg yolks

3 tablespoons unsifted all-purpose flour

2 tablespoons cornstarch

¼ teaspoon salt

2 tablespoons dark Jamaican rum

1½ teaspoons pure vanilla extract

1 to 1½ teaspoons rum extract

1 tablespoon unsalted butter, softened

½ recipe Flaky Pie Pastry, rolled out, fitted into the pie plate, and baked (page 152)

2 to 3 firm, ripe medium bananas

2 teaspoons fresh lemon juice

GARNISH

¾ cup well chilled heavy cream

1 tablespoon strained confectioners' sugar

¼ teaspoon pure vanilla extract

Nut Brittle, made with pecans, coarsely chopped

AT A GLANCE

PAN: 9-inch ovenproof glass pie plate

PAN PREP: Buttered

PASTRY PREP: Baked

DIFFICULTY: 2

1. Place the milk and ¼ cup of the granulated sugar in a large saucepan and stir to blend. Cook over low heat without stirring until the mixture is just under the boil or until a skin forms on the surface. Remove from the heat and set aside.

2. Beat the yolks in a large bowl with a hand mixer or whisk until light in color, about 1 minute. Add the remaining ¼ cup sugar, 1 tablespoon at a time, and beat until thick and very light. Combine the flour, cornstarch, and salt, and stir into the yolk mixture.

3. Temper the yolk mixture by adding one-quarter of the hot milk mixture and stirring well to blend. Pour the yolk mixture back into the saucepan and, using a whisk, blend the mixtures.

4. Bring to a boil over low heat, stirring constantly with a whisk. As it begins to thicken, stir more vigorously until smooth. Be sure to reach into the bend of the saucepan. After it reaches the boil, continue to cook the pastry cream for about 1 minute, stirring gently to prevent the cream from scorching. Do not overmix.

5. Remove the filling from the heat. Stir in the rum and vanilla and rum extracts. Dot the top of the filling with the butter and set aside to cool until tepid.

6. Cut the bananas in ¼-inch slices, and drizzle with lemon juice. Gently fold them into the pastry cream. Fill the baked pie shell and smooth the top as best you can with the back of a large tablespoon. Refrigerate the pie at least 4 hours before serving.

7. In a chilled bowl with chilled beaters, whip the cream, confectioners' sugar, and vanilla on medium speed until the cream is thick. Empty the cream into a 16-inch pastry bag fitted with a #824 large, open-star tip. Pipe the cream in a lattice design. When ready to serve, sprinkle the top with the chopped brittle. This pie is best eaten the day it is made.

STORAGE: Refrigerate, covered with aluminum foil, for up to 1 day. Freezing is not recommended.

nut brittle

MAKES ABOUT ½ CUP

Caramelized nuts create a delightful contrast in textures and flavors when used to garnish fruit tarts or creamy pie and tart fillings. Use skinned hazelnuts, pecans, walnuts, sliced almonds (with or without the skin), and skinned peanuts. Be sure to sprinkle them on just before serving to retain their appealing crunch.

¼ cup superfine sugar
1 tablespoons water

⅓ cup nuts

1. Butter a 15-inch sheet of heavy-duty aluminum foil. Butter a metal tablespoon to stir the nuts into the caramel. Set aside.

2. Place the sugar and water in a small, heavy saucepan. Cover the pot and cook over low heat. Before it reaches the boiling point, check the bottom of the pot to be sure all of the sugar has dissolved. If not, *gently stir* the mixture, but *do not stir after the boil.*

3. Uncover the pot and continue to cook the sugar syrup. Brush the side of the saucepan occasionally with a pastry brush dipped in water to remove any sugar crystals that may be clinging to the side. Cook until the syrup begins to caramelize. This can take anywhere from 10 to 30 minutes, depending on the thickness of the pot and the quantity you are cooking. As the syrup changes color, to ensure even browning, tilt the pot and move it in a gentle swirling motion. *When making caramel, always use extreme caution as the syrup can cause serious bums.*

4. Add the nuts (whole or broken) and stir quickly with the buttered spoon to coat with the caramel. Immediately spread the mixture onto the buttered aluminum foil. Let the nuts stand at room temperature until hardened. This will take only a few minutes.

5. When the caramelized nuts are hard, place them on a cutting board and coarsely chop with a chef's knife. Chop only what you need.

STORAGE: Store in an airtight container in a cool place. Nut brittle can be kept for up to 4 to 6 months, provided it is not stored in a humid environment.

fruity viennese linzer tart

MAKES 8 TO 10 SERVINGS

My recipe for this Middle European specialty has long been a favorite with my students. What made this tart such a hit was the filling of cooked frozen raspberries mixed with raspberry preserves. It is more fruity and less sweet than the classic jam-filled Linzer torte.

The crumbly texture of the crust comes from sieved hard-boiled egg yolks and lots of ground nuts. Be sure to use unblanched nuts. The skin imparts a rich nutty taste. Because the dough is fragile, it is best to form the lattice top by shaping balls of pastry into ropes with your hands. Balls of dough are also used to trim the edge of the pan. The dough will spread during baking, creating an eye-appealing top.

FILLING

1 (10-ounce) package frozen unsweetened raspberries

1/3 cup granulated sugar

About 1/3 cup raspberry preserves

1/2 teaspoon fresh lemon juice

PASTRY

1 cup unblanched almonds

1/2 cup unblanched hazelnuts

1 1/2 cups unsifted all-purpose flour

1/4 teaspoon salt

3/4 teaspoon ground cinnamon

1/8 teaspoon ground cloves

1 cup (2 sticks) unsalted butter, at room temperature

1/2 teaspoon grated lemon zest

2/3 cup granulated sugar

2 hard-boiled large egg yolks

1 large egg

1 teaspoon fresh lemon juice

1 tablespoon confectioners' sugar, for garnish

AT A GLANCE

PAN: 10-inch extra-deep metal tart pan with removable bottom

PAN PREP: Buttered

RACK LEVEL: Lower third

OVEN TEMP: 350°F

BAKING TIME: 45–50 minutes

DIFFICULTY: 3

MAKE THE FILLING

1. Place the frozen raspberries and granulated sugar in a small, heavy saucepan. Bring to a slow boil over medium-low heat. Reduce the heat and simmer for 15 to 20 minutes, or until most of the liquid has evaporated. *Watch carefully* to avoid burning. Empty the raspberries into a liquid measuring cup. You should have about 1 cup. Add enough preserves to equal 1 1/3 cups. Stir in the lemon juice. Set aside to cool.

MAKE THE PASTRY

2. Place the almonds, hazelnuts, and 1/2 cup of the flour in the bowl of a food processor fitted with the steel blade. Process until the mixture resembles very fine meal. Add the remaining flour, the salt, cinnamon, and cloves. Pulse until well blended. Set aside.

3. Fit an electric mixer with the paddle attachment and blend the butter, lemon zest, and sugar on low speed. Sieve the yolks through a strainer and add to the butter mixture along with $\frac{1}{2}$ cup of the nut-flour mixture. Lightly beat together the egg and lemon juice and add to the butter mixture. Blend in remaining nut-flour mixture, forming a soft dough. *Do not overmix.*

4. Butter the tart pan. With floured hands, press slightly more than half of the dough into the bottom of the tart pan. Chill while preparing the balls for the lattice top.

5. Make 10 graduated balls for the lattice from the remaining dough. The first two should be the size of large walnuts, the next four should be slightly smaller, and the final four should be a bit smaller still. The rest of the pastry will be used to complete the edge. Chill the dough balls and remaining pastry for 10 to 15 minutes, or until firm enough to handle without sticking to your hands.

ASSEMBLE AND BAKE THE TART

6. Position the rack in the lower third of the oven. Heat the oven to 350°F.

7. Spread the raspberry filling on the tart shell, leaving a $\frac{1}{2}$-inch border of dough. Take one of the largest balls of dough and roll it back and forth on a lightly floured surface with floured hands to form a rope approximately 10 inches long. Position the rope down the center of the pan. Make two 9-inch ropes using two medium balls of dough. Position them to the left and right of the center rope, approximately $1\frac{1}{4}$ inches apart. Make two 8-inch ropes from the smallest balls of pastry. Position them $1\frac{1}{4}$ inches to the left and right of the medium length ropes.

8. Rotate the pan about an eighth of a turn and, starting at the center, repeat with the remaining balls of dough, forming a lattice.

9. Shape 32 balls from the remaining dough. Place each ball into a groove in the pan. There will be 32 grooves. Bake the tart for 45 to 50 minutes, or until golden brown. Cool at least 4 hours before cutting. Dust the edge with confectioners' sugar before serving.

STORAGE: Refrigerate, loosely covered with a sheet of wax paper then aluminum foil, for up to 5 days. Warm briefly before serving. This tart can be frozen.

fluted cream cheese flan with fresh berries

MAKES 8 TO 10 SERVINGS

Here is an upside-down, crustless cheese tart that resembles a flan. The filling is made with a combination of cream cheese and crème fraîche, a thick, slightly cultured heavy cream available in some gourmet shops and upscale supermarkets. The moist, velvety texture comes from baking the tart in a water bath. Be careful not to overbeat the filling, as too much air may cause it to crack during baking.

When I'm ready to serve the flan, I mound lots of fresh berries in the center and top them with raspberry coulis. I like the sauce to drip down the scalloped edge of the tart. The presentation is gorgeous, and it's sheer heaven to eat.

---

1 pound cream cheese, at room temperature

²/₃ cup superfine sugar

4 large eggs, separated

²/₃ cup crème fraîche (or ¹/₃ cup heavy cream plus ¹/₃ cup sour cream)

1 teaspoon pure vanilla extract

3 to 4 cups mixed berries, washed and thoroughly dried (see page 357)

Raspberry Coulis

A few fresh mint leaves, for garnish

AT A GLANCE

PAN: Deep 10-inch metal tart pan, or deep 9½-inch ovenproof glass pie plate

PAN PREP: Generously buttered and lined with buttered parchment

RACK LEVEL: Lower third

OVEN TEMP: 325°F

BAKING TIME: 45–50 minutes

DIFFICULTY: 1

1. Position the rack in the lower third of the oven. Heat the oven to 325°F. Generously butter the tart pan or pie plate and line the bottom with baking parchment. Butter the parchment. Have some boiling water ready in a tea kettle.

2. Place the cream cheese and sugar in the large bowl of an electric mixer fitted with the paddle attachment. Cream the cheese and sugar on low speed until light. Blend in the egg yolks, two at a time. Add the crème fraîche and vanilla, mixing just until smooth. Empty the batter into a large bowl.

3. In a separate, clean bowl, whip the egg whites until they stand in firm peaks. Fold the whites into the cheese mixture. Pour the batter into the pan.

4. Set the pan on an 18-inch square of aluminum foil. Trim the corners of the foil with scissors, then mold the foil around the pan. Be careful not to tear the foil. Set the tart pan into a roasting pan about 2½ inches deep. Place both in the oven. Fill the roasting pan with 1 inch of boiling water.

5. Bake the tart for 45 to 50 minutes, or until set around the edges. It is OK if it is somewhat soft in the center. It will firm as it cools. Turn the oven off. Wedge a wooden spoon handle in the door of the oven and then close the door. This will allow some of the hot air to escape and let the tart cool down slowly.

6. After 1 hour, remove the tart from the oven and set on a rack to cool further. When it is completely cool, invert it onto a serving plate. Shake gently to release it from the pan (see Note). Peel off the parchment. If necessary, smooth the top with an offset spatula dipped in hot water. Cover with plastic wrap and refrigerate until ready to serve. This tart can be made up to 4 days ahead.

7. When ready to serve, mound the berries in the center of the tart, leaving a 1½-inch border. Spoon the raspberry coulis at random over the berries. Garnish with mint leaves and serve at once.

STORAGE: Refrigerate, covered with wax paper then aluminum foil, for up to 1 day. This tart can be frozen, without the berries and coulis.

NOTE: If the tart is difficult to release from the pan, mold a piece of heavy-duty aluminum foil tightly around the bottom of the pan, then place it in a sink filled with 1 inch of warm water for 1 to 2 minutes and try again. Repeat if necessary.

raspberry coulis

MAKES 1 CUP

2 tablespoons water

¼ cup sugar

1 tablespoon light corn syrup

12-ounce package frozen unsweetened raspberries, thawed

1 tablespoon framboise liqueur or kirschwasser, or to taste

1 teaspoon fresh lemon juice

1. Place the water, sugar, and syrup in a heavy, medium saucepan. Cover and bring to a slow boil. When the sugar is dissolved, add the raspberries, reduce the heat, and simmer, uncovered, for 2 to 3 minutes.

2. Puree the mixture in a blender or food processor until very smooth. Using a rubber spatula, press the puree through a fine-mesh strainer, pushing as much pulp as possible through the sieve. Discard the seeds.

3. Add the framboise and lemon juice, cover, and refrigerate until 30 minutes before using.

STORAGE: Refrigerate in a tightly covered container for up to 3 days.

easy does it yeasted coffee cakes

two master doughs

cinnamon buns

crumb buns

swedish tea ring

holiday stollen

rustic cinnamon walnut horns

scalloped chocolate pecan strip

sticky buns

apple and dried-cranberry coffee cake

golden raisin poppy seed twist

dimpled sugar cake

two master doughs

You will find the following two yeasted sweet dough recipes a cinch to prepare. The directions are written for both stand mixer and hand methods. Making the dough takes less time than you think, especially if you use a stand mixer with a paddle attachment. Preparing the dough by hand can give equally marvelous results; however, the amount of flour must be increased slightly.

The recipes for Simple Sweet Dough (below) and Rich Sour Cream Dough (page 184) are interchangeable and both produce excellent pastries; the only difference is that the latter is richer. Both dough recipes require overnight refrigeration because they are enriched with butter and eggs and are too soft to handle when freshly made. After the dough is chilled, it is easy to handle and a snap to roll and shape.

When you cube the butter, lay the butter on the open wrapper. Using a dough scraper or thin, sharp knife, halve the butter lengthwise, give it a quarter turn and cut it again lengthwise, forming four "sticks." Then cut across the sticks, making ½-inch cubes.

If the recipe you are preparing uses only half of the dough, prepare the full master recipe. This gives you the opportunity to make more than one variety, or to freeze half for later use (see Freezing Yeasted Doughs, page 185).

simple sweet dough

**MAKES 2 POUNDS DOUGH, ENOUGH FOR 1 LARGE OR 2 MEDIUM COFFEE CAKES,
OR 2 TO 3 DOZEN INDIVIDUAL COFFEE CAKES**

4 tablespoons sugar, divided

¼ cup warm water (110° to 115°F)

1 package active dry yeast

3 cups unbleached all-purpose flour, spooned in and leveled (plus ¼ cup for Hand Method)

1 teaspoon salt

1 cup (2 sticks) unsalted butter, cut into ½-inch cubes (see Two Master Doughs, above), plus 1 teaspoon soft butter for brushing top of dough

½ cup milk

3 large egg yolks

1 teaspoon pure vanilla extract

1. Rinse a small bowl in hot water to warm it. Add 1 tablespoon of the sugar and the warm water to the bowl. Sprinkle the yeast over the water. *Do not stir.* Cover the bowl with a saucer and let the mixture stand for 5 minutes. Stir it briefly with a fork, cover again, and let it stand for 2 to 3 minutes more, or until bubbly. (See Working with Yeast, page 197.)

STAND MIXER METHOD

2. In the bowl of an electric mixer fitted with the paddle attachment, mix on low speed the 3 cups of flour, remaining 3 tablespoons of sugar, and the salt. Add the *slightly* firm cubed butter and continue to mix until meal-size crumbs form, 2 to 4 minutes, depending upon the temperature of the butter. Stop the mixer.

3. Using a fork, in a separate bowl, mix the milk, egg yolks, and vanilla. Add the milk mixture to the flour, along with the dissolved yeast, and mix on low speed for about 15 seconds. Stop the mixer and scrape down the side of the bowl with a rubber spatula. Mix on low speed for another 30 seconds, or until a smooth dough is formed. *Note:* This is a soft dough. Continue to step 4 below.

HAND METHOD

2. In a large mixing bowl, whisk together the 3 cups of flour, remaining 3 tablespoons of sugar, and the salt. Add the *soft* cubed butter, and using a pastry blender or your fingertips, work in the butter until the mixture resembles fine meal.

3. Make a well in the center. Using a fork, blend together in a small bowl the milk, egg yolks, and vanilla. Pour the milk mixture into the well and add the dissolved yeast. With a wooden spoon, gradually work the crumbs into the liquids, mixing until all the crumbs are incorporated and a rough dough is formed. Sprinkle the work surface with about 2 tablespoons of the remaining flour. Turn the dough onto the floured surface and knead lightly, adding the remaining 2 tablespoons of flour, kneading until smooth. *Note:* This is a soft dough. Continue to step 4 below.

4. Lightly butter a medium bowl for storing the dough. Empty the dough into the prepared bowl, smoothing the top with lightly floured hands. Spread a thin layer of softened butter over the top. Cover tightly with plastic wrap and refrigerate overnight.

STORAGE: Refrigerate, tightly covered with plastic wrap, for up to 3 days. For longer storage, see Freezing Yeasted Doughs, page 185.

rich sour cream dough

**MAKES 2 POUNDS DOUGH, ENOUGH FOR 1 LARGE OR 2 MEDIUM COFFEE CAKES,
OR 2 TO 3 DOZEN INDIVIDUAL COFFEE CAKES**

4 tablespoons sugar, divided

¼ cup warm water (110° to 115°F)

1 package active dry yeast

3 cups unbleached all-purpose flour, spooned in and leveled (plus ¼ cup for Hand Method)

1 teaspoon salt

¾ cup (1½ sticks) unsalted butter, cut into ½-inch cubes (see Two Master Doughs, page 182), plus 1 teaspoon soft butter for brushing top of dough

2 large eggs

½ cup sour cream

1 teaspoon pure vanilla extract

1. Rinse a small bowl in hot water to warm it. Add 1 tablespoon of the sugar and the warm water to the bowl. Sprinkle the yeast over the water. *Do not stir.* Cover the bowl with a saucer and let the mixture stand for 5 minutes. Stir it briefly with a fork, cover again, and let it stand for 2 to 3 minutes, or until bubbly. (See Working with Yeast, page 197.)

STAND MIXER METHOD

2. In the bowl of an electric mixer fitted with the paddle attachment, mix on low speed the 3 cups of flour, remaining 3 tablespoons of sugar, and the salt. Add the *slightly* firm butter and continue to mix until meal-size crumbs form, 2 to 4 minutes, depending upon the temperature of the butter. Stop the mixer.

3. Using a fork, in a large bowl, mix the eggs, sour cream, and vanilla. Add the sour cream mixture to the flour, along with the dissolved yeast, and mix on low speed until a rough dough is formed. *Note:* This is a soft dough. Continue to step 4 on the opposite page.

HAND METHOD

2. In a large mixing bowl, whisk together the 3 cups of flour, remaining 3 tablespoons of sugar, and the salt. Add the *soft* cubed butter, and using a pastry blender or your fingertips, work in the butter until the mixture resembles fine meal.

3. Make a well in the center. Using a fork, blend together in a small bowl the eggs, sour cream, and vanilla. Pour the sour cream mixture into the well and add the dissolved yeast. With a wooden spoon, gradually work the crumbs into the liquids, mixing until all the crumbs are incorporated and a rough dough is formed. Sprinkle the work surface with about 2 tablespoons of the remaining flour. Turn the dough onto the floured surface, add the remaining 2 tablespoons of flour, and knead until smooth. *Note:* This is a soft dough. Continue to step 4 on the opposite page.

4. Lightly butter a medium bowl for storing the dough. Turn the dough into the prepared bowl, smoothing the top with lightly floured hands. Brush the top lightly with the soft butter. Cover tightly with plastic wrap and refrigerate overnight.

STORAGE: Refrigerate, tightly covered with plastic wrap, for up to 3 days. For longer storage, see Freezing Yeasted Doughs, below.

Freezing Yeasted Doughs

The yeasted dough recipes in this book freeze extremely well because of their richness. This is of great benefit when you wish to prepare dough to be kept on hand for later use. The dough can either be frozen without shaping, or shaped and frozen, ready for baking.

When dough is to be frozen, it is essential that it have its first rise before freezing. The first rise, though not always significant, takes place under refrigeration. After the first rise, the dough must be deflated to eliminate the air. Then it is ready for freezing.

To prepare the dough for freezing, always divide it beforehand so you can use smaller pieces as needed. Cut the dough into halves or thirds, or according to the recipe you anticipate making. Cover each piece tightly in plastic wrap, date it, and place in plastic bags. Be sure to squeeze out the excess air, then secure the bag well. The dough can be frozen for at least 3 months, depending upon the temperature of your freezer; zero degrees or below is optimum.

When ready for use, if the dough has been frozen without shaping, it should be placed in the refrigerator to thaw slowly overnight. If the dough has already been shaped, remove it from the freezer and let it thaw at room temperature. After thawing, refer to each individual recipe for the amount of time the dough should rise.

cinnamon buns

MAKES 9 BUNS

Get ready for Sunday morning breakfast with these scrumptious cinnamon buns. With the sweet scent of cinnamon swirling through the house, these buns are sure to awaken even the deepest of sleepers. Children and adults alike will dash to the kitchen to devour the buns.

½ recipe (about 1 pound) Simple Sweet Dough (page 182) or Rich Sour Cream Dough (page 184)

3 tablespoons unsalted butter, softened

3 tablespoons granulated sugar

3 tablespoons firmly packed dark brown sugar

2 tablespoons Lyle's Golden Syrup (see page 352) or light corn syrup

1 tablespoon ground cinnamon

⅛ teaspoon salt

1 large egg lightly beaten with 1 teaspoon water, for egg wash

1 small recipe Vanilla Glaze (page 368; optional)

AT A GLANCE

PAN: 8- × 8- × 2-inch square baking pan

PAN PREP: Buttered generously and lined with baking parchment

RISING TIME: 45–60 minutes

RACK LEVEL: Center

OVEN TEMP: 350°F

BAKING TIME: 30–35 minutes

DIFFICULTY: 1

1. Remove the dough from the refrigerator 1 to 1½ hours before using.

2. Generously butter the pan. Line the bottom with parchment. Set aside.

3. In a medium bowl, using a wooden spoon, mix the butter, granulated and brown sugars, syrup, cinnamon, and salt until smooth.

4. Place the dough on a lightly floured surface. Gently knead six or eight times to coat with flour. Pat or shape the dough into a rectangle. Roll the dough into a 9- × 12-inch rectangle with a 9-inch side parallel to the edge of the counter.

5. Spoon dollops of the cinnamon filling evenly across the dough, making three rows across and three rows down. Using a small, offset metal spatula, spread the filling evenly across the dough, leaving a 1½-inch border on the far edge. Lightly brush the border with the egg wash. Starting at the side of the rectangle closest to you, roll the dough tightly. Pinch the seam well to seal the flap. Roll the log back and forth a few times to seal the layers. With your hands, gently stretch the log until it measures about 12 inches.

6. Cut the log into nine 1¼-inch pieces, and place them cut side up in the baking pan, spacing them evenly, three rows across and three rows down. Press the tops of the buns gently to even the surface.

7. Cover the pan with a tea towel and set it in a warmish place to allow the buns to rise until puffy and almost doubled, 45 to 60 minutes.

8. Fifteen minutes before baking, position the rack in the center of the oven. Heat the oven to 350°F.

9. Gently brush the tops of the buns with the egg wash. Bake for 30 to 35 minutes, or until golden brown. If the buns are browning too quickly, lay a sheet of aluminum foil over the top to allow the center of the buns to bake through. Remove the buns from the oven and allow them to sit for 15 minutes. While the buns are cooling, make the glaze.

10. To remove the buns from the pan, cover it with a cooling rack, invert the buns and carefully lift off the pan. Remove the parchment, then cover the buns with another rack and turn the buns top side up. If the buns have risen unevenly while baking, gently press the tops to level them. While the buns are still warm, drizzle the glaze over the top by dipping a small whisk or fork into the icing and waving it rapidly back and forth over the surface of the buns.

STORAGE: Store at room temperature, tightly wrapped in aluminum foil, for up to 3 days. Heat before serving. These buns may be frozen (see Refreshing Yeasted Coffee Cakes, page 193).

crumb buns

MAKES 9 BUNS

If you are addicted to streusel toppings as much as I am, try your hand at these irresistible crumb buns. These classic buns, with their thick crown of melt-in-your-mouth crumbs, are always a crowd pleaser. I have yet to see anyone resist plucking away at the crunchy crumbs.

½ recipe (about 1 pound) Simple Sweet Dough (page 182) or Rich Sour Cream Dough (page 184)

Carole's Favorite Streusel (small recipe)

1 large egg lightly beaten with 1 teaspoon water, for egg wash

Confectioners' sugar, for dusting

AT A GLANCE

PAN: 9 × 9 × 2-inch square pan

PAN PREP: Generously buttered

RISING TIME: 45 minutes

RACK LEVEL: Lower third

OVEN TEMP: 350°F

BAKING TIME: 30–35 minutes

DIFFICULTY: 1

1. Remove the dough from the refrigerator 1 to 1½ hours before shaping.

2. Generously butter the pan. On a lightly floured surface, knead the dough gently six to eight times, or until smooth, then pat it into a square. Using a dough scraper or a sharp knife, divide the dough evenly into nine pieces. Cupping your hand over each piece, roll the dough on a barely floured surface, continuously rotating it until it forms a ball.

3. Arrange the balls in the pan, placing three pieces across and three pieces down. Be sure to space them evenly. Flatten the balls slightly until they are about ¼ inch apart; they do not have to touch. Cover the pan with a tea towel and set in a warmish place to rise for 45 minutes, or until the balls begin to touch each other. While the buns are rising, prepare the streusel.

4. Fifteen minutes before baking, position the rack in the lower third of the oven. Heat the oven to 350°F.

5. Gently brush the tops of the buns with the egg wash. Sprinkle the crumb mixture heavily over the dough. Press the streusel slightly into the dough. Bake for 30 to 35 minutes, or until the streusel is lightly browned. Remove from the oven and place on a rack to cool. To remove the buns from the pan, place a 12-inch piece of aluminum foil on top of the pan, cupping it around the side to hold the streusel in place. Cover with a cooling rack, invert, and carefully lift off the pan. Cover with another rack, invert again, remove the aluminum foil, and cool right side up. When the buns are almost cool, dust the tops heavily with confectioners' sugar. Reheat before serving. Break apart when ready to serve.

STORAGE: Store at room temperature, tightly wrapped in aluminum foil, for up to 3 days. These buns may be frozen (see Refreshing Yeasted Coffee Cakes, page 193).

SHAVED CHOCOLATE AND PISTACHIO BISCOTTI AND JEWELED ALMOND BISCOTTI

FLUTED CREAM CHEESE FLAN WITH FRESH BERRIES

BANANA CREAM PIE WITH PECAN BRITTLE

COCONUT LEMON-LIME TASSIES

PEANUT BUTTER BALLS

FAVORITE LEMON SQUARES

ALMONDATES

FRENCH LACE WHAT-NOTS

CRUMB BUNS

GRANDMA JENNIE'S DATE AND NUT BREAD

SOUTHERN PECAN PIE

SCALLOPED CHOCOLATE PECAN STRIP

SNOW-CAPPED CHOCOLATE CREAM CAKE

MAJESTIC MANDARIN CAKE

CLASSIC SOUR CREAM CINNAMON AND NUT COFFEE CAKE

CARROT HONEY CAKE

LEMON MERINGUE PIE

BOSTON CREAM PIE

PEPPERMINT CLOUD

ZUCCHINI LOAF WITH APRICOTS AND DATES

CHOCOLATE MARBLE CHEESECAKE

CRISPY GINGERSNAPS

POPPY SEED THUMBPRINTS

CHOCOLATE SNOWCAPS

OLD-FASHIONED BUTTERMILK BISCUITS

FAVORITE VANILLA MUFFINS

JEFF'S CHOCOLATE-GLAZED MIDNIGHT MUFFINS

ULTRA-RICH CORN MUFFINS

THREE BERRY CRISP WITH BUTTER-NUT CRUMB TOPPING

FRUIT AND NUT APPLESAUCE CAKE

PINEAPPLE UPSIDE-DOWN CAKE

FLORENTINES

MINNA'S APRICOT SQUARES

CRACKLY CINNAMON WAFERS

PIGNOLI LEMON CAKE

ROCKY ROAD GARGANCHEWAS

RUSTIC CINNAMON WALNUT HORNS

SESAME COINS

LEMON POPPY SEED SHORTBREAD

CHOCOLATE SHORTBREAD NUGGETS

COCONUT LAYER CAKE

STICKY BUNS

SOUR CREAM MARBLE CAKE

COCONUT-CRUSTED KEY LIME NAPOLEONS

ZACH'S CHOCOLATE COCONUT DEVILS

**CAROLE'S REALLY GREAT
CHOCOLATE CHIP COOKIES**

CAROLE'S BEST BROWNIES

BLUEBERRY CRUMB PIE WITH WARM BLUEBERRY SAUCE

carole's favorite streusel

MAKES ENOUGH FOR ONE 8-INCH SQUARE OR 9-INCH ROUND COFFEE CAKE, OR 12 MUFFINS

This has been my tried-and-true streusel recipe for as long as I can remember. The key here is to melt the butter, but only to the point where it does not overheat. Once the butter has cooled to tepid, the remaining ingredients are added. If the crumb mixture appears to be too dry or too crumbly, add a bit more butter.

Making the streusel in the same pot in which the butter was melted is very convenient. If the crumb mixture requires additional butter, push some of the crumbs aside and place the butter in the cleared spot. Place the saucepan on low heat, positioning it so that the butter is over the heat.

SMALL RECIPE

6 to 7 tablespoons unsalted butter

1 cup all-purpose flour, spooned in and leveled

½ cup sugar

½ teaspoon ground cinnamon

¼ teaspoon baking powder

¼ teaspoon salt

3 tablespoons finely chopped walnuts or pecans (see page 356; optional)

LARGE RECIPE

⅔ cup (10⅔ tablespoons) unsalted butter

1½ cups all-purpose flour, spooned in and leveled

¾ cup sugar

¾ teaspoon ground cinnamon

½ teaspoon baking powder

scant ½ teaspoon salt

¼ cup finely chopped walnuts or pecans (see page 356, optional)

1. Place the butter in a 2-quart heavy-bottomed saucepan for small recipe or 3-quart for large recipe and heat until almost melted; remove from the heat and *cool to tepid*.

2. Whisk together the flour, sugar, cinnamon, baking powder, salt, and nuts if using. Add to the butter and stir with a fork until blended and mixture begins to form crumbs. Gently squeeze the mixture with your hand to form larger lumps, then break them apart with your fingertips. Before using, let the streusel stand for 10 to 15 minutes.

swedish tea ring

MAKES ONE 11- TO 12-INCH TEA RING, 8 TO 10 SERVINGS

When I made this tea ring during my teenage years, this was my favorite way to shape the dough. The cake, filled with brown and white sugars, cinnamon, nuts, and sometimes raisins, was rolled into a log and then shaped into a ring on a cookie sheet. With a simple snip of the scissors, the ring was cut at intervals. The slices were turned on their side to form a ring of "petals." After baking, a drizzle of vanilla glaze gives just the right finishing touch. This beautiful coffee cake promises to be a hit every time you serve it.

¼ cup granulated sugar

¼ cup light brown sugar

1 teaspoon ground cinnamon

½ recipe (about 1 pound) Simple Sweet Dough (page 182) or Rich Sour Cream Dough (page 184), cold

1 large egg white lightly beaten with 1 teaspoon water, for egg wash

¾ cup medium-finely chopped toasted pecans (see page 356)

½ cup golden raisins, plumped (see page 358; optional)

1 small recipe Vanilla Glaze (page 368)

AT A GLANCE

PAN: Large cookie sheet

PAN PREP: Baking parchment

RISING TIME: 45–60 minutes

RACK LEVEL: Lower third

OVEN TEMP: 350°F

BAKING TIME: 25–28 minutes

DIFFICULTY: 1

1. In a small bowl, combine the granulated and brown sugars and cinnamon. Set aside.

2. Butter the corners of a large cookie sheet to secure the baking parchment, then line the pan with the parchment.

3. On a lightly floured surface, knead the *cold* dough gently six to eight times. Roll the dough into a 9- × 16-inch rectangle with the 16-inch side parallel to the edge of the counter. Brush the dough with the egg wash. Sprinkle the top with the sugar/cinnamon mixture, leaving a 1-inch border on the far side. Scatter the chopped nuts and raisins, if using, over the dough and gently pat them into the surface.

4. Beginning at the side of the rectangle closest to you, roll the dough tightly, jelly roll style, to form a log. As you roll, be sure to square the ends of the log with a dough scraper to even the thickness of the log. Pinch the seam, sealing it well and gently roll the log back and forth, elongating the log until it measures 16 to 18 inches.

5. Place the log *seam side down* on the cookie sheet and form it into a circle, 7 to 8 inches round. To make the ring, brush one of the ends with the egg wash and seal it to the opposite end by pinching them together. Invert a 4½-inch (8-ounce) heatproof custard cup, with 1 inch of the outer rim buttered, into the center of the ring. This will help to keep the shape of the circle. Adjust the shape and flatten the circle slightly with the palm of your hand.

6. Using sharp scissors, cut 16 to 18 slits about three-quarters of the way through the dough, spacing them about 1 inch apart. Turn the slices out so the cut portions lay flat against the pan (see illustrations). Cover the ring with a tea towel and set in a warmish place to rise for 45 to 60 minutes, or until puffy and almost doubled.

7. Fifteen minutes before baking, position the rack in the lower third of the oven. Heat the oven to 350°F.

8. Brush the top of the ring with the egg wash and bake for 25 to 28 minutes, or just until golden brown. *Do not overbake.*

9. While the ring is baking, prepare the glaze. Drizzle the glaze over the top of the warm cake by dipping a small whisk or fork into the icing and waving it rapidly back and forth over the surface of the cake.

STORAGE: Store at room temperature, tightly wrapped in aluminum foil, for up to 3 days. This cake may be frozen (see Refreshing Yeasted Coffee Cakes, page 193).

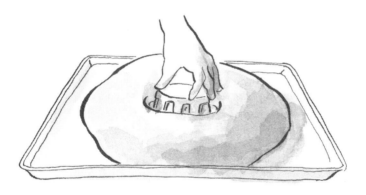

holiday stollen

MAKES TWO 13- TO 14-INCH STOLLEN, 8 TO 10 SERVINGS PER STOLLEN

Stollen, the classic German sweet bread of Dresden, is traditionally served at Christmas and has more than 500 years of history. This bread-like yeast cake is characteristically made with citron and other dried fruits, almonds, and spices. It has a crescent shape with tapered ends; the dough is folded over itself, resembling a giant Parker House roll. A classic stollen is not sweet and the texture is somewhat dry.

My adaptation is a lighter version of this classic pastry. It is made with candied orange and lemon peel along with dried apricots and raisins. While this recipe is not a traditional stollen, the final result is a delicious cake.

1 recipe Simple Sweet Dough (page 182) or Rich Sour Cream Dough (page 184)

½ cup golden raisins, plumped (see page 358)

½ cup dark raisins, plumped (see page 358)

¼ cup dried apricots (not organic), diced into ¼-inch pieces, plumped (see page 358)

¼ cup candied orange peel

¼ cup candied lemon peel

½ cup brandy, such as Courvoisier, Hennessy, St. Rémy Napoleon, or applejack

¾ cup sliced blanched almonds, lightly toasted (see page 356)

6 tablespoons unsalted butter, melted

¼ cup confectioners' sugar, for dusting

AT A GLANCE

PANS: Two 14- × 17-inch cookie sheets

PAN PREP: Baking parchment

RISING TIME: 1 hour

RACK LEVELS: Upper and lower thirds

OVEN TEMP: 375°F

BAKING TIME: 20–25 minutes

DIFFICULTY: 2

1. Remove the dough from the refrigerator 1½ hours before using.

2. Place the plumped raisins and apricots in a 1-quart bowl. Add the candied orange and lemon peels and the brandy, then mix well to distribute the brandy through the fruit. Let macerate for at least 1 hour, mixing occasionally.

3. Drain the excess brandy from the fruit. Transfer the fruit to a double thickness of paper towels. Blot the top of the fruit with more paper towels. Empty into a bowl and set aside.

4. Butter the corners of the cookie sheets to secure the baking parchment, then line the pans with the parchment.

5. Divide the dough in half. On a lightly floured surface, working with half at a time, gently knead in half of the macerated fruits and half of the toasted almonds. Pat the dough into an oval. With a floured rolling pin, roll the dough into a larger 8- × 12-inch oval, keeping the 12-inch side parallel to the edge of the counter. Make a slight depression lengthwise in the center of the 12-inch side with the rolling pin. Fold the dough over, leaving 1 inch of the bottom half exposed, like a huge Parker House roll, patting the top gently.

6. Place the stollen on a cookie sheet and reshape it. Repeat with the second half of dough. Cover the stollen with tea towels and let them rise in a warmish place until puffy and almost doubled, about 1 hour.

7. Fifteen minutes before baking, position the racks in the upper and lower thirds of the oven. Heat the oven to 375°F.

8. Gently brush each stollen with 2 tablespoons of the melted butter. Bake for 20 to 25 minutes, or until golden brown. To ensure even browning, toward the end of baking time, rotate the pans top to bottom and front to back. Remove from the oven and brush the tops with the remaining melted butter. Place the confectioners' sugar in a strainer or sugar shaker and coat the tops of the stollen with half of the sugar. When the stollen are cool, dust again with the remaining sugar.

STORAGE: Store at room temperature, tightly covered with aluminum foil, for up to 3 days. These cakes may be frozen (see Refreshing Yeasted Coffee Cakes below).

Refreshing Yeasted Coffee Cakes

Nothing is as irresistible as the taste of homemade yeasted pastries, warm from the oven with their freshly baked fragrance swirling through the air. Surely these treats are at their best soon after baking. However, because they do not contain preservatives, they will lose their freshness much sooner than store-bought.

To restore their fresh-baked goodness, these types of pastries should be reheated before serving. Whether a whole cake or bread, in an individual serving, it should be *loosely* wrapped in aluminum foil and reheated in a low oven, about 300°F. The amount of time depends upon the size of the pastry; individual pastries should be ready in 6 to 8 minutes, while larger ones can take up to 20 or more minutes. If the pastry was heated while still frozen, allow some extra time (see Freezing Yeasted Doughs, page 185).

To determine when the pastry is ready, lightly press the aluminum foil with your fingertip to test the softness of the pastry. Tear open the foil and bake the pastry for 1 to 2 minutes longer. If it yields easily, the pastry is ready. After removing it from the oven, let the pastry cool, because if eaten too hot, it will be doughy and unpleasant. When tepid, it is ready to be enjoyed—and when it was made will be your best kept secret.

rustic cinnamon walnut horns

MAKES TWENTY 3½- TO 4-INCH HORNS

These rustic crescents differ from a typical yeasted pastry in that they have a somewhat crispy texture. The dough is rolled in a mixture of coarsely chopped walnuts, sugar, and cinnamon. During baking, the sugar caramelizes, leaving an enticing crust. When I tested the recipe, the only difficulty my assistant and I had was that it was impossible to stop eating the horns. As we broke off a piece or two to sample, before we knew it they were devoured.

Take note that the walnuts are chopped into two different consistencies. First, the dough is rolled in coarsely chopped walnuts, then it is sprinkled with medium chopped nuts. It's okay if the dough tears when it is rolled in the larger nuts. This adds to the rustic charm of the horns.

1⅔ cups walnuts

5 tablespoons granulated sugar, divided

3 tablespoons light brown sugar

1¼ teaspoons ground cinnamon, divided

½ recipe (about 1 pound) Simple Sweet Dough (page 182) or Rich Sour Cream Dough (page 184), cold

1 large egg lightly beaten with 2 teaspoons water, for egg wash

Confectioners' sugar, for dusting

AT A GLANCE

PANS: Two rimmed cookie sheets

PAN PREP: Baking parchment

RISING TIME: 45–60 minutes

RACK LEVELS: Upper and lower thirds

OVEN TEMP: 350°F

BAKING TIME: 18–20 minutes

DIFFICULTY: 3

1. Place the walnuts in the bowl of a food processor fitted with a steel blade. Pulse five or six times, or until the nuts are coarsely chopped. Remove 1 cup of the walnuts and set aside for rolling. Add 3 tablespoons of the granulated sugar, the brown sugar, and ¾ teaspoon of the cinnamon to the processor bowl, and pulse with the remaining nuts 6 to 8 times, or until the nuts are medium chopped. Empty the filling into a bowl.

2. In a small bowl, combine the remaining 2 tablespoons granulated sugar and remaining ½ teaspoon cinnamon for rolling.

3. Dab the corners of the cookie sheets with butter and line with baking parchment.

4. Divide the dough in half and shape each piece into a log. Return one log to the refrigerator. Sprinkle the work surface with one-fourth of the coarsely chopped walnuts and one-fourth of the cinnamon/sugar mixture for rolling. Working with one log at a time and using your hands, roll the log in this mixture. As you roll, sprinkle the work surface with another one-fourth of the walnuts and one-fourth of the cinnamon/sugar mixture. After the dough is coated on both sides, roll it into a 6- × 15-inch parallelogram, with the 15-inch side parallel to the edge of the counter. To do this, as you roll, angle the bottom right-hand corner outwards and the upper left-hand corner outwards until the parallelogram measures about 6 × 15 inches. This will enable you to shape the horns without wasting the ends.

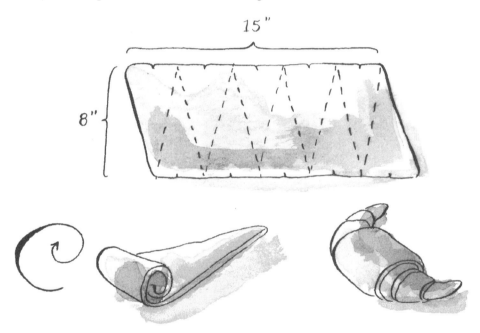

5. Brush the surface of the dough with the egg wash. Sprinkle with half of the nut filling, and lightly press it into the dough. Lay a ruler against the long side of the dough closest to you. With a dough scraper or a pizza cutter, make a small (¼-inch) indentation in the dough every 3 inches. You will have four indentations. Turn the ruler upside down and lay it along the top of the dough. Make four (¼-inch) indentations, spacing them 3 inches apart. With the indentations as a guide, cut the dough into 10 triangles. Using the dough scraper or a paring knife, make a ½-inch knick in the center of the 3-inch side of each triangle. This will enable you to stretch the triangles as they are rolled (see illustrations).

(continued)

6. Starting at the 3-inch side of the triangle, tightly roll the dough, stretching the crescent to elongate it as you roll. When you reach the end of the triangle, continue to roll the horn two or three times toward the narrow end to seal the layers. To prevent the dough from unraveling, *do not roll the dough back and forth*—only roll in one direction. Place the horn on the pan and bend the ends to form a crescent. Repeat with the remaining dough.

7. Cover the pans with tea towels and set in a warmish place to rise for 45 to 60 minutes. The horns should feel puffy when lightly touched with your fingertip.

8. Fifteen minutes before baking, position the racks in the upper and lower thirds of the oven. Heat the oven to 350°F.

9. Bake the horns for 18 to 20 minutes, or until golden brown. To ensure even browning, toward the end of baking time, rotate the pans top to bottom and front to back. Remove from the oven and place on cooling racks. While the horns are still warm, dust them with confectioners' sugar. When ready to serve, dust again with confectioners' sugar.

STORAGE: Store at room temperature, tightly wrapped in aluminum foil, for up to 3 days. These horns may be frozen (see Refreshing Yeasted Coffee Cakes, page 193).

Working with Yeast

The kind of yeast I like to use is active dry yeast. Some people shy away from recipes that use this product because they have poor success with reconstituting it. Begin by ignoring the package directions.

Yeast loves to live in a warm environment, and it thrives on sweeteners such as sugar or honey. Dissolving a bit of sugar in the warm liquid causes the yeast mixture to bubble or foam, a process that is known as proofing. These bubbles tell you that the yeast is activated and ready to go to work.

Here are a few simple steps to follow:

- Start with a small bowl, preferably stainless steel, that is at least 3 inches across the bottom to give enough surface area for the yeast to proof. Warm the bowl by rinsing it with hot water.

- Measure the liquid, taking care that the temperature is correct. It should fall between 110° and 115°F. Use an instant-read thermometer to determine this. The thermometer should not register below 110°F because as the liquid is poured into the bowl, the temperature will drop several degrees and be too cool.

- Add the sugar to the bowl and pour in the warm liquid. Sprinkle the yeast over the top, and without stirring, cover the bowl with a saucer and let it stand for 5 minutes.

- After 5 minutes, stir the mixture with a small whisk or fork. Cover the bowl again, and let it stand for an additional 2 to 3 minutes or until bubbly. Now the yeast is proofed and ready to use. Note: Yeast dissolved in warm milk may take longer to proof.

- At times, the dissolved yeast will multiply five or six times its original volume. This will depend on the amount of liquid called for in the recipe. If the yeast begins to overflow the bowl, stir it down and let it rise again. It's OK for the yeast mixture to wait for you.

scalloped chocolate pecan strip

MAKES ONE 15- TO 16-INCH STRIP, 8 TO 10 SERVINGS

If you've never tasted a yeasted cake made with a chocolate filling, you are in for a pleasant surprise. This sweet dough, spread with bittersweet chocolate filling and toasted pecans, is rolled into a log and cut into scallops. The top of the cake is finished with a sprinkling of pearl sugar. Take the time to seek this sugar out: it adds crunch and eye appeal. This gorgeous coffee cake will surely impress even the most discriminating audience.

¼ cup water

2 tablespoons granulated sugar

½ teaspoon espresso powder

2½ ounces fine-quality bittersweet chocolate, such as Lindt, chopped

¼ teaspoon lemon juice

¼ teaspoon pure vanilla extract

1 tablespoon unsalted butter, softened

½ recipe (about 1 pound) Simple Sweet Dough (page 182) or Rich Sour Cream Dough (page 184), cold

½ cup pecans, toasted and coarsely chopped (see page 356)

1 large egg lightly beaten with 2 teaspoons water, for egg wash

2 teaspoons opaque pearl sugar (see page 152; optional)

1 small recipe Vanilla Glaze (page 368)

AT A GLANCE

PAN: Large cookie sheet

PAN PREP: Baking parchment

RISING TIME: 45–60 minutes

RACK LEVEL: Lower third

OVEN TEMP: 350°F

BAKING TIME: 30 minutes

DIFFICULTY: 2

1. In a small, heavy saucepan, combine the water, granulated sugar, espresso powder, and chocolate. Cook over low heat, stirring occasionally, for 8 to 10 minutes, or until large bubbles form. Remove from the heat and stir in the lemon juice, vanilla, and butter. Set aside to cool completely. The mixture should have the consistency of soft fudge.

2. Butter the corners of the cookie sheet to secure the baking parchment, then line the pan with the parchment.

3. Place the dough on a lightly floured work surface and gently knead it six to eight times, or until smooth. Roll it into an 9- × 14-inch rectangle with the 14-inch side parallel to the edge of the counter. Using a small, offset spatula, spread the cooled chocolate filling over the surface of the dough, leaving a 1-inch border on all sides. Sprinkle the chopped pecans on the chocolate, and using your hand, press the nuts gently into the chocolate. Lightly brush the far edge of the dough with egg wash.

4. Starting at the bottom edge, roll the dough tightly into a log, pinching the seam to seal. Place the log *seam side down,* on the cookie sheet and square the ends with a dough scraper or metal spatula. Flatten the log slightly with the palm of your hand.

5. Using scissors, cut about 12 slits at approximately 1-inch intervals on the right side of the dough, cutting about three-fourths of the way through. For the left side, also cut about 12 slits; however, space the slits so that you are cutting in between the slits on the opposite side. Gently turn the slices to expose the filling, and pull them slightly downward, starting with the right side first. After the right side is done, turn the left side. Flatten the top of the cake gently with your hand, and then lightly press the slices so they lay flat against the pan. Cover the cake with a tea towel and set in a warmish place to rise for 45 to 60 minutes, or until puffy and almost doubled.

6. Fifteen minutes before baking, position the rack in the lower third of the oven. Heat the oven to 350°F.

7. Lightly brush the strip with the egg wash and sprinkle the top with pearl sugar. Bake for 30 minutes, or just until golden brown.

8. While the cake is baking, make the glaze. Remove the cake from the oven and place on a rack to cool. While the strip is still warm, loosen it from the parchment with a long, thin spatula. Drizzle the warm cake with the glaze.

STORAGE: Store at room temperature, tightly wrapped in aluminum foil, for up to 3 days. This cake may be frozen (see Refreshing Yeasted Coffee Cakes, page 193).

sticky buns

MAKES 15 BUNS

Sticky buns! Everyone, including my son-in-law, Andy, loves them. And no surprise, Andy was raised in Pennsylvania, which is sticky bun country. These honey-glazed rolls are sweet with sugar, cinnamon, and often lots of crunchy pecans.

Sticky buns have a long history dating back to the Middle Ages, with the advent of cinnamon. These sweet little buns are believed to have traveled from Europe to the United States. The Pennsylvania Dutch, whose cuisine was influenced by their German ancestry, introduced us to *schnecken*, now known as sticky buns. Their popularity has been steadfast over many generations, and I suspect that this will continue for many more. When preparing the pans, *do not* use nonstick spray, as the topping will not adhere to the sides of the tins. These sticky buns are topped with a generous amount of pecans and finished with a caramelized honey glaze.

PECAN TOPPING

¼ cup (½ stick) unsalted butter, softened

¾ cup packed very fresh light brown sugar

2 tablespoons honey

2 tablespoons light corn syrup

⅔ cup broken pecans (see page 356)

½ recipe (about 1 pound) Simple Sweet Dough (page 182) or Rich Sour Cream Dough (page 184), cold

FILLING

2 tablespoons unsalted butter, very soft

2 tablespoons granulated sugar

2 tablespoons packed light brown sugar

½ teaspoon ground cinnamon

½ cup medium-chopped pecans (see page 356)

2 to 3 tablespoons golden raisins, plumped (see page 358)

1 large egg lightly beaten with 2 teaspoons water, for egg wash

AT A GLANCE

PAN: Two standard muffin pans

PAN PREP: Generously buttered

RISING TIME: 45 minutes

RACK LEVELS: Upper and lower thirds

OVEN TEMP: 350°F

BAKING TIME: 18–20 minutes

DIFFICULTY: 2

MAKE THE TOPPING

1. Generously butter 15 muffin tin cavities. Place the softened butter in a medium bowl and gradually add the brown sugar, honey, and corn syrup, mixing until a smooth paste is formed. Divide the mixture evenly into the cavities, using about 2 teaspoons for each. Using the back of a teaspoon, spread the topping as best you can around the bottom and three-fourths of the way up the sides. Sprinkle the bottom of the cavities with the broken pecans.

SHAPE AND FILL THE BUNS

2. Remove the dough from the refrigerator, place it onto a lightly floured rolling surface, and press it into a 4- × 6-inch rectangle. Roll the dough into a 10- × 15-inch rectangle with the 15-inch side parallel to the edge of the counter.

3. Using a small, offset spatula, spread the dough with the softened butter, leaving a 1½-inch border at the top. In a small bowl, combine the granulated and brown sugars with the cinnamon. Sprinkle the mixture over the dough along with the nuts and raisins, again leaving a 1½-inch border at the top. Brush the border with the egg wash.

4. Roll the dough tightly, starting with the edge closest to you. Pinch the seam well with your fingertips to seal it. Then roll the cylinder back and forth a few times to compress the layers. The finished roll should measure about 15 inches. Using a dough scraper or a thin-bladed, sharp knife, cut the dough into 15 even slices. Place the slices into the prepared muffin tins cut-side down and press the tops gently with your fingertips to even the surface. Cover with a tea towel and set aside in a warmish place to rise for about 45 minutes, or until puffy and almost doubled.

BAKE AND FINISH THE BUNS

5. Fifteen minutes before baking, position the racks in the upper and lower thirds of the oven. Heat the oven to 350°F. Bake the buns for 18 to 20 minutes, or until they just begin to turn golden brown. To ensure even browning, toward the end of the baking time, rotate the pans top to bottom and front to back. Watch carefully; these should not be overbaked.

6. While the buns are baking, place two cooling racks over sheets of wax paper. Remove the buns from the oven, let stand for 2 to 3 minutes, then invert onto the cooling racks. *Do not remove the pans for 10 minutes to allow the honey syrup to coat the buns.* Carefully remove the pans. If any of the nut topping remains in the pans, spoon it onto the appropriate bun, handling the mixture carefully as it may be hot.

STORAGE: Store at room temperature, tightly wrapped in aluminum foil, for up to 3 days. Heat before serving. These sticky buns may be frozen (see Refreshing Yeasted Coffee Cakes, page 193).

apple and dried-cranberry coffee cake

MAKES ONE 9-INCH CAKE, 8 TO 10 SERVINGS

Sautéed apples and dried cranberries, delicately spiced, are nestled in a sweet yeasted dough that is pressed into a springform pan. After baking, the fruit that adorns the top is glazed with apricot preserves. This is a pretty cake and one that highlights autumn's best flavors.

½ recipe (about 1 pound) Simple Sweet Dough (page 182) or Rich Sour Cream Dough (page 184)

2 tablespoons unsalted butter

1 pound Golden Delicious apples (2 large), peeled, halved, cored, and sliced ¼ inch thick

¼ cup dried cranberries (not organic)

3 tablespoons sugar

½ teaspoon ground cinnamon

Pinch of ground allspice

2 teaspoons fresh lemon juice

GLAZE

¼ cup apricot preserves

2 teaspoons water

AT A GLANCE

PAN: 9-inch springform pan

PAN PREP: Buttered and lined with baking parchment

RISING TIME: 25–30 minutes

RACK LEVEL: Lower third

OVEN TEMP: 375°/350°F

BAKING TIME: 50–55 minutes

DIFFICULTY: 1

1. Remove the dough from the refrigerator 1 to 1½ hours before using.

2. In a heavy, 10-inch sauté pan, melt the butter over low heat. Add the apples, cranberries, sugar, cinnamon, and allspice. Sauté the mixture until the apples are soft, translucent, and caramelized, 20 to 25 minutes. Remove from the heat and add the lemon juice. Set aside to cool completely.

3. Butter the pan and line the bottom with parchment. Set aside. On a lightly floured work surface, gently knead the dough six to eight times, and shape it into a disk. With lightly floured hands, press the dough into the prepared pan, stretching it to completely cover the bottom. Push the dough up against the side of the pan, forcing it up to form a wall ¼ inch thick and ¾ inch high. Be sure to press it well into the crease of the pan. If the dough becomes too elastic, let it rest for a few minutes. Prick the surface of the dough ten to twelve times with a fork. Cover the pan with a tea towel and set it in a warmish place to rise until puffy but not *doubled*, 25 to 30 minutes.

4. Fifteen minutes before baking, position the rack in the lower third of the oven. Heat the oven to 375°F. Redefine the lip of the dough with your thumb and gently depress the center with your hand.

5. Carefully spoon the *cooled* filling over the dough, leaving a ¾-inch border around the edge and then filling in the center. Place the pan on a sheet of heavy-duty aluminum foil and wrap the pan with the foil to catch any leakage. Cover the pan loosely with aluminum foil and bake for 10 minutes. Remove the top foil and *reduce* the oven temperature to 350°F. Bake for an additional 40 to 45 minutes, or until the top is golden brown and the sides begin to release.

6. While the cake is baking, make the apricot glaze. Place the apricot preserves and water in a microwave-safe bowl. Stir to combine. Heat on medium power until the mixture is bubbly, then pass it through a medium-gauge strainer.

7. Remove the cake from the oven and let it stand on a cooling rack for 20 minutes. Release and remove the side of the pan and cool for 30 minutes longer. To remove the bottom of the pan and the parchment, place a 12-inch strip of aluminum foil directly onto the top of the cake, cupping the foil around the side to hold the topping in place. Cover with a cooling rack, invert the cake, and carefully lift off the bottom of the pan and remove the parchment. *Immediately* cover with another rack, turn the cake top side up, and remove the foil. While the cake is still warm, brush the fruit with the apricot glaze. This cake is best served slightly warm.

STORAGE: Refrigerate, lightly wrapped in aluminum foil, for up to 3 days. Reheat before serving in a 325°F oven for 10 to 15 minutes, or until slightly warm. This cake may be frozen (see Refreshing Yeasted Coffee Cakes, page 193).

golden raisin poppy seed twist

MAKES ONE 15- TO 16-INCH TWIST, 10 TO 12 SERVINGS

Poppy seeds and raisins are an Old World combination. The whole seeds are commonly ground for these types of pastries. Since most kitchens do not have a poppy seed grinder, for this recipe I omitted the grinding and cooked the whole seeds with raisins, along with sweet and fragrant ingredients such as honey and orange. The tasty filling is braided through the pastry, making a striking finish. If you like poppy seeds as much as I do, you must try this wonderful recipe.

1¼ cups golden raisins

¼ cup (1 ounce) poppy seeds

¼ cup toasted almonds, finely chopped (see page 356)

2 tablespoons sugar

2 tablespoons honey

2 tablespoons unsalted butter

½ teaspoon freshly grated navel orange zest

½ teaspoon pure vanilla extract

1 large egg white

½ recipe (about 1 pound) Simple Sweet Dough (page 182) or Rich Sour Cream Dough (page 184), cold

2 to 3 tablespoons fresh navel orange juice, for thinning

1 large egg white lightly beaten with 1 teaspoon water, for egg wash

Clear Shiny Glaze (page 368)

AT A GLANCE

PAN: Large cookie sheet

PAN PREP: Baking parchment

RISING TIME: 45–60 minutes

RACK LEVEL: Lower third

OVEN TEMP: 350°F

BAKING TIME: 30–35 minutes

DIFFICULTY: 2

1. Dab each corner of the cookie sheet lightly with butter and line with baking parchment.

2. Place the raisins in a food processor fitted with the steel blade, and pulse until coarsely chopped. Empty them into a heavy-duty medium saucepan and add the poppy seeds, almonds, sugar, honey, butter, orange zest, vanilla, and egg white. Over medium-low heat, stir the mixture until the sugar dissolves, 3 to 4 minutes. Watch carefully to prevent scorching. Set aside to cool.

3. Place the dough on a lightly floured work surface and shape it into a log. Roll the log into a 10- × 15-inch rectangle, with the 15-inch side parallel to the edge of the counter.

4. Add enough orange juice to the poppy seed filling to achieve a spreading consistency. Spread a 3-inch-wide strip of filling in the center of the dough, spreading it from right to left across the 15-inch side of the dough. Smooth the filling with a small, offset spatula or moistened fingertips. Lightly brush the far edge of the dough with the egg wash. Roll the dough up jelly roll style. Pinch the seam to seal, then roll the log back and forth two or three times. Carefully lift the roll onto the parchment-lined cookie sheet, placing it seam side down, angling it as necessary. Using a rolling pin or the palm of your hand, flatten the log until it measures about 3½ × 15 inches.

5. Using a dough scraper or thin-bladed, sharp knife, score the log lengthwise into three equal strips, then cut through. Starting in the center, braid the strips, then repeat with the opposite side (see illustrations). Pinch the ends together well and tuck under. Cover the pan with a tea towel and set in a warmish place to rise for 45 to 60 minutes, until puffy and almost doubled.

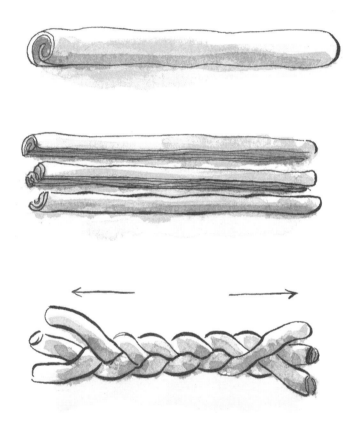

6. Fifteen minutes before baking, position the rack in the lower third of the oven. Heat the oven to 350°F. Bake for 30 to 35 minutes, or until golden brown.

7. About 15 minutes before the twist is done, prepare the glaze. Remove the braid from the oven and immediately brush the surface with the hot glaze. After 10 minutes, loosen with a large metal spatula. When firm enough to handle, transfer to a cooling rack.

STORAGE: Store at room temperature, tightly wrapped in aluminum foil, for up to 3 days. This cake may be frozen (see Refreshing Yeasted Coffee Cakes, page 193).

dimpled sugar cake

MAKES ONE 8-INCH CAKE, SIXTEEN 2-INCH SQUARES

If you want to make a quick yeasted coffee cake, this recipe is for you. The dough is pressed into the pan and dimpled much like focaccia bread. The holes are filled with brown sugar and butter, and the top is sprinkled generously with granulated sugar and cinnamon. When the sugars melt during baking, the top develops a sweet, crusty surface. This cake is perfect not only as a mid-morning snack, but any time of day.

$\frac{1}{2}$ recipe (about 1 pound) Simple Sweet Dough (page 182) or Rich Sour Cream Dough (page 184)

$\frac{1}{3}$ cup golden raisins, plumped (see page 358)

6 tablespoons dark brown sugar

$\frac{1}{4}$ cup ($\frac{1}{2}$ stick) cold unsalted butter, cut into 32 cubes

2 tablespoons granulated sugar mixed with $\frac{1}{2}$ teaspoon ground cinnamon

AT A GLANCE

PAN: 8- × 8- × 2-inch baking pan

PAN PREP: Buttered generously and lined with baking parchment

RISING TIME: 60 minutes

RACK LEVEL: Center

OVEN TEMP: 375°F

BAKING TIME: 25–28 minutes

DIFFICULTY: 1

1. Remove the dough from the refrigerator 1 to 1$\frac{1}{2}$ hours before using.

2. Butter the pan and line the bottom with parchment. On a lightly floured work surface, knead the raisins into the dough. Let the dough rest for a few minutes and then shape it into a 7- to 8-inch rectangle. Place the dough in the prepared pan and press it with your hand until the entire bottom is evenly covered. Place a tea towel over the top and set it in a warmish place to rise for about 1 hour, or until puffy and almost doubled.

3. Fifteen minutes before baking, position the rack in the middle of the oven. Heat the oven to 375°F.

4. Using two fingers, make depressions randomly in the dough about every 1$\frac{1}{2}$ to 2 inches. You should make 32 holes. Drop about $\frac{1}{2}$ teaspoon of brown sugar into each hole as best you can. Press a cube of butter deeply into the sugar. It's okay if some of the sugar spreads onto the top of the dough. Sprinkle the top of the cake heavily with the cinnamon/sugar mixture.

5. Bake the cake for 25 to 28 minutes. Remove from the oven and place on a cooling rack for 20 minutes. To remove the baking parchment, cover the pan with a square of aluminum foil, cupping it around the side to hold it in place. Place the cooling rack on top of the cake, invert it, and lift off the pan. Remove the parchment, then cover the cake with another rack and turn the cake top side up.

STORAGE: Store at room temperature, tightly wrapped in aluminum foil, for up to 3 days. This cake may be frozen (see Refreshing Yeasted Coffee Cakes, page 193).

• Strawberry Dimpled Sugar Cake

Here is a play on the Dimpled Sugar Cake: Instead of brown sugar, fill the dimples with strawberry preserves. During baking, the melted preserves and sugary top coating form an appealing pink-and-white marbled surface. In step 4 of the recipe, substitute ¼ cup strawberry preserves for the brown sugar. Place ½ teaspoon of preserves in each hole, as best you can. Press a cube of butter deeply into the preserves and sprinkle the top of the cake heavily with the cinnamon/sugar mixture. Proceed with step 5 of the recipe.

perfect pound cakes, homestyle coffee cakes, and quick breads

powdered sugar pound cake

neil's whipped cream pound cake

butter pecan pound cake

chocolate crown pound cake

lemon cream cheese pound cake

dried cherry almond pound cake

classic sour cream cinnamon and nut coffee cake

banana chocolate chip cake

chocolate chocolate streusel squares

sour cream marble cake

pineapple squares with toasted coconut streusel

fruit and nut applesauce cake

carrot honey cake

golden apple upside-down gingerbread cake

irish soda bread

grandma jennie's date and nut bread

pumpkin pecan loaf

zucchini loaf with apricots and dates

candied maple walnut pancake loaf

powdered sugar pound cake

MAKES ONE 10-INCH CAKE, 16 TO 20 SERVINGS

If you are looking for a really terrific pound cake, you can stop here. Kept in my recipe box for years, this pound cake recipe was inspired by Nell Slagle, a dear friend from Fort Worth, Texas. Nell was a marvelous baker, and any recipe she ever recommended was always special.

The cake is made with powdered (confectioners') sugar, which gives it an extremely velvety texture. In Nell's day, cakes were sweeter, so I took the liberty of reducing some of the sugar. I also replaced a small amount of the butter with canola oil, which gives the cake added moistness. Be sure to drizzle in the oil slowly to retain the emulsion of the butter, and also follow the directions for adding the sugar slowly. The little extra touches will be well worth the effort. With one bite of this pound cake, I'm sure you will love it as much as I do.

4 cups sifted cake flour, spooned in and leveled

2 teaspoons baking powder

$\frac{1}{2}$ teaspoon salt

6 large eggs

$1\frac{1}{2}$ cups (3 sticks) unsalted butter, slightly firm

$\frac{1}{4}$ cup canola or vegetable oil

$3\frac{1}{2}$ cups strained confectioners' sugar, spooned in and leveled, plus additional for dusting

2 teaspoons pure vanilla extract

$\frac{1}{8}$ teaspoon lemon oil (see page 351)

AT A GLANCE

PAN: 10-inch angel food cake pan

PAN PREP: Buttered generously and lined with buttered parchment

RACK LEVEL: Lower third

OVEN TEMP: 325°F

BAKING TIME: 1 hour, 20–25 minutes

DIFFICULTY: 1

1. Position the rack in the lower third of the oven. Heat the oven to 325°F. Generously butter the angel food cake pan, line the bottom with baking parchment, then butter the parchment. Set aside.

2. In a large bowl, thoroughly whisk together the flour, baking powder, and salt. Set aside.

3. Place the eggs in a medium bowl and whisk until well blended. Set aside.

4. Cut the butter into 1-inch pieces and place in the bowl of an electric mixer fitted with the paddle attachment. Mix on medium speed until smooth and lightened in color, about 2 minutes. Slowly drizzle in the oil, taking about 1 minute, then beat for 2 minutes longer. Scrape down the side of the bowl.

5. Reduce the mixer speed to medium-low. *If your mixer has a splatter shield attachment, now is a good time to use it.* Add the confectioners' sugar, 2 to 3 tablespoons at a time, taking 8 to 10 minutes. Gradually add $\frac{1}{2}$ cup of the eggs and beat for 2 minutes longer, scraping down the side of the bowl as needed. Blend in the vanilla and lemon oil.

6. Add the flour mixture alternately with the remaining eggs, dividing the flour into four parts and the eggs into three parts, beginning and ending with the flour, mixing until well blended after each addition. Scrape down the side of the bowl as needed.

7. Empty the batter into the pan and smooth the top with the back of a large soupspoon. Bake for 1 hour and 20 to 25 minutes. The cake is done when the top is golden brown and firm to the touch, and a wooden skewer inserted deeply in the center comes out clean.

8. Remove the cake from the oven and let stand on a cooling rack for 25 to 30 minutes. Holding the tube, lift the cake from the outer ring and place it on the cooling rack. Let stand for another 20 to 30 minutes. Cover the cake with a cooling rack, invert, and carefully lift off the tube section of the pan and the parchment paper. Cover with another rack and turn the cake top side up to finish cooling. Dust with confectioners' sugar before serving.

STORAGE: Store under a glass cake dome or tightly covered with plastic wrap for up to 5 days. This cake may be frozen.

neil's whipped cream pound cake

MAKES ONE 9-INCH BUNDT CAKE, 10 TO 12 SERVINGS

If you've never tried a cake made with whipped cream instead of butter, you are missing a special treat. Just ask my grandson Neil—it's his most requested cake. Thickly whipped cream, folded throughout the vanilla batter, imparts an especially delicate flavor and fine texture. When you whip the cream, be sure to chill the bowl and the mixer's whip attachment beforehand. It's also a good idea to place the carton of cream in the freezer for 15 minutes before whipping to ensure that it is well chilled.

Check out the variations listed below. Shaved bittersweet chocolate added to the batter offers a marvelous flavor contrast to the sweetness of the cream. The cinnamon-nut variation will please those who love nuts and like a little spice in their life.

---

1 cup heavy cream, well chilled

1½ cups strained all-purpose flour, spooned in and leveled

1½ teaspoons baking powder

⅛ teaspoon salt

4 large eggs, at room temperature

1⅓ cups superfine sugar

1 teaspoon pure vanilla extract

Confectioners' sugar, for dusting

AT A GLANCE

PAN: 9-inch Bundt pan

PAN PREP: Buttered generously and floured

RACK LEVEL: Lower third

OVEN TEMP: 350°F

BAKING TIME: 55–60 minutes

DIFFICULTY: 2

1. In a chilled bowl with a chilled whip attachment, whip the cream on medium-low speed until firm peaks form. *Take care not to overwhip the cream, or it will become grainy and will not blend smoothly into the batter.*

2. Position the rack in the lower third of the oven. Heat the oven to 350°F. Generously butter the Bundt pan, dust with flour, then invert it over the kitchen sink and tap firmly to remove the excess flour. Set aside.

3. In a medium bowl, thoroughly whisk together the flour, baking powder, and salt. Set aside.

4. In the large bowl of an electric mixer fitted with the whip attachment, beat the eggs on medium-high speed for 5 minutes. Add the sugar, 1 tablespoon at a time, taking about 4 minutes, then blend in the vanilla. Reduce the mixer speed to low and add the dry ingredients in two additions, mixing just until blended. Scrape down the side of the bowl as needed.

5. Remove the bowl from the mixer. Using an oversize rubber spatula, fold in the whipped cream, one-third at a time. Be sure the cream is thoroughly folded through the batter.

6. Spoon the batter into the pan and smooth the top with the back of a large soupspoon. Bake for 55 to 60 minutes. The cake is done when the top is golden brown and firm to the touch, and a wooden skewer inserted deeply in the center comes out clean.

7. Remove the cake from the oven and place on a cooling rack for 20 minutes. Invert the pan onto the rack and carefully lift it off. Let the cake cool completely. Dust lightly with confectioners' sugar before serving.

STORAGE: Store under a glass cake dome or covered with plastic wrap for up to 5 days. This cake may be frozen.

Whipped Cream Pound Cake with Shaved Chocolate

At the end of step 4, gently fold in 1 (3.5-ounce) shaved bar of fine-quality bittersweet chocolate, such as Lindt. Proceed with the recipe as written.

Whipped Cream Pound Cake with Cinnamon and Nuts

Place ¾ cup walnuts, 2 tablespoons sugar, ½ teaspoon ground cinnamon, and ⅛ teaspoon ground mace or nutmeg in the bowl of a food processor fitted with the steel blade. Process until the nuts are finely chopped. Fold the mixture gently into the batter at the end of step 4. Proceed with the recipe as written.

butter pecan pound cake

MAKES ONE 9-INCH BUNDT CAKE, 10 TO 12 SERVINGS

The scent of pecans toasting in the oven always causes my taste buds to tingle. For me, the combination of these crunchy nuts, rich sweet butter, and dark brown sugar is irresistible. Be sure to use Lyle's Golden Syrup for this recipe. The honey-like syrup, so popular in England, adds moistness, color, and a unique flavor to this delectable cake.

2¼ cups sifted cake flour, spooned in and leveled

¾ teaspoon baking powder

½ teaspoon salt

¼ teaspoon baking soda

1 cup (2 sticks) unsalted butter, slightly firm

2 tablespoons Lyle's Golden Syrup (see page 352)

¾ cup superfine sugar

¾ cup lightly packed very fresh dark brown sugar

3 large eggs

¾ teaspoon pure vanilla extract

¾ teaspoon caramel extract

½ cup sour cream

1½ cups toasted pecans, coarsely chopped (see page 356)

AT A GLANCE

PAN: 9-inch Bundt pan

PAN PREP: Buttered generously and floured

RACK LEVEL: Lower third

OVEN TEMP: 325°F

BAKING TIME: 1 hour, 5–10 minutes

DIFFICULTY: 1

1. Position the rack in the lower third of the oven. Heat the oven to 325°F. Generously butter the Bundt pan, dust with flour, then invert it over the kitchen sink and tap firmly to remove the excess flour. Set aside.

2. In a large bowl, thoroughly whisk together the flour, baking powder, salt, and baking soda. Set aside.

3. Cut the butter into 1-inch pieces and place in the bowl of an electric mixer fitted with the paddle attachment. Mix on medium speed until smooth and lightened in color, about 2 minutes. Stop the machine, add the syrup, and blend for about 2 minutes.

4. Add the superfine sugar, 1 to 2 tablespoons at a time, taking 3 to 4 minutes. Blend in the dark brown sugar, taking another 3 to 4 minutes. Add the eggs, one at a time, about 1 minute apart, scraping down the side of the bowl as needed. Blend in the vanilla and caramel extracts.

5. Reduce the mixer speed to low. Add the flour mixture alternately with the sour cream, dividing the flour into three parts and the sour cream into two parts, beginning and ending with the flour, mixing just until blended after each addition. Scrape down the side of the bowl and mix for about 10 seconds longer.

6. Remove the bowl from the machine and, using a large rubber spatula, fold in the pecans. Empty the batter into the pan and smooth the top with the back of a large soupspoon. Bake for 1 hour and 5 to 10 minutes, or until the top is firm to the touch and a wooden skewer inserted deeply in the center comes out clean.

7. Remove the cake from the oven and place on a cooling rack for 20 minutes. Invert the pan onto the rack and carefully lift it off. Let the cake cool completely.

STORAGE: Store under a glass cake dome or covered with plastic wrap for up to 5 days. This cake may be frozen.

chocolate crown pound cake

MAKES ONE 9-INCH BUNDT CAKE, 10 TO 12 SERVINGS

Deep, dark, and decadent, this cake is loaded with chocolate flavor. Be sure to use fine-quality chocolate in this recipe—it will make a difference. Chose the accompaniment of your choice—a frosty glass of milk or a scoop of vanilla ice cream—and enjoy.

6 ounces fine-quality bittersweet chocolate, such as Lindt, chopped

1 tablespoon espresso powder

¼ cup boiling water

2 tablespoons honey

2 cups strained all-purpose flour, spooned in and leveled

⅓ cup strained Dutch-process cocoa powder, spooned in and leveled

¾ teaspoon baking powder

½ teaspoon salt

¼ teaspoon baking soda

⅔ cup (1⅓ sticks) unsalted butter, slightly firm

1¼ cups superfine sugar

3 large eggs

1½ teaspoons pure vanilla extract

¾ cup sour cream

Midnight Chocolate Glaze (page 370), or confectioners' sugar for dusting

AT A GLANCE

PAN: 9-inch Bundt pan

PAN PREP: Buttered generously and floured

RACK LEVEL: Lower third

OVEN TEMP: 350°F

BAKING TIME: 55–60 minutes

DIFFICULTY: 1

1. Position the rack in the lower third of the oven. Heat the oven to 350°F. Generously butter the Bundt pan, dust with flour, then invert it over the kitchen sink and tap firmly to remove the excess flour. Set aside.

2. Place the chocolate in a medium, heatproof bowl. Dissolve the espresso powder in the boiling water and add it to the chocolate along with the honey. Place the bowl over a pot of simmering water, making sure the bottom of the bowl does not touch the water. Heat until the chocolate is melted, stirring occasionally to blend. Remove the pot from the heat, keeping the bowl over the hot water. (The mixture should remain warm.)

3. In a large bowl, thoroughly whisk together the flour, cocoa powder, baking powder, salt, and baking soda. Set aside.

4. Cut the butter into 1-inch pieces and place in the bowl of an electric mixer fitted with the paddle attachment. Mix on medium speed until smooth and lightened in color, about 2 minutes. Add the sugar, 1 to 2 tablespoons at a time, taking 6 to 8 minutes. Add the eggs, one at a time, about 1 minute apart, scraping down the side of the bowl as needed. Blend in the vanilla.

5. Stop the machine and add the warm chocolate mixture, then mix on medium-low speed until blended, scraping down the side of the bowl as needed.

6. Add the dry ingredients alternately with the sour cream, dividing the flour into three parts and the sour cream into two parts, beginning and ending with the flour, mixing well after each addition. Scrape down the side of the bowl again as needed.

7. Empty the batter into the pan and smooth the top with the back of a large soupspoon. Bake for 55 to 60 minutes. The cake is done when the top is firm to the touch and a wooden skewer inserted deeply in the center comes out clean.

8. Remove the cake from the oven and let stand on a cooling rack for 20 minutes. Invert the pan onto the rack and carefully lift it off. While the cake is cooling, make the glaze.

9. While the cake is slightly warm, set the rack on a rimmed cookie sheet lined with wax paper. Spoon the glaze on top of the cake, letting it trickle down the side at random. Let the cake stand until the glaze has completely set. Alternately, simply dust the top with confectioners' sugar just before serving.

STORAGE: Store under a glass cake dome or tented with aluminum foil for up to 5 days. This cake may be frozen before glazing.

lemon cream cheese pound cake

MAKES ONE LARGE LOAF CAKE, 8 TO 10 SERVINGS

Take the zing of lemon, the tang of cream cheese, and the sweetness of sugar and you have an addictive trio of flavors. When you make the batter, be sure the cream cheese is soft; otherwise, it will not blend smoothly with the butter. Serve this dynamite loaf cake for brunch or afternoon tea, or enjoy a slice on the sly when everyone has gone to bed.

1¾ cups sifted cake flour, spooned in and leveled

1 teaspoon baking powder

½ teaspoon salt

¾ cup (1½ sticks) unsalted butter, slightly firm

4 teaspoons freshly grated lemon zest

¼ teaspoon lemon oil (see page 351)

4 ounces cream cheese, at room temperature, cut into 1-inch pieces

1¼ cups superfine sugar

3 large eggs, separated

2 tablespoons fresh lemon juice

1 teaspoon pure vanilla extract

⅛ teaspoon cream of tartar

AT A GLANCE

PAN: 9- × 5- × 2¾-inch loaf pan

PAN PREP: Buttered generously and lined with buttered parchment

RACK LEVEL: Lower third

OVEN TEMP: 325°F

BAKING TIME: 1 hour, 10–15 minutes

DIFFICULTY: 1

1. Position the rack in the lower third of the oven. Heat the oven to 325°F. Generously butter the loaf pan, line the bottom with baking parchment, then butter the parchment. Set aside.

2. In a medium bowl, thoroughly whisk together the flour, baking powder, and salt. Set aside.

3. Cut the butter into 1-inch pieces and place in the bowl of an electric mixer fitted with the paddle attachment. Add the lemon zest and lemon oil, and mix on medium speed until smooth. Add the cream cheese, one piece at a time, and continue to mix until smooth and creamy. Blend in the sugar, 1 tablespoon at a time, taking 6 to 8 minutes. Add the egg yolks, one at a time, beating well after each addition, scraping down the side of the bowl as needed.

4. Combine the lemon juice and vanilla in a small bowl. Reduce the mixer speed to low and mix in one-half of the dry ingredients, then the lemon juice mixture, and then the remaining dry ingredients, mixing just to incorporate. Empty into a large bowl.

5. In a clean bowl of an electric mixer fitted with the whisk attachment, beat the egg whites on medium speed until frothy. Add the cream of tartar and continue to beat until soft peaks form. Using an oversize rubber spatula, fold one-third of the egg whites into the batter, using about 20 strokes to blend. Fold in the remaining whites, one-half at a time, using about 40 strokes to incorporate.

6. Spoon the batter into the pan and smooth the top with the back of a large soupspoon. Bake for 1 hour and 10 to 15 minutes. The cake is done when the top is golden brown and firm to the touch, and a wooden skewer inserted deeply in the center comes out clean.

7. Remove the cake from the oven and let stand on a cooling rack for 20 minutes. Turn the loaf pan on its side and carefully ease the cake from the pan. When the cake is cool enough to handle, remove the parchment paper, turn the loaf top side up, and cool completely on the rack.

STORAGE: Store under a glass cake dome or tightly covered with plastic wrap for up to 5 days. This cake may be frozen.

Poppy Seed Lemon Cream Cheese Pound Cake

Whisk 3 tablespoons poppy seeds into the flour mixture in step 2 and proceed with the recipe.

dried cherry almond pound cake

MAKES ONE 10-INCH BUNDT CAKE, 10 TO 12 SERVINGS

This pound cake is loaded with really good stuff! The sour cream batter, made with almond paste and orange zest, is studded with amaretto-plumped dried cherries and crunchy toasted almonds. You will find that the flavors become even better as this cake mellows with age.

1 cup sliced unblanched almonds, toasted (see page 356)

2/3 cup dried cherries (not organic)

3 tablespoons amaretto liqueur

2 cups strained all-purpose flour, spooned in and leveled

1/2 teaspoon baking powder

1/4 teaspoon salt

1/8 teaspoon baking soda

1 cup (2 sticks) unsalted butter, slightly firm

2 teaspoons freshly grated navel orange zest

1/2 cup (2 1/2 ounces) shredded almond paste (see page 355)

1 1/4 cups superfine sugar

4 large eggs

1 teaspoon pure vanilla extract

1/4 teaspoon pure almond extract

1/2 cup sour cream

Confectioners' sugar, for dusting

AT A GLANCE

PAN: 10-inch Bundt pan

PAN PREP: Buttered generously and floured

RACK LEVEL: Lower third

OVEN TEMP: 325°F

BAKING TIME: 1 hour, 10 minutes

DIFFICULTY: 1

1. Position the rack in the lower third of the oven. Heat the oven to 325°F. Generously butter the Bundt pan, dust with flour, then invert it over the kitchen sink and tap firmly to remove the excess flour. Set aside.

2. Place the toasted almonds in a medium bowl and crumble them with your hands. Sprinkle 2 to 3 tablespoons of the crumbled nuts evenly on the bottom of the pan. Set the remaining almonds aside.

3. Place the cherries in a small bowl. Add enough boiling water to cover the cherries and let stand for 5 minutes to soften. Drain and blot dry on paper towels. Coarsely chop the cherries, then return to the bowl and add the amaretto. Cover the bowl and let steep while preparing the batter.

4. In a medium bowl, thoroughly whisk together the flour, baking powder, salt, and baking soda. Set aside.

5. Cut the butter into 1-inch pieces and place in the bowl of an electric mixer fitted with the paddle attachment. Add the orange zest and mix on medium speed until smooth. Add the almond paste in three additions and beat until smooth and lightened in color, about 2 minutes.

6. Add the superfine sugar, 2 to 3 tablespoons at a time, taking 4 to 6 minutes and scraping down the side of the bowl as needed. Add the eggs, one at a time, beating thoroughly after each addition, then blend in the vanilla and almond extracts.

7. Reduce the mixer speed to low. Add the dry ingredients alternately with the sour cream, dividing the flour into three parts and the sour cream into two parts, beginning and ending with the flour, mixing *just* until blended after each addition. Scrape down the side of the bowl again.

8. Drain the cherries well. Remove the bowl from the machine and, using a large rubber spatula, fold in the almonds and cherries. Empty the batter into the pan and smooth the top with the back of a large soupspoon. Bake for about 1 hour and 10 minutes. The cake is done when the top is golden brown and firm to the touch, and a wooden skewer inserted deeply in the center comes out clean.

9. Remove the cake from the oven and place on a cooling rack for about 20 minutes. Invert the pan onto the rack and carefully lift it off. Let the cake cool completely. Dust with confectioners' sugar before serving.

STORAGE: Store under a glass cake dome or tightly covered with plastic wrap for up to 5 days. This cake may be frozen.

classic sour cream cinnamon and nut coffee cake

MAKES ONE 10-INCH CAKE, 16 TO 20 SERVINGS

When I began this book, this was one recipe that I knew I wanted to include. It was given to me by my good friend Mariette Bronstein, a superb cook and baker. The memory of my first taste of this cake in her home stayed with me for years. The brown sugar and toasted pecans form a crunchy crust that is absolutely addictive. Although many recipes for this type of cake exist, I think this one is extra special.

1½ cups sour cream

1 teaspoon baking soda

NUT MIXTURE

1¼ cups toasted pecans (see page 356)

3 tablespoons granulated sugar

2 tablespoons dark brown sugar

½ teaspoon ground cinnamon

BATTER

3 cups strained all-purpose flour, spooned in and leveled

2 teaspoons baking powder

1 teaspoon salt

1 cup (2 sticks) unsalted butter, slightly firm

1¾ cups superfine sugar

3 large eggs

1 teaspoon pure vanilla extract

AT A GLANCE

PAN: 10-inch angel food cake pan

PAN PREP: Buttered generously and lined with buttered parchment

RACK LEVEL: Lower third

OVEN TEMP: 350°F

BAKING TIME: 1 hour, 10–15 minutes

DIFFICULTY: 1

1. In a small bowl, stir together the sour cream and baking soda. Let stand at room temperature for 1 hour.

2. Position the rack in the lower third of the oven. Heat the oven to 350°F. Generously butter the angel food pan, line the bottom with baking parchment, then butter the parchment. Set aside.

MAKE THE NUT MIXTURE

3. Place the pecans, granulated and dark brown sugars, and cinnamon in the work bowl of a food processor fitted with the steel blade. Pulse 5 to 6 times, or until the nuts are medium chopped. Set aside.

MAKE THE BATTER

4. In a large bowl, thoroughly whisk together the flour, baking powder, and salt, and set aside.

5. Cut the butter into 1-inch pieces and place in the bowl of an electric mixer fitted with the paddle attachment. Mix on medium speed until smooth and lightened in color, about 2 minutes. Add the superfine sugar, 1 to 2 tablespoons at a time, taking 6 to 8 minutes. Add the eggs,

one at a time, beating for 1 minute after each addition, scraping down the side of the bowl as needed. Blend in the vanilla.

6. Reduce the mixer speed to low. Add the flour mixture alternately with the sour cream mixture, dividing the flour into four parts and the sour cream into three parts, beginning and ending with the flour, mixing until just blended after each addition. Scrape down the side of the bowl again.

7. Spoon two-thirds of the batter into the pan. Sprinkle one-half of the nut mixture evenly over the batter. Cover the mixture with the remaining batter, distributing it evenly over the nuts. Smooth the batter with the back of a large soupspoon or a small offset spatula, spreading it to the side of the pan first, before spreading it toward the center. *(To prevent the nut mixture from being disturbed, do not pick up the spoon as the batter is spread.)* Sprinkle with the remaining nut mixture, pressing it gently into the batter with a clean soupspoon.

BAKE THE CAKE

8. Bake for 1 hour and 10 to 15 minutes. The cake is done when the top is golden brown and springy to the touch, and a wooden skewer or toothpick inserted deeply in the center comes out clean.

9. Remove the cake from the oven and let stand on a cooling rack for 25 to 30 minutes. Holding the tube, lift the cake from the outer ring and place it on the cooling rack. Let stand for another 20 to 30 minutes. To remove the cake from the tube section, cut a 2-inch hole in the center of a 12-inch piece of aluminum foil and place it directly on top of the cake, cupping the foil around the side to hold the topping in place. Cover with a cooling rack, invert the cake, and carefully lift off the tube section and the parchment paper. Cover with another rack and invert again. Remove the aluminum foil and cool right side up.

STORAGE: Store under a glass cake dome or tightly covered with plastic wrap for up to 5 days. This cake may be frozen.

banana chocolate chip cake

MAKES ONE 10-INCH BUNDT CAKE, 10 TO 12 SERVINGS

One of my assistants, Judy Epstein, has two teens with terrific taste buds. After we sent home various cakes for them to sample, Cory and Hannah wanted to know when I was finally going to make their favorite, a Banana Chocolate Chip Cake. When I did, it passed muster with flying colors, and that was good enough for me.

Be sure to use mini chips because larger ones will sink to the bottom of the pan. And, for an even-textured cake, take the time to strain the pureed bananas. The finished cake will be so much better. Just ask Cory and Hannah!

2½ cups sifted cake flour, spooned in and leveled

1 teaspoon baking soda

½ teaspoon salt

½ teaspoon mace

2 large, very ripe bananas

1 teaspoon lemon juice

¾ cup sour cream

1 teaspoon pure vanilla extract

¾ teaspoon banana extract

¾ cup (1½ sticks) unsalted butter, slightly firm

1¼ cups superfine sugar

3 large eggs

½ cup chocolate mini-morsels

1 large recipe Vanilla Glaze (page 368)

AT A GLANCE

PAN: 10-inch Bundt pan

PAN PREP: Buttered generously and floured

RACK LEVEL: Lower third

OVEN TEMP: 350°F

BAKING TIME: 55–60 minutes

DIFFICULTY: 1

1. Position the rack in the lower third of the oven. Heat the oven to 350°F. Generously butter the Bundt pan, dust with flour, then invert it over the kitchen sink and tap firmly to remove the excess flour. Set aside.

2. In a large bowl, thoroughly whisk together the flour, baking soda, salt, and mace. Set aside.

3. Cut the bananas into 1-inch pieces and place with the lemon juice in the work bowl of a food processor fitted with the steel blade. Process for 30 seconds, then stop the machine and scrape down the side of the bowl. Process for another 10 seconds, or until the bananas are pureed. Strain the puree through a medium-gauge strainer. You should have a generous cupful. Stir the sour cream and vanilla and banana extracts into the bananas and set aside.

4. Cut the butter into 1-inch pieces and place in the bowl of an electric mixer fitted with the paddle attachment. Mix on medium speed until smooth and lightened in color, about 2 minutes. Add the sugar, 1 to 2 tablespoons at a time, taking 6 to 8 minutes. Blend in the eggs, one at a time, beating thoroughly after each addition, scraping down the side of the bowl as needed.

5. Reduce the mixer speed to low and add the dry ingredients alternately with the banana/sour cream mixture, dividing the flour mixture into four parts and the liquid into three parts, beginning and ending with the flour. Scrape down the side of the bowl, then mix for 10 to 15 seconds longer. Remove the bowl from the machine and, using a large rubber spatula, fold in the chocolate morsels.

6. Spoon the batter into the pan. Smooth the surface with the back of a large soupspoon and bake for 55 to 60 minutes. The cake is done when the top is golden brown and firm to the touch, and a wooden skewer inserted deeply in the center comes out clean.

7. Remove the cake from the oven and let stand on a cooling rack for 10 minutes. Invert the pan onto the rack and carefully lift it off. As the cake is cooling, prepare the vanilla glaze. While the cake is still warm, place a piece of parchment or wax paper under the rack and spoon the glaze onto the cake. The glaze will harden as the cake cools.

STORAGE: Store under a glass cake dome or tightly covered with aluminum foil for up to 7 days. This cake may be frozen before glazing.

Glazed Banana Nut Cake

Omit the mini-morsels and fold in ½ to ¾ cup medium-chopped pecans or walnuts.

chocolate chocolate streusel squares

MAKES ONE 9- × 13- × 2-INCH CAKE, 2 DOZEN 2-INCH SERVINGS

This chocolate-packed coffee cake is a chocoholic's dream. Rich sour cream pairs with cocoa powder and unsweetened chocolate to make a cake with a tender, melt-in-your-mouth crumb. In keeping with the chocolate theme, I top the batter with buttery chocolate streusel and then add mini chocolate chips and chopped walnuts for a bit of pizzazz.

1¼ cups strained all-purpose flour, spooned in and leveled

¼ cup strained Dutch-process cocoa powder

¾ teaspoon baking powder

¼ teaspoon salt

3 ounces unsweetened chocolate, coarsely chopped

6 tablespoons (¾ stick) unsalted butter

2 tablespoons canola or vegetable oil

2 large eggs

⅔ cup granulated sugar

⅓ cup lightly packed very fresh dark brown sugar

1 teaspoon pure vanilla extract

¾ cup sour cream

Chocolate Streusel

FINISHING

⅓ cup chocolate mini-morsels

½ cup medium-chopped walnuts (see page 356)

AT A GLANCE

PAN: 9- × 13- × 2-inch baking pan

PAN PREP: Generously buttered

RACK LEVEL: Center

OVEN TEMP: 350°F

BAKING TIME: 30–35 minutes

DIFFICULTY: 1

1. Position the rack in the center of the oven. Heat the oven to 350°F. Generously butter the pan and set aside.

2. In a medium bowl, thoroughly whisk together the flour, cocoa powder, baking powder, and salt. Set aside.

3. Place the chocolate, butter, and oil in a medium, heatproof bowl and set over a pot of simmering water. (The bottom of the bowl should not touch the water.) Heat until the chocolate is melted, stirring occasionally. Keep warm.

4. Place the eggs in the bowl of an electric mixer fitted with the whip attachment. Beat on medium-high speed for 2 minutes. Add the granulated sugar, then the dark brown sugar, 1 to 2 tablespoons at a time, taking 2 minutes for each. Add the vanilla and beat for 1 minute longer. The mixture should be thick.

5. Reduce the speed to medium and add the warm chocolate mixture, mixing for 2 minutes to blend. Scrape down the side of the bowl as needed.

6. Reduce the mixer speed to low. Add the dry ingredients alternately with the sour cream, dividing the flour mixture into three parts and the sour cream into two parts, beginning and ending with the flour. Scrape down the side of the bowl.

7. Spread the batter evenly into the pan. Take a handful of the streusel mixture and squeeze gently to form a large clump. Then break the clump apart, and sprinkle the crumbs onto the batter. Repeat until all of the streusel mixture has been used. Gently press the crumbs onto the top of the batter, sprinkle with the mini chips and walnuts, and press *gently* again.

8. Bake for 30 to 35 minutes. The cake is done when a toothpick inserted in the center comes out clean and the sides begin to pull away from the pan.

9. Remove the cake from the oven and let stand on a cake rack until cool. When ready to serve, cut into 2-inch squares.

STORAGE: Store in the pan at room temperature, well wrapped with aluminum foil, for up to 5 days. This cake may be frozen.

chocolate streusel

MAKES ENOUGH FOR ONE 9-INCH ROUND OR 9- × 13- × 2-INCH COFFEE CAKE, OR 12 TO 14 MUFFINS

Have you ever tried a chocolate streusel? If not check out this recipe. While it is used with Chocolate Chocolate Streusel Squares, it would be equally delicious with Favorite Vanilla Muffins (page 126) or Jeff's Chocolate-Glazed Midnight Muffins (page 136).

6 to 7 tablespoons unsalted butter

1 cup all-purpose flour, spooned in and leveled

¼ cup granulated sugar

¼ cup lightly packed very fresh dark brown sugar

2 tablespoons strained Dutch-process cocoa powder

¼ teaspoon baking powder

¼ teaspoon salt

¼ teaspoon ground cinnamon

1. Place the butter in a 2-quart heavy-bottomed saucepan and heat until almost melted; remove from the heat and *cool until tepid.* Whisk together the flour, granulated and brown sugars, cocoa powder, baking powder, salt, and cinnamon.

2. Add the dry ingredients to the butter, tossing with a fork until crumbs are formed. Gently squeeze the mixture with your hand to form larger lumps, then break them apart with your fingertips. Before using, let the streusel stand for 10 to 15 minutes.

sour cream marble cake

MAKES ONE 9-INCH BUNDT CAKE, 10 TO 12 SERVINGS

Weaving together swirls of deep chocolate and creamy vanilla, this sour cream marble cake is an irresistible taste combination any time your sweet tooth calls. It never ceases to amaze me that so many people are drawn to these contrasts of flavors and colors. To achieve a beautiful marbled affect, be sure to follow the directions carefully. If the batter is overworked, the layers of chocolate and vanilla will not be clearly defined.

MARBLING

3 ounces fine-quality bittersweet chocolate, such as Lindt, coarsely chopped

4 teaspoons unsalted butter

3 tablespoons Dutch-process cocoa powder

2 tablespoons light corn syrup

3 tablespoons water

¼ teaspoon baking soda

BATTER

2½ cups sifted cake flour, spooned in and leveled

1½ teaspoons baking powder

½ teaspoon baking soda

½ teaspoon salt

1¼ cups sour cream

¼ cup milk

1½ teaspoons pure vanilla extract

¾ cup (1½ sticks) unsalted butter, slightly firm

1½ cups superfine sugar

4 large eggs

Confectioners' sugar for dusting

AT A GLANCE

PAN: 9-inch Bundt pan

PAN PREP: Buttered generously and floured

RACK LEVEL: Lower third

OVEN TEMP: 350°F

BAKING TIME: 55–60 minutes

DIFFICULTY: 3

1. Position the rack in the lower third of the oven. Heat the oven to 350°F. Generously butter the Bundt pan, dust with flour, then invert the pan over the kitchen sink and tap firmly to remove the excess flour. Set aside.

MAKE THE MARBLING

2. Melt the chocolate and butter in a 2-quart bowl set over a pot of simmering water. (The bottom of the bowl should not touch the water.) Stir in the cocoa powder, corn syrup, and water, mixing until smooth. Remove from the heat and blend in the baking soda. Keep the chocolate mixture warm over the water bath while you prepare the batter.

MAKE THE BATTER

3. In a large bowl, thoroughly whisk together the flour, baking powder, baking soda, and salt and set aside.

4. In a medium bowl, combine the sour cream, milk, and vanilla. Set aside.

5. Cut the butter into 1-inch pieces and place in the bowl of an electric mixer fitted with the paddle attachment. Mix on medium speed for 2 minutes, then add the superfine sugar, 1 to 2 tablespoons at a time, taking 6 to 8 minutes. Scrape down the side of the bowl as needed. Add the eggs, one at a time, at 30-second intervals, scraping down the side of the bowl again.

6. Reduce the mixer speed to low. Add the dry ingredients alternately with the sour cream mixture, dividing the flour into three parts and the sour cream into two parts, and beginning and ending with the flour. Mix just until blended after each addition. Scrape down the side of the bowl as needed.

7. Remove the marbling mixture from the water bath. Measure $1\frac{1}{2}$ cups of the batter, and add it to the marbling mixture, folding the two mixtures together gently.

FINISH THE CAKE

8. Spoon one-half of the vanilla batter into the pan and smooth the top with the back of a large soupspoon. Using about one-third of the chocolate batter, distribute spoonfuls evenly over the vanilla batter, smoothing it carefully to the edge and covering as much vanilla batter as possible. Spoon one-half of the remaining vanilla batter over the chocolate batter. Spread the remaining chocolate batter over the vanilla, then finish with the remaining vanilla batter. As each layer of vanilla batter is spread, cover as much of the chocolate as you can.

9. Insert a table knife almost to the bottom of the pan and gently lift the knife up, over, and down again to fold the batters together, making about 15 folds as you rotate the pan. Smooth the top of the batter with the back of a large soupspoon.

10. Bake for 55 to 60 minutes. The cake is done when the top is golden brown and firm to the touch, and a wooden skewer inserted in the center comes out clean.

11. Remove the cake from the oven and let stand on a cooling rack for 15 to 20 minutes. Cover with a cooling rack, invert the cake, and carefully lift off the pan. Cool the cake completely on the rack. Just before serving, dust the top with confectioners' sugar.

STORAGE: Store under a glass cake dome or covered with plastic wrap for up to 5 days. This cake may be frozen.

pineapple squares with toasted coconut streusel

MAKES ONE 9- × 13- × 2-INCH CAKE, 2 DOZEN 2-INCH SERVINGS

If you love pineapple as much as I do, be sure to try these tasty, streusel-topped squares. The citrus-scented batter is laced with sweet pineapple, which gives the cake a wonderful moistness. These pretty crumb cake squares with their generous coating of chewy, buttery streusel make a refreshing tropical treat at any time of the year.

1 (8-ounce) can crushed pineapple in pineapple juice, well drained

1¾ cups sifted cake flour, spooned in and leveled

1 teaspoon baking powder

¼ teaspoon baking soda

¼ teaspoon salt

½ cup (1 stick) unsalted butter, slightly firm

1 teaspoon freshly grated navel orange zest

1 teaspoon freshly grated lemon zest

⅔ cup plus 3 tablespoons superfine sugar, divided

2 large eggs, separated

⅓ cup sour cream

3 tablespoons fresh navel orange juice

¾ teaspoon pure vanilla extract

Toasted Coconut Streusel

AT A GLANCE

PAN: 9- × 13- × 2-inch baking pan

PAN PREP: Generously buttered

RACK LEVEL: Center

OVEN TEMP: 350°F

BAKING TIME: 30–35 minutes

DIFFICULTY: 1

1. Position the rack in the center of the oven. Heat the oven to 350°F. Generously butter the pan and set aside. Set aside.

2. Place the pineapple in the work bowl of a food processor fitted with the steel blade. Process for 10 seconds, or until finely chopped.

3. In a large bowl, thoroughly whisk together the flour, baking powder, baking soda, and salt. Set aside.

4. Cut the butter into 1-inch pieces and place in the bowl of an electric mixer fitted with the paddle attachment. Add the orange and lemon zests and mix on medium speed until smooth and lightened in color, about 2 minutes. Add ⅔ cup of the sugar, 1 tablespoon at a time, taking 4 to 6 minutes.

5. Add the egg yolks, one at a time, beating until blended after each addition and scraping down the side of the bowl as needed. Reduce the mixer speed to low and blend in the pineapple.

6. Combine the sour cream, orange juice, and vanilla in a small bowl. Add the dry ingredients alternately with the sour cream mixture, dividing the flour into three parts and the sour cream into two parts, beginning and ending with the flour, scraping down the side of the bowl as needed. Mix just to incorporate after each addition.

7. Place the egg whites in the bowl of an electric mixer fitted with the whip attachment. Whip on medium speed until soft peaks form, then add the remaining 3 tablespoons sugar, 1 tablespoon at a time, and beat for 30 seconds until thoroughly blended. Do not overbeat.

8. Using an oversize rubber spatula, fold about one-third of the whipped egg whites into the batter, taking about 20 turns. Fold in the remaining egg whites, taking about 40 turns. Scrape the batter into the pan. Smooth the top with the back of a large soupspoon. Distribute the streusel evenly over the batter, patting lightly to adhere.

9. Bake for 30 to 35 minutes. The cake is done when the top is golden brown and springy to the touch, and a toothpick inserted in the center comes out clean.

10. Remove the cake from the oven and let stand on a cooling rack for about 20 minutes. Place a 15-inch strip of aluminum foil directly on top of the cake, cupping it around the sides to hold the topping in place. Cover with a cooling rack, invert the cake, and carefully lift off the pan. Cover with another rack, invert again, remove the foil, and cool right side up. (Alternatively, the cake may be stored in the pan and cut directly into 2-inch squares.)

STORAGE: Store in the pan in the refrigerator, well wrapped with aluminum foil, for up to 5 days. This cake may be frozen.

toasted coconut streusel

MAKES ENOUGH FOR ONE 10-INCH ROUND OR 9- × 13- × 2-INCH COFFEE CAKE, OR 18 TO 20 MUFFINS

This streusel makes an especially nice topping for cakes made with pineapple or citrus flavors.

1 cup flaked, sweetened coconut

6 tablespoons (¾ stick) unsalted butter

½ teaspoon freshly grated navel orange zest

1 cup all-purpose flour, spooned in
   and leveled

½ cup strained confectioners' sugar, spooned
   in and leveled

⅛ teaspoon freshly grated nutmeg

1. Position the rack in the center of the oven. Heat the oven to 325°F. Place the coconut in a shallow pan and bake for 8 to 10 minutes, or until golden brown. Watch carefully and stir occasionally, as it burns quickly. When the coconut has cooled, crush into smaller pieces with your hand.

2. Place the butter and orange zest in a 3-quart, heavy-bottomed saucepan and heat until almost melted; remove from the heat and *cool to tepid.*

3. Add the crushed coconut, flour, confectioners' sugar, and nutmeg, then stir with a fork to form coarse crumbs. Before using, let the streusel stand for 10 to 15 minutes.

fruit and nut applesauce cake

MAKES ONE 9- × 13- × 2-INCH CAKE, 2 DOZEN 2-INCH SERVINGS

If you like applesauce cake, you must try this recipe. The batter is made with fresh apples, raisins, and dried cranberries accented with cinnamon and nutmeg. Don't be tempted to substitute jarred applesauce because it is too watery and the end result will not be the same. Fresh apples add superior flavor and just the right amount of moisture.

APPLESAUCE

3 Granny Smith apples (about 1 pound), peeled, halved, and cored

2 tablespoons unsalted butter

1/4 cup water

1 teaspoon fresh lemon juice

BATTER

2 1/2 cups strained all-purpose flour, spooned in and leveled

1 1/2 teaspoons ground cinnamon

1 teaspoon baking soda

1/2 teaspoon baking powder

1/2 teaspoon ground nutmeg

1/2 teaspoon salt

1/2 cup (1 stick) unsalted butter, slightly firm

1 teaspoon freshly grated lemon zest

3/4 cup granulated sugar

3/4 cup lightly packed very fresh dark brown sugar

2 large eggs

1 teaspoon pure vanilla extract

1/2 cup low-fat plain yogurt or buttermilk

1 cup medium-chopped walnuts (see page 356)

1/2 cup golden raisins, plumped (see page 358)

1/4 cup dried cranberries (not organic), plumped and coarsely chopped (page 358)

Applejack Glaze (page 358)

AT A GLANCE

PAN: 9- × 13- × 2-inch baking pan

PAN PREP: Generously buttered

RACK LEVEL: Lower third

OVEN TEMP: 350°F

BAKING TIME: 35–40 minutes

DIFFICULTY: 2

MAKE THE APPLESAUCE

1. Using a food processor fitted with the medium shredding disk, shred the apples. (Alternatively, the apples can be shredded on the half-moon side of a box grater.) Melt the butter in a heavy, 10-inch sauté pan. Stir in the apples, water, and lemon juice. Cover the pan and reduce the heat to low; cook the apples until tender, about 25 minutes. (The apples should retain some texture.) Empty from the pan and set aside to cool. You should have about 1 cup of applesauce.

MAKE THE BATTER

2. Position the rack in the lower third of the oven. Heat the oven to 350°F. Generously butter the pan and set aside.

3. In a large bowl, strain together the flour, cinnamon, baking soda, baking powder, nutmeg, and salt. Set aside.

4. Cut the butter into 1-inch pieces and place it in the bowl of an electric mixer fitted with the paddle attachment. Add the lemon zest and mix on medium speed until smooth and lightened in color, about 2 minutes. Add the granulated sugar, 1 tablespoon at a time, taking 2 to 3 minutes, then add the brown sugar, taking another 2 to 3 minutes. Beat for 1 minute longer. Add the eggs, one at a time, beating for 1 minute after each addition, then mix in the vanilla. Scrape down the side of the bowl as needed.

5. Reduce the mixer speed to medium-low and blend in the applesauce. Add the dry ingredients alternately with the yogurt, dividing the flour mixture into three parts and the yogurt into two parts, beginning and ending with the flour. Scrape down the side of the bowl.

6. Remove the bowl from the machine and, using an oversize rubber spatula, fold in the walnuts, raisins, and cranberries. Spoon the batter into the pan and smooth the top with the bottom of a large soupspoon.

BAKE THE CAKE

7. Bake for 35 to 40 minutes. The cake is done when the top is springy to the touch and a toothpick inserted deeply in the center comes out clean. Remove the cake from the oven and place on a cooling rack. Fifteen minutes before the cake is done, prepare the glaze.

8. While the cake is still hot, *immediately* pour the glaze over the cake, spreading evenly with an offset spatula. The glaze will harden within minutes. Cool the cake completely on the rack.

STORAGE: Store in the pan at room temperature, lightly covered with aluminum foil for up to 5 days. This cake may be frozen before glazing.

carrot honey cake

MAKES ONE 9- × 9-INCH CAKE, SIXTEEN 2¼-INCH SERVINGS

The addition of honey to carrot cake not only adds flavor but also gives the cake a very moist texture. Cinnamon, cardamom, and orange zest complement the sweetness of the carrots and honey, making a cake that promises to please.

When you prepare the batter, be sure to have your cake pan ready and your oven preheated because this is a batter that cannot stand after mixing.

3 large carrots (about 8 ounces), peeled and trimmed

1½ cups all-purpose flour, spooned in and leveled

2 teaspoons ground cinnamon

1 teaspoon baking soda

¾ teaspoon ground cardamom

½ teaspoon salt

3 large eggs

½ cup granulated sugar

½ cup lightly packed very fresh light brown sugar

1 teaspoon freshly grated navel orange zest

¾ cup canola oil

¼ cup honey

1 teaspoon pure vanilla extract

½ cup medium-chopped toasted pecans (see page 356)

1 large recipe Cream Cheese Frosting (page 374)

AT A GLANCE

PAN: 9- × 9- × 2-inch square baking pan

PAN PREP: Generously buttered

RACK LEVEL: Center

OVEN TEMP: 350°F

BAKING TIME: 40–45 minutes

DIFFICULTY: 1

1. Position the rack in the center of the oven. Heat the oven to 350°F. Generously butter the pan and set aside.

SHRED THE CARROTS

2. To shred the carrots in a food processor: Fit the machine with the medium shredding disk. Cut the carrots into 1-inch chunks and place in the feeder tube. Shred using very light pressure. Remove the shredding disk and insert the steel blade. Pulse 4 to 5 times, then process for 5 to 6 seconds. (You should have 1½ to 1⅔ cups.) Set aside.

3. To shred the carrots by hand: Finely shred the carrots using the smallest (scant ⅛-inch) half-moon side of a box grater. (You should have 1½ to 1⅔ cups.) Set aside.

MAKE THE BATTER

4. In a medium bowl, thoroughly whisk together the flour, cinnamon, baking soda, cardamom, and salt. Set aside.

5. Place the eggs in the bowl of an electric mixer fitted with the whip attachment. Beat for 2 minutes on medium speed, then add the granulated sugar, 1 tablespoon at a time, taking 2 to 3 minutes. Add the brown sugar, 1 tablespoon at a time, taking another 2 to 3 minutes, then beat in the orange zest.

6. Using a small whisk, mix together the oil, honey, and vanilla in a 1-quart mixing bowl, beating until the honey is thoroughly incorporated with the oil. Immediately pour into the egg/ sugar mixture in a steady stream and beat well. Reduce the speed to medium-low and mix in the carrots. Add the dry ingredients in two additions, mixing only to blend after each addition. Scrape down the side of the bowl as needed. Then, quickly mix in the pecans. *Note:* This batter cannot stand before baking because the oil and honey will settle to the bottom of the bowl.

BAKE THE CAKE

7. Immediately pour the batter into the pan and bake for 40 to 45 minutes. The cake is done when it is firm to the touch, the sides begin to release, and a toothpick inserted in the center comes out clean.

8. While the cake is baking, prepare the frosting.

9. Remove the cake from the oven and place on a cooling rack. When the cake is cool, spread with the frosting, swirling it with the bottom of a soupspoon. Cut into sixteen 2¼-inch squares.

STORAGE: Refrigerate, covered with aluminum foil, for up to 7 days. The frosted cake may be frozen.

golden apple upside-down gingerbread cake

MAKES ONE 9- × 9-INCH CAKE, 8 TO 10 SERVINGS

This recipe comes from Kathie Finn Redden, a cooking teacher and caterer, who was blessed with an extraordinary sense of taste. Her zesty gingerbread is complemented by a topping of sweet sautéed apples. When the cake is inverted, the juices of the fruit enhance the tender crumb of the cake. Be sure to serve this with a scoop of vanilla ice cream.

APPLES

5 tablespoons unsalted butter, divided

5 medium Golden Delicious apples (about 2¼ pounds), peeled, cored, and cut into eighths

¼ cup lightly packed dark brown sugar

¼ cup Calvados or applejack brandy

CAKE

1½ cups all-purpose flour, spooned in and leveled

2 teaspoons ground ginger

1 teaspoon baking soda

1 teaspoon ground cinnamon

½ teaspoon salt

¼ teaspoon ground nutmeg

¼ teaspoon ground cloves

½ cup (1 stick) unsalted butter, slightly firm

½ cup lightly packed very fresh dark brown sugar

2 large eggs

½ cup light molasses

¼ cup crystallized ginger, cut into ¼-inch pieces

¼ cup milk

AT A GLANCE

PAN: 9- × 9- × 2-inch square baking pan

PAN PREP: Generously buttered

RACK LEVEL: Center

OVEN TEMP: 350°F

BAKING TIME: 50–55 minutes

DIFFICULTY: 1

1. Position the rack in the center of the oven. Heat the oven to 350°F. Generously butter a 9-inch square (preferably nonstick) pan and set aside.

PREPARE THE APPLES

2. Melt 2 tablespoons of the butter in a heavy 12-inch sauté pan. Arrange half of the apples cut side down in a single layer, and sauté over medium heat until lightly browned. Using a thin, metal spatula, turn the apples and brown on the other side. Have ready a large, rimmed cookie sheet lined with a double thickness of paper towels. When the apples are done, using the metal spatula, transfer them to the rimmed cookie sheet. Add 1 more tablespoon of butter to the pan, sauté the remaining apples, and transfer them to the rimmed cookie sheet. (It's OK to add a bit more butter to the pan if needed.)

3. Add the remaining 2 tablespoons of butter, the brown sugar, and the brandy to the sauté pan. Cook over medium heat until the sugar is melted. Simmer for 2 to 3 minutes, or until large bubbles and a thick syrup form. Pour the syrup into the cake pan and tilt it to distribute evenly. (It's okay if the liquid does not cover the entire bottom of the pan.) Arrange the apples in rows on top of the syrup.

MAKE THE BATTER

4. In a medium bowl, whisk together the flour, ginger, baking soda, cinnamon, salt, nutmeg, and cloves. Set aside.

5. Cut the butter into 1-inch pieces and place in the bowl of an electric mixer fitted with the paddle attachment. Mix on medium speed until smooth, $1\frac{1}{2}$ to 2 minutes. Add the brown sugar and mix until well blended. Add the eggs, one at a time, about 1 minute apart. With the machine off, add the molasses and the crystallized ginger. Scrape down the side of the bowl.

6. With the mixer on low speed, blend in half of the dry ingredients, add the milk, then add the remaining dry ingredients. Mix just until blended after each addition. Pour the batter over the apples and smooth the top with a small, offset spatula.

BAKE THE CAKE

7. Bake for 50 to 55 minutes, or until the top of the gingerbread is springy to the touch and begins to release from the side of the pan. Remove the cake from the oven and place on a cooling rack for 10 minutes. Run a knife around the side of the pan, then set aside until ready to serve. Serve warm.

STORAGE: Store at room temperature loosely wrapped in aluminum foil for up to 2 days. Freezing is not recommended.

NOTE: Since upside-down cakes are best served shortly after inverting, do not invert the cake until you are ready to serve it. If you make this cake early in the day, reheat the cake in a 350°F oven for 10 to 15 minutes to melt the juices again. Invert the cake onto a serving platter. To allow the caramelized juices to coat the top of the cake, do not remove the pan for a few minutes. When you remove the pan, if any apples remain, replace them on top of the cake.

irish soda bread

MAKES TWO 8-INCH ROUND BREADS, 6 TO 8 SERVINGS PER BREAD

Every March, before St. Patrick's Day, I look forward to preparing this simple-to-make Irish soda bread. It is absolutely the best that I have ever come across. This recipe came to me by way of Ellen Meehen, whose family hails from the Emerald Isle.

The characteristic cross that appears on top of Irish soda bread is made by cutting deeply into the round of dough before it is baked. This is best done with the blade of a single-edge razor blade, available in most drug stores. A sharp, thin-bladed paring knife will do in a pinch, but it tears the dough and you won't achieve the same result.

4 cups strained unbleached all-purpose flour, spooned in and leveled, plus additional for kneading

$1/4$ cup sugar

1 tablespoon caraway seeds

2 teaspoons baking powder

$1/2$ teaspoon salt

$1/2$ cup (1 stick) unsalted butter, cut into $1/2$-inch cubes, at room temperature

1 to 2 cups dark raisins, plumped (see page 358)

$1\frac{1}{3}$ cups buttermilk

1 teaspoon baking soda

2 large eggs

1 large egg white

1 large egg yolk beaten with 1 teaspoon water, for egg wash

AT A GLANCE

PANS: Two 8-inch round layer cake pans

PAN PREP: Generously buttered

RACK LEVEL: Lower third

OVEN TEMP: 375°F

BAKING TIME: 45–50 minutes

DIFFICULTY: 1

1. Position the rack in the lower third of the oven. Heat the oven to 375°F. Generously butter the two cake pans and set aside.

2. In a large bowl, thoroughly whisk together the flour, sugar, caraway seeds, baking powder, and salt.

3. Add the butter to the flour mixture and, using a pastry blender, work the butter into the dry ingredients until the mixture resembles coarse meal. Stir in the raisins.

4. In a small bowl, blend together the buttermilk, baking soda, whole eggs, and egg white. Stir the liquid into the flour mixture, blending together with a fork. When the liquid is absorbed, turn the batter onto a floured work surface. The mixture will be sticky. With floured hands, knead lightly just until the dough is smooth.

5. Divide the dough in half. Working with one piece of dough at a time, lightly flour the cut side and shape into a ball. Place into a pan and flatten slightly. Using a single-edge razor blade or a sharp knife held at a 25° angle, cut a 4-inch cross, about ½-inch deep, in the center of each ball.

6. Combine the egg yolk with the water and brush over the surface of the dough, brushing from the bottom up. Bake for 45 to 50 minutes, or until golden brown. Remove from the oven and place on a rack to cool. To slice, cut the soda bread in half with a serrated knife. Working with one half at a time, place the cut side down on a cutting board and slice across into ½- to ¾-inch pieces.

STORAGE: Store at room temperature, tightly wrapped in aluminum foil, for up to 3 days.

grandma jennie's date and nut bread

MAKES 4 ROUND BREADS, 3 TO 4 SERVINGS PER BREAD; OR 2 MEDIUM LOAVES, 6 TO 8 SERVINGS PER LOAF

I came across this 1940s recipe quite by accident when shopping in a local handbag store. I was discussing my latest venture with Bernice Frankel, my saleswoman, who enthusiastically recalled her Grandma Jennie's delectable date and nut bread.

During that era, date and nut breads were often baked in cans with the lids removed. When unmolded, the finished bread revealed the ridges of the can. If you want to re-create the original look of this bread, be sure to use 19-ounce cans (such as those used for Progresso canned products). Avoid cans with pop-top lids, as they do not work, and be sure to butter the cans extremely well. As an alternative, Grandma Jennie's bread can be baked in loaf pans.

1 pound pitted dates, cut into $\frac{1}{2}$-inch pieces

2 cups boiling water

2 teaspoons baking soda

3 cups strained all-purpose flour, spooned in and leveled

$\frac{1}{2}$ teaspoon salt

$\frac{1}{2}$ teaspoon ground allspice

$\frac{1}{2}$ cup (1 stick) unsalted butter, slightly firm

1 teaspoon grated navel orange zest

$\frac{3}{4}$ cup granulated sugar

$\frac{1}{2}$ cup lightly packed very fresh dark brown sugar

2 large eggs

1 teaspoon pure vanilla extract

$1\frac{1}{4}$ cups walnuts, cut into $\frac{1}{2}$-inch pieces

AT A GLANCE

PANS: Four empty 19-ounce cans (not pop-top) with tops removed or two 8½- × 4½- × 2¾-inch loaf pans

PAN PREP: Buttered generously and lined with buttered parchment

RACK LEVEL: Lower third

OVEN TEMP: 350°F

BAKING TIME: 60–65 minutes for loaves, 50–55 minutes for cans

DIFFICULTY: 1

1. Position the rack in the lower third of the oven. Heat the oven to 350°F. Generously butter four 19-ounce tin cans using a pastry brush, line the bottoms with baking parchment circles, then butter the parchment. Or generously butter two 8½- × 4½- × 2¾-inch loaf pans, line the bottoms with baking parchment, then butter the parchment.

2. Place the dates in a 2-quart bowl. Stir in the boiling water and the baking soda. Set aside.

3. In a large bowl, thoroughly whisk together the flour, salt, and allspice. Set aside.

4. Cut the butter into 1-inch pieces and place in the bowl of an electric mixer fitted with the paddle attachment. Add the orange zest and mix on medium speed until lightened in color, 1½ to 2 minutes. Add the granulated sugar, 1 to 2 tablespoons at a time, taking about 2 minutes, then add the brown sugar, taking another 2 minutes, scraping down the side of the bowl as necessary, and mix for 1 minute longer.

5. Add the eggs, one at a time, mixing for 1 minute after each addition, then blend in the vanilla. Scrape down the side of the bowl.

6. Reduce the mixer speed to low and add the flour mixture alternately with the date mixture, dividing the flour into four parts and the dates into three parts, beginning and ending with the flour. Remove the bowl from the mixer and, using an oversize rubber spatula, fold in the walnuts.

7. If baking in tin cans, fill each can with 1½ cups of batter. Tap the cans firmly on the counter to level the batter. Bake for 50 to 55 minutes. Alternatively, divide the batter between the loaf pans and bake for 60 to 65 minutes. The bread is done when it is firm to the touch, the sides begin to release, and a toothpick inserted in the center comes out clean.

8. Remove from the oven and let cool on racks for about 20 minutes. Invert each bread onto a rack and gently lift off the cans or pans and the parchment. When the breads are cool enough to handle, carefully turn them right side up.

STORAGE: Store at room temperature, tightly covered with plastic wrap, for up to 5 days, or refrigerate for up to 10 days. These breads may be frozen.

pumpkin pecan loaf

MAKES 1 LARGE LOAF, 8 TO 10 SERVINGS

Here is a terrific recipe for a pumpkin quick bread. The pleasantly spiced batter has orange and lemon zests, which enhance the flavor of pumpkin. Be sure to use pure pumpkin puree, not ready-made pumpkin pie filling; a popular brand is Libby's. This is a quick bread that gets better with age. However, in my experience, it is always devoured in the blink of an eye.

1¾ cups all-purpose flour, spooned in and leveled

1½ teaspoons ground cinnamon

1 teaspoon baking powder

1 teaspoon baking soda

½ teaspoon salt

½ teaspoon ground nutmeg

¼ teaspoon ground allspice

2 large eggs

¾ cup lightly packed very fresh dark brown sugar

⅓ cup granulated sugar

2 teaspoons freshly grated navel orange zest

1 teaspoon freshly grated lemon zest

½ cup canola oil

1¼ cups canned pure pumpkin puree

½ cup medium-chopped toasted pecans (see page 356)

AT A GLANCE

PAN: 9- × 5- × 2½-inch loaf pan

PAN PREP: Buttered generously and lined with buttered parchment

RACK LEVEL: Center

OVEN TEMP: 325°F

BAKING TIME: 60–65 minutes

DIFFICULTY: 1

1. Position the rack in the center of the oven. Heat the oven to 325°F. Generously butter the loaf pan, line the bottom with baking parchment, then butter the parchment. Set aside.

2. Combine the flour, cinnamon, baking powder, baking soda, salt, nutmeg, and allspice in a medium bowl and whisk until thoroughly combined. Set aside.

3. In the bowl of an electric mixer fitted with the whip attachment, beat the eggs on medium-high speed for 2 minutes, or until lightened in color. Add the brown sugar, 1 to 2 tablespoons at a time, taking about 2 minutes, and the granulated sugar, taking about 1 minute. Add the orange and lemon zests and beat for 1 minute longer. Scrape down the side of the bowl as needed.

4. Reduce the mixer speed to medium-low and drizzle in the oil in a steady stream, taking about 2 minutes. Reduce the mixer speed to low and add the pumpkin puree. Mix until thoroughly combined. Add the dry ingredients in two additions and blend for 10 to 15 seconds, *just* until incorporated. Remove the bowl from the mixer and, using a large rubber spatula, fold in the pecans.

5. Spoon the batter into the pan and bake for 60 to 65 minutes, or until the top feels springy to the touch, or a wooden skewer or a toothpick inserted deeply into the center comes out clean.

6. Remove from the oven and place on a cooling rack. When the loaf is almost cool, invert it onto the rack. Remove the pan, peel off the parchment paper, and turn the loaf top side up. When ready to serve, cut with a serrated knife into ½-inch slices.

STORAGE: Store at room temperature, tightly covered with plastic wrap, for up to 5 days. This loaf may be frozen.

zucchini loaf with apricots and dates

MAKES 1 MEDIUM LOAF, 6 TO 8 SERVINGS

Zucchini is a vegetable that marries well with other flavors because of its neutral taste. Here, the batter is mingled with tangy dried apricots, sweet dates, and a zesty assortment of spices. Toasted walnuts add a touch of crunch. When all of these flavors mellow, this becomes a marvelous tea loaf that you won't want to miss. When preparing the fruit, do not cut the pieces too large.

3 small zucchini (about 1 pound)

1 teaspoon salt

¼ cup (about 2 ounces) dried apricots (not organic), cut into ¼-inch pieces, packed

1½ cups all-purpose flour, spooned in and leveled, plus 2 tablespoons for fruit and nuts

1 teaspoon baking powder

1 teaspoon ground cinnamon

½ teaspoon baking soda

½ teaspoon ground ginger

½ teaspoon ground coriander

2 large eggs

½ cup lightly packed very fresh dark brown sugar

½ cup granulated sugar

¼ cup (½ stick) unsalted butter, melted

¼ cup canola oil

1 teaspoon pure vanilla extract

½ cup (about 4 ounces) diced dates, cut into ¼-inch pieces, packed

¾ cup coarsely chopped toasted walnuts (see page 356)

AT A GLANCE

PAN: 8½- × 4½- × 2¾-inch loaf pan

PAN PREP: Buttered generously and lined with buttered parchment

RACK LEVEL: Lower third

OVEN TEMP: 325°F

BAKING TIME: 65–70 minutes

DIFFICULTY: 1

1. Position the rack in the lower third of the oven. Heat the oven to 325°F. Generously butter the loaf pan, line the bottom with baking parchment, then butter the parchment. Set aside

2. Scrub the zucchini well using a vegetable brush, trim the ends, but do not peel. Cut the zucchini into 1-inch chunks. Shred the zucchini in a food processor fitted with the medium shredder blade using *light* pressure on the pusher. You should have about 4 cups. (Alternatively, the zucchini may be shredded on the half-moon side of a box grater.)

3. Transfer the zucchini to a colander and sprinkle with the salt, working it through to distribute evenly. Place an 8-inch plate directly on top of the zucchini and weigh it down with a heavy object, such as a large can of tomatoes. Let stand for 30 minutes to exude the liquid, then take handfuls of the zucchini and squeeze firmly to remove additional liquid. Set aside.

4. Place the diced apricots in a microwave-safe bowl and add enough water to cover. Microwave on high power for 2 minutes. Empty into a strainer and rinse under cold water to cool. Drain well on paper towels. Set aside.

5. In a large mixing bowl, whisk together $1\frac{1}{2}$ cups of the flour, the baking powder, cinnamon, baking soda, ginger, and coriander. Set aside.

6. Place the eggs in the bowl of a standing mixer fitted with the whip attachment and beat on medium-high speed for 3 minutes. Scrape down the side of the bowl as needed.

7. Add the brown sugar, then the granulated sugar, 1 tablespoon at a time, taking 2 to 3 minutes for each one. Beat for 2 minutes longer, or until the mixture is thickened and lightened in color. Scrape the side of the bowl as needed.

8. Combine the butter and oil. With the mixer on, pour in the butter/oil mixture in a steady stream. Reduce the mixer speed to low and add the zucchini and vanilla. Add the flour mixture all at once, mixing *just* until incorporated. Remove the bowl from the machine.

9. Toss the apricots, dates, and walnuts with the remaining 2 tablespoons of flour. Using an oversize rubber spatula, fold gently into the batter.

10. Pour the batter into the pan and bake for 65 to 70 minutes, or until the top is golden brown and springy to the touch. A wooden skewer or toothpick inserted into the center should come out clean.

11. Remove from the oven and place on a rack to cool. When the loaf is almost cool, invert onto the rack. Remove the pan, peel off the parchment paper, and turn the loaf top side up and cool completely. To serve, cut the loaf into $\frac{1}{2}$-inch slices with a serrated knife, using a back-and-forth sawing motion.

STORAGE: Store at room temperature, tightly covered in aluminum foil or plastic wrap, for up to 5 days, or refrigerate for up to 10 days. This loaf may be frozen.

candied maple walnut pancake loaf

MAKES 1 MEDIUM LOAF, 6 TO 8 SERVINGS

This terrific recipe comes from Yocheved Hirsch, my very talented friend who teaches cooking in Tel Aviv, Israel. I named the cake "Pancake Loaf" because the batter is made with self-rising flour, a flour often used for pancakes, and the finished loaf is soaked with maple syrup. A mixture of chunky walnuts and cinnamon is used as a topping, as well as laced through the batter.

Be sure to poke lots of holes in the top and apply the syrup several times to allow it to be absorbed through the buttery crumb. As the syrup is spooned, the nuts become glazed, giving the finished cake an addictive candied topping.

1 large egg

1 large egg yolk

1 cup sugar

1 teaspoon pure vanilla extract

¼ cup vegetable oil

1 cup self-rising cake flour, spooned in and leveled, sifted

6 tablespoons sour cream

⅔ cup coarsely chopped walnuts (see page 356)

½ teaspoon ground cinnamon

½ cup pure maple syrup

AT A GLANCE

PAN: 8½- × 4½- × 2¾-inch loaf pan

PAN PREP: Buttered generously and lined with buttered parchment

RACK LEVEL: Center

OVEN TEMP: 325°F

BAKING TIME: 40 minutes

DIFFICULTY: 1

1. Position the rack in the center of the oven. Heat the oven to 325°F. Generously butter the loaf pan, line the bottom with baking parchment, then butter the parchment. Set aside.

2. In the bowl of an electric mixer fitted with the whip attachment, beat the whole egg and egg yolk on medium speed for 1 minute. Add the sugar, 1 to 2 tablespoons at a time, taking about 2 minutes, and continue to beat until thickened, about 2 minutes longer. Blend in the vanilla. Drizzle in the oil in a steady stream, taking about 30 seconds. Beat for 15 seconds longer.

3. Reduce the mixer speed to low. Add one-half of the flour, then blend in the sour cream, then the remaining flour, mixing only until combined after each addition. Remove the bowl from the mixer.

4. Combine the walnuts and cinnamon. Using a rubber spatula, fold ¼ cup of the nut mixture into the batter.

5. Spoon the batter into the pan, smoothing the top with the back of a large soupspoon. Sprinkle the remaining walnut mixture over the top. Bake for about 40 minutes, or until the top of the loaf is golden brown and springy to the touch, and a toothpick inserted deeply in the center comes out clean. *Note:* This loaf will not rise to the top of the pan. The shallow cake allows the maple syrup to be fully absorbed.

6. Remove from the oven and place on a cooling rack. Poke the cake at 1-inch intervals using a wooden or metal skewer, or a toothpick (see headnote). Spoon the maple syrup over the top *very slowly* to allow the cake to absorb the syrup. Do this several times until all the syrup has been absorbed. Let stand for 30 minutes.

7. To remove the pan, place a 10-inch piece of aluminum foil directly on top of the loaf, cupping it around the side to hold the topping in place. Cover with the cooling rack, invert the cake, and carefully lift off the pan and the parchment paper. Cover with another rack, invert again, and cool right side up. To serve, cut the loaf into ½-inch slices using a serrated knife.

STORAGE: Store at room temperature, tightly wrapped in aluminum foil, for up to 3 days. This loaf may be frozen.

all the
classic cakes

absolutely the best yellow cake

zach's chocolate marble cake

devil's food cake with shiny fudge frosting

snow-capped chocolate cream cake

pignoli lemon cake

praline crunch cake

maple walnut cake

chunky chocolate chip cake

chocolate macaroon cake

sweet mays' green mountain apple cake

applesauce spice cake

banana nut cake

golden peach cake

rosy rhubarb cake

pineapple upside-down cake

apple walnut upside-down cake

chocolate pear upside-down cake

orange sponge cake

starmount sponge cake

hot milk sponge cake

absolutely the best yellow cake

MAKES 12 TO 16 SERVINGS

One of the most popular yellow cakes baked in this country is undoubtedly the 1-2-3-4 cake. It derives from the original pound cake formula of one pound each of butter, sugar, eggs, and flour. With the addition of more leavening and more liquid, that formula becomes the best butter cake that I know. The ingredients are perfectly balanced. It is the ideal birthday cake.

3 cups sifted cake flour

1 tablespoon baking powder

$\frac{1}{2}$ teaspoon salt

1 cup (2 sticks) unsalted butter

2 cups superfine or strained sugar

4 large eggs

$1\frac{1}{2}$ teaspoons pure vanilla extract

1 cup milk

Confectioners' sugar for dusting

AT A GLANCE

PAN: 10-inch angel food cake pan (4-quart capacity; see Note)

PAN PREP: Buttered or buttered and floured (see Note)

RACK LEVEL: Lower third

OVEN TEMP: 350°F

BAKING TIME: 65–70 minutes

DIFFICULTY: 1

1. Position the rack in the lower third of the oven. Heat the oven to 350°F. Butter the angel food pan (see Note).

2. Using a triple sifter, sift together the flour, baking powder, and salt. Set aside.

3. Cut the butter into 1-inch pieces and place in the large bowl of an electric mixer fitted with beaters or the paddle attachment. Soften on low speed. Increase the speed to medium-high and cream until smooth and light in color, $1\frac{1}{2}$ to 2 minutes.

4. Add the superfine sugar, 1 tablespoon at a time, taking 8 to 10 minutes to blend it in well. Scrape the side of the bowl occasionally.

5. Add the eggs, one at a time at 1-minute intervals. Scrape the side of the bowl as necessary. Blend in the vanilla.

6. Reduce the mixer speed to medium-low. Add the dry ingredients alternately with the milk, dividing the flour mixture into four parts and the liquid into three parts, and starting and ending with the flour. Mix just until incorporated after each addition. Scrape the side of the bowl and mix for 10 seconds longer.

7. Spoon the batter into the pan and smooth the surface with the back of a tablespoon. Center the pan on the rack and bake for 65 to 70 minutes, or until the cake is golden brown on top and comes away from the sides of the pan. A toothpick inserted into the center should come out dry.

8. Remove the cake from the oven and set the pan on a cake rack to cool to room temperature. If you are using a pan with a removable bottom, remove the pan by lifting up the center tube and running a thin-bladed knife under the cake and around the inner tube to loosen the cake. Invert the cake onto the cake rack. If your pan does not have a removable bottom, run a sharp knife around the outer side and inner tube, then invert the cake onto the rack. Place on a cake platter top side up. Just before serving, dust the top of the cake with confectioners' sugar.

STORAGE: Store at room temperature under a glass cake dome or in an airtight container for up to 5 days.

NOTE: This is a large cake. If you prefer, you can substitute three 9-inch layers for the angel food cake pan. Or the recipe can easily be cut in half and baked in any ring or flat-bottomed 2-quart pan. Another alternative would be to make the whole recipe and bake it in 2 smaller pans, one to eat now, and one to freeze to enjoy at a later date. Remember to reduce the baking time when using smaller pans. Let your nose be the guide in judging the time. About 3 to 5 minutes after you notice a wonderful aroma coming from the oven, the cake should be just about done.

If the cake is baked in a fluted ring pan, be sure to butter and *flour* the pan. Let the baked cake cool in the pan for 10 to 15 minutes, then remove the pan while the cake is still warm. Serve bottom side up.

zach's chocolate marble cake

MAKES 10 TO 12 SERVINGS

As my children were growing up, a rousing yuh-m-m came from them whenever I made this cake. I knew it was their favorite because it vanished so fast. Now my grandson Zach is following in their footsteps. I can tell by how fast his little fingers put the cake into his mouth that it's his number-one choice as well. This is a variation of Absolutely the Best Yellow Cake. As with that one, you may divide the batter and bake it in two 6-cup ring pans. Be sure to butter and flour the pans. This wonderful cake needs nothing more than a dusting of confectioners' sugar to be perfect, but you may also give it a chocolate glaze. Whatever you choose, it is a winner.

CAKE

$1\frac{1}{2}$ ounces unsweetened chocolate, coarsely chopped

$1\frac{1}{2}$ tablespoons vegetable shortening

2 tablespoons honey

Scant $\frac{1}{2}$ teaspoon baking soda

1 teaspoon espresso powder

2 tablespoons boiling water

$2\frac{1}{3}$ cups sifted cake flour

2 teaspoons double-acting baking powder

$\frac{1}{2}$ teaspoon salt

$\frac{1}{4}$ teaspoon freshly ground nutmeg

$\frac{3}{4}$ cup ($1\frac{1}{2}$ sticks) unsalted butter

$1\frac{1}{2}$ cups superfine or strained sugar

4 large eggs

1 teaspoon pure vanilla extract

$\frac{3}{4}$ cup milk

GLAZE

$\frac{1}{2}$ cup heavy cream

1 tablespoon light corn syrup

4 ounces semisweet or bittersweet chocolate, coarsely chopped

1 to 2 tablespoons coffee liqueur

$\frac{1}{2}$ teaspoon pure vanilla extract

AT A GLANCE

PAN: 10-inch Bundt pan (12-cup capacity)

PAN PREP: Generously buttered and floured

RACK LEVEL: Lower third

OVEN TEMP: 350°F

BAKING TIME: 55–65 minutes

DIFFICULTY: 1

1. Position the rack in the lower third of the oven. Heat the oven to 350°F. Generously butter the Bundt pan. Dust with all-purpose flour and invert over the sink, tapping out excess.

MAKE THE CAKE

2. In a small bowl, melt the chocolate and vegetable shortening over hot water or in a microwave oven, using a medium setting. Stir well to be sure the chocolate is completely melted. Blend in the honey. Sprinkle the baking soda over the top of the chocolate and blend well. Dissolve the espresso powder in the boiling water and add to the chocolate mixture, stirring until completely smooth. Set aside. The mixture will thicken as it stands.

3. Using a triple sifter, sift together the flour, baking powder, salt, and nutmeg. Set aside.

4. Cut the butter into 1-inch pieces and place in the large bowl of an electric mixer fitted with beaters or the paddle attachment to soften on low speed. Increase the speed to medium-high and cream until smooth and light in color, 1½ to 2 minutes.

5. Add the sugar 1 tablespoon at a time, taking 6 to 8 minutes to blend it in well. Scrape the side of the bowl occasionally.

6. Add the eggs, one at a time at 1-minute intervals. Scrape the side of the bowl as necessary. Blend in the vanilla.

7. Reduce the mixer speed to low. Add the dry ingredients alternately with the milk, dividing the flour into three parts and the liquid into two parts, and starting and ending with the flour. Mix only until incorporated after each addition. Scrape the side of the bowl and mix for 10 seconds longer.

8. Transfer 1 generous cup of batter to a separate bowl. Stir the chocolate mixture, then blend it into the cup of vanilla batter, gently folding the two together.

LAYER THE CHOCOLATE AND VANILLA BATTERS

9. Spoon one-half of the remaining vanilla batter into the bottom of the pan, smoothing the surface with the bottom of a tablespoon. Using a tablespoon, drop one-half of the chocolate batter by spoonfuls around the pan. With the bottom of the tablespoon, spread the chocolate batter, working from the middle to the side, until the vanilla batter is completely covered. Top with a second layer of vanilla, reserving about 1 cup for the last layer. Spread the batter again from the middle, then drop the remaining chocolate batter over the vanilla, spreading it to the edges. End the layering with the remaining vanilla batter, spreading the batter over the chocolate as best as you can. You should have three layers of vanilla and two layers of chocolate.

MARBLEIZE THE CAKE

10. Insert a table knife into the batter with the tip pointed downward and *almost* touching the bottom. Then lift the knife up and gently fold the two batters together. Repeat by inserting the knife down again, going around the pan at about 2-inch intervals for a total of 10 to 12 times. For a less marbled effect, simply run the knife around the pan three times at 1-inch intervals. Smooth the top of the batter. Center the pan on the rack and bake for 55 to 65 minutes, or until the cake is golden brown on top, and begins to come away from the sides of the pan. A toothpick inserted into the center should come out dry.

(continued)

11. Remove the cake from the oven and set the pan on a wire rack to cool for 15 or 20 minutes. Place a wire rack over the top of the pan and invert. Let the cake stand for about 30 seconds and then gently remove the pan. Allow the cake to cool completely. Glaze the cake or dust the top with confectioners' sugar.

MAKE THE GLAZE

12. Place the heavy cream, corn syrup, and coarsely chopped chocolate in a small *heavy* saucepan. Over low heat, stir constantly until the chocolate is completely melted. Do not beat. Watch for bubbles to appear on the side of the pot. The mixture should *just* come to a boil.

13. Set the saucepan in a larger pan filled with ice water. When the mixture is tepid, blend in the liqueur and vanilla. As the glaze cools, it should thicken to the consistency of thick chocolate sauce. Pour the glaze through a fine-mesh strainer to remove any air bubbles. If the glaze fails to thicken, place it in the refrigerator for 4 to 5 minutes.

14. Set the wire rack with the cake over a shallow pan to catch the dripping glaze. Spoon the glaze over the cake, allowing the icing to drip gently at random down the side, leaving parts of the cake exposed.

STORAGE: Store at room temperature under a glass cake dome or in an airtight container for up to 5 days.

devil's food cake with shiny fudge frosting

MAKES 10 TO 12 SERVINGS

Devil's food cake is an American classic impossible to resist if you are a chocophile. This triple-layered version is dramatically high and absolutely mouth watering.

¾ cup strained unsweetened cocoa, such as Hershey's (do not use Dutch-process cocoa)

½ cup hot water

¾ cup cold water

2¾ cups sifted cake flour

1 teaspoon baking soda

¼ teaspoon salt

¾ cup (1½ sticks) unsalted butter

1 cup superfine sugar

1 cup lightly packed light brown sugar

3 large eggs

1 teaspoon pure vanilla extract

Chocolate Custard Filling (page 257)

Shiny Fudge Frosting (page 374)

1. Position racks in the lower and upper third of the oven. Heat the oven to 350°F. Butter the pans. Line the bottoms and sides with wax paper and lightly butter the wax paper.

2. Put the cocoa in a small bowl. Slowly add the hot water, stirring until smooth, then blend in the cold water. Set aside.

3. Sift together the flour, baking soda, and salt, using a triple sifter. Set aside.

4. Place the butter, cut into 1-inch pieces, in the large bowl of an electric mixer fitted with beaters or the paddle attachment. Soften on low speed. Increase the mixer speed to medium-high and cream the butter until smooth and light in color, 1½ to 2 minutes.

5. Add the superfine sugar, 1 tablespoon at a time, taking 3 to 4 minutes to blend it in well. Then add the brown sugar, 1 tablespoon at a time, over an additional 3 to 4 minutes. Scrape the side of the bowl occasionally.

6. Add the eggs, one at a time at 1-minute intervals, scraping the side of the bowl as necessary. Blend in the vanilla.

7. Reduce the mixer speed to low. Add the dry ingredients alternately with the cocoa liquid, dividing the flour into three parts and the liquid into two parts, and starting and ending with the flour. Mix only until incorporated after each addition. Scrape the side of the bowl. Mix 10 seconds longer.

AT A GLANCE

PANS: Three 9-inch layer pans (see Note)

PAN PREP: Buttered and lined with buttered wax paper

RACK LEVELS: Lower and upper thirds

OVEN TEMP: 350°F

BAKING TIME: 25–30 minutes

DIFFICULTY: 1

(continued)

BAKE THE LAYERS

8. Spoon the batter into the pans, smoothing the surface with the back of a tablespoon. Place two pans on the lower rack of the oven and center the third pan on the upper rack. Bake for 25 to 30 minutes, or until the cakes begin to come away from the sides of the pans and the tops are springy to the touch. While the cakes are baking, prepare the filling.

9. Remove the pans from the oven. Set onto cake racks for 10 minutes to cool slightly, then invert onto the racks sprayed with nonstick coating and remove the pans. Carefully peel off the paper. Allow to cool completely before assembling.

ASSEMBLE THE CAKE

10. Place the first layer top side down on a serving plate. Slide 4 strips of wax paper between the plate and the bottom of the cake and cover the cake with half of the chocolate custard, leaving a ½-inch border around the edge.

11. Place the second layer top side down and spread with the remaining half of the custard. Arrange the third layer over the second, top side up, and align the three layers so the side of the cake is straight. Place the filled cake in the refrigerator to set while you prepare the frosting.

12. When ready to frost the cake, hold the container 10 inches above the cake and pour on enough frosting to cover the top. Using a 10-inch metal spatula, spread it across, allowing excess to drip down the side. *Do this only once, as the frosting sets quickly.* The frosting should be fluid enough to drip, but not too runny. Holding the spatula vertically, run it around the side of the cake to smooth the frosting.

13. For an attractive melted tallow effect, drop spoonfuls of the remaining frosting down the side of the cake, beginning at the top edge. Drizzle 2 to 3 tablespoons randomly over the top of the cake.

14. When the frosting is completely set, carefully remove the wax paper from the plate. Allow the cake to stand uncovered until the frosting is very firm.

STORAGE: This cake may be kept in a cool place under a glass dome if you plan to eat it shortly after it is made. For longer storage, cover loosely with an aluminum foil tent and refrigerate. Allow to stand at room temperature 2 to 3 hours before serving. The cake will keep up to 5 days.

NOTE: You may bake this in two 9-inch layer pans, then divide the baked layers into four disks. The filling will be spread a little more thinly than with 3 layers, and the cake may take an additional 5 minutes of baking time.

chocolate custard filling

MAKES ABOUT 2 CUPS, ENOUGH TO FILL TWO 9-INCH LAYERS

1½ cups milk

⅓ cup heavy cream

2 ounces unsweetened chocolate, finely chopped

½ cup sugar

2 tablespoons cornstarch

4 teaspoons flour

⅛ teaspoon salt

3 large egg yolks

1½ teaspoons pure vanilla extract

1. Fill the bottom of a double boiler with 1 to 1½ inches of water. Bring to a boil and reduce the flame to low.

2. Put the milk, cream, and chocolate in the top portion of the double boiler. Set over the boiling water and heat, stirring with a whisk, until the chocolate is completely melted and the mixture is smooth.

3. In a medium-sized mixing bowl, whisk together the sugar, cornstarch, flour, and salt. Whisk the dry ingredients rapidly into the hot milk, blending until smooth.

4. Stir constantly with a wooden spoon and, as the mixture thickens to the consistency of warm chocolate pudding, use the whisk again to remove any lumps that may have formed, but do not overmix. Cover the pot and cook the filling for 10 to 12 minutes, stirring occasionally. Be sure to reach into the corners of the saucepan to remove any lumps that may have accumulated.

5. In a small bowl, lightly beat the egg yolks. Add about ⅓ cup of the hot filling to the yolks to temper them. Then return the yolk mixture to the remaining hot filling and stir thoroughly with a wooden spoon. Continue to cook over low heat for 2 to 3 minutes, stirring occasionally. The custard will thicken further. If the filling is not smooth, whisk again briefly.

6. Remove the custard from the top of the double boiler and blend in the vanilla. Empty the filling into a bowl, cover the top with buttered wax paper or parchment, and let stand at room temperature for 15 minutes. Then refrigerate until cold.

STORAGE: Refrigerate, tightly covered, for up to 3 days.

snow-capped chocolate cream cake

MAKES 10 TO 12 SERVINGS

In this unusual cake, coarsely cut nonpareil candies are sprinkled over the top of a chocolate–whipped cream batter. As the cake bakes, the candy sinks slightly and forms a rippled surface with an attractive snow-capped effect.

Be sure to purchase a fine-quality chocolate nonpareil, such as those sold in specialty candy stores. Do not try to chop them in the processor; too many of the tiny beads will separate from the wafers, while the candy will remain almost whole. Even with a minimum of handling, some beads will fall from the candies. Put aside these extra beads to sprinkle over the top of the glazed cake.

1 cup (6 ounces) semisweet chocolate nonpareil candies

4 ounces semisweet chocolate, such as Lindt Excellence, Tobler Tradition, or Baker's German's Sweet, broken into pieces

¼ cup hot water

2 teaspoons instant espresso powder

2 cups sifted cake flour

1½ teaspoons baking powder

⅛ teaspoon baking soda

3 large eggs

1¼ cups superfine or strained sugar

1½ teaspoons pure vanilla extract

1¼ cups heavy cream, whipped to firm peaks

1 small recipe Quick Chocolate Glaze (page 369)

AT A GLANCE

PAN: 9- × 13- × 2-inch oblong baking pan

PAN PREP: Buttered

RACK LEVEL: Lower third

OVEN TEMP: 350°F

BAKING TIME: 40–45 minutes

DIFFICULTY: 1

1. Position the rack in the lower third of the oven. Heat the oven to 350°F. Butter the pan.

2. Cut the nonpareil candies by hand into ¼- to ½-inch pieces, and set aside.

3. Put the chocolate, hot water, and espresso in a small dish. Melt in the microwave on medium power, or set the dish in a skillet containing ½ inch of hot water. Stir until the chocolate melts. Blend with a whisk until completely smooth. Set aside to cool.

4. Using a triple sifter, sift together the flour, baking powder, and baking soda. Set aside.

5. Place the eggs in the large bowl of an electric mixer fitted with beaters or the whip attachment. Beat on medium-high speed until light in color and thickened, approximately 2 minutes. Add the sugar, 1 tablespoon at a time, taking 3 to 4 minutes to blend it in well.

6. Reduce the mixer speed to low. Add the vanilla. Blend in the melted chocolate mixture, mixing just until incorporated. Scrape the side of the bowl as necessary.

7. Add the dry ingredients alternately with the whipped cream, dividing the flour mixture into three parts and the cream into two parts, and starting and ending with the flour. Mix just until incorporated after each addition. Scrape the side of the bowl as necessary.

8. Spoon the batter into the buttered pan and smooth the surface with the back of a tablespoon. Sprinkle the nonpareils evenly over the top, but do not press them into the batter. Place the pan in the center of the rack and bake for 40 to 45 minutes, or until the cake is springy to the touch and begins to come away from the side of the pan.

9. Remove the cake from the oven and place the pan on a cake rack to cool to room temperature. Dip a teaspoon into the chocolate glaze and drizzle randomly over the top of the cake. Be sure to leave parts of the rippled surface of the cake exposed. Immediately sprinkle the extra nonpareil beads over the cake. Shake the pan two or three times so the beads will cling to the glaze. Cut the cake into squares just before serving.

STORAGE: Store at room temperature, covered with aluminum foil, for up to 5 days.

pignoli lemon cake

MAKES 10 TO 12 SERVINGS

Pignolis, pine nuts, or Indian nuts—whatever you choose to call these small, cream-colored oval nuts—are versatile and delicious. Recipes containing pine nuts usually come from countries along the Mediterranean and Balkan Seas, where they adorn all sorts of baked goods in addition to providing accent in a variety of savory dishes and salads.

This cake is pleasingly tart, with a smooth-textured crumb and a sugar-glazed surface.

1 cup pine nuts (pignolis)	1⅓ cups superfine or strained sugar
2¼ cups sifted cake flour	2 large egg yolks
1 teaspoon baking powder	2 large whole eggs
½ teaspoon baking soda	1 tablespoon fresh lemon juice
¼ teaspoon salt	1 teaspoon pure vanilla extract
½ cup (1 stick) unsalted butter	1 cup unsweetened plain low-fat yogurt
1½ to 2 teaspoons freshly grated lemon zest	

AT A GLANCE

PAN: 10-inch Bundt pan
(12-cup capacity)

PAN PREP: Generously
buttered and sugared

RACK LEVEL: Lower third

OVEN TEMP: 325°/350°F

BAKING TIME: 50–55 minutes

DIFFICULTY: 1

1. Position the rack in the lower third of the oven. Heat the oven to 325°F. Generously butter the Bundt pan. Dust heavily with granulated sugar, invert over the kitchen sink, and tap to remove excess.

2. Place the pine nuts in a shallow pan and toast in the oven for 6 to 8 minutes. Watch carefully so that they don't burn. Set aside to cool. Increase the oven temperature to 350°F.

3. Using a triple sifter, sift together the flour, baking powder, baking soda, and salt. Set aside.

4. Cut the butter into 1-inch pieces and place in the large bowl of an electric mixer fitted with beaters or the paddle attachment, add the lemon zest, and soften on low speed. Increase to medium-high and cream until smooth and light in color, 1½ to 2 minutes.

5. Add the sugar, 1 tablespoon at a time, taking 6 to 8 minutes to blend it in well. Scrape the side of the bowl as necessary.

6. Add the egg yolks and beat for 1 minute, scraping the side of the bowl occasionally. Add the whole eggs at 1-minute intervals. Beat for 1 minute longer. Blend in the lemon juice and vanilla.

7. Reduce the mixer speed to low. Add the dry ingredients alternately with the yogurt, dividing the flour mixture into three parts and the yogurt into two parts, and starting and ending with the flour. Mix just until incorporated after each addition. Scrape the side of the bowl as necessary, and mix for 10 seconds longer.

8. Remove the bowl from the mixer. Fold in the pine nuts.

9. Spoon the cake batter into the sugar-coated pan, smoothing the surface with the back of a tablespoon. Center the pan on the rack and bake for 50 to 55 minutes, or until the cake begins to come away from the sides of the pan. A toothpick inserted into the center should come out dry.

10. Remove the cake from the oven. Set on a cake rack to cool for 15 to 20 minutes, then invert the cake onto the rack. Gently remove the pan and allow the cake to cool completely. When ready to serve, cut into 1-inch slices.

STORAGE: Store at room temperature under a glass dome or in an airtight container for up to 5 days.

praline crunch cake

MAKES 8 TO 10 SERVINGS

Praline, a candy made by caramelizing pecans with sugar, is traditional to New Orleans Creole cuisine. In this recipe, the candy is crushed and stirred into the buttery sugar batter along with additional chopped pecans. The batter is then marbleized with a crunchy pecan filling. This is a pecan lover's dream.

NUT FILLING

1 cup pecans

¼ cup granulated sugar

¼ cup lightly packed light brown sugar

2 teaspoons ground cinnamon

CAKE

2 cups sifted cake flour

1 teaspoon baking soda

¼ teaspoon salt

½ cup (1 stick) unsalted butter

1 cup lightly packed light brown sugar

2 large eggs

1 teaspoon pure vanilla extract

¾ cup buttermilk

½ cup crushed praline (page 380)

½ cup pecans, chopped medium-fine (see page 356)

Confectioners' sugar for dusting (optional)

AT A GLANCE

PAN: Fluted ring pan (8-cup capacity)

PAN PREP: Buttered and floured

RACK LEVEL: Lower third

OVEN TEMP: 350°F

BAKING TIME: 45–50 minutes

DIFFICULTY: 2

1. Position the rack in the lower third of the oven. Heat the oven to 350°F. Butter the ring pan and dust with all-purpose flour. Invert the pan over the kitchen sink and tap to remove excess flour.

MAKE THE FILLING

2. Place the nuts, granulated and brown sugars, and cinnamon in the container of a food processor fitted with a steel blade. Pulse six to eight times, or until the nuts are medium chopped. Transfer to a small bowl and set aside.

MAKE THE CAKE

3. Sift the flour, baking soda, and salt together in a triple sifter. Set aside.

4. Cut the butter into 1-inch pieces and put in the large bowl of an electric mixer fitted with beaters or the paddle attachment. Soften on low speed, then increase to medium-high and cream until smooth and light in color, 1½ to 2 minutes.

5. Add the brown sugar, 1 tablespoon at a time, taking 6 to 8 minutes to blend it in well. Scrape the side of the bowl occasionally.

6. Add the eggs, one at a time at 1-minute intervals, scraping the side of the bowl as necessary. Beat for 1 minute longer. Blend in the vanilla.

7. Reduce the mixer speed to low. Add the dry ingredients alternately with the buttermilk, dividing the dry ingredients into three parts and liquid into two parts, and starting and ending with the flour. Scrape the side of the bowl and mix for 10 seconds longer. Remove the bowl from the mixer. Fold in the crushed praline and chopped pecans.

8. Spoon about one-third of the batter into the bottom of the pan. Sprinkle with half of the chopped nut filling. Repeat, alternating batter and filling, ending with a layer of batter. You should have three layers of batter and two layers of nut filling.

9. Using a table knife, cut into the batter almost to the bottom of the pan. Rotating the pan, gently fold about eight times.

10. Bake for 45 to 50 minutes, or until the cake begins to leave the sides of pan. A toothpick inserted into center will come out dry.

11. Remove the cake from the oven and place the pan on a cake rack to cool for 10 to 15 minutes. Invert onto the rack and gently remove the pan. Allow the cake to cool completely. Just before serving, dust the top of the cake with confectioners' sugar, if you wish. When ready to serve cut into 1-inch slices.

STORAGE: Store at room temperature under a glass cake dome for up to 4 days.

maple walnut cake

MAKES 10 TO 12 SERVINGS

During the early years of my marriage, I lived in Burlington, Vermont, and learned to appreciate the beauty of Vermont's sugar maple trees. In the early spring, when the snow still chills the ground, the sap from the trees begins to run. Among the workers it is traditional to celebrate the end of the tapping season at "sugar-in-snow" parties, where the intensely sweet hot syrup is poured over clean white snow to form a candy-like maple ice enjoyed by children and adults alike.

Maple sap is processed into several grades of syrup. Fancy Grade, which is light amber in color with a delicate flavor, is considered prime, but many native Vermonters prefer the stronger-flavored Grade A. If you have the opportunity, try this thick sweet syrup. I, too, think it has more character.

Although I recommend that you make this with pure Vermont maple syrup, you may substitute any store brand of genuine (not imitation) maple syrup. I think you'll find the combination of walnuts and maple syrup intriguing: This cake does not just appeal to adults. As with the maple ice, children will love it too.

$^2/_3$ cup sour cream

$^2/_3$ cup maple syrup

$^1/_4$ teaspoon baking soda

$2^1/_2$ cups sifted cake flour

2 teaspoons baking powder

$^1/_2$ teaspoon salt

$^3/_4$ cup ($1^1/_2$ sticks) unsalted butter

$^1/_2$ cup granulated sugar

$^2/_3$ cup lightly packed light brown sugar

3 large eggs

$1^1/_2$ teaspoons pure vanilla extract

$^1/_2$ teaspoon imitation maple extract

$1^1/_2$ cups walnuts, chopped medium-fine

1 large recipe Vanilla Glaze (page 368), flavored with $^1/_2$ teaspoon imitation maple extract; or confectioners' sugar for dusting

AT A GLANCE

PAN: 10-inch Bundt pan (12-cup capacity)

PAN PREP: Buttered and floured

RACK LEVEL: Lower third

OVEN TEMP: 350°F

BAKING TIME: 55–60 minutes

DIFFICULTY: 1

1. Position a rack in the lower third of the oven. Heat the oven to 350°F. Butter the Bundt pan, dust the pan with all-purpose flour, and invert it over the kitchen sink to tap out excess.

2. In a small bowl whisk together the sour cream, maple syrup, and baking soda. Set aside.

3. Using a triple sifter, sift together the flour, baking powder, and salt. Set aside.

4. Cut the butter into 1-inch pieces and place in the large bowl of an electric mixer fitted with beaters or the paddle attachment to soften on low speed. Increase to medium-high and cream until smooth and light in color, $1^1/_2$ to 2 minutes.

5. Add the granulated sugar, 1 tablespoon at a time, taking 3 to 4 minutes to blend it in well. Then add the brown sugar, 1 tablespoon at a time, taking an additional 3 to 4 minutes. Scrape the side of the bowl as necessary.

6. Add the eggs, one at a time at 1-minute intervals, scraping the side of the bowl. Blend in the vanilla and maple extracts.

7. Reduce the mixer speed to low. Add the dry ingredients, alternating with the sour cream mixture, dividing the flour mixture into three parts and the sour cream into two parts, and starting and ending with the flour. Mix just until incorporated after each addition. Scrape the side of the bowl as necessary, and mix for 10 seconds longer.

8. Remove the bowl from the mixer and fold in the walnuts with a rubber spatula. Spoon the batter into the pan, smoothing the surface with the back of a tablespoon. Center the pan on the rack and bake for 55 to 60 minutes, or until the cake begins to come away from the sides of the pan and a toothpick inserted into the center comes out dry.

9. Remove the cake from the oven. Set it on a cake rack to cool for 15 to 20 minutes. Invert the cake onto the rack and gently lift the pan off the cake. While the cake is still slightly warm, frost with the vanilla glaze. Or simply dust the top of the cake with confectioners' sugar just before serving.

STORAGE: Store at room temperature under a glass dome or in an airtight container for up to 5 days.

chunky chocolate chip cake

MAKES 10 TO 12 SERVINGS

Full of semisweet chocolate bits and coarsely chopped walnuts, this soft-textured cake is especially delicious when served with ice cream.

3 ounces unsweetened chocolate, coarsely chopped

¾ cup plus 2 tablespoons boiling water

2 cups sifted cake flour

1 teaspoon baking soda

½ teaspoon salt

⅔ cup (1⅓ sticks) unsalted butter

1¼ cups superfine or strained sugar

2 large eggs

1 teaspoon pure vanilla extract

1 (6-ounce) package semisweet chocolate chips

1 cup walnuts, coarsely chopped (see page 356)

Confectioners' sugar for dusting, or 1 large recipe Quick Chocolate Glaze (page 369)

AT A GLANCE

PAN: 9- × 13- × 2-inch oblong baking pan

PAN PREP: Buttered

RACK LEVEL: Lower third

OVEN TEMP: 350°F

BAKING TIME: 35–40 minutes

DIFFICULTY: 1

1. Position the rack in the lower third of the oven. Heat the oven to 350°F. Butter the baking dish.

2. Put the chocolate in a small bowl and add the boiling water. Let stand 5 minutes to soften the chocolate, then stir with a whisk until the chocolate is completely melted and the mixture is smooth. Set aside.

3. Using a triple sifter, sift together the flour, baking soda, and salt. Set aside.

4. Cut the butter into 1-inch pieces and place in the large bowl of an electric mixer fitted with beaters or the paddle attachment to soften on low speed. Increase to medium-high and cream until smooth and light in color, 1½ to 2 minutes.

5. Gradually add the sugar, 1 tablespoon at a time, taking 6 to 8 minutes to blend it in well. Scrape the side of the bowl as necessary.

6. Add the eggs one at a time at 1-minute intervals. Beat 1 minute longer. Scrape the side of the bowl again. Blend in the vanilla.

7. Reduce the mixer speed to low. Stir the chocolate mixture. Add the dry ingredients alternating with the chocolate, dividing the flour mixture into four parts and the chocolate into three parts, and starting and ending with the flour. Mix just until incorporated after each addition. Scrape the side of the bowl as necessary, and mix for 10 seconds longer.

8. Remove the bowl from the mixer. With a rubber spatula, fold in the chocolate chips and walnuts. Spoon the batter into the pan, smoothing the surface with the back of a tablespoon. Center the pan on the rack and bake for 35 to 40 minutes, or until the cake begins come away from the side of the pan and a toothpick inserted into the center comes out dry.

9. Remove the cake from the oven and set the pan on a cake rack to cool. Just before serving, dust the top with confectioners' sugar or frost with the chocolate glaze. Since the cake is stored in the pan, the first piece may be difficult to remove because the chocolate and nuts may cause it to crumble. The trick to removing it easily is to cut the first piece with a wet knife, using a gentle sawing motion. Lift the square of cake with a small metal spatula pressed flat against the bottom of the pan. The remaining pieces will lift out easily.

STORAGE: Store at room temperature, covered with aluminum foil, for up to 5 days.

chocolate macaroon cake

MAKES 10 TO 12 SERVINGS

A mixture of meringue, coconut, and toasted pecans swirled through the batter gives this chocolate cake a chewy texture that makes it an excellent choice for cake à la mode. It calls for really top-quality vanilla ice cream.

Take care not to reach too deeply into the pan when marbleizing this cake. It is important that a layer of batter remain on the bottom to keep the thick filling from sinking all the way through to the pan and sticking.

MERINGUE FILLING

¾ cup pecans

1 (3½-ounce) can flaked coconut

2 large egg whites

½ cup superfine sugar

½ teaspoon pure vanilla extract

¼ teaspoon almond extract

CAKE

2¼ cups sifted cake flour

1 teaspoon baking powder

¼ teaspoon baking soda

½ teaspoon salt

⅔ cup (1⅓ sticks) unsalted butter

1 cup superfine or strained sugar

3 large eggs

1½ ounces unsweetened chocolate, melted

1 teaspoon pure vanilla extract

1 (16-ounce) can Hershey's chocolate syrup

1 large recipe Quick Chocolate Glaze (page 369), or confectioners' sugar for dusting

AT A GLANCE

PAN: 10-inch Bundt pan (12-cup capacity)

PAN PREP: Buttered generously and floured

RACK LEVEL: Lower third

OVEN TEMP: 325°/350°F

BAKING TIME: 65–70 minutes

DIFFICULTY: 2

1. Position the rack in the lower third of the oven. Heat the oven to 325°F. Generously butter the Bundt pan. Dust with all-purpose flour, invert the pan over the kitchen sink, and tap out the excess.

MAKE THE FILLING

2. Place the pecans in a shallow pan in the oven for 6 to 8 minutes, or until lightly toasted.

3. Put the coconut and pecans in the container of a food processor fitted with a steel blade. Pulse six to eight times, or until the pecans are chopped medium. Set aside.

4. Put the egg whites in the small bowl of an electric mixer fitted with beaters or the whisk attachment. Beat on medium-low speed until frothy. Increase the speed to medium-high, and beat to firm peaks. Add the superfine sugar, 1 tablespoon at a time, taking 45 to 60 seconds. Add the vanilla and almond extracts, and beat 1 minute longer to form a stiff meringue. Remove the bowl from the mixer and fold in the coconut/pecan mixture. Set aside. Increase the oven temperature to 350°F.

MAKE THE CAKE

5. Using a triple sifter, sift together the flour, baking powder, baking soda, and salt. Set aside.

6. Cut the butter into 1-inch pieces and place in the large bowl of an electric mixer fitted with beaters or the paddle attachment. Soften on low speed. Increase to medium-high and cream until smooth and light in color, 1½ to 2 minutes.

7. Add the superfine sugar, 1 tablespoon at a time, taking 6 to 8 minutes to blend it in well. Scrape the side of the bowl.

8. Add the eggs one at a time at 1-minute intervals, scraping the side of the bowl as necessary. Blend in the melted chocolate and vanilla and scrape the side of the bowl again.

9. Reduce the mixer speed to low. Add the dry ingredients alternating with the chocolate syrup, dividing the flour mixture into three parts and the syrup into two parts, and starting and ending with the flour. Mix just until incorporated after each addition. Scrape the side of the bowl as necessary.

10. Remove the bowl from the mixer. Spoon one-fourth of the batter into the bottom of the pan. Run the back of a tablespoon around the batter to form a well. Spoon one-third of the meringue filling into the well. Repeat, alternating the batter and filling, ending with a layer of batter. You should have four layers of batter and three layers of filling. Smooth the surface with the bottom of a tablespoon, spreading from the center out.

MARBLEIZE THE BATTER

11. Using a table knife, cut into the batter, but do not go completely to the bottom of the pan. Gently fold about eight times, rotating the pan.

12. Center the pan on the rack and bake for 65 to 70 minutes, or until the cake begins to come away from the sides of the pan and the top is springy to the touch. A toothpick inserted into the center should come out dry.

13. Remove the cake from the oven and set the pan on a cake rack to cool for 20 to 30 minutes. Invert the pan onto the rack and carefully remove it. While the cake is still slightly warm, frost with the chocolate glaze. Or simply dust the top with confectioners' sugar just before serving.

STORAGE: Store at room temperature under a glass dome or in an airtight container for up to 5 days.

sweet mays' green mountain apple cake

MAKES 6 TO 8 SERVINGS

This recipe was created by the mother of May Sutter, my friend of many years. May's mother, also named May, lives in the rural Green Mountains of Vermont. Daughter May, a marvelous cook and baker in her own right, refined her mother's "dump and pour" recipe into this moist, delicious apple cake. I named this cake after them both.

2 medium-large cooking apples (about 1 pound), such as Northern Spy, McIntosh, Rome, or Empire

1¼ cups sifted unbleached all-purpose flour

1 teaspoon baking soda

1 teaspoon ground cinnamon

¼ teaspoon ground nutmeg

¼ teaspoon salt

¼ cup (½ stick) unsalted butter

½ cup granulated sugar

1 large egg

1 teaspoon pure vanilla extract

½ cup plumped raisins (see page 358)

½ cup walnuts, chopped medium-fine (see page 356)

Confectioners' sugar for dusting

AT A GLANCE

PAN: 8- × 8- × 2-inch square baking pan

PAN PREP: Buttered

RACK LEVEL: Lower third

OVEN TEMP: 350°F

BAKING TIME: 35–40 minutes

DIFFICULTY: 1

1. Position the rack in the lower third of the oven. Heat the oven to 350°F. Butter the baking pan.

2. Quarter, core, and peel the apples. Divide each apple into eighths and place in the container of a food processor fitted with the steel blade. Pulse four or five times, or until the pieces are about ¼ inch in size. Be careful not to overprocess, or the pieces will be too small. You should have about 2 cups of chopped apples. Set aside.

3. Sift together the flour, baking soda, cinnamon, nutmeg, and salt in a triple sifter.

4. Cut the butter into 1-inch pieces and place in the small bowl of an electric mixer fitted with beaters or the paddle attachment. Soften on low speed. Increase the speed to medium-high, and cream until smooth and light in color, about 1 minute.

5. Add the granulated sugar, 1 tablespoon at a time, taking 2 to 3 minutes to blend it in well. Scrape the side of the bowl occasionally.

6. Add the egg, and beat for 1 minute, scraping the side of the bowl as necessary. Blend in the vanilla.

7. Reduce the mixer speed to low. Add the apples and mix for about 10 seconds. Then blend in the dry ingredients, half at a time. Mix 10 seconds longer.

8. Remove the bowl from the mixer. Fold in the raisins and nuts. Spoon the batter into the pan and smooth the surface. Center the pan on the rack and bake for 35 to 40 minutes, or until the cake is springy to the touch and begins to come away from the sides of the pan.

9. Remove from the oven and set the pan on a cake rack to cool. Just before serving, dust the top with confectioners' sugar. Cut the cake into squares in the pan.

STORAGE: Store at room temperature, covered loosely with aluminum foil, up to 2 days or refrigerate for up to 5 days.

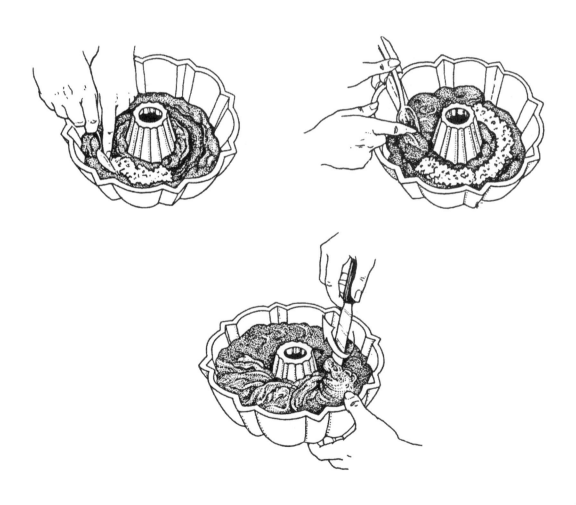

applesauce spice cake

MAKES 8 TO 10 SERVINGS

This moist cake contains both applesauce and tart, freshly grated green apple. Chopped, toasted pecans add texture and flavor. The combination is unbeatable, especially accompanied by a mug of mulled apple cider.

2¼ cups sifted unbleached all-purpose flour

1 teaspoon baking soda

1½ teaspoons ground cinnamon

1 teaspoon ground allspice

1 teaspoon ground nutmeg

½ teaspoon salt

¾ cup pecans, lightly toasted and chopped medium-fine (see page 356); plus additional chopped nuts for garnish (optional)

⅓ cup (⅔ stick) unsalted butter

1 teaspoon grated lemon zest

⅓ cup vegetable shortening

¾ cup granulated sugar

⅔ cup lightly packed light brown sugar

2 large eggs

1 medium-sized tart greening or Granny Smith apple, peeled and chopped medium-small (about ⅔ cup)

1 teaspoon pure vanilla extract

1 cup sweetened bottled applesauce

Brown Sugar Glaze (optional; opposite page)

AT A GLANCE

PAN: 9-inch fluted tube pan (10-cup capacity)

PAN PREP: Buttered and floured

RACK LEVEL: Lower third

OVEN TEMP: 350°F

BAKING TIME: 55–60 minutes

DIFFICULTY: 1

1. Position the rack in the lower third of the oven. Heat the oven to 350°F. Butter the tube pan, dust it lightly with flour, and invert over the kitchen sink to tap out excess flour.

2. Sift together the flour, baking soda, cinnamon, allspice, nutmeg, and salt in a triple sifter. Stir in the chopped pecans. Set aside.

3. Cut the butter into 1-inch pieces and place in the large bowl of an electric mixer fitted with beaters or the paddle attachment. Soften on low speed. Add the lemon zest. Increase the speed to medium-high and cream until smooth, about 1 minute. Add the shortening and mix for 1 minute longer.

4. Add the granulated sugar, 1 tablespoon at a time, taking 3 to 4 minutes to blend it in well. Add the brown sugar over an additional 3 to 4 minutes. Scrape the side of the bowl occasionally.

5. Add the eggs one at a time at 1-minute intervals. Reduce the speed to medium-low. Add the fresh apple and the vanilla.

6. Reduce the mixer speed to low. Add the flour/nut mixture alternating with the applesauce, dividing the flour mixture in three parts and the applesauce in two parts, and starting and ending with the flour. Beat just until incorporated after each addition. Scrape the side of the bowl occasionally.

7. Spoon the batter into the pan and smooth the top. Center the pan on the rack and bake for 55 to 60 minutes, or until the cake begins to leave the side of the pan and a toothpick inserted into the center comes out dry.

8. Remove from the oven. Place the pan on a cake rack to set for 10 to 15 minutes, then invert the cake onto the rack and remove the pan. If you like, while the cake is still warm, pour brown sugar glaze over the top, letting it drip naturally down the side. Garnish the top with chopped pecans, if you wish.

STORAGE: Store at room temperature under a glass cover or in an airtight container for up to 2 days. For longer storage, wrap the unglazed cake in plastic wrap and refrigerate for up to 10 days.

brown sugar glaze

MAKES ABOUT ½ CUP, ENOUGH TO GLAZE A 9-INCH FLUTED RING CAKE

This caramel-flavored glaze is delicious on cakes made with brown sugar, spices, or nuts. Or try it on chocolate- or coffee-flavored cakes and top with chocolate shavings.

3 tablespoons butter

3 tablespoons light brown sugar

3 tablespoons heavy cream

¾ cup strained confectioners' sugar

½ teaspoon vanilla extract

1. In a small saucepan, melt the butter and sugar together over low heat. Stir in the heavy cream and cook slowly until the mixture comes to a gentle boil. Simmer 1 to 2 minutes.

2. Off the heat, gradually add the confectioners' sugar in three additions, whisking until smooth. Blend in the vanilla. The icing should be pourable. If it is too thick, thin with drops of extra cream.

banana nut cake

MAKES 10 TO 12 SERVINGS

My earliest recollection of homemade cake was my grandmother's banana cake. I was no more than three years old when I sat perched on her kitchen table and watched her open the oven door, carefully sliding out what seemed to my child's eyes to be an enormous flat pan with a cake that had the most wonderful aroma. It wasn't until I was much older that it occurred to me that it was not the pan that was so big but that I was so small. I still have my grandmother's handwritten recipe with her scrawled measurements and notes, which I am sure she knew by heart. Here is my version of her delicious cake.

3 small bananas (to make 1 cup puree)

½ cup sour cream

2¼ cups sifted cake flour

1 teaspoon baking soda

1 teaspoon salt

¼ teaspoon ground nutmeg

1 cup walnuts or pecans, chopped medium-size (see page 356)

½ cup (1 stick) unsalted butter

1 cup granulated sugar

½ cup lightly packed light brown sugar

2 large eggs

1 teaspoon pure vanilla extract

Confectioners' sugar for dusting

AT A GLANCE

PAN: 9- × 13- × 2-inch oblong baking pan

PAN PREP: Buttered

RACK LEVEL: Lower third

OVEN TEMP: 350°F

BAKING TIME: 40–45 minutes

DIFFICULTY: 1

1. Position the rack in the lower third of the oven. Heat the oven to 350°F. Butter the pan.

2. Break the bananas into 1-inch pieces and place in the container of a food processor. Pulse a few times until the bananas are pureed but not watery. Alternatively, press them through a strainer with medium-large holes. Stir the puree into the sour cream.

3. Sift together the flour, baking soda, salt, and nutmeg in a triple sifter. Stir in the chopped nuts and set aside.

4. Cut the butter into 1-inch pieces and put in the large bowl of an electric mixer fitted with beaters or the paddle attachment. Soften on low speed. Increase the speed to medium-high and cream until smooth and light color, 1½ to 2 minutes.

5. Add the granulated and brown sugars, starting with the granulated sugar, 1 tablespoon at a time, taking 6 to 8 minutes to blend both in well. Scrape the side of the bowl occasionally.

6. Add the eggs one at a time at 1-minute intervals, scraping the side of the bowl as necessary. Blend in the vanilla.

7. Reduce the mixer speed to low. Add the flour/nut mixture alternately with the sour cream/ banana mixture, dividing the flour mixture into three parts and the banana mixture into two parts, and starting and ending with the flour. Scrape the side of the bowl and mix for 10 seconds longer.

8. Spoon the batter into the pan and smooth the surface with the back of a tablespoon. Bake for 40 to 45 minutes, or until cake is golden brown on top, springy to the touch, and comes away from the sides of the pan.

9. Remove from the oven and set the pan on a cake rack to cool. Just before serving, dust the top with confectioners' sugar. When ready to serve, cut into squares in the pan.

STORAGE: Store at room temperature, covered loosely with aluminum foil, for up to 5 days.

golden peach cake

MAKES 8 TO 10 SERVINGS

Peaches are my favorite summer fruit. It is impossible for me to pass a bin of fragrant, ripe peaches without stopping. I always pick up one or two to get a closer whiff, then I gently press the brilliant red, orange, and gold skins to see if they are ready for baking.

TOPPING

¼ cup walnuts

1 teaspoon sugar

¼ teaspoon ground cinnamon

CAKE

3 medium peaches

1 teaspoon freshly squeezed lemon juice

1¾ cups sifted cake flour

2 teaspoons baking powder

½ teaspoon salt

½ cup (1 stick) unsalted butter

½ teaspoon grated lemon zest

¾ cup plus 2 tablespoons sugar

4 large egg yolks or 2 large eggs

1 teaspoon pure vanilla extract

⅓ cup milk

Yogurt Topping (optional; page 281)

AT A GLANCE

PAN: 9-inch springform pan

PAN PREP: Buttered

RACK LEVEL: Lower third

OVEN TEMP: 350°F

BAKING TIME: 55–60 minutes

DIFFICULTY: 1

1. Position the rack in the lower third of the oven. Heat the oven to 350°F. Butter the pan.

MAKE THE TOPPING

2. Place the nuts, sugar, and cinnamon in container of a food processor fitted with the steel blade. Pulse until the nuts are medium chopped. Set aside.

MAKE THE CAKE

3. Wipe the peaches with a damp paper towel. Peel only if you wish. Cut the peaches into 1-inch chunks, to make about 2 cups. Sprinkle the peaches with the lemon juice. Set aside.

4. Sift together the flour, baking powder, and salt in a triple sifter. Set aside.

5. Cut the butter into 1-inch pieces and place in the large bowl of an electric mixer fitted with beaters or the paddle attachment. Soften on low speed, then add the lemon zest. Increase the speed to medium-high and cream until smooth and light in color, 1½ to 2 minutes.

6. Add the sugar, 1 tablespoon at a time, taking 6 to 8 minutes to blend it in well. Scrape the side of the bowl occasionally. Add the yolks one at a time at 30-second intervals. Beat for 2 minutes longer, scraping the side of the bowl as necessary. Blend in the vanilla.

7. Reduce the mixer speed to low. Add the dry ingredients alternately with the milk, dividing the flour mixture into three parts and the liquid into two parts, and starting and ending with the flour. Beat just until incorporated after each addition. Scrape the side of the bowl and mix for 10 more seconds.

8. Spread two-thirds of the batter in the pan. Arrange the peaches over the top in a single layer. Drop the remaining batter by tablespoons evenly around the pan. Working from the center outward, gently spread the batter over the fruit with the back of the tablespoon as best you can. It is not necessary to cover the peaches completely. Do not press too hard or fruit will cling to the spoon.

9. Sprinkle the topping evenly over the batter. Center the pan on the rack and bake for 55 to 60 minutes, or until the cake begins to come away from side of pan and is golden brown on top.

10. Remove from the oven and set the pan on a cake rack to cool. When ready to serve, remove the side of the pan. Cut into wedges and serve plain or with the yogurt topping.

STORAGE: Store at room temperature, covered loosely with aluminum foil, for the first day after baking. For longer storage, refrigerate for up to 4 additional days. Reheat before serving in a 350°F oven for about 10 minutes, until slightly warm.

Nectarine Cake

Substitute nectarines for the peaches, preparing them as in step 3.

Blueberry Cake

Substitute 1¼ cups fresh blueberries for the peaches. Prepare as follows: Wash and dry thoroughly on paper towels. Sprinkle berries with 2 teaspoons all-purpose flour. Omit the lemon juice.

Green Grape Cake

Substitute 1¼ cups seedless Thompson grapes for the peaches. Prepare as follows: Spread the grapes in a single layer on a flat pan lined with paper toweling. Wipe the grapes with damp paper toweling, shaking the pan occasionally to move the grapes. Omit the lemon juice.

Purple Plum Cake

Substitute ¾ pound purple plums for the peaches. Prepare as follows: Wipe with damp paper toweling, slice in half, and remove the pits. Cut the plums into ½-inch pieces.

rosy rhubarb cake

MAKES 8 TO 10 SERVINGS

This wonderful recipe comes from my friend Virginia McKinley, a fine baker with a treasury of homespun recipes. Her rhubarb cake recipe intrigued me, since rhubarb is more commonly used for pies and pastries.

Rhubarb can be considered a fruit or a vegetable. Actually, it is the stalk of an aromatic plant. Although the top leaves are poisonous, the stems are used in cooking, for making aperitifs, and for medicinal purposes. Rhubarb is very nutritious, but it is also extremely tart and must be cooked with more sugar than is necessary for most fruits.

1 pound fresh rhubarb

1½ cups sugar, divided

1 cup sifted unbleached all-purpose flour

1 teaspoon baking soda

1 teaspoon ground cinnamon

¼ teaspoon salt

1 cup whole wheat flour, preferably stone-ground

½ cup (1 stick) unsalted butter

2 large eggs

1 teaspoon pure vanilla extract

1 cup plain low-fat yogurt

Whipped cream for serving

AT A GLANCE

PAN: 9- × 13- × 2-inch oven-proof glass baking dish

PAN PREP: Buttered

RACK LEVEL: Lower third

OVEN TEMP: 325°F

BAKING TIME: 40–45 minutes

DIFFICULTY: 1

1. Wash and dry the rhubarb. Cut off the ends, making sure no trace of the poisonous leaves remains. Scrape the strings from the rhubarb with a sharp knife or a vegetable peeler, pulling any remaining loose strings with your fingertips. Cut the rhubarb stalks into ¼- to ½-inch slices (you should have about 2 cups) and put in a medium-size glass or stainless steel bowl. (Do not use aluminum.) Sprinkle with ½ cup of the sugar and let stand while you prepare the batter. The rhubarb will soften and release some juice. Do not prepare the fruit more than ½ hour in advance or the sugar will extract too much liquid from the rhubarb.

2. Position the rack in the lower third of the oven. Heat the oven to 325°F. Butter the baking dish.

3. Sift together the all-purpose flour, baking soda, cinnamon, and salt, using a triple sifter. Stir in the whole wheat flour, blending it in thoroughly. Set aside.

4. Cut the butter into 1-inch pieces and place in the large bowl of an electric mixer fitted with beaters or the paddle attachment. Soften on low speed, then increase the speed to medium-high. Cream until smooth and light in color, 1½ to 2 minutes.

5. Add the remaining 1 cup sugar, 1 tablespoon at a time, taking 6 to 8 minutes to blend it in well. Scrape the side of the bowl occasionally. Add the eggs one at a time at 1-minute intervals, scraping the side of the bowl as necessary. Blend in the vanilla.

6. Reduce the mixer speed to low. Add the dry ingredients alternately with the yogurt, dividing the flour mixture into three parts and the yogurt into two parts, and starting and ending with the flour. Mix only until incorporated after each addition. Scrape the side of the bowl as necessary.

7. Remove the bowl from mixer. Fold the rhubarb and its juices into the batter.

8. Spoon the batter into the baking dish, smoothing the surface with the back of a tablespoon. Bake for 40 to 45 minutes, or until cake begins to come away from the sides of dish, is springy to the touch, and is browned on the bottom.

9. Remove from the oven and set the pan on a cake rack to cool completely. When ready to serve, cut into squares and top with whipped cream.

STORAGE: Store at room temperature, covered loosely with aluminum foil, for up to 5 days.

Variation

Combine ⅔ cup lightly toasted, broken pecans with 1 tablespoon flour and fold into the batter with the rhubarb.

pineapple upside-down cake

MAKES 9 SERVINGS

If you wish to keep this cake for later use, do not invert it immediately. Instead, let it cool in the pan; the fruit and juices will stick, but this can be remedied. Return the cake to a 350°F oven for 10 to 15 minutes or using very low heat, reheat the pan on a stove burner. After the bottom of the pan is well warmed, invert the cake and let it stand 5 minutes before removing the pan.

TOPPING

3 to 4 tablespoons unsalted butter

⅓ to ½ cup lightly packed dark brown sugar

9 pineapple rings, well drained on paper toweling (reserve ½ cup juice)

9 maraschino or canned Bing cherries, pitted

Pecan halves

CAKE

1½ cups sifted cake flour

2½ teaspoons baking powder

¼ teaspoon salt

⅓ cup (⅔ stick) sweet butter

½ cup sugar

2 large eggs

1 teaspoon pure vanilla extract

½ cup reserved pineapple juice

Whipped cream or Yogurt Topping (opposite)

AT A GLANCE

PAN: 9- × 9- × 2-inch square baking pan

PAN PREP: None

RACK LEVEL: Lower third

OVEN TEMP: 350°F

BAKING TIME: 30–35 minutes

DIFFICULTY: 1

1. Position the rack in the lower third of the oven. Heat the oven to 350°F.

MAKE THE TOPPING

2. Put the butter in the ungreased baking pan and heat over a very low flame just to melt the butter. Remove from the heat, and tilt the pan to coat the bottom completely with the melted butter. Sprinkle the brown sugar over the butter and press it evenly across the surface. Arrange the pineapple slices, three to a row, making three rows. Place a cherry in the center of each ring. Neatly fill in the empty spaces around the cherries with pecan halves, rounded side down. Set aside.

MAKE THE CAKE

3. Sift together the flour, baking powder, and salt, using a triple sifter. Set aside.

4. Cut the butter into 1-inch pieces and place in the large bowl of an electric mixer fitted with beaters or the paddle attachment. Soften on low speed. Increase the speed to medium and cream until smooth and light in color, 1 to 1½ minutes.

5. Add the sugar, 1 tablespoon at a time, taking 3 to 4 minutes to blend it in well. Scrape the side of the bowl occasionally.

6. Add the eggs one at a time at 1-minute intervals, scraping the side of bowl as necessary. Blend in the vanilla.

7. Reduce the mixer speed to low. Add the dry ingredients alternately with the pineapple juice, dividing the flour mixture into three parts and the liquid into two parts, and starting and ending with the flour. Mix just until incorporated after each addition. Scrape the side of the bowl and mix for 10 seconds longer.

8. Spoon the batter into pan, spreading from the sides to the center. Smooth the top surface with the back of a tablespoon.

9. Bake for 30 to 35 minutes, or until the edges of the cake are brown and the juices around the sides of the pan begin to bubble. Remove from the oven and place on a cake rack. Let the cake cool in the pan for 5 to 10 minutes. Then run a thin knife around the edges of the pan to loosen the sides. Invert the pan onto a serving platter. *Let stand for 5 minutes before removing the pan.* Carefully lift the pan. If any fruit clings to the pan, remove and arrange on top of the cake. When ready to serve, slice into squares and accompany with dollops of whipped cream or yogurt topping. This cake is best served slightly warm.

STORAGE: Store at room temperature, covered loosely with aluminum foil, for up to 1 day.

yogurt topping

MAKES 1 CUP

Yogurt topping is a refreshing alternative to cream-based sauces and is the ideal choice for those who wish to keep their calories down. The topping is at its best used shortly after it's made.

½ pint low-fat unsweetened plain yogurt

2 to 3 tablespoons strained confectioners' sugar

½ teaspoon pure vanilla extract

In a small bowl, combine the yogurt and sugar, stirring briefly to blend. Stir in the vanilla. Cover and store in the refrigerator until ready to use. Serve within 1 hour.

apple walnut upside-down cake

MAKES 8 TO 10 SERVINGS

Slices of Golden Delicious apples in butter, walnuts, and brown sugar form the base of a delightful topping accented with a dash of dark Jamaican rum.

TOPPING

1½ pounds (about 3 large) Golden Delicious apples

¼ cup (½ stick) unsalted butter

⅓ cup lightly packed light brown sugar

¼ teaspoon freshly grated lemon zest

½ teaspoon ground cinnamon

1 tablespoon dark Jamaican rum

⅓ cup coarsely chopped walnuts

CAKE

1⅔ cups sifted cake flour

2 teaspoons baking powder

½ teaspoon salt

⅓ cup (⅔ stick) unsalted butter

¼ teaspoon freshly grated lemon zest

½ cup sugar

2 large eggs

1 teaspoon pure vanilla extract

½ cup apple juice

Whipped cream or Yogurt Topping (page 281)

AT A GLANCE

PAN: 10-inch skillet with ovenproof handle

PAN PREP: None

RACK LEVEL: Lower third

OVEN TEMP: 375°F

BAKING TIME: 30–35 minutes

DIFFICULTY: 1

MAKE THE TOPPING

1. Core and peel the apples and cut each into eighths. In a 10-inch skillet with an ovenproof handle, melt the butter over low heat. Blend in the brown sugar, lemon zest, and cinnamon. Add the apples and stir to coat with the syrup. Spread the fruit in a single layer. Cover the pan, and simmer for 3 to 5 minutes, or until the apples are tender. Remove the lid, raise the heat to medium-high, and cook for 1½ to 2 minutes to thicken the syrup. Remove from the heat. Arrange the apples in a circle, leaving a few in the center. Sprinkle them with the rum and nuts. Set aside while you prepare the cake.

2. Position the rack in the lower third of the oven. Heat the oven to 375°F.

MAKE THE CAKE

3. Sift together the flour, baking powder, and salt, using a triple sifter. Set aside.

4. Cut the butter into 1-inch pieces and place in the large bowl of an electric mixer fitted with beaters or the paddle attachment to soften on low speed. Add the lemon zest. Increase the speed to medium. Cream until smooth and light in color, 1 to 1½ minutes.

5. Add the sugar, 1 tablespoon at a time, taking 3 to 4 minutes to blend it in well. Scrape the side of the bowl occasionally.

6. Add the eggs one at a time at 1-minute intervals, scraping the side of the bowl as necessary. Blend in the vanilla.

7. Reduce the mixer speed to low. Add the dry ingredients alternately with the apple juice, dividing the flour mixture into three parts and the liquid into two parts, and starting and ending with the flour. Mix just until incorporated after each addition. Scrape the side of the bowl and mix for 10 seconds longer.

8. Spoon the batter into the skillet, spreading from the side to the center. Smooth the top with the back of a tablespoon.

9. Center the skillet on the rack and bake for 30 to 35 minutes, or until the edges are brown. Remove from the oven and set on a cake rack to cool for 5 to 10 minutes. Run a thin knife around the edge of the skillet to loosen the sides. Invert the pan onto a serving platter. *Let stand 5 minutes before removing the skillet,* to release the fruit and syrup. Carefully remove the skillet. If any fruit remains in the skillet, remove and arrange on top of cake. When ready to serve, slice into wedges and accompany with dollops of whipped cream or yogurt topping. This cake is best served slightly warm.

STORAGE: Store at room temperature, covered loosely with aluminum foil, for up to 1 day.

chocolate pear upside-down cake

MAKES 8 TO 10 SERVINGS

Chocolate and pears are a heavenly combination. The honey glaze gives the top of this delectable cake an attractive sheen.

TOPPING

¼ cup (½ stick) unsalted butter

¼ cup sugar

2 tablespoons honey

1 (29-ounce) can pear halves, well drained on paper toweling

1 walnut half for each pear

CAKE

1¼ cups sifted cake flour

1 teaspoon baking powder

½ teaspoon salt

⅓ cup (⅔ stick) unsalted butter

¾ cup sugar

2 large eggs

2 ounces unsweetened chocolate, melted

1 teaspoon pure vanilla extract

⅔ cup milk

Whipped cream or Yogurt Topping (page 281)

AT A GLANCE

PAN: 10-inch skillet with ovenproof handle

PAN PREP: None

RACK LEVEL: Lower third

OVEN TEMP: 350°F

BAKING TIME: 50–55 minutes

DIFFICULTY: 1

MAKE THE TOPPING

1. In the skillet, melt the butter over a very low flame. Stir in the sugar and honey and cook just until the sugar melts. Remove from the heat. Set aside. Fit one walnut half into each pear cavity. With the narrow ends toward center, arrange the pears in a circle in the skillet, cavity side down. Fill the space in the center with one pear half. Set aside.

2. Position the rack in the lower third of the oven. Heat the oven to 350°F.

MAKE THE CAKE

3. Sift together the flour, baking powder, and salt, using a triple sifter. Set aside.

4. Cut the butter into 1-inch pieces and place in the large bowl of an electric mixer fitted with beaters or the paddle attachment. Soften on low speed, then increase the speed to medium and cream until smooth and light in color, 1 to 1½ minutes.

5. Add the sugar, 1 tablespoon at a time, taking 3 to 4 minutes to blend it in well. Scrape the side of the bowl occasionally.

6. Add the eggs one at a time at 1-minute intervals, scraping the side of the bowl again. Blend in the melted chocolate and vanilla.

7. Reduce the mixer speed to low. Add the dry ingredients alternately with the milk, dividing the flour mixture into three parts and the liquid into two parts, and starting and ending with the flour. Mix just until incorporated after each addition. Scrape the side of the bowl and mix for 10 seconds longer.

8. Spoon the batter into the skillet, spreading from the side toward the center. Smooth the surface with the back of a tablespoon.

9. Center the skillet on the rack and bake for 50 to 55 minutes, or until the top of the cake feels springy to the touch. Remove from the oven and place on a cake rack. Let cool in the pan for 5 to 10 minutes. Run a thin knife around the edge of the skillet to loosen the sides, and invert onto a serving platter. *Let stand for 5 minutes before removing the pan,* to release the fruit. Remove the skillet. If any fruit remains in the skillet, remove and arrange on top of the cake. When ready to serve, slice into wedges and accompany with dollops of whipped cream or yogurt topping. This cake is best when served slightly warm.

STORAGE: Store at room temperature, covered loosely with aluminum foil, for up to 1 day.

orange sponge cake

MAKES 14 TO 16 SERVINGS

Every baker's repertoire should contain a special cake that can stand on its own merits or be modified into other delectable creations. This is such a recipe: an airy cake, refreshing and moist, tinged with a lovely orange flavor. It is satisfying whether eaten plain or fancied up into a party presentation, such as in Majestic Mandarin Cake (page 328).

7 large eggs, separated

1 large whole egg

²/₃ cup plus ½ cup superfine or strained sugar

1 teaspoon freshly grated navel orange zest

1 teaspoon freshly grated lemon zest

¼ cup fresh navel orange juice

1 cup plus 2 tablespoons sifted cake flour

1 teaspoon cream of tartar

¼ teaspoon salt

AT A GLANCE

PAN: 10-inch angel food cake pan with a removable bottom (4-quart capacity)

PAN PREP: Ungreased

RACK LEVEL: Lower third

OVEN TEMP: 325°F

BAKING TIME: 40–45 minutes

DIFFICULTY: 1

1. Position the rack in the lower third of the oven. Heat the oven to 325°F.

2. Place the egg yolks and the whole egg in the small bowl of an electric mixer fitted with beaters or the whip attachment. Whip on medium speed for about 2 minutes. Add ²/₃ cup of the sugar, 1 tablespoon at a time, taking 5 to 6 minutes to blend it in well. Scrape the side of the bowl occasionally. The mixture will be thick and light yellow in color.

3. Reduce the mixer speed to medium-low. Add the grated orange and lemon zests and orange juice and beat about 1 minute longer.

4. Reduce the mixer speed to low. Add the flour and mix just until incorporated. Remove the bowl from the mixer and transfer the yolk mixture to a large mixing bowl. Set aside.

5. Wash and dry the beaters. In the large bowl of the mixer, whip the egg whites at medium speed until frothy. Add the cream of tartar and salt. Increase the speed to medium high and beat just until the whites form soft peaks. Gradually add the remaining ½ cup sugar over 15 seconds, and then continue beating for 30 seconds longer to form a glossy, soft meringue. Remove the bowl from the machine.

6. With a 2¾-inch-wide rubber spatula, fold one-fourth of the meringue into the yolk mixture, taking about 20 turns. Add the remaining meringue, using about 50 turns to incorporate the two together.

7. Gently spoon the batter into the cake pan, smoothing the top with the back of a tablespoon. Insert a knife into the batter and circle the pan twice to remove any air pockets. Smooth the surface again. Bake for 40 to 45 minutes, or until the cake is golden brown on top and springy to the touch.

8. Remove the cake from the oven and *immediately* invert onto a cake rack. Let the cake cool completely in the pan.

9. To remove the pan, turn the cake upright and carefully run a sharp, thin-bladed knife in two or three strokes around the side of pan to loosen the cake. Then run it around the center tube. Lift the cake by the center tube and remove the outer rim. Run the knife under the cake in two or three strokes, then invert onto a cake rack and remove the tube. Place on a cake platter, top or bottom side up.

STORAGE: Store at room temperature under a glass dome or covered with aluminum foil for up to 1 week.

starmount sponge cake

MAKES 14 TO 16 SERVINGS

I have a special fondness for the city of Greensboro, North Carolina, because just after I was married my parents moved there. On my frequent visits I was often entertained by a number of extraordinary cooks, many of whom lived in the Starmount section of that city. The sumptuous foods and pastries that I sampled there have been a source of inspiration to me throughout my culinary career. This cake is named in remembrance of the gracious hospitality of those cooks and in respect for their talents.

Starmount Sponge Cake, as high as the pan, is feather-light and has a lovely lemon flavor. It comes from my friend Shirley Lynch of Greensboro. No doubt you will agree that her cake is a grand one.

1²⁄₃ cups sifted cake flour

1 teaspoon baking powder

¹⁄₈ teaspoon salt

5 large eggs, separated

1 large whole egg

1¹⁄₂ cups superfine or strained sugar, divided

2 teaspoons freshly grated lemon zest

2 tablespoons fresh lemon juice

¹⁄₄ cup plus 1 teaspoon water, divided

¹⁄₂ teaspoon cream of tartar

AT A GLANCE

PAN: 10-inch angel food cake pan with removable bottom (4-quart capacity)

PAN PREP: Ungreased

RACK LEVEL: Lower third

OVEN TEMP: 325°F

BAKING TIME: 45–50 minutes

DIFFICULTY: 1

1. Position the rack in the lower third of the oven. Heat the oven to 325°F.

2. Sift together the flour, baking powder, and salt in a triple sifter. Set aside.

3. Place the egg yolks and the whole egg in the small bowl of an electric mixer fitted with beaters or the whip attachment. Whip on medium speed for about 2 minutes. Add 1¹⁄₄ cups of the sugar, 1 tablespoon at a time, taking 5 to 6 minutes to blend it in well. Scrape the side of the bowl occasionally. The mixture will thicken and turn light yellow in color.

4. Reduce the mixer speed to medium-low. Add the lemon zest and juice. Beat 1 minute longer.

5. Reduce the mixer speed to low. Gradually add the dry ingredients alternately with ¹⁄₄ cup of the water, dividing the flour mixture into three parts and the water into two parts, and starting and ending with the flour. Mix just until incorporated after each· addition. Transfer the yolk mixture to a large mixing bowl.

6. Wash and dry the beaters. In the large bowl of the mixer, beat the egg whites and the remaining 1 teaspoon of water on medium speed until frothy. Add the cream of tartar. Increase the speed to medium-high and beat until the whites form soft peaks. Gradually add the remaining $\frac{1}{4}$ cup sugar, taking about 15 seconds, and continue beating for 30 seconds longer to form a glossy, soft meringue. Remove the bowl from the machine.

7. With a $2\frac{3}{4}$-inch-wide rubber spatula, fold one-fourth of the meringue into the yolk mixture, taking about 20 turns to lighten. Then fold in the remaining meringue, taking about 50 additional turns.

8. Gently spoon the batter into the pan, smoothing the top with the back of a tablespoon. Insert a knife into the batter and circle the pan twice to remove any air pockets. Smooth the surface again. Bake for 45 to 50 minutes, or until the cake is golden brown on the top and springy to the touch.

9. Remove the cake from the oven and immediately invert the pan onto a cake rack. Let the cake cool completely in the pan. To remove the pan, turn the cake upright and carefully run a sharp, thin-bladed knife two or three times around the pan to loosen the side. Then run the knife two or three times around the center tube. Lift the cake by the center tube and remove the outer rim. Run the knife under cake in two or three strokes and invert onto a cake rack to remove the tube. Place on a cake platter, top or bottom side up.

STORAGE: Store at room temperature under a glass dome or covered with aluminum foil for up to 1 week.

hot milk sponge cake

MAKES 6 TO 8 SERVINGS

The hot milk gives this thin layer sponge cake a somewhat denser crumb that makes it ideal for shortcakes or cake à la mode. It is also the perfect foundation for classic Boston Cream Pie (page 320) or Washington Pie (see variation opposite).

This cake can be made in under 15 minutes, but be sure to follow the directions carefully. To ensure proper volume, the hot milk must be beaten rapidly into the batter, and the flour added immediately. When correctly made, the cake should rise to the top of the pan.

½ cup milk	½ teaspoon salt
1 tablespoon unsalted butter	2 large eggs
1 cup sifted cake flour	¾ cup superfine or strained sugar
1 teaspoon baking powder	1 teaspoon pure vanilla extract

AT A GLANCE

PAN: 9-inch round layer pan

PAN PREP: Generously buttered and lined with parchment

RACK LEVEL: Lower third

OVEN TEMP: 350°F

BAKING TIME: 30–35 minutes

DIFFICULTY: 1

1. Position the rack in the lower third of the oven. Heat the oven to 350°F. Generously butter the cake pan and line with parchment.

2. In a small saucepan, heat the milk and butter to almost boiling. Set aside.

3. Sift together the flour, baking powder, and salt in a triple sifter. Set aside.

4. Beat the eggs on medium-high speed in an electric mixer fitted with beaters or the whip attachment for about 2 minutes. Gradually add the sugar, 1 tablespoon at a time, taking 4 to 5 minutes to blend it in well. Scrape the side of the bowl occasionally. The mixture will thicken and turn light yellow in color.

5. Reduce the mixer speed to medium. Add the vanilla, then pour in the hot milk *in a steady stream*, taking about 10 seconds. Immediately add the dry ingredients all at once, and beat just until blended, scraping the side of the bowl as necessary. Increase the mixer speed to medium-high and beat 10 seconds. The batter will be very thin. Remove the bowl from the mixer and quickly pour the batter into the pan. Bake for 30 to 35 minutes, or until the cake begins to come away from the side of pan and is golden brown and springy to the touch.

6. Set on a cake rack to cool for about 10 minutes. Run a thin knife around the side of the pan to loosen. Invert the pan onto a rack sprayed with nonstick coating and peel off the parchment paper. Invert again to finish cooling right side up.

STORAGE: Store at room temperature under a glass dome or covered with aluminum foil for up to 3 days. For longer storage, freeze.

Washington Pie

Divide the sponge layer into three thin rounds (see page 366). Spread each layer with raspberry jam and dust the top generously with confectioners' sugar. For those who have difficulty handling jelly rolls, this is a nice alternative.

special occasion cakes

lemon roulade

french jelly roll

royal chiffon cake

golden citrus chiffon cake

fudgy chiffon ring

sweet angel cake

powdered sugar angel food cake

peppermint cloud

sweetmeat angel cake

coconut layer cake

raspberry ribbons

georgia peanut cake

double trouble fudge cake

boston cream pie

burnished sugar layer cake

hazelnut blitz torte with praline cream filling

majestic mandarin cake

ann's cheesecake

manhattan cheesecake

a great italian cheesecake

pineapple cheese squares

praline cheesecake

chocolate marble cheesecake

black-bottom mint cheesecake

lemon roulade

MAKES 10 TO 12 SERVINGS

This golden-yellow sponge cake filled with a tart lemon filling is especially appealing to those who do not like their desserts too sweet. If you wish, orange zest and juice can be substituted for the lemon. Finely crushed toasted coconut (about $\frac{1}{3}$ cup) added to the batter is also a nice touch.

$\frac{2}{3}$ cup sifted cake flour

2 tablespoons strained cornstarch

$\frac{1}{4}$ teaspoon baking powder

5 large eggs, separated

$\frac{1}{2}$ cup plus 2 tablespoons superfine or strained sugar, divided

$\frac{1}{2}$ teaspoon pure vanilla extract

$\frac{1}{2}$ teaspoon freshly grated lemon zest

1 tablespoon fresh lemon juice

Pinch of salt

3 tablespoons confectioners' sugar, plus additional for dusting

Clear Lemon Filling (page 377)

AT A GLANCE

PAN: 11- × 17- × 1-inch jelly roll pan

PAN PREP: Buttered and lined with buttered parchment

RACK LEVEL: Lower third

OVEN TEMP: 375°F

BAKING TIME: 12–14 minutes

DIFFICULTY: 2

1. Position the rack in the lower third of the oven. Heat the oven to 375°F. Butter the jelly roll pan and line the bottom with baking parchment. Lightly butter the parchment.

2. Sift together the flour, cornstarch, and baking powder. Set aside.

3. Put the egg yolks in the small bowl of an electric mixer fitted with beaters or the whip attachment. Beat on medium speed for 3 to 4 minutes, or until thick and light in color. Add $\frac{1}{2}$ cup of the superfine sugar, 1 tablespoon at a time, taking 3 to 4 minutes to blend it in well. Reduce the speed to medium-low and beat in the vanilla, lemon zest, and lemon juice. Remove the bowl from the mixer and set aside.

4. Wash and dry the beaters. In the large bowl of the mixer, whip the egg whites on medium speed until frothy. Add the salt and increase the speed to medium-high. Beat until the whites form soft peaks. Add the remaining 2 tablespoons superfine sugar, taking about 15 seconds, and continue beating 15 seconds longer.

5. Pour the yolk mixture into the whites and beat for 2 minutes longer.

6. Remove the bowl from the mixer. Slowly sift the dry ingredients over the egg mixture, folding them in with a $2\frac{3}{4}$-inch-wide rubber spatula.

7. Pour the batter into the pan. Gently smooth the top with the back of a tablespoon, being sure to spread evenly at corners. Tap the pan gently on the counter to even out the batter. Bake for 12 to 14 minutes, or until the top feels set and is springy to the touch. While the cake is baking, cut a 20-inch piece of parchment for inverting the cake. Put it on a flat workspace and dust heavily with the confectioners' sugar passed through a fine strainer.

8. Remove the cake from the oven and *immediately* invert the cake onto the parchment. Protecting your hands with pot holders, remove the pan and gently peel off the parchment that lined the pan. Roll up the cake and sugar-dusted paper together tightly, starting on the long side closest to you. Place seam side down to cool.

9. Carefully unroll the cake, but not completely flat. The edge closest to you should remain curled. Spoon the filling under the curled edge first, then evenly over the rest of the cake, leaving a 1-inch border on the far side.

10. Tuck the curled edge under and roll the cake up gently. Place seam side down on a wooden breadboard or oblong platter and cover loosely with aluminum foil. Refrigerate until 1 hour before serving time. Just before serving, dust the top lightly with confectioners' sugar.

STORAGE: Refrigerate, loosely covered with aluminum foil, for up to 3 days.

french jelly roll

MAKES 8 TO 10 SERVINGS

This is made with a classic French sponge batter, *biscuit au beurre*. It is not as moist as a typical sponge, but a thick jam filling tenderizes the cake. The superb flavor of the biscuit comes from the small amount of clarified butter in the batter.

You may fill this with any buttercream frosting or fruit-flavored whipped cream instead of jam. If you do, be sure to moisten the cake with a sugar syrup (see page 372) or it will be too dry.

3 large eggs

1 large egg yolk

$\frac{1}{2}$ cup granulated sugar

$\frac{1}{2}$ teaspoon pure vanilla extract

$\frac{1}{2}$ cup unsifted all-purpose flour

$\frac{1}{4}$ teaspoon baking powder

2 tablespoons warm (100° to 110°F) clarified butter (see page 359)

Confectioners' sugar for dusting

$\frac{1}{2}$ cup seedless raspberry preserves, or any other jam or jelly of your choice

AT A GLANCE

PAN: 10½- × 15½- × 1-inch jelly roll pan

PAN PREP: Buttered and lined with buttered parchment

RACK LEVEL: Lower third

OVEN TEMP: 350°F

BAKING TIME: 14–16 minutes

DIFFICULTY: 2

1. Position the rack in the lower third of the oven. Heat the oven to 350°F. Butter the bottom of the jelly roll pan and line with parchment. Lightly butter the parchment.

2. Select a saucepan that will hold the large bowl of an electric mixer without the bowl touching the 2 inches of water in the pan. Heat until the water simmers but does not boil rapidly.

3. Place the eggs and the additional egg yolk in the large bowl of the electric mixer. Using a wire whisk, stir in the granulated sugar and vanilla, just to blend. Mix briefly; do not beat. Set the bowl over the hot water. Slowly and continuously stir with the whisk until the sugar is completely dissolved and the mixture feels quite warm. Test by rubbing a small amount of the warm egg mixture between your fingers. You should not feel the grain of the sugar crystals.

4. Remove the pan from the heat and dry the bottom of the bowl. With the beaters or the whip attachment, beat the mixture on medium-high speed for about 6 minutes, or until thick and light in color. Remove the bowl from the mixer.

5. Place the flour and baking powder in a triple sifter and sift into the egg mixture, folding in with a 2¾-inch-wide rubber spatula. Pour in the clarified butter in a steady stream, folding it in quickly. Immediately transfer the batter into the pan. Smooth with the back of a tablespoon, spreading it evenly into the corners. Tap the pan gently on the counter to even out the batter. Bake for 14 to 16 minutes, or until the cake begins to come away from the side of the pan and the top is lightly browned.

6. While the cake is baking, generously sprinkle a linen kitchen towel or a 20-inch sheet of parchment with confectioners' sugar passed through a fine strainer.

7. Remove the pan from the oven and allow to stand for 1 minute. Run a thin knife around the edges to release. Invert onto the prepared towel or parchment. Protecting your hands with pot holders, gently lift off the pan. Brush the lining paper with warm water, let stand for 2 minutes, then peel off the paper. Trim $\frac{1}{4}$ inch off the sides of the sponge sheet with a sharp knife to remove dry or uneven edges. Tightly roll together the cake and towel away from you, starting on a long side. Place seam side down on a cake rack to cool.

8. Carefully unroll the cake, but do not unroll completely flat. The edge closest to you should remain curled.

9. Spread the sponge sheet with the preserves, leaving a $\frac{1}{2}$-inch border on the side farthest away from you.

10. Tuck the curled edge under and roll tightly. Place seam side down on a wooden breadboard or oblong platter. Cover loosely with aluminum foil and let stand at room temperature for up to 6 hours. Just before serving, dust the top with confectioners' sugar. Accompany with a selection of fruit sorbets and garnish with mint leaves, if desired.

STORAGE: Refrigerate, loosely covered with aluminum foil, for up to 3 days.

royal chiffon cake

MAKES 14 TO 16 SERVINGS

An especially light chiffon cake with a hint of almond. For interesting flavor variations, try adding coffee zest or espresso zest (see page 350), finely chopped nuts, or perhaps combinations of spices.

2¼ cups sifted cake flour

1 tablespoon baking powder

½ teaspoon salt

5 large eggs, separated

1 large egg

1⅓ cups superfine or strained sugar, divided

½ cup safflower oil

2 teaspoons pure vanilla extract

1 teaspoon almond extract

¾ cup water

¼ teaspoon cream of tartar

AT A GLANCE

PAN: 10-inch angel food cake pan with a removable bottom (4-quart capacity)

PAN PREP: Ungreased

RACK LEVEL: Lower third

OVEN TEMP: 325°F

BAKING TIME: 60–70 minutes

DIFFICULTY: 1

1. Position the rack in the lower third of the oven. Heat the oven to 325°F.

2. Sift together the flour, baking powder, and salt, using a triple sifter. Set aside.

3. Place the egg yolks and the whole egg in the large bowl of an electric mixer fitted with the beaters or the whip attachment. Beat on medium-high speed for 3 minutes. Add 1 cup of the sugar, 1 tablespoon at a time, taking 4 to 5 minutes to blend it in well. The mixture will be thick and light yellow in color.

4. Pour in the oil in a steady stream over 15 seconds. Add the vanilla and almond extracts and whip 1 minute longer. Reduce the speed to medium-low.

5. Add the dry ingredients alternately with the water, dividing the flour into three parts and the water into two parts, and starting and ending with the flour. Scrape the side of the bowl and beat for 10 seconds longer. Set aside.

6. Wash and dry the beaters. In the large bowl of the mixer, whip the egg whites on medium speed until frothy. Add the cream of tartar and increase the speed to medium-high. When the whites form soft peaks, add the remaining ⅓ cup sugar, 1 tablespoon at a time, over 30 seconds to form a glossy soft meringue. Whip 1 minute longer.

7. Remove the bowl from the mixer. Using a 2¾-inch-wide rubber spatula, fold one-fourth of the yolk mixture into the whites, taking about 15 turns to lighten. Then reverse and fold the whites into the yolk mixture, taking an additional 40 to 50 turns.

8. Gently spoon or pour the batter into the pan. Center the pan on the rack and bake for 60 to 70 minutes, or until the cake is golden brown on top and springy to the touch.

9. Remove from the oven and *immediately* invert the pan onto a cake rack. Let the cake cool completely in the pan. To remove, run a sharp, thin-bladed knife in two or three strokes around the side of the pan to loosen the cake, then run it around center tube. Holding the center tube, lift the cake and remove it from the outer rim. Run the knife under the cake in two or three strokes, invert the cake onto a rack, and remove the tube section. Transfer to a cake platter, top or bottom side up.

STORAGE: Store at room temperature under a glass dome or covered with aluminum foil for up to 5 days.

Cinnamon Chiffon Cake

Add 2 teaspoons ground cinnamon and $\frac{1}{4}$ teaspoon powdered cloves to the dry ingredients. Reduce the vanilla to 1 teaspoon. Substitute 1 ($5\frac{1}{2}$-ounce) can apple juice for the water.

golden citrus chiffon cake

MAKES 14 TO 16 SERVINGS

The refreshing flavors of orange and lemon are wonderful in combination and add a nice accent to this delicate chiffon cake. Watch how quickly it disappears when you serve it.

2¼ cups sifted cake flour	½ cup safflower oil
1 tablespoon baking powder	2 teaspoons grated navel orange zest
½ teaspoon salt	½ teaspoon grated lemon zest
6 large eggs, separated	⅔ cup orange juice
1 large whole egg	4 teaspoons fresh lemon juice
1⅓ cups superfine or strained sugar, divided	¼ teaspoon cream of tartar

AT A GLANCE

PAN: 10-inch angel food cake pan with a removable bottom (4-quart capacity)

PAN PREP: Ungreased

RACK LEVEL: Lower third

OVEN TEMP: 325°F

BAKING TIME: 60–65 minutes

DIFFICULTY: 1

1. Position the rack in the lower third of the oven. Heat the oven to 325°F.

2. Sift together the flour, baking powder, and salt, using a triple sifter, and set aside.

3. Put 5 of the egg yolks and the whole egg in the large bowl of an electric mixer fitted with the beaters or the whip attachment. (Reserve the remaining yolk for another use.) Beat on medium-high speed for 3 minutes. Add 1 cup of the sugar, 1 tablespoon at a time, taking 4 to 5 minutes to blend it in well. The mixture will be thick and light yellow in color.

4. Pour in the oil in a steady stream over 15 seconds. Add the orange and lemon zests and whip 1 minute longer. Reduce the speed to medium-low.

5. Combine the orange and lemon juices. Add the juices to the yolk mixture alternately with the dry ingredients, dividing the flour mixture into three parts and the juices into two parts, and starting and ending with the flour. Scrape the side of the bowl and beat for 10 seconds longer. Set aside.

6. Wash and dry the beaters. In the large bowl of the mixer, whip the 6 egg whites on medium speed until frothy. Add the cream of tartar, increase the speed to medium-high, and whip until the whites form soft peaks. Add the remaining ⅓ cup sugar, 1 tablespoon at a time, over 30 seconds to form a glossy soft meringue. Whip 1 minute longer.

7. Remove the bowl from the mixer. Using a 2¾-inch-wide rubber spatula, fold one-fourth of the yolk mixture into the whites, taking about 15 turns to lighten, then fold the whites into the yolk mixture, taking an additional 40 to 50 turns.

8. Gently spoon or pour the batter into the pan. Center the pan on the rack and bake for 60 to 65 minutes, or until the cake is golden brown on top and springy to the touch.

9. Remove from the oven and *immediately* invert the pan onto a cake rack. Let the cake cool completely in the pan. To remove, run a thin, sharp-bladed knife in two or three sweeps around the side of the pan to loosen the cake, then run it around the center tube. Holding the center tube, lift the cake and remove it from the outer rim. Run the knife under the cake in two or three strokes, invert the cake onto a rack, and remove the tube section. Transfer to a cake platter, top or bottom side up.

STORAGE: Store at room temperature under a glass dome or covered with aluminum foil for up to 5 days.

fudgy chiffon ring

MAKES 14 TO 16 SERVINGS

This dark chocolate cake receives its rich color from nonalkaline cocoa, generally a domestic cocoa such as Hershey's. It has a more robust flavor than European-style Dutch-process cocoas, and produces a slightly darker cake. If you wish to substitute a Dutch-process alkaline cocoa like Droste, omit the baking soda. (For more information, see pages 349–350.)

For this recipe, I use the traditional chiffon cake method of beating the egg yolks, oil, and flavoring into the dry ingredients all at once in order to achieve a denser, fudgy texture. This is wonderful with a scoop of vanilla ice cream.

2 teaspoons instant espresso powder

²⁄₃ cup boiling water

¹⁄₂ cup nonalkaline cocoa, such as Hershey's

1²⁄₃ cups sifted cake flour

2 teaspoons baking powder

¹⁄₄ teaspoon baking soda

¹⁄₂ teaspoon salt

1¹⁄₃ cups superfine or strained sugar

6 large eggs, at room temperature, separated

¹⁄₃ cup safflower oil

1¹⁄₂ teaspoons pure vanilla extract

¹⁄₄ teaspoon cream of tartar

AT A GLANCE

PAN: 10-inch angel food cake pan with a removable bottom (4-quart capacity)

PAN PREP: Ungreased

RACK LEVEL: Lower third

OVEN TEMP: 325°F

BAKING TIME: 55–60 minutes

DIFFICULTY: 1

1. Position the rack in the lower third of the oven. Heat the oven to 325°F.

2. In a small bowl, dissolve the espresso powder in the water. Add to the cocoa, stirring until very smooth. Set aside to cool.

3. Using a triple sifter, sift together the flour, baking powder, baking soda, salt, and sugar into the large bowl of an electric mixer fitted with beaters or the whip attachment. Add the cocoa mixture, 5 of the egg yolks, the oil, and vanilla. (Reserve the remaining yolk for another use.) Beat on medium speed for 3 minutes, or until smooth and creamy. Scrape the side of the bowl occasionally. Set aside.

4. Wash and dry the beaters. In a separate large bowl of the electric mixer, whip the 6 egg whites on medium speed until frothy. Add the cream of tartar. Increase the speed to medium-high. Beat until the whites form firm, shiny peaks, but are not dry.

5. Remove the bowl from the machine. With a 2³⁄₄-inch-wide rubber spatula fold one-fourth of the batter into the whites, taking 20 turns to lighten. Then fold the whites back into the batter, taking an additional 40 turns.

6. Spoon or pour the batter into the pan. Bake for 55 to 60 minutes, or until the cake is springy to the touch. Remove from the oven and immediately invert the pan onto a cake rack. Let the cake cool completely in the pan. To remove the pan, run a sharp, thin-bladed knife in two or three strokes around the side of the pan to loosen, then run the knife around the center tube. Holding the cake by the center tube, run the knife under the cake in two or three sweeps to loosen the bottom, invert onto a cake rack, and remove the tube section. Transfer to a serving platter, top or bottom side up.

STORAGE: Store at room temperature under a glass dome or covered with aluminum foil for up to 5 days.

sweet angel cake

MAKES 12 TO 14 SERVINGS

I like to serve this after a heavy dinner. It is light and fluffy and wonderfully refreshing with freshly cut fruit.

Take care when incorporating the flour/sugar mixture into the meringue, as the weight of these ingredients can cause the meringue to deflate. I get the best results using a wire whisk instead of a rubber spatula for folding. *Never* use an electric mixer.

1 cup sifted cake flour

1½ cups superfine sugar, divided

½ teaspoon baking powder

1½ cups egg whites (about 12), defeathered (see pages 358–359), at room temperature

1 tablespoon warm water

1½ teaspoons cream of tartar

¼ teaspoon salt

1½ teaspoons pure vanilla extract

½ teaspoon almond extract

AT A GLANCE

PAN: 10-inch angel food with a removable bottom (4-quart capacity)

PAN PREP: Ungreased

RACK LEVEL: Lower third

OVEN TEMP: 375°F

BAKING TIME: 30–35 minutes

DIFFICULTY: 2

1. Position the rack in the lower third of the oven. Heat the oven to 375°F.

2. On a 12-inch square of wax paper, sift together the cake flour, ½ cup of the superfine sugar, and the baking powder four times, using a triple sifter. Set aside.

3. Place the egg whites and warm water in the large bowl of an electric mixer fitted with beaters or the whip attachment. Beat on medium speed until frothy. Add the cream of tartar, salt, and vanilla and almond extracts. Increase the speed to medium-high and continue beating until the whites form soft peaks. To ensure that you catch the whites at just the right point, watch for a design similar to the ripples on the back of a seashell.

4. Immediately begin to sprinkle in the remaining 1 cup of superfine sugar, 2 tablespoons at a time, taking about 2 minutes to blend it in well, sprinkling it toward the side of the bowl. Scrape the side of the bowl occasionally. Beat 30 seconds longer, until you have a very stiff meringue. Do not overbeat.

5. Transfer the meringue to a very large, slope-sided mixing bowl. (Do not use a straight-sided bowl.) Put the flour/sugar mixture into the sifter or a strainer set on a 12-inch square of wax paper. Gradually shake the flour/sugar mixture in five or six additions over the meringue, gently folding with a large wire whisk. Fold just as you would if you were using a rubber spatula. The dry ingredients do not have to disappear completely after each addition. Folding will take 60 to 70 turns. Take care not to overmix, and never stir the batter. It will deflate if you do.

6. Using a 2¾-inch-wide rubber spatula, carefully push the batter into the angel food pan. Press the batter gently with a tablespoon to smooth. Lower a table knife into the batter with the blade reaching almost to the bottom of the pan. Circle the pan twice to remove air pockets, then smooth the surface with the back of a spoon.

7. Bake for 30 to 35 minutes, or until the cake is golden brown on top and springy to the touch. *Do not overbake or the cake will deflate.* Remove the cake from the oven and *immediately* invert onto a cake rack. Let cool completely in the pan.

8. To remove the pan, insert a sharp thin-bladed knife about ½ inch down the side of the pan and sweep around the pan in two or three strokes. Do the same around the center tube. Tilt the pan on its side, and rotate, giving it several firm taps against the countertop until the cake releases. Lift the cake from the outer rim. With the blade of the knife slanted slightly downward, run the knife under the cake while turning the center tube. Invert onto a cake rack and remove the tube section. Transfer the cake to a serving platter.

STORAGE: Store at room temperature under a glass dome or covered with aluminum foil for up to 5 days.

powdered sugar angel food cake

MAKES 12 TO 14 SERVINGS

Confectioners' sugar gives this angel food cake a smoother, more velvety texture than Sweet Angel. The cake will not rise as high, but its finer texture makes it an ideal choice for tunnel cakes.

1 cup strained cake flour

1 cup strained confectioners' sugar, divided

1/2 teaspoon baking powder

1 cup strained superfine sugar

1 1/2 cups large egg whites (about 12) defeathered (see pages 358–359), at room temperature

1 tablespoon warm water

1 1/2 teaspoons cream of tartar

1 1/2 teaspoons pure vanilla extract

1/2 teaspoon almond extract

1/2 teaspoon salt

AT A GLANCE

PAN: 10-inch angel food with a removable bottom (4-quart capacity)

PAN PREP: Ungreased

RACK LEVEL: Lower third

OVEN TEMP: 375°F

BAKING TIME: 30–35 minutes

DIFFICULTY: 2

1. Position the rack in the lower third of the oven. Heat the oven to 375°F.

2. On a 12-inch square of wax paper, strain together the cake flour, 1/2 cup of the confectioners' sugar, and the baking powder four times, using a fine-mesh strainer. Do not use a triple sifter; the confectioners' sugar will clog it. Set aside.

3. On another 12-inch square of wax paper, strain together the superfine sugar and the remaining 1/2 cup confectioners' sugar four times. Set aside.

4. Place the egg whites and warm water in the large bowl of an electric mixer fitted with beaters or the whip attachment. Beat on medium speed until frothy. Add the cream of tartar, vanilla and almond extracts, and the salt. Increase the speed to medium-high and continue beating until the whites form soft peaks. To ensure that you catch the whites at just the right point, watch for a design similar to the ripples on the back of a seashell.

5. Immediately begin to add the superfine/confectioners' sugar mixture, 1 tablespoon at a time, sprinkling it in toward the side of the bowl. Take 3 to 4 minutes to blend it in well, scraping the side of the bowl occasionally. Beat 30 seconds longer until you have a very stiff meringue. Do not overbeat.

6. Transfer the meringue to a very large, slope-sided mixing bowl. (Do not use a straight-sided bowl.) Put the flour/sugar mixture into a strainer set on a 12-inch square of wax paper. Gradually shake the cake flour/sugar mixture in five or six additions over the meringue, gently folding with a large balloon whisk. Fold just as you would if you were using a rubber spatula. The dry ingredients do not have to disappear completely after each addition. This will take a total of 60 to 70 turns. Take care not to overmix, and never stir the batter. It will deflate if you do.

7. Using a 2¾-inch-wide rubber spatula, carefully push the batter into the pan. Press the batter gently with the back of a tablespoon to smooth. Lower a table knife into the batter, reaching almost to the bottom of the pan. Circle the pan twice to remove air pockets, then smooth the surface with the back of a spoon.

8. Bake for 30 to 35 minutes, or until the cake is golden brown on top and springy to the touch. Do not overbake or the cake will deflate. Remove the cake from the oven and invert *immediately* onto a cake rack. Let the cake cool completely in the pan.

9. To remove the pan, insert a sharp, thin-bladed knife about ½ inch down the side of the pan and sweep around the pan in two or three strokes. Do the same around the inner tube. Tilt the pan on its side and rotate, giving it several firm taps against the countertop until the cake releases. Lift the cake from the outer rim and with the blade of the knife slanted slightly downward, run the knife under the cake while turning the center tube. Invert onto a cake rack and remove the tube section. Transfer to a serving platter.

STORAGE: Store at room temperature under a glass dome or covered with aluminum foil for up to 5 days.

peppermint cloud

MAKES 12 TO 14 SERVINGS

A confetti of crushed peppermint candies is mingled throughout this billowy batter. The punch of peppermint adds a refreshing lift and turns the cake into a pretty peppermint cloud.

CAKE

½ teaspoon pure mint extract

2 tablespoons crushed peppermint candies (see Note)

Sweet Angel Cake (page 304), modified as follows:
1. Substitute the mint extract for the almond extract in step 4.
2. Sprinkle in the crushed peppermint at step 6, when sifting the dry ingredients over the meringue.

PINK PEPPERMINT GLAZE

1¼ cups strained confectioners' sugar

1½ teaspoons light corn syrup

5 teaspoons boiling water

½ teaspoon pure peppermint extract

Red food coloring

2 teaspoons crushed peppermint candies (optional)

1. Make the adapted cake and allow the baked cake to cool completely.

2. To make the glaze: In a small mixing bowl, combine the confectioners' sugar, corn syrup, water, and peppermint extract. Whisk until smooth and pourable.

3. Dip the tip of a toothpick into the bottle of food coloring. Dip the toothpick into the glaze, then stir to blend. This will give the glaze a lovely subtle pink hue; one drop of food coloring is far too much. Repeat two or three times until you achieve the desired color.

4. Spoon the glaze over the top of the cake, allowing it to drip randomly down the sides. If the glaze becomes too thick, add a few drops of water. If desired, immediately sprinkle the crushed peppermint over the top, before the glaze hardens.

STORAGE: Store at room temperature under a glass dome or covered with aluminum foil for up to 1 day with candy on top or 3 days without candy.

NOTE: To crush peppermint candy, put candies in a plastic bag and twist top of bag, allowing room for candy to spread. Set the bag on your work surface. Hit with the bottom of a small pot or a hammer until the candy is broken into pieces.

About Angel Food Cakes

Angel food cakes are believed to have originated with the Pennsylvania Dutch sometime during the mid-nineteenth century. They are made primarily with egg whites, sugar, flour, and flavorings. They are totally fat-free when unadorned, perfect for those on a low-cholesterol and low-fat diet.

An angel food cake made from scratch has a pleasantly sweet taste, totally unlike that of the packaged cake mixes, which I think taste acrid. Many people who claim they dislike angel food cakes have a complete change of heart once they taste one made with pure ingredients.

Few recipes for angel food cakes exist because the base recipe is very sensitive and leaves little margin for ingredient variation other than a change of flavorings or the addition of spices. Nonetheless these cakes lend themselves to many marvelous recipe spin-offs.

This chapter contains two base recipes upon which to expand. Sweet Angel Cake (page 304) is modeled after the classic formula, which calls for superfine sugar. Powdered Sugar Angel Food Cake (page 306) uses confectioners' sugar, which contains a small amount of cornstarch.

You can achieve variety with the imaginative use of fillings. Because the texture of angel food cake is dense, it is easy to carve out and fill the center. Sweetmeat Angel Cake (page 310) is a wonderful recipe for a tunnel cake. These cakes are also scrumptious garnished with flavored whipped cream.

• Angel food cakes are generally baked in ungreased tube pans. The batter must cling to the ungreased surface in order to maintain its volume. If your tube pan does not have a removable bottom, line the bottom with parchment to make releasing the cake easier.

• Use only freshly separated egg whites. Separate egg whites when you remove them from the refrigerator. Let them stand at room temperature for about 20 minutes before using.

• Use superfine sugar in angel food cakes. Regular granulated or table sugar is too coarse. If lumpy, strain before measuring.

• When combining superfine sugar and flour, or superfine sugar and other dry ingredients such as confectioners' sugar, strain them through a fine-mesh strainer—preferably four times—to combine thoroughly.

• Do not overbeat the egg whites before adding the sugar or the cake with flop.

• Angel food cake batter will not hold. After the flour/sugar mixture has been added to the meringue, spoon it immediately into the pan. Pass a knife through the batter to remove air pockets and be sure to smooth the surface of the batter again with the back of a spoon. Since the batter is quite thick, the top of the cake will be very uneven if this is not done.

• Overbaking can cause angel food cakes to deflate even before you've removed them from the oven. As little as a minute or two can make the difference, so watch the baking time carefully.

• Unless instructed otherwise, invert an angel food cake as soon as it comes out of the oven to help keep it from shrinking.

sweetmeat angel cake

MAKES 12 TO 14 SERVINGS

As its name indicates, this cake harbors lots of treats in its luscious filling.

1/3 cup dried apricots, cut into 1/2-inch pieces

1 cup plus 2 tablespoons water, divided

2/3 cup pitted dates, cut into 1/2-inch pieces

3 tablespoons amaretto liqueur

1 teaspoon plain unflavored gelatin

2 1/2 cups heavy cream, well chilled

1/3 cup strained confectioners' sugar

1 1/2 teaspoons pure vanilla extract

1/2 cup coarsely chopped walnuts (see page 356)

2 tablespoons red glacé cherries, cut into 1/4-inch pieces

1 ounce semisweet chocolate, coarsely chopped; plus additional chocolate for shaving (optional)

Powdered Sugar Angel Food Cake (page 306), baked and cooled

1. Place the apricots and 1 cup of the water into a small saucepan. Bring to a boil, reduce the heat, and simmer for 8 to 10 minutes, or just until tender. Add the dates, return to the boil, and simmer 1 minute longer. Transfer to a bowl, add the amaretto, cover, and let stand for about 20 minutes while you prepare the whipped cream.

2. Sprinkle the gelatin over the remaining 2 tablespoons of water in a small heatproof glass bowl and let stand 5 minutes. Place the bowl in a small skillet filled with 1/2 inch of boiling water. Stir until the gelatin is clear and completely dissolved. Remove from the skillet and allow to cool to tepid.

3. Put the cream in a large chilled bowl of an electric mixer fitted with beaters or the whip attachment. Whip on medium speed until the cream begins to thicken, then pour in the gelatin and add the sugar and vanilla. Continue beating until the cream forms soft peaks.

4. Remove the bowl from the mixer. Reserve about 2 cups of whipped cream for frosting. Fold the cooked fruit mixture into the remaining cream, along with the walnuts, cherries, and chopped chocolate. You should have about 4 cups of filling.

ASSEMBLE THE CAKE

5. Place the cake, bottom side up, on a cake plate. Using a serrated knife, gently cut a 3/4-inch layer off of the top and set aside on a square of wax paper. You are now ready to make the tunnel.

6. To judge the depth of the cut for the tunnel, hold the knife upright along the outside of the cake with the point ¾ inch from the bottom. Position your thumb on the knife level with the top of the cake. Holding that position, insert the knife ¾ inch in from the side of the cake, going only as far down as your thumb. Using a gentle up-and-down motion, cut a circle around the outer edge of the cake to form a wall. Repeat around the inner circle to form a second ¾-inch wall.

7. Cut wedges from the center portion approximately every 2 inches. Pull out the wedges and set aside for another use. Be sure the bottom of the well is fairly smooth.

8. Fill the tunnel with the fruit/cream mixture. If the cavity is not completely filled, use some of the reserved whipped cream. Place the top layer over the filling and press gently to adhere.

9. Whisk the reserved whipped cream several times to thicken. Then use it to cover the side and top of the cake generously. Garnish the cake with semisweet chocolate shavings if desired.

STORAGE: Store in the refrigerator loosely covered with aluminum foil. This cake will keep up to 3 days.

coconut layer cake

MAKES 10 TO 12 SERVINGS

Finely chopped, unsweetened coconut is steeped in milk and then pureed to give this golden butter cake a scrumptious coconut flavor. Place a single bright red strawberry rose to the side of the cake for an eye-catching finish.

¾ cup milk

½ cup shredded coconut, fresh, desiccated or canned flakes (see Note)

2⅓ cups sifted cake flour

2 teaspoons baking powder

½ teaspoon salt

⅔ cup (1⅓ sticks) unsalted butter

1⅓ cups superfine or strained sugar

3 large eggs

1 teaspoon pure vanilla extract

FROSTING AND GARNISH

Quick Buttercream Frosting (page 373)

1⅓ cups shredded coconut, fresh, desiccated or canned flakes

1 extra-large well-shaped strawberry

AT A GLANCE

PAN: Two 9-inch round cake pans

PAN PREP: Buttered and lined with buttered wax paper

RACK LEVEL: Lower third

OVEN TEMP: 350°F

BAKING TIME: 25–30 minutes

DIFFICULTY: 1

PREPARE THE COCONUT

1. In a small saucepan, scald the milk. Add the coconut, cover, and let steep for 30 minutes. Pour the milk and coconut into the container of a food processor fitted with the steel blade and pulse eight to ten times, or until the coconut is finely chopped. Transfer to a measuring cup and set aside.

BAKE THE LAYERS

2. Position the rack in the lower third of the oven. Heat the oven to 350°F. Butter the cake pans, line the bottoms and sides with wax paper, and lightly butter the wax paper.

3. Sift together the flour, baking powder, and salt in a triple sifter. Set aside.

4. Cut the butter into 1-inch pieces and put in the large bowl of an electric mixer fitted with beaters or the paddle attachment. Soften on low speed. Increase the speed to medium-high. Cream until smooth and light in color, 1½ to 2 minutes.

5. Add the sugar, 1 tablespoon at a time, taking 6 to 8 minutes to blend it in well. Scrape the side of the bowl occasionally.

6. Add the eggs, one at a time at 1-minute intervals, scraping the side of the bowl as necessary. Blend in the vanilla.

7. Reduce the mixer speed to low. Add the flour mixture in three additions alternately with the coconut/milk mixture in two additions, starting and ending with the flour. Mix only until incorporated after each addition. Scrape the side of the bowl and mix for 10 seconds longer.

8. Spoon the batter into the pans, smoothing the surfaces with the back of a tablespoon. Bake for 25 to 30 minutes, or until the cakes begin to come away from the sides of the pans, are golden brown on top, and springy to the touch.

9. Remove from the oven. Set the pans on cake racks to cool for 10 minutes. Invert the pans onto racks sprayed with nonstick coating and remove the pans and paper. Cool completely.

ASSEMBLE, FROST, AND GARNISH THE CAKE

10. Place one layer on a plate top side down. Cut four 4-inch strips of wax paper and slide the strips under the edge of the layer to keep the plate clean. Spread the top with frosting, leaving a ½-inch unfrosted border around the edge. Put the second layer, top side up, on the first. Using a long, metal spatula, spread a thin layer of frosting around the side of the cake.

11. Cover the top of the cake with frosting, swirling it with the rounded bottom of a tablespoon. Recoat the side of cake with the remaining frosting.

12. Generously sprinkle the top and side of the cake with coconut, pressing it gently into the frosting. Some of the coconut will fall onto the wax paper. Carefully remove the paper and sprinkle the excess coconut over the top of the cake.

13. Garnish with a strawberry rose. To make the rose, cut the berry as you would a radish rose: Start with five slits on the bottom to resemble petals, make four slits in the next layer, and three slits in the third layer.

STORAGE: The cake may be kept in a cool place under a glass dome if you plan to eat it shortly after it is made. For longer storage, cover loosely with an aluminum foil tent and refrigerate. Allow to stand at room temperature 2 to 3 hours before serving. The cake will keep for up to 5 days.

NOTE: Desiccated coconut is unsweetened and can be purchased in health food stores. You may substitute regular sweetened, canned coconut if you wish. To substitute the sweetened, canned variety for fresh, add the canned coconut to the scalded milk. Then drain off the sugary milk and discard. Scald fresh milk, using the same measurement. Add the coconut and proceed with the recipe.

raspberry ribbons

MAKES 14 TO 16 SERVINGS

Think pink! Here is an absolutely irresistible combination of raspberry cream and lightly almond-flavored angel food cake. It's also especially pretty, fancy enough for guests but surprisingly easy to decorate.

2 (10-ounce) boxes frozen raspberries with syrup, thawed and drained

3 tablespoons cold water

2 teaspoons unflavored gelatin

1½ cups heavy cream, chilled

½ cup strained confectioners' sugar

1 to 2 tablespoons kirsch

Sweet Angel (page 304) or Powdered Sugar Angel Food Cake (page 306), baked and cooled

1 pint (1½ cups) fresh raspberries

1. Puree the thawed raspberries in a blender. Strain through a fine-mesh strainer to remove the seeds. You should have about ¾ cup puree.

2. Put the water in a small, heatproof dish and sprinkle on the gelatin. Let stand for 5 minutes, then set the dish in a small skillet filled with ½ inch of boiling water. Stir until the gelatin is dissolved and completely clear. Allow to cool slightly, then stir into the raspberry puree.

3. Put the cream in a small chilled bowl of an electric mixer. Whip on medium speed. As it thickens, gradually add the sugar. Continue beating until very thick. Remove the bowl from the mixer. With a 2¾-inch-wide rubber spatula, fold in the raspberry puree and kirsch. If the raspberry cream is too thin, chill for about 1 hour, or until firm enough to spread. At this point, the filling can be spread, but *do not mix* or it will thin out.

4. With the bottom side up, divide the cake into three layers (see page 366). Reserve half of the raspberry cream for outer frosting and decorating the cake.

5. Place the widest layer on a serving plate cut side up. Cover with a little more than half of the remaining raspberry cream. Position the middle layer over the first, wide side down, and cover with the rest of the cream. Arrange the top layer cut side down over the middle layer. Frost the side and top of the cake with the reserved raspberry cream, setting aside about one-third for decoration. Arrange the fresh raspberries at random over the top of the cake, pressing them gently into the cream.

6. Fit a 14-inch pastry bag with a #114 large leaf tube. Fill the bag with the remaining raspberry cream. Holding the bag at a 90-degree angle, with the tip almost touching the top of the cake, make 1- to 2-inch-long ribbons of cream, partially covering the raspberries. Turn the bag to the left or to the right as you lift it to make an attractive end to each ribbon. Allow some of the ribbons to fall about $\frac{1}{2}$ inch over the side of the cake. If desired, trim the plate with fresh lemon leaves or other nonpoisonous greenery. Refrigerate for 3 to 4 hours. Remove from the refrigerator $\frac{1}{2}$ hour before serving.

STORAGE: Refrigerate, covered loosely with an aluminum foil tent, for up to 3 days.

georgia peanut cake

MAKES 10 TO 12 SERVINGS

Peanut butter and crunchy chopped peanuts make a cake packed with peanut flavor. The bourbon-flavored creamy peanut icing is an outstanding complement. The layers are extremely delicate, so handle with care when assembling.

2¼ cups sifted cake flour

2 teaspoons baking powder

½ teaspoon salt

½ cup (1 stick) unsalted butter

⅓ cup smooth peanut butter

½ cup granulated sugar

1 cup lightly packed light brown sugar

2 large eggs

½ cup sour cream

1 teaspoon pure vanilla extract

⅔ cup milk

⅔ cup unsalted plain peanuts (not dry-roasted), chopped medium-fine (see page 356), plus additional for garnish

Creamy Peanut Bourbon Frosting (opposite page)

AT A GLANCE

PANS: Two 9-inch round cake pans

PAN PREP: Buttered and lined with buttered wax paper

RACK LEVELS: Lower thirds

OVEN TEMP: 350°F

BAKING: 30–35 minutes

DIFFICULTY: 1

1. Position the rack in the lower third of the oven. Heat the oven to 350°F. Butter the cake pans, line the bottoms and sides with wax paper, and lightly butter the wax paper.

2. Sift together the flour, baking powder, and salt, using a triple sifter. Set aside.

3. Cut the butter into 1-inch pieces and place in the large bowl of an electric mixer fitted with beaters or the paddle attachment. Soften on low speed. Increase the speed to medium-high. Cream until smooth and light in color, about 1 minute. Add the peanut butter and cream for 30 seconds longer.

4. Add the granulated sugar, 1 tablespoon at a time, taking 3 to 4 minutes to blend it in well. Add the brown sugar over an additional 3 to 4 minutes. Scrape the side of the bowl occasionally.

5. Add the eggs, one at a time at 1-minute intervals, scraping the side of the bowl as necessary. Blend in the sour cream and vanilla.

6. Reduce the mixer speed to low. Add the flour mixture alternately with the milk, dividing the flour into three parts, the milk into two parts, and starting and ending with the flour. Scrape the side of the bowl and mix for 10 seconds longer. Blend in the nuts; *do not overmix*.

7. Spoon the batter into the pans, smoothing the surface with the back of a tablespoon. Bake for 30 to 35 minutes, or until the cakes begin to come away from the sides of the pans and are springy to the touch.

8. Remove from the oven. Set the pans on cake racks for 10 minutes to cool slightly, then invert onto the racks sprayed with nonstick coating and lift off the pans. Carefully remove the wax paper and continue to cool completely.

ASSEMBLE THE CAKE

9. Place one cake layer on a serving plate top side down. Spread with frosting, leaving a ½-inch unfrosted border around the edge. Set the second layer, top side up, on the first. Spread a thin layer of frosting around the side of the cake using a long metal spatula. Thin the remaining frosting with additional milk or cream to reach a soft, creamy consistency.

10. Cover the top of the cake with frosting, swirling it with the bottom of a tablespoon. To create a swirled design on the sides, recoat the side of the cake with the remaining frosting. Sprinkle chopped peanuts over the top. If you wish, you can swirl a touch of smooth peanut butter on the back of a teaspoon over the surface of cake for an interesting two-toned effect.

STORAGE: Store at room temperature under a glass cake cover or in an airtight container for up to 5 days.

creamy peanut bourbon frosting

MAKES ABOUT 3 CUPS, ENOUGH TO FILL OR FROST TWO 9-INCH LAYERS

½ cup smooth peanut butter

¼ cup (½ stick) unsalted butter, at room temperature

1 (3-ounce) package cream cheese, at room temperature

3 tablespoons bourbon

1 to 2 tablespoons milk or cream, plus additional if necessary

1 teaspoon pure vanilla extract

4 to 4½ cups (1 pound) strained confectioners' sugar

3 to 4 tablespoons coarsely chopped peanuts for garnish

1. Place the peanut butter, butter, and cream cheese in a medium-sized bowl. Blend with a wooden spoon until very smooth.

2. In a small bowl, combine the bourbon, milk, and vanilla. Add the sugar to the peanut butter mixture alternately with the bourbon mixture, about four additions of sugar to three additions of liquid, mixing until smooth and creamy. If the frosting is too stiff, add additional drops of milk until desired spreading consistency is reached. After frosting, sprinkle the chopped peanuts over the top of the cake.

double trouble fudge cake

MAKES 10 TO 12 SERVINGS

Here's one that is absolutely addictive. A delicious candy-like filling baked into the cake creates a chewy contrast to the melt-in-your-mouth chocolate layers and silky frosting.

CHOCOLATE-NUT FILLING

1/4 cup unsweetened Dutch-process cocoa

1/3 cup sugar

3/4 cup walnuts

2 tablespoons melted butter

CAKE

3 ounces unsweetened chocolate, broken into small pieces

3/4 cup hot water

1 tablespoon freeze-dried coffee crystals

2 cups sifted cake flour

1 1/4 teaspoons baking soda

1/2 teaspoon salt

1/2 cup (1 stick) unsalted butter

1 1/2 cups superfine or strained sugar

3 large eggs

1 teaspoon pure vanilla extract

1/2 cup sour cream

CHOCOLATE CUSTARD FROSTING

2 ounces unsweetened chocolate, coarsely chopped

2 ounces semisweet chocolate, coarsely chopped

1 tablespoon freeze-dried coffee crystals

1/2 cup boiling water

1 cup sugar

3 tablespoons cornstarch

1/8 teaspoon salt

1 cup half-and-half

1 tablespoon unsalted butter

1 1/2 teaspoons pure vanilla extract

AT A GLANCE

PANS: Two 9-inch round cake pans

PAN PREP: Buttered and lined with buttered parchment

RACK LEVEL: Lower third

OVEN TEMP: 350°F

BAKING TIME: 30–35 minutes

DIFFICULTY: 2

1. Position the rack in the lower third of the oven. Heat the oven to 350°F. Butter the cake pans. Line the bottoms with parchment and butter again.

MAKE THE CHOCOLATE-NUT FILLING

2. Place the cocoa, sugar, and walnuts in the container of a food processor fitted with a steel blade. Process until the nuts are medium-sized. Add the melted butter, and pulse *just* until the crumbs are coated. Set aside.

MAKE THE CAKE

3. In a small saucepan, combine the chocolate, water, and coffee. Stir over low heat until the chocolate is completely melted and the mixture is smooth. Set aside.

4. Sift together the flour, baking soda, and salt, using a triple sifter. Set aside.

5. Cut the butter into 1-inch pieces and place in the large bowl of an electric mixer fitted with beaters or the paddle attachment. Soften on low speed. Increase the speed to medium-high and cream until smooth and light in color, 1½ to 2 minutes.

6. Add the sugar, 1 tablespoon at a time, taking 6 to 8 minutes to blend it in well. Scrape the side of the bowl occasionally.

7. Add the eggs, one at a time at 1-minute intervals, scraping the side of the bowl as needed. Reduce the mixer speed to medium. Blend in the chocolate mixture, then the vanilla.

8. Reduce the mixer speed to low. Add the dry ingredients alternately with the sour cream, dividing the flour mixture into three parts and the sour cream into two parts, and starting and ending with the flour. Mix only until incorporated after each addition. Scrape the side of the bowl.

9. Divide two-thirds of the batter between the two pans, smoothing the surface with the back of a tablespoon. Sprinkle half of the chocolate/nut mixture into each pan. Dab the remaining batter over the top of each layer, spreading it lightly over the crumbs with the back of the spoon. It is not necessary for the batter to cover the crumbs completely. Bake for 30 to 35 minutes, or until the cakes begin to come away from the sides of the pans and are springy to the touch.

10. Remove from the oven. Place the pans on cake racks for 10 minutes to cool and set the layers. Spray the rack with nonstick coating, then invert and lift the pans off the cakes. Remove the wax paper. Continue to cool to room temperature.

MAKE THE CHOCOLATE CUSTARD FROSTING

11. In a small heavy saucepan, combine the unsweetened and semisweet chocolates, the coffee, and boiling water. Stir until the chocolate is completely melted and the coffee dissolved. In a separate small bowl, combine the sugar, cornstarch, and salt and add to chocolate mixture, stirring until blended. Slowly add the half-and-half, whisking gently until well combined.

12. Bring to a boil over low heat, stirring continuously with a wooden spoon. Cook gently about 1 minute longer, stirring occasionally, then remove from the heat. Off the heat, blend in the butter and vanilla. To cool quickly, set saucepan in cold water. Stir gently, do not beat, until the frosting is thick enough to spread. This will only take a few minutes.

ASSEMBLE THE CAKE

13. Place one layer on a plate, top side down. Cut four 4-inch strips of wax paper and slide them under the edge of the layer to protect the plate. Spread the layer with frosting, leaving a ½-inch unfrosted border around the edge. Place the second layer, top side up, on the first. Using a long, metal spatula, spread a thin layer of frosting around the side of the cake.

14. Cover the top of the cake with frosting, swirling it with the rounded bottom of a tablespoon. Recoat the side of the cake with the remaining frosting.

STORAGE: Store at room temperature under a glass cake cover or in an airtight container for up to 5 days.

boston cream pie

In the mid-1850s, a German pastry chef who worked at the Parker House Hotel in Boston served his rendition of a popular cake known as pudding-cake pie.

Traditionally, this "pie" consisted of a single sponge layer, split into two thin disks filled with a thick layer of vanilla custard and dusted with confectioners' sugar. The Parker House chef broke with tradition and replaced the confectioners' sugar with a thin chocolate icing. The sides were left unfrosted, exposing the custard filling. His version became the rage of Boston and for years it was called Parker House Cream Pie. Eventually, the name of the hotel was dropped and the cake became known simply Boston Cream Pie. My version of this perennial favorite calls for dripping the chocolate icing down the side. This is a bonus for chocolate lovers and also makes a prettier presentation.

VANILLA CUSTARD FILLING

1 1/3 cups milk, divided

1/3 cup granulated sugar

2 tablespoons cornstarch

1 tablespoon all-purpose flour

1 large whole egg

1 large egg yolk

1 tablespoon butter

1 teaspoon pure vanilla extract

CHOCOLATE ICING

1 ounce unsweetened chocolate, coarsely chopped

1 ounce semisweet chocolate, coarsely chopped

1 1/4 cups strained confectioners' sugar

3 tablespoons boiling water, plus a few extra drops for thinning

1 tablespoon light corn syrup

1/2 teaspoon pure vanilla extract

Hot Milk Sponge Cake (page 290)

MAKE THE FILLING

1. In a medium saucepan, combine 1 cup of the milk and the granulated sugar, and bring to a slow boil over low heat.

2. In a small bowl, combine the cornstarch and flour. Gradually stir in the remaining 1/3 cup milk, whisking until very smooth. Then whisk in the whole egg and the egg yolk. Add to the hot milk mixture. Bring to a boil over low heat, whisking constantly, until the mixture is thick and smooth. Cook 30 to 45 seconds after the mixture reaches a boil, stirring gently with a wooden spoon to prevent scorching.

3. Remove from the heat and stir in the butter and vanilla. Press a piece of buttered wax paper onto the filling to prevent a skin from forming. Refrigerate until the filling is chilled.

MAKE THE CHOCOLATE ICING

4. Place the unsweetened and semisweet chocolates in a medium mixing bowl. Melt slowly over a low flame in a skillet containing ½ inch of hot water.

5. Remove the bowl from the skillet. Stir the chocolate to blend. Add the confectioners' sugar alternately with the hot water, four parts sugar to three parts water, beating well after each addition.

6. Beat in the corn syrup and vanilla. The icing should be pourable, the consistency of chocolate syrup. If too tight, add a few drops of boiling water until the desired consistency is reached. The icing will tighten as it cools. If you are making it ahead of time, place the bowl in skillet filled with ½ inch of hot water to keep warm.

ASSEMBLE THE CAKE

7. Divide the sponge cake horizontally into two layers. Set the bottom layer cut side up on a serving plate. Cut four strips of wax paper, each 4 inches wide, and slide under the edge of the cake to keep the plate clean while you frost.

8. Cover the cake with a ½-inch layer of custard. Then position the second layer over the first, cut side down. Holding the bowl 10 inches over the center of the cake, pour on the chocolate icing. Using a 10-inch metal spatula, *quickly* ease the icing to the edge of the cake. Allow it to drip randomly down the side; the icing will set almost immediately.

STORAGE: Refrigerate uncovered for 15 to 20 minutes to set. If you wish, the cake can be made ahead and refrigerated for up to 6 to 8 hours before serving. Remove ½ hour before serving. Leftover cake should be refrigerated, loosely covered with a foil tent. The cake will keep up to 3 days.

burnished sugar layer cake

MAKES 10 TO 12 SERVINGS

Caramelized sugar is used in various ways for a large variety of pastries and desserts. Here caramel syrup is blended into a vanilla batter, giving the cake a wonderful golden brown color and a marvelous burnished sugar taste.

The syrup may be made many days in advance and stored in a jar at room temperature; however, it will harden upon standing. When ready to use it, reheat the syrup to about 100°F in a microwave at medium setting or in a water bath (see page 355). It should be the consistency of thick maple syrup.

A word of caution: Do not attempt to make caramel with young children or pets underfoot. While the end result is delicious, the procedure for making caramel is serious business.

CARAMEL SYRUP

1⅓ cups granulated sugar

¼ cup water

3 to 4 drops lemon juice

¼ cup hot water

CAKE

1 cup sour cream

½ cup warm caramel syrup

¼ teaspoon baking soda

2½ cups sifted cake flour

2 teaspoons baking powder

¾ teaspoon salt

¾ cup (1½ sticks) unsalted butter

1⅓ cups superfine or strained sugar

3 large eggs

1 teaspoon pure vanilla extract

BURNISHED SUGAR FROSTING

½ cup (1 stick) unsalted butter, at room temperature

3 cups strained confectioners' sugar, divided

3 tablespoons warmed caramel syrup

⅛ teaspoon salt

2 to 3 tablespoons sour cream

1 teaspoon pure vanilla extract

3 or 4 drops maple extract (optional)

AT A GLANCE

PAN: Two 9-inch round cake pans

PAN PREP: Buttered and lined with buttered wax paper

RACK LEVEL: Lower third

OVEN TEMP: 350°F

BAKING TIME: 30–35 minutes

DIFFICULTY: 2

MAKE THE CARAMEL SYRUP

1. Put the granulated sugar in a heavy, 2-quart saucepan. (Do not use a smaller pan.) Add ¼ cup water and bring to a slow boil. Simmer until the sugar is dissolved. Stir briefly only if undissolved sugar clings to the bottom of the pot. Brush the side of the saucepan with water to remove any sugar crystals, then add the lemon juice. Cook until the mixture turns deep golden brown, 320° to 330°F. This will take from 10 to 20 minutes, depending upon the thickness of the saucepan. Watch carefully, as the sugar syrup burns easily. If it gets too black, it will taste bitter.

2. When the desired color and temperature are reached, *immediately* remove the pan from the heat and set in a sink filled to a shallow depth with cold water to stop the cooking. *At once* pour the ¼ cup hot water into the syrup. The caramel will bubble up.

3. Return the saucepan to low heat briefly, stirring until smooth and syrupy. Pour into a measuring cup. Scrape the drippings from the pan with a buttered spoon. (The butter keeps the syrup from sticking to the spoon.) This recipe yields about ¾ cup syrup, enough to prepare the cake and glaze.

MAKE THE CAKE

4. Position the rack in the lower third of the oven. Heat the oven to 350°F. Butter the cake pans. Line the bottoms and sides with wax paper and butter the paper lightly.

5. In a small bowl, combine the sour cream, ½ cup warm caramel syrup, and baking soda. Set aside.

6. Using a triple sifter, sift together the flour, baking powder, and salt. Set aside.

7. Cut the butter into 1-inch pieces and place in the large bowl of an electric mixer fitted with beaters or the paddle attachment. Soften on low speed. Increase the speed to medium-high and cream until smooth and light in color, 1½ to 2 minutes.

8. Add the superfine sugar, 1 tablespoon at a time, taking 6 to 8 minutes to blend it in well. Scrape the side of the bowl occasionally.

9. Add the eggs, one at a time at 1-minute intervals. Scrape the side of the bowl as necessary. Beat for 1 minute longer. Blend in the vanilla.

10. Reduce the mixer speed to low. Add the dry ingredients alternating with the caramel-flavored sour cream, dividing the flour mixture into three parts and the sour cream into two parts, and starting and ending with the flour. Mix only until incorporated after each addition. Scrape the side of the bowl and mix for 10 seconds longer.

11. Spoon the batter into the pans and smooth the surface with the back of a tablespoon. Center the pans on the rack and bake for 30 to 35 minutes, or until the cakes are browned on top and springy to the touch.

12. Remove from the oven and place the pans on cake racks to cool for 15 minutes. Invert the pans onto the racks, and gently remove the pans and paper.

(continued)

MAKE THE FROSTING

13. In a medium-sized bowl, cream the butter with a wooden spoon until very smooth. Gradually add 1½ cups of the confectioners' sugar in three or four additions, blending well after each addition.

14. Blend in the 3 tablespoons caramel syrup, stirring until smooth. Add the remaining 1½ cups confectioners' sugar and the salt, alternating with the sour cream. Flavor with the vanilla and maple extracts. The frosting should be creamy, but do not overmix. If too thin, chill briefly in the refrigerator.

ASSEMBLE THE CAKE

15. Place a layer on a plate top side down. Cut four strips of wax paper, 4 inches wide, and slide under the edge to keep the plate clean. Using a metal spatula, spread frosting on the top about ¼ inch thick, leaving a ½-inch unfrosted border all around. Place the second layer, top side up, on top of the first, aligning the layers evenly. Apply a thin layer of frosting to the side with the spatula. Cover the top completely. Use the remaining frosting for a second application around the side.

16. Gently press the bottom of a teaspoon into the frosting, then pull it out to create little ¼- to ½-inch peaks. Continue on the top and side at ½-inch intervals. Chill in the refrigerator for ½ hour or until the peaks are set.

STORAGE: Store at room temperature under a glass dome or in an airtight container for up to 5 days.

hazelnut blitz torte with praline cream filling

MAKES 8 TO 10 SERVINGS

During my childhood in the South, my mother frequently made a blitz torte. This unusual cake consists of two thin butter cake layers covered with a stiff meringue and topped with crushed hazelnuts. The meringue rises high above the side of the pan during baking, but shrinks and forms a crusty, uneven surface as the cake cools.

The wonderful custard filling is flavored with praline paste, a delicious nut butter made from candied hazelnuts. Since the golden meringue crust is so pretty, frosting becomes unnecessary.

For a quick alternative to the praline filling, prepare an espresso-flavored filling by omitting the nut paste and adding 2 teaspoons of espresso zest (see pages 350–351) to the hot milk. When I use the espresso flavoring, I like to substitute pecans for the hazelnuts.

Whatever you choose to use as a filling, this torte is absolutely scrumptious, and I can assure you it will be a conversation piece every time you serve it.

CAKE

1 cup sifted cake flour

1 teaspoon baking powder

1/8 teaspoon salt

1/2 cup (1 stick) unsalted butter

1/2 cup superfine or strained sugar

4 large eggs yolks (reserve whites for meringue)

1 teaspoon pure vanilla extract

3 tablespoons milk

MERINGUE

1/2 cup superfine or strained sugar

1/3 cup strained confectioners' sugar

4 egg whites

1/2 teaspoon pure vanilla extract

1/2 cup hazelnuts, coarsely chopped (see page 356)

1 tablespoon granulated sugar

Praline Cream Filling (page 378)

MAKE THE CAKE BATTER

1. Position the rack in the lower third of the oven. Heat the oven to 325°F. Generously butter the cake pans.

2. Sift together the flour, baking powder, and salt, using a triple sifter. Set aside.

3. Cut the butter into 1-inch pieces and place in the small bowl of an electric mixer fitted with beaters or the paddle attachment. Soften on low speed. Increase the mixer speed to medium. Cream until smooth and light in color, 1 1/2 to 2 minutes.

AT A GLANCE

PAN: Two 9-inch round cake pans with removable bottoms (see Note)

PAN PREP: Generously buttered

RACK LEVEL: Lower third

OVEN TEMP: 325°F

BAKING TIME: 30–35 minutes

DIFFICULTY: 2

(continued)

4. Add the superfine sugar, 1 tablespoon at a time, taking 3 to 4 minutes to blend it in well. Scrape the side of the bowl occasionally.

5. Add the egg yolks, two at a time at 1-minute intervals; beat 1 minute longer, scraping the side of the bowl as necessary. Blend in the vanilla.

6. Reduce the mixer speed to low. Add the flour mixture alternately with the milk, dividing the flour into three parts and the milk into two parts, and starting and ending with the flour. Scrape the side of the bowl. Mix 10 seconds longer.

7. Spoon the batter into the center of the pans. Using the back of a tablespoon, spread the batter from the center out to the side. This will be a very thin layer of batter. Set aside.

MAKE THE MERINGUE

8. Strain the superfine sugar and the confectioners' sugar together three times through a fine strainer. Place the egg whites in the large bowl of an electric mixer fitted with beaters or the whip attachment. Beat on medium speed until the whites are frothy. Increase the speed to medium-high and continue to beat until the whites form firm, moist peaks, but are not dry. Add the sugars, 1 tablespoon at a time, over 3 to 4 minutes. Blend in the vanilla and beat 1 minute longer, until you have a very stiff, glossy meringue.

BAKE THE CAKES

9. Spoon the meringue over the batter in the pans, making sure the entire surface is covered and the meringue clings to the side of the pan. With the back of a tablespoon, swirl the meringue to form a few peaks. It should not be smooth. Sprinkle each layer with the hazelnuts, then top both with the granulated sugar. Bake for 30 to 35 minutes, or until the meringue is golden brown and feels dry to the touch.

10. Remove the cakes from the oven and set the pans on cake racks to cool completely. The meringue will shrink and sink as it stands. When the cakes are completely cool, run a thin knife around the sides of pans to release any meringue that clings.

ASSEMBLE THE CAKE

11. To remove the pans, place each layer on top of a coffee can—the outer ring will drop to the counter. Run a long sharp knife under the bottom of each cake to release the metal disk. Slide one layer gently onto a serving platter and the other onto a cake rack. If you have used springform or standard layer pans, cut a 12-inch piece of aluminum foil and place it gently over the meringue, molding the sides of the foil around the pan. Invert onto a second cake rack and carefully lift off the pan. Center a serving plate over the layer and invert again. The meringue side will be up. Do this carefully to avoid crushing the meringue. Repeat with the second layer; however, after removing the pan, turn the meringue right side up onto a cake rack instead of a plate.

12. Spoon the filling over the bottom layer on the platter, leaving a $\frac{1}{2}$-inch unfrosted border around the edge. Carefully slide the top layer from the rack onto the first layer. This cake is at its best served shortly after assembling. However, it can be filled and refrigerated, covered, for up to 6 to 8 hours. Let stand at room temperature $\frac{1}{2}$ hour before serving.

STORAGE: Refrigerate, covered loosely with aluminum foil, for up to 3 days.

NOTE: If layer pans with removable bottoms are not available, you may substitute two 9-inch springform pans or two 9-inch standard layer pans. However, special handling will be required to remove the cakes.

majestic mandarin cake

MAKES 16 TO 18 SERVINGS

If you wish to create a party cake that makes a statement, I can think of no better choice than this. It is dramatically high, feather-light, and has a heavenly orange-cream frosting garnished with crunchy golden flakes of toasted coconut. This cake is baked in an angel food pan. It is a nice touch to fill the center hole with an appropriate decoration. For a bridal shower you may choose a miniature doll; for Christmas, try an arrangement of seasonal decorations; or at any time of year, a cluster of fresh shrubbery greens.

3 (11-ounce) cans mandarin oranges

¾ cup sugar

⅓ cup all-purpose flour

⅛ teaspoon salt

⅔ cup fresh navel orange juice

2 to 3 tablespoons fresh lemon juice

2 large eggs, lightly beaten

1½ to 2 tablespoons grated navel orange zest

1 teaspoon grated lemon zest

2½ cups heavy cream, well chilled

3 tablespoons Grand Marnier, Cointreau, or Triple Sec; plus 3 to 4 tablespoons for brushing (optional)

1 (3½-ounce) can shredded coconut, toasted

Orange Sponge Cake (page 286), baked and cooled

1. Drain the oranges and set aside to dry thoroughly on several layers of paper toweling.

2. In the top of a double boiler, combine the sugar, flour, and salt. Slowly whisk in the orange and lemon juices, then blend in the eggs. Place the pan over 1 inch of simmering water and stir constantly with a wooden spoon until the mixture thickens, 8 to 10 minutes. Remove from the heat and whisk briefly just to smooth the mixture. Stir in the grated orange and lemon zests. Place a buttered round of wax paper directly on the surface to prevent a film from forming. Chill for 2 to 3 hours, or until very cold. This mixture can be made up to 3 days in advance.

3. Place the heavy cream in a large, chilled bowl of an electric mixer fitted with chilled beaters or whip attachment. Whip on medium speed until it begins to thicken. Add the Grand Marnier and beat until the cream forms firm peaks. Remove from the machine and whisk one-fourth of the whipped cream into the orange filling, until smooth and well blended. Using a 2¾-inch-wide rubber spatula, fold the filling into the remaining cream. Divide the filling in half.

4. Set aside 40 of the nicest mandarin orange sections for garnish. Dice the remaining oranges and fold into one-half of the filling. The remaining filling will be used to frost the cake.

5. Place the cake on a serving plate bottom side up and cut horizontally into four layers (see page 366). Set the widest layer cut side up on a serving plate. Cut four strips of wax paper, each 4 inches wide, and slip them under the cake to keep the plate clean. If desired, brush the layer lightly with Grand Marnier. Cover with one-third of the filling containing the diced oranges. Position the second-widest layer over the first, narrowest side up. Brush with liqueur and cover with one-third of the filling. Repeat with the third layer. Place the top layer cut side down. Press the cake gently to align the side.

6. If you wish, set aside one-fourth of the reserved mandarin cream for piped decoration. However, this step is entirely optional. Cover the side and the top of the cake with the cream, using a long, metal spatula to smooth the surface. Sprinkle the top and side of cake with toasted coconut.

7. Fit a 14-inch pastry bag with a large, #2 open-star tube. Fill one-third full with the remaining mandarin cream. Garnish the cake with rosettes spaced 1 inch apart, beginning with the top outer edge, then the inner edge, and finally the bottom edge.

8. Press reserved mandarin orange slices between the rosettes. Chill uncovered in the refrigerator for up to 8 hours. When ready to serve, arrange fresh lemon leaves (available at most florists) or other clean greenery in the center. To serve, slice with a serrated knife, using a gentle sawing motion.

STORAGE: Refrigerate, lightly covered with an aluminum foil tent, for up to 4 days.

ann's cheesecake

MAKES 10 TO 12 SERVINGS

Ann Amendolara Nurse teaches Italian cooking in the New York metropolitan area. Ann is an authority on fine food and I take special notice of any dish she prepares. Her cheesecake is one of the finest that I have ever tasted.

This crustless cake is made with a combination of cream cheese and ricotta and flavored with healthy amounts of lemon juice and pure vanilla extract. It is light and velvety, and impossible to stop eating. With each bite I tell myself, "This must be your last," but somehow it never is.

I have included Ann's recipe because if it is a collector's item with Ann, you know it is going to be exceptional.

½ cup (1 stick) unsalted butter

3 tablespoons all-purpose flour

3 tablespoons cornstarch

2 (8-ounce) packages cream cheese, at room temperature

1 (15-ounce) carton whole milk ricotta cheese, liquid drained from the top

1½ cups sugar

4 large eggs

1½ tablespoons fresh lemon juice

1 tablespoon pure vanilla extract

1 pint (2 cups) sour cream

AT A GLANCE

PAN: 9-inch springform pan

PAN PREP: Buttered

RACK LEVEL: Lower third

OVEN TEMP: 325°F

BAKING TIME: 1 hour, plus additional 1 hour for oven cooling

DIFFICULTY: 2

1. Position the rack in the lower third of the oven. Heat the oven to 325°F. Butter the springform pan.

2. In a small saucepan, melt the butter over low heat. Set aside to cool.

3. Mix together the flour and cornstarch and strain onto a sheet of wax paper. Set aside.

4. Place the cream cheese and ricotta in the large bowl of an electric mixer fitted with beaters or the paddle attachment. Mix on medium speed until smooth and creamy.

5. Add the sugar in three additions over 1 minute, scraping the side of the bowl as necessary. Beat for 30 seconds longer.

6. Add the eggs one at a time at 30-second intervals, mixing well after each addition. Blend in the flour/cornstarch mixture, lemon juice, and vanilla.

7. Add the melted butter and sour cream. Continue beating for 30 seconds, or until all ingredients are well blended. Scrape the side of the bowl and mix for 10 seconds longer.

8. Set the pan on an 18-inch square of heavy-duty aluminum foil. Mold the foil snugly around the pan to catch any batter that might leak. Pour the batter into the pan and bake for 1 hour.

9. At the end of the hour, turn off the heat and, without opening the oven door, leave the cake in the oven for 1 hour longer. Remove from the oven. Set the pan on a cake rack to cool completely. Refrigerate. Remove from the refrigerator 1 hour before serving. Run a thin knife around the edge of the pan to loosen the cake, and carefully remove the rim. Transfer to a cake platter.

STORAGE: Refrigerate, covered with aluminum foil, for up to 5 days.

manhattan cheesecake

MAKES 10 TO 12 SERVINGS

New York–style cheesecake has a luscious, dense consistency and a very creamy texture. This type of cheesecake is often called Lindy's cheesecake, named after the famous Broadway restaurant. While researching recipes for this book, I came upon no less than a dozen lists of similar ingredients claiming to be the original.

This recipe varies from traditional versions in that the pan is lined with a quick-to-make crumb crust instead of the more time-consuming sweet pastry dough. Tiers of sliced strawberries arranged on top make it picture-perfect.

CRUST

10 double graham crackers, or enough to make about 1½ cups of crumbs

2 tablespoons sugar

⅓ cup (⅔ stick) unsalted butter, melted

CAKE

1½ pounds cream cheese, at room temperature

1¼ cups sugar, divided

5 large egg yolks

½ cup heavy cream

2 teaspoons pure vanilla extract

1½ teaspoons freshly grated lemon zest

1½ teaspoons freshly grated orange zest

3 large egg whites

STRAWBERRY TOPPING

¾ cup apricot preserves

1 tablespoon kirschwasser or Grand Marnier

3 to 4 cups large, deep-red strawberries

AT A GLANCE

PAN: 9-inch springform pan

PAN PREP: Generously buttered

RACK LEVEL: Lower third

OVEN TEMP: 325°F

BAKING TIME: 40 minutes, plus additional 1 hour for oven cooling

DIFFICULTY: 2

1. Position the rack in the lower third of the oven. Heat the oven to 325°F. Generously butter the springform pan.

MAKE THE CRUST

2. Break the crackers into the container of a food processor fitted with a steel blade. Add the sugar and pulse until you get fine crumbs. Pour in the melted butter, pulsing just to blend.

3. Empty the crumbs into the pan. Using a spoon, press a thick layer (⅛ to ¼ inch) of crumbs against the side, extending about two-thirds of the way up. Using a flat-bottomed glass, press the remaining crumbs evenly over the bottom of the pan. Be sure to flatten the crumbs where the side meets the bottom. Refrigerate.

MAKE THE FILLING

4. Wash the processor bowl and steel blade. Put the cream cheese and 1 cup of the sugar in processor and process for 15 seconds, then scrape down the side of the bowl and process 5 seconds longer. While the machine is running, pour the egg yolks through the feeder tube and process 10 seconds. Add the cream, vanilla, and the lemon and orange zests. Process 10 seconds longer.

5. In the large bowl of an electric mixer fitted with beaters or the whip attachment, beat the egg whites to soft peaks. Add the remaining ¼ cup of sugar, 1 tablespoon at a time, beating until the whites are shiny, about 45 seconds. With a 2¾-inch-wide rubber spatula, fold one-fourth of the cheese mixture into the whites, taking about 10 turns to lighten. Fold in the remaining cheese mixture, taking an additional 30 turns.

6. Pour the batter into the pan. Set the pan on an 18-inch square of heavy-duty aluminum foil. Mold it around the side of the pan to catch any batter that might leak. Bake for 40 minutes.

7. At the end of the baking time, turn off heat and prop the oven door ajar with the handle of a wooden spoon. Cool the cake in the oven for 1 hour longer. Remove from the oven, discard the foil, and place the pan on a cake rack to cool for at least 3 hours. Refrigerate until ready to prepare strawberry topping.

MAKE THE STRAWBERRY TOPPING

8. In a small saucepan, combine the apricot preserves and liqueur, bring to a slow boil over low heat, and continue to cook until the preserves are completely melted. Remove from the heat. Strain through a fine strainer to remove the large pieces. Return to the saucepan. Set aside.

9. Wash, hull, and dry the berries well on several layers of paper toweling (see page 357). Slice them in half lengthwise.

10. Arrange the berries cut sides down around the edge of the cheesecake with the points of the berries facing outward. Arrange a second circle inside the first, with points of the berries extending inward. The bottoms of the berries should touch. Fill in the center randomly.

11. Arrange a second layer of berries on top of the first, beginning ½ inch from the edge of the cake. Extend the points outward, placing them in the spaces between the points of the first layer of berries. Arrange the second layer with points extending outward also. Fill in the top with the berries' points extended outward. Continue circling the top with the points of the berries outward, making a third and fourth layer if necessary. The design will resemble a rosette (see illustrations page 334). The cake may now be refrigerated for up to 4 to 6 hours, covered loosely with wax paper.

(continued)

12. Remove the cake from the refrigerator 1 hour before serving. Shortly before you are ready to serve it, warm the apricot preserves over low heat. (Do not glaze the berries until just before serving or they will become soft and runny.) With a pastry brush, lightly coat the berries, taking care not to disturb the design. If the preserves are too thick, thin them with a few drops of hot water.

STORAGE: Refrigerate, covered loosely with a foil tent, for up to 3 days.

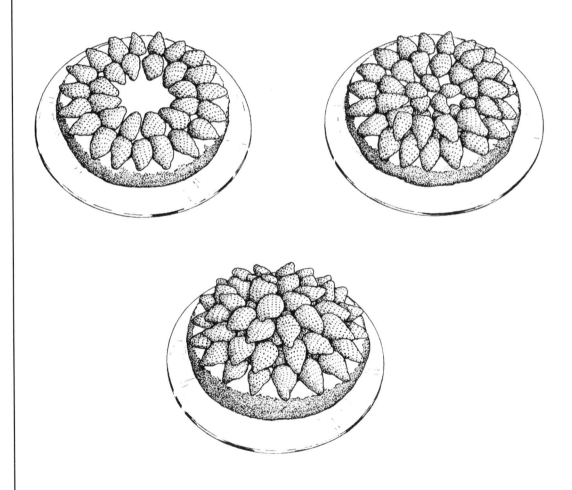

About Cheesecakes

If one were to take a vote on the most popular cake served in this country, the cheesecake would probably be the winner. It is rich, high in calories, and beloved.

There are two main types of cheesecake—what is commonly known as the New York type, made with cream cheese and sour or heavy cream, and the Italian or curd cheese variety, made with ricotta or, occasionally, cottage cheese. New York cheesecake is the richer of the two, with a smooth, velvety texture. Italian cheesecakes are usually less creamy and somewhat lighter in texture.

Cheesecake crusts can range from crusts made with graham crackers, zwieback, and chocolate wafers, and at times mixed with nuts. Some cheesecakes are made without a separate crust at all, as the cheesecake itself forms a light outer crust as it bakes.

Cheesecakes are not only delicious, they are quite simple to prepare. They are best made a day or two before you plan to serve them. The flavor improves as they mature, and they become easier to slice. They also have a very long shelf life.

- Be sure the cream cheese is very soft before you start mixing; lumps are difficult to eliminate once they have formed. Blending the sugar into the cream cheese before adding other ingredients helps to smooth it out.

- Take care not to overbeat cheesecake batter. While the ingredients should be well blended, excessive beating creates too many air cells, which expand in the oven, causing the surface of the cheesecake to crack.

- The texture of the cheesecake will be creamier if it is not overbaked. Remember, cheesecakes continue to bake as they cool down in the oven. Overbaking can also cause the top of the cheesecake to crack.

- Cheesecakes should mature in the refrigerator for at least 24 hours before serving, and since most cheesecakes keep well, you can make them as many as 2 or 3 days ahead. Only the finishing touches, such as fruit toppings, should be completed shortly before serving.

- Cheesecake tastes best at room temperature. Remove the cake from the refrigerator at least 1 hour or more before serving, depending upon weather conditions.

- Most cheesecakes are difficult to slice because of their creamy texture. To make clean slices, dip a sharp knife into warm water each time you make a cut. (If you are cutting the cake at the table, put the water in an opaque container so that the cloudy water will not show.) A wire cheese cutter also works quite well.

a great italian cheesecake

MAKES 8 TO 10 SERVINGS

Italian cheesecakes are prepared with ricotta, a high-moisture cheese made from milk or a combination of milk and whey, which is heated to extract the proteins.

When ricotta is baked it releases a substantial amount of liquid, which will make the filling watery if not dealt with in some fashion. Many recipes call for adding generous amounts of flour or cornstarch to absorb the moisture. However, this can make the cheesecake rather heavy and dry. A better method is to drain the ricotta in linen towels before using it, as specified in this recipe.

I created this creamy Italian cheesecake with the help of two fine Italian cooks, Joanne Roppate, who learned the secret of removing the water from the cheese from her Sicilian mother, and Sarah Melillo, whose contribution was to add a pureed whole navel orange to the batter, giving the cheesecake a refreshing citrus taste. The smooth texture comes from the use of confectioners' sugar in place of granulated.

Unlike most cheesecakes, this cake does not have to stand overnight. In fact, it's fabulous when freshly made. Try it and see if you don't agree.

3 pounds fresh, whole-milk ricotta

18 amaretti biscuits

2 tablespoons unflavored, dried bread crumbs

3 tablespoons unsalted butter, melted and cooled

1 medium-sized navel orange (about 6 ounces)

8 large eggs

2 cups strained confectioners' sugar

3 tablespoons all-purpose flour

2 teaspoons pure vanilla extract

¼ teaspoon salt

⅔ cup heavy cream

AT A GLANCE

PAN: 9-inch springform pan

PAN PREP: Buttered

RACK LEVEL: Lower third

OVEN TEMP: 325°F

BAKING TIME: 70–75 minutes, plus an additional 30 minutes for oven cooling

DIFFICULTY: 2

1. To extract the excess water from the ricotta: Arrange two linen or 100 percent cotton dish towels (do not use terrycloth) on top of each other on the kitchen counter. Spread the cheese lengthwise on the doubled towels into a rectangle measuring about 14 × 5 inches. Bring the sides of the towels to the center and roll the cheese tightly in the towels, jelly-roll fashion. Let the cheese stand for ½ hour. Unroll the towels and replace them with two clean, dry towels. Repeat the procedure, letting the cheese stand for another ½ hour.

2. Butter the springform pan. Break the biscuits into pieces and add with the bread crumbs to the container of a processor fitted with the steel blade. Pulse six to eight times or until fine crumbs form. You should have ¾ cup crumbs. Stop the machine and pour in the melted butter. Pulse three times just to blend.

3. Empty the crumb mixture into the pan. With the bottom of a glass, press the crumbs evenly onto the bottom of the pan. (Do not extend the crumbs up the side.) Refrigerate while you prepare the filling.

4. Position the rack in the lower third of the oven. Heat the oven to 325°F.

5. Cut the entire orange, including rind and pith, into 2-inch chunks. You should have about 2 cups. Place the eggs and orange chunks into the container of a food processor fitted with the steel blade. Process for 2 minutes, or until the mixture is thick and light in color and the orange pieces are finely chopped.

6. Stop the machine and add the ricotta, sugar, flour, vanilla, and salt. The volume of the ingredients will reduce in mixing. Process for 10 seconds, or just until smooth and creamy. Scrape down the side and process for 5 seconds longer.

7. With the machine running, pour in the cream through the feeder tube. Immediately pour the filling into the pan.

8. Set the pan on a 12-inch square of aluminum foil, molding the foil around the side of the pan to catch leakage. Bake for 70 to 75 minutes, or until the top of the cake is golden brown. Turn off the heat and prop the oven door ajar with the handle of a wooden spoon. Cool the cake in the oven for 30 minutes longer.

9. Remove the cake from the oven. Set the pan on a cake rack to cool completely. Refrigerate at least 3 to 4 hours to set, but remove the cake from the refrigerator at least 1 hour before serving. Run a thin knife around the side of the pan and carefully remove the rim.

STORAGE: Refrigerate, covered loosely with aluminum foil, for up to 1 week.

pineapple cheese squares

MAKES 8 TO 10 SERVINGS

Here, a buttery shortbread-like cookie dough crust is spread with a crushed pineapple mixture before the cheesecake ingredients are poured in. The baked cake is coated with a sour cream topping and briefly returned to the oven until the topping sets. These cheese squares are best served just slightly warm, but I find it difficult to resist eating them straight from the oven.

CRUST

1¼ cups all-purpose flour

¼ cup sugar

¼ teaspoon salt

½ cup (1 stick) cold unsalted butter, cut into ¼-inch cubes

1 large egg

PINEAPPLE LAYER

1 (20-ounce) can crushed pineapple in light syrup

1 tablespoon sugar

1 tablespoon cornstarch

2 teaspoons lemon juice

CHEESE LAYER

1 pound cottage cheese

8 ounces farmer cheese, at room temperature

¾ cup sugar, divided

3 tablespoons all-purpose flour

2 teaspoons grated lemon zest

1 teaspoon pure vanilla extract

⅔ cup heavy cream

4 large eggs

SOUR CREAM TOPPING

1 cup sour cream

2 tablespoons sugar

½ teaspoon pure vanilla extract

AT A GLANCE

PAN: 8- × 12- × 2-inch heat-proof oblong glass baking dish

PAN PREP: Buttered

RACK LEVEL: Lower third

OVEN TEMP: 350°/400°F

BAKING TIME: Crust:16–18 minutes; Cheese filling: 30 minutes, plus an additional 1 hour for oven cooling; Topping: 8–10 minutes

DIFFICULTY: 1

MAKE THE CRUST

1. Position the rack in the lower third of the oven. Heat the oven to 350°F. Butter the baking dish.

2. Place the flour, sugar, and salt into the bowl of a food processor fitted with the steel blade. Pulse three or four times. Add the butter, then process 10 seconds, or until fine crumbs form.

3. In a small bowl, beat the egg lightly with a fork. Add to the processor, and pulse only until the mixture begins to form a ball. Remove and shape the dough into a flat rectangle. Wrap in wax paper and chill for 10 minutes.

4. Press the dough evenly over the bottom of the baking dish. Bake for 16 to 18 minutes, or until the edge begins to brown. Remove the crust from oven and set aside.

PREPARE THE PINEAPPLE LAYER

5. Drain the pineapple well, reserving $1/2$ cup of the juice. In a medium-size saucepan, combine the sugar and cornstarch. Blend in the pineapple juice and drained pineapple. Bring to a slow boil and cook, stirring constantly, until the mixture thickens. Remove from the heat and stir in the lemon juice. Set aside to cool for 5 minutes.

6. Spoon the pineapple filling over the crust, spreading it evenly with the back of a spoon. Set aside.

MAKE THE CHEESE FILLING

7. Press the cottage and farmer cheeses through a food mill or a colander into a large mixing bowl. Stir in $1/2$ cup of the sugar, the flour, lemon zest, and vanilla, blending well. Slowly pour in the heavy cream.

8. Place the eggs in the container of a food processor fitted with the steel blade. Process 1 minute. With the machine running, pour the remaining $1/4$ cup sugar through feeder tube and process 1 minute longer. Stop the machine and add the cheese mixture, one-half at a time if the container is small. Pulse three or four times just to blend. *Do not overprocess.*

9. Pour the cheese mixture over the pineapple filling. Bake for 30 minutes.

10. Turn off the heat and prop the oven door open with the handle of a wooden spoon. Continue to cool in the oven for 1 hour. Remove from the oven and cool for $1/2$ hour on a rack while you prepare the topping. The cake will sink slightly as it cools.

MAKE THE TOPPING

11. Preheat the oven to 400°F.

12. Put the sour cream in a medium-size bowl. Whisk in the sugar and vanilla. Spread on the top of the cheesecake, leaving a $1/4$-inch margin of cheese filling showing around edge. Bake for 8 to 10 minutes. Serve slightly warm.

STORAGE: Refrigerate, covered loosely with aluminum foil, for up to 4 days.

praline cheesecake

MAKES 10 TO 12 SERVINGS

Here, a delicious mixture of chopped, toasted pecans and brown sugar bakes on the bottom of the cake to become a terrific, crunchy topping when the cake is inverted. The cheesecake is sensational served with in-season sliced, fresh peaches or navel orange sections.

1½ cups toasted pecans (see page 356)

2 zwieback crackers, broken into pieces

1¼ cups lightly packed light brown sugar, divided

¼ cup (½ stick) unsalted butter, melted

2 pounds cream cheese, at room temperature

⅓ cup granulated sugar

4 large eggs

1 cup sour cream

1½ teaspoons pure vanilla extract

½ teaspoon maple extract

1 teaspoon freshly grated lemon zest

1 teaspoon freshly grated navel orange zest

Confectioners' sugar for dusting

AT A GLANCE

PAN: 9-inch springform pan

PAN PREP: Generously buttered and lined with buttered parchment

RACK LEVEL: Lower third

OVEN TEMP: 325°F

BAKING TIME: 70 minutes, plus an additional 1 hour for oven cooling

DIFFICULTY: 2

1. Position the rack in the lower third of the oven. Heat the oven to 325°F. Generously butter the springform pan and line the bottom with a parchment circle. Butter the parchment.

2. Put the pecans, zwieback, and ¼ cup of the brown sugar in the bowl of a food processor fitted with the steel blade. Process until the nuts are ground medium-fine. Stop the machine and pour in the melted butter, then pulse just to combine. Empty the crumb mixture into the pan. Press the nut mixture thickly up the side with the back of a spoon, making a 1½- to 2-inch border. Use a glass to press the remaining nut mixture onto the bottom of the pan, being sure to press into the corners of the pan to get an even layer. Refrigerate the pan while you prepare the filling.

3. Wash and dry the processor bowl and steel blade. Place the cream cheese, the remaining 1 cup brown sugar, and the granulated sugar into the processor container and process with the steel blade for 30 seconds. Scrape the bowl and process 10 seconds longer. Add the eggs one at a time through the feeder tube and process for 10 seconds longer. Stop the machine.

4. Add the sour cream, vanilla and maple extracts, and lemon and orange zests. Process for 10 seconds longer. *Do not overprocess.* Pour into the pan.

5. Cut an 18-inch square of heavy-duty aluminum foil and set the pan on the foil. Bring the edges of the foil up and mold it around the pan.

6. Place a larger and wider shallow pan on the oven rack and set the foil-lined pan into it. Fill the larger pan with 1 inch of boiling water. Bake the cake for 70 minutes.

7. Turn the oven off and prop the door open with the handle of a wooden spoon. Cool the cheesecake in the oven for 1 hour longer. Remove the cake, still wrapped in aluminum foil, from the oven and set the cake on a rack to cool completely. When the cake is cool, change the aluminum foil to a clean piece, as it will be oily. Refrigerate the cake for 4 to 6 hours or overnight.

8. To unmold the cake, dip a sharp, thin-bladed knife into hot water and run the knife around the edge of the pan to loosen the crust. Remove the side of the springform pan and invert the cheesecake onto a cake plate. Carefully ease the metal disk off the cake, using the tip of a sharp knife, and remove the parchment. If any of the nut crust sticks to the parchment, scrape it off with a metal spatula and press onto the cake. Dipping the spatula into hot water will help to smooth the surface. Refrigerate, covered with aluminum foil. Remove the cake from the refrigerator 1 hour before serving. When ready to serve, dust the top lightly with confectioners' sugar.

STORAGE: Refrigerate, covered with aluminum foil, for up to 1 week.

chocolate marble cheesecake

MAKES 10 TO 12 SERVINGS

Marbleizing a cheesecake batter is fun. You may also experiment with patterns. Try alternating patches of vanilla and chocolate batter instead of the typical swirled effect. For best results, the batter should be very thick. Do not make this in a food processor, as it overthins the batter so that it will not hold a design.

For hard-core chocophiles, this recipe is easily turned into a fabulous chocolate cheesecake. See the variation below.

---

3 ounces imported bittersweet chocolate, such as Lindt Courante, Tobler, or Poulain

1 ounce unsweetened chocolate

½ cup heavy cream

1 teaspoon coffee zest (see pages 350–351)

2 pounds cream cheese, at room temperature

1⅓ cups sugar

4 large eggs

1 cup sour cream

1½ teaspoons pure vanilla extract

AT A GLANCE

PAN: 9-inch springform pan

PAN PREP: Buttered

RACK LEVEL: Lower third

OVEN TEMP: 325°F

BAKING TIME: 1 hour, plus additional 1 hour to cool in oven

DIFFICULTY: 2

1. Position the rack in the lower third of the oven. Heat the oven to 325°F. Butter the springform pan.

2. Break the bittersweet and unsweetened chocolates into pieces and place in a small heatproof bowl. Set the bowl in a pan of shallow simmering water and stir until melted, or melt in a microwave at medium setting. Blend in the cream. Add the coffee zest and stir until smooth. Set aside.

3. Place the cream cheese in the large bowl of an electric mixer fitted with beaters or the paddle attachment. Mix on medium speed for 30 to 45 seconds, until smooth and creamy.

4. Add the sugar in a steady stream, taking 45 to 60 seconds. Scrape the side of the bowl as necessary. Mix for 1 minute longer.

5. Reduce the mixer speed to medium-low. Add the eggs one at a time at 30-second intervals, mixing well after each addition. Add the sour cream and vanilla and mix for 30 seconds longer. Scrape the side of bowl again.

6. Measure out 2 cups of the batter and transfer to a separate bowl. Add to it the chocolate mixture, stirring until thoroughly blended.

7. Spoon one-fourth of the vanilla batter over the bottom of the pan. Then, working from the edge to the center, circle the pan with alternating spoonfuls of chocolate and vanilla batters. Reserve one-fourth of the vanilla batter and $1/2$ cup of the chocolate batter to finish off the top. To complete the top, smooth on the reserved vanilla batter, working from the edge to the center, then dab on the remaining chocolate batter at random. Insert the handle of a wooden spoon into the batter and gently swirl around the pan to create an attractive, marbleized surface. Center the pan on an 18-inch square of heavy-duty aluminum foil and mold the foil around the side of the pan.

8. Select a pan large enough to allow at least 1 inch of water to circulate around the batter-filled pan. A shallow stainless steel roasting pan or a disposable aluminum foil roasting pan measuring about $12 \times 17^{1}/_{2} \times 2$ inches is ideal. Pull out the oven rack to its full extension and set the empty pan on the rack. Place the batter-filled pan in the larger pan. Using a kettle or a 1-quart measuring cup, carefully pour very hot water into the larger pan to a level of about 1 inch. Gently ease the rack holding the pans into the preheated oven and bake for 1 hour.

9. Turn off the heat and prop the oven door open with the handle of a wooden spoon. Leave cake undisturbed for an additional hour. Remove the cake from the oven, discard the foil, and set the pan on a cake rack to cool completely. Refrigerate the cooled cake at least 24 hours before serving.

10. To unmold the cake, run a thin knife around the edge of the pan and carefully remove the rim. Place the cheesecake on a cake platter. Let the cake stand at room temperature until ready to slice.

STORAGE: Refrigerate, covered with an aluminum foil tent, for up to 1 week.

Chocolate Cheesecake

Increase the bittersweet chocolate to 6 ounces, the heavy cream to 1 cup, the coffee zest to 2 teaspoons, and the sugar to $1^{1}/_{2}$ cups. At step 6, add the chocolate mixture to the vanilla batter, stirring until thoroughly blended. Omit the marbling and proceed with recipe.

black-bottom mint cheesecake

MAKES 10 TO 12 SERVINGS

Here, a cream cheese batter is flavored with Vandermint liqueur and baked in a candy-coated chocolate wafer crumb crust. When the cake is unmolded from the pan, the dark chocolate crust forms a beautiful contrast to the pale creamy top. Chocolate crème de menthe wafers inserted at angles around the edge of the cake make a dynamite presentation. (The classic procedure would be to prepare chocolate triangles from scratch; however, these candies offer a quick and tasty substitute.) This is one recipe that makes even a novice look like real pro.

CRUMB CRUST

1 (9-ounce) box chocolate wafers

⅓ cup (⅔ stick) unsalted butter, melted and cooled

FILLING

1 cup mint chocolate chips

3 tablespoons water

1½ to 2 tablespoons Vandermint liqueur

1½ pounds cream cheese, at room temperature

1 cup sugar

4 large eggs

2 cups sour cream

2 teaspoons pure vanilla extract

16 Andes crème de menthe candies, for garnish

AT A GLANCE

PAN: 9-inch springform pan

PAN PREP: Generously buttered

RACK LEVEL: Lower third

OVEN TEMP: 325°F

BAKING TIME: 50 minutes, plus an additional 1 hour for oven cooling

DIFFICULTY: 2

MAKE THE CRUST

1. Generously butter the springform pan. Break the chocolate wafers into a food processor fitted with the steel blade. Pulse until you have fine crumbs. Add the melted butter, pulsing just to blend. Empty the contents into the pan and press the crumbs onto the side with the back of a spoon, making a 1½- to 2-inch border. Use a flat-bottomed glass to press the remaining crumbs onto the bottom of the pan, being sure to press firmly into the corners. Refrigerate while you prepare the filling.

2. Position the rack in the lower third of the oven. Heat the oven to 325°F.

MAKE THE FILLING

3. Place the chocolate chips and water in a small heat-proof bowl. Set the bowl in a pan of simmering water and stir until melted, or melt in a microwave on medium setting. Blend in the liqueur. Spoon the chocolate over the cooled crust, spreading it evenly with the back of a spoon. Set aside.

4. Put the cream cheese in the large bowl of an electric mixer fitted with beaters or the paddle attachment. Mix for 30 to 45 seconds on medium speed, until smooth and creamy.

5. Add the sugar in a steady stream, taking 30 to 45 seconds. Scrape the side of the bowl as necessary. Mix 1 minute longer or until very smooth.

6. Reduce the mixer speed to medium-low. Add the eggs one at a time at 30-second intervals, mixing well after each addition. Add the sour cream and vanilla and blend for 30 seconds longer, scraping the side of the bowl again as necessary.

BAKE THE CHEESECAKE

7. Pour the cheese filling over the chocolate, starting around the side, then filling in the middle. Smooth the surface with the back of a spoon. Be careful not to disturb the crumb crust. Bake for 50 minutes.

8. Turn off the heat and *without opening* the oven door, leave the cake in the oven for 1 hour longer. Remove from the oven. Set on a cake rack to cool 3 hours or longer. Refrigerate at least 24 hours before serving.

9. About 1 hour before serving, run a thin knife around the edge of the pan and carefully remove the rim. Transfer the cheesecake to a cake platter and, if you wish, garnish as follows: Imagine that the surface of the cake is the face of a clock. Starting at 12 o'clock, press the long side of the candy gently against the cake. Push the inner end of the mint all the way into the cake so that the edge is completely flush with the surface, while the outer end of the mint is standing high. The mint will form an elongated triangle. Continue with three more mints, inserting them at 3, 6, and 9 o'clock. Then insert the remaining mints evenly around the top of the cake. Leave the cake at room temperature until ready to serve.

STORAGE: Refrigerate, covered with aluminum foil, for up to 1 week.

special baking information

SPECIAL EQUIPMENT

Many of the items used for everyday baking are already in your kitchen. If you need to make a purchase or want to try a new tool, remember that high-quality equipment will pay off in the end.

Pastry (or Dough) Scraper

A pastry scraper performs many tasks in the preparation of cookie dough. If you have difficulty handling dough, this is the purchase to make. Uses include leveling the cup when measuring dry ingredients, cutting and portioning dough, releasing pastry that sticks to the rolling surface, cleaning the rolling surface, moving pastry, turning the dough, and even slicing or cutting cookies. Select one that feels weighty, with a stainless steel blade and a wooden or plastic handle. Avoid those with metal handles, as they are slippery and hard to grip.

Pastry Cloth and Rolling Pin Cover

Once you own a pastry cloth, your troubles with rolling dough will be a thing of the past. I highly recommend my custom canvas pastry cloth made by Ateco, paired with a knitted rolling pin cover or "stocking" (see Sources, page 381). Rubbing flour into the weave of the cloth and stocking creates an almost nonstick surface. This greatly reduces the amount of flour absorbed by the dough. In addition, dough sticking, breaking, or tearing is virtually eliminated. Washing the pastry cloth and rolling pin cover after each use will make them softer over time. After drying, store the cloth and cover rolled flat around a rolling pin. Do not fold the cloth because folding creates creases that will mark future batches of dough.

Rolling Pins and Surfaces

For rolling cookie dough, I recommend a heavy-duty, 12-inch, ball-bearing rolling pin made by Ateco (see Sources, page 381) for basic rolling needs and a tapered French rolling pin, 19 to 21 inches long, without handles, for rolling thin doughs.

Cookie dough can be rolled on any flat surface; however, the one you choose may help or hinder your efforts. My favorite rolling surface is a large wooden pastry board that I cover with a canvas cloth to prevent the dough from sticking. To keep the board from sliding while working, I anchor it with a 12-inch square of rubber shelf liner. A dampened linen towel or several layers of moist paper towels are good alternatives. If you don't have a pastry board, roll the dough on your kitchen counter, be it granite, Formica, Corian, or wood.

Silpat

Silpat is a French baking mat, silicone treated, with a nonstick surface and flexible fiber encased in the silicone. It's ideal for baking lace and other delicate cookies. Silpat is pricey, but it is worth the investment.

Graters

To zest citrus fruits and grate whole nutmeg, the size and shape of the cutting edges are of utmost importance. I prefer a small, flat, stainless steel shredder with an easy-to-grasp handle and tiny, scalloped cutting edges.

This grater is safe for your knuckles and produces the perfect size zest. A flat hand grater with medium-sized scalloped edge is a good choice for shredding ingredients such as almond pastes.

Strainers and Sifters

Strainers are essential for removing lumps and aerating flour. They also incorporate leavenings and salt. For incorporating dry ingredients with leavening, I recommend using an 8-inch, medium-gauge strainer, preferably double-mesh. It is worthwhile to invest in those that are well constructed.

Most of the sifters manufactured today, both single- and triple-mesh, suffer from poor construction and materials. The handles break easily under the stress of sifting and the mesh layers clog readily. If you use a triple-mesh sifter, rather than stressing the handle through repeated squeezing, it is better to firmly tap the sifter with the side of your hand to shake the dry ingredients through. Never wash a sifter. Wipe it with damp paper towels. Use it only for flour, never powdered sugar or cocoa powder; a strainer is recommended for these ingredients.

How to Line a Pie Plate with Pastry

1. Thoroughly butter the bottom, sides, and rim of an oven-proof glass pie plate.

2. Roll out the pastry to a 13-inch circle. To do so, imagine the pastry disk is the face of a clock. Start from the center and roll toward 12 o'clock. Then roll in the opposite direction to 6 o'clock, then to 3 o'clock, and finally to 9 o'clock. *Each time you roll, the starting position of the rolling pin should be from the center.*

3. Position the rolling pin 4 inches from the *top* of the pastry. Lift the dough over the top of the rolling pin and gently roll the dough toward you.

4. Lift the pastry up. Be sure to keep a finger pressed against the barrel of the rolling pin to keep it from slipping. Position the pastry over a 9-inch pie plate, leaving about 2 inches of dough hanging over the edge of the pan on the side closest to you. Then unroll the pastry over the pie plate, moving the pin away from you.

5. Drape the dough loosely into the pan, molding it into the crease. To do this, place your fingers against the side of the pan, and gently push the dough down toward the crease. Do this around the entire pan. *Be careful not to stretch the dough.*

6. Trim the edge with scissors leaving a $1/4$- to 1-inch overhang. The size is determined by the type of finished edge you plan to use.

NOTE: If the pie shell is to be filled before baking be sure to leave some additional dough around the edge because the weight of the filling will cause the dough to "draw in" or contract.

SPECIAL INGREDIENTS

Using high-quality ingredients will not only make things easier when baking, it will also improve the flavor, texture, and presentation of all of your desserts.

Chocolate

Today's baker can choose from a wealth of chocolates, both domestic and imported. Whether the chocolate is melted, chunked, or chipped in a dough or batter, or used as a finishing touch, I can't imagine a baking book without a healthy helping of this seductive ingredient.

Bittersweet and Semisweet Chocolate

The authentic (or "real") chocolates must, by federal regulations, contain no less than 27 percent chocolate liquor.

Each manufacturer's distinct formula produces varying degrees of sweetness, intensity, and smoothness. Both semisweet and bittersweet chocolates contain sugar, chocolate liquor, cocoa butter, lecithin (a natural soybean product), and vanilla. Because they are sold under a variety of names (including semisweet, bittersweet, extra bittersweet, bitter, special dark, Eagle Sweet, dark sweet, and German's sweet), purchasing these chocolates is sometimes confusing, since the labels do not indicate the amount of sugar added to a particular brand. It is entirely possible that a semisweet chocolate may be less sweet than a bittersweet. The only way to tell is by tasting.

Well-known domestic brands include Nestle Semisweet Chocolate, Baker's Semisweet Chocolate, Baker's German's Sweet, which is sweeter than the basic semisweet, and Ghirardelli Semisweet. Premium domestic chocolates include Merckens,

How to Bake an Empty Pie Shell

1. After the pastry is fitted into the pan, *lightly* prick the bottom and side with a fork at ¹/₂- to 1-inch intervals. Do not pierce too deeply or the filling may seep through the crust. Place the pie plate on a half-sheet or jelly roll pan and refrigerate for at least 15 minutes.

2. Tear an 18-inch square of heavy-duty aluminum foil. Make a buttered circle in the center of the foil 2 inches larger than the size of the pan. Place the foil buttered side down, centering it into the baking pan. Using your hands, press the foil completely flush against the side. Fill with enough ordinary dried beans (any kind or size will do) or baking nuggets to *just* cover the surface of the pan.

3. Bake the crust on the lower rack of a 425°F oven for 15 to 18 minutes, or until the sides begin to brown. Let stand for 30 seconds, then gently remove the foil and beans.

4. Reduce the oven temperature to 375°F. Continue to bake for 3 to 5 minutes, or until golden brown.

Peter's Burgundy, Scharffen Berger, and Guittard.

These are some of the more widely known, luxurious imported chocolates on the market: Lindt Bittersweet, Tobler Tradition, and Godiva, all from Switzerland, Callebaut Semisweet or Bittersweet from Belgium; Valrhona and Cacao Barry from France; Perugina from Italy; El Rey from Venezuela, and Maillard Eagle Sweet Chocolate from England.

Many of the recipes in this book call for "best quality" bittersweet or semisweet chocolate. Because the quantity of sugar varies in many chocolates, it is not always wise to make substitutions. Should you have trouble locating premium chocolate in your supermarket baking aisle, be sure to check the candy section.

Milk Chocolate

Also termed a "real" chocolate, milk chocolate is recognizable by its light color. It must be made from at least 10 percent chocolate liquor and 12 percent milk solids. Sugar and vanilla are also added. Although not commonly used melted in batters, milk chocolate, cut into bits, can be added to cookie doughs.

Unsweetened Chocolate (Bitter or Baking)

This chocolate contains between 53 percent and 55 percent cocoa butter and 45 percent to 47 percent chocolate liquor. Because it does not contain sugar, do not substitute bittersweet or semisweet chocolate for unsweetened chocolate. Popular brands are Nestle's, Baker's, Hershey's, and Ghirardelli. Premium

chocolates such as Scharffen Berger, Guittard, and Callebaut are worth seeking out.

White Chocolate

Because it does not contain chocolate liquor, white chocolate is not classified as "real" chocolate. It is made of cocoa butter, butterfat, sugar, milk solids, lecithin, and vanilla, and is extremely sweet. It contains about 30 percent milk and is rich in fat. White chocolate is extremely perishable, so buy it in small quantities unless you use it frequently. Some premium brands found in the candy aisles of many supermarkets are Lindt Swiss White, Perugina White, Lindt Blancor, Tobler Narcisse, and Valrhona Ivoire.

Chocolate Chips

When you buy chocolate chips, buy *real* chocolate. Chocolate chips are available in sizes and shapes that are different from the familiar dollop. Mini-chips or morsels give you more chocolate pieces per measure. You can also find jumbo chips and chocolate chunks.

You'll find semisweet chocolate chips, milk chocolate chips, white chocolate chips, and flavored chips in the baking section.

Unsweetened Cocoa Powder

Two types of cocoa powder are available for bakers: nonalkaline and Dutch-processed, or alkaline. When chocolate liquor is placed under hydraulic pressure, it is possible to remove at least 75 percent of the cocoa butter. The remaining cocoa solids, called a presscake, are ground into a powder. Even though most of the cocoa butter has been removed, the resulting cocoa powder still contains 8 to 24 percent fat.

The most popular cocoa sold in the United States is nonalkaline cocoa, manufactured by Hershey's, Baker's, or Ghirardelli. This acidic cocoa has a strong, full-bodied flavor. Since nonalkaline cocoa does not have the acid removed, baked goods that contain leavening generally use baking soda in order to neutralize the acid.

In Dutch-processed cocoa, the acid is neutralized with alkali. This dark powder is favored by baking professionals for its rich, delicate flavor. Here, baking powder may be used for leavening. Popular Dutch-processed cocoas are Dröste, Poulain, Feodora, and Van Houten, along with Hershey's, who introduced its own Dutch-processed cocoa powder, boxed in a silver tin.

Fresh Coconut

When purchasing a fresh coconut, choose one that feels heavy in your hand, then shake it and listen for the sound of liquid swishing. The weight and sound indicate that the center still contains the watery liquid and has not dried out.

To open the coconut, hold it so it will not roll (a rubber dish drainer is an ideal place to do this). Turn the coconut so the three black dots or "eyes" are at the top. Using an ice pick or a small screwdriver, pierce the eyes completely through the flesh. Invert the coconut over the sink or a bowl and drain the juice. The watery liquid that comes out is not the coconut milk. It can be strained and used for a drink, but it is not recommended for cooking.

To crack the coconut in half, turn it on its side and draw a line around the middle of the coconut. Forcefully hit the coconut with a hammer along the line, turning the coconut until you have pounded all around its girth. Repeat 2 or 3 times or until the coconut splits.

Removing the barklike skin is optional. Use a small screwdriver to remove the flesh from the shell. If you want the coconut to be snowy white, then peel the thin skin with a small paring knife. Rinse the coconut to clean the surface of any small pieces of skin, then dry the meat with paper toweling.

Shred the coconut in a food processor fitted with a fine medium or shredding blade. If it is too coarse, chop it again with the steel blade, pulsing until you get the desired size. One coconut yields about 4 cups of shredded coconut. Fresh coconut is highly perishable. Refrigerate leftover coconut in an airtight container for up to 5 days or freeze for up to 3 months.

Flavorings, Spirits, and Coloring

Coffee and Espresso

Coffee and espresso, when used in concentrated form, is a wonderful flavor accent for chocolate, spice, and nut treats. I like to make a coffee or espresso "zest": for coffee zest, dissolve three parts instant coffee with one part boiling water; for espresso zest, dissolve two parts espresso powder with one part boiling water. Use coffee and espresso zests as you would an extract flavoring—that is, judiciously. Be sure to store your opened jars in the refrigerator to retain freshness.

Flavored Extracts

Check out the baking aisle or any cook's catalog and you will find a wide variety of pure, flavored extracts along with imitation flavors. Pure almond, lemon, orange, banana, raspberry, hazelnut, spearmint, and peppermint are available, as well as imitation maple and coconut. If you do not see the pure extract, you can substitute an imitation with reasonable success for most flavorings; the one exception is vanilla.

Flavored Oils

Flavored oils are highly concentrated and should be used in small amounts. The fruit oil is squeezed from the rind with no other oils added, hence the intensity. The Baker's Catalogue (see page 381) sells a "dropper cap," which screws onto bottles and can precisely measure a drop or two when a quarter teaspoon is too much. Some of the more popular flavors are orange, lemon, lime, peppermint, and anise. Because these oils are highly concentrated, use them sparingly. A few drops will go a long way. After opening, it is best to store them in the refrigerator. You'll find flavored oils in specialty grocers or gourmet shops.

Food Coloring

Various dyes are used to tint batter and/or icings. Liquid food coloring is available in almost any supermarket, while the paste form is sold in specialty stores.

Liqueurs

Liqueurs can add a fruity nuance to dried fruit fillings used in desserts. Liqueurs are prepared by redistilling various spirits with flavoring materials such as herbs, seeds, berries, and roots. An average liqueur can contain up to 35 percent sweetening agent. This accounts for the slightly syrupy consistency.

Vanilla

Vanilla is produced from the tropical vanilla orchid, the only orchid to produce an edible fruit. The orchid flowers are hand-pollinated and the newly harvested bean must be cured for six months before it can be processed into pure vanilla extract. Pure vanilla extract is made from vanilla beans combined with at least 35 percent alcohol, water, and sugar, which acts as a preservative. Vanilla flavor extract and natural vanilla flavor are natural vanilla products, but are weaker in flavor than the pure extract. Imitation vanilla flavorings or vanillin, a by-product of paper making, do not begin to compare with the natural vanilla flavorings and should not be used in fine baking.

Vanilla, as all extracts, is very concentrated, and should be measured carefully and used judiciously to avoid overwhelming your baked goods.

Lyle's Golden Syrup

This honey-colored liquid sweetener, imported from England, may be used in place of corn syrup and provides a unique, toasty flavor to baked goods. It is sold under the Lyle's label and can be purchased domestically in specialty food stores and some supermarkets. See Sources on page 381.

Candies and Decorative Sugars

Many candies and sprinkles are available for embellishing cookies and desserts, transforming ordinary to magic.

NONPAREILS: These are tiny sugar balls that commonly come in white and also a rainbow of colors.

CHOCOLATE NONPAREIL CANDIES: These are a cluster of tiny nonpareils, usually white, on chocolate disks. Candy-store versions are superior to the mass-produced, tasteless compound-chocolate varieties.

COARSE SUGARS: Available in brown (Demerara) and sparkling white, these lend an attractive finish and add crunch to your cookie.

PEARL SUGAR: With super-white, large, irregular-shaped sugar grains, pearl sugar's main attraction, beyond appearance, is that it does not melt in baking.

SPARKLING WHITE SUGAR: Clear, large-crystal sugar grains, commonly from Scandinavia, slow-melting, used to decorate cookies and pastries.

SPECIAL TECHNIQUES

My primary goal throughout my years of teaching has been to stress the importance of techniques. At first glance, a recipe may seem straightforward, but numerous pitfalls hide within the text of a recipe that lead to mediocre results or even failures. Good baking relies on checks and balances of ingredients. How they are measured, how they are combined, how they are baked, how they are stored, all make a difference in the final result.

I teach primarily participation classes and my kitchen is my classroom. In this environment I have had the privilege to observe my students in action. This has given me the opportunity to zero in on procedures written in a recipe that can stymie even the most seasoned bakers.

Measuring Flour and Dry Ingredients

Flour is the "muscle man" in baking. It forms the structure to support key ingredients like butter, sugar, and eggs. Throughout my baking career, I have always sifted flour before measuring. And my cardinal rule is to *always* spoon the flour into the cup. *Never* dip the cup into the flour. Dipping the cup compacts the flour, and you will have far too much flour in the cookies.

Start with an accurate set of dry or graduated measuring cups and a sheet of wax paper, approximately 15 inches in length, placed on your work surface. Spoon the dry ingredients into the appropriate-size dry or graduated measuring cup. (If measuring flour, be sure to fluff it first with a spoon.) Using a straight-bladed object, such as a dough scraper, straight spatula, or dull side of a knife, level the flour by sweeping the utensil straight across the top of the cup.

If you are a "shaker," a person accustomed to shaking the measuring cup while spooning in flour, stop. Put your measuring cup down on the wax paper and then spoon the dry ingredient into the cup. The simple motion of shaking compacts the flour too much.

Straining, Sifting, and Whisking Dry Ingredients

Although it is common practice for manufacturers to label bags of flour "pre-sifted," if a recipe calls for sifting, ignore this. The benefits of aerating flour or other dry ingredients cannot be minimized. "Aerating" means passing the dry ingredients through the mesh; the mesh removes lumps and makes the dry ingredients lighter and more powdery. Straining or sifting sets the stage for better blending and absorption of other ingredients. But, most important, straining or sifting blends the dry ingredients with leavening more thoroughly, which is key to achieving a successful result.

It is irrelevant whether you use a sifter or a strainer as long as the dry ingredients pass through a mesh. That mesh can be a medium-gauge strainer or the traditional, cylinder-shaped sifter. Because sifters today are so poorly made, I personally prefer a strainer. Generally, I strain over a sheet of wax paper about 15 inches in length.

Working with Chocolate

Chocolate should be treated with respect. It is temperature sensitive; it reacts to moisture, odors, and to overmixing. If chocolate is overheated, the flavor and texture are compromised. When chocolate is melted, merely a few drops of liquid can change its texture from satiny to gritty. When stored in a cold environment, its beautiful sheen is destroyed; if stored near pungent flavors, chocolate will absorb their essence. Why bother with this temperamental ingredient? Because, there is not other like it!

How to Chop Chocolate

Chocolate should always be cut into small pieces to ensure even melting. This is crucial

to retaining its good flavor and velvety texture. If the chocolate pieces are too large, the surface area becomes overheated before the center has an opportunity to melt.

You should chop chocolate into varying sizes according to its texture. Unsweetened chocolate is the hardest of the dark chocolate, followed by bittersweet and semisweet chocolate. Bulk or block chocolate should be shaved on a cutting board using a chef's knife. Dark chocolates can also be chopped in a food processor because they are firm enough to withstand the heat. If using a processor, for even consistency and to avoid damaging the blade, the chocolate should be cut into pieces no larger than 1 inch before processing. Milk and white chocolate are soft chocolates and should not be chopped in a processor. These delicate chocolates can easily be cut into small pieces with a chef's knife on a cutting board.

Here is a neat trick for cutting up pre-wrapped squares or bars of chocolate. Do not remove the wrapper from the chocolate. Place the paper-wrapped square or bar on a cutting board and pierce it several times with an ice pick. When the paper is removed, the chocolate will be broken into pieces, ready to melt with no mess. The same method works effectively for breaking up small candy bars.

Melting Dark Chocolates

USING A WATER BATH: Select a wide, shallow pan, such as a 10-inch skillet, and fill it with $1/2$ inch of hot water, no more. Over low heat, bring the water to a simmer. Place the chopped chocolate in a heat-proof bowl deep and wide enough to prevent water or steam from reaching the chocolate. Place the bowl in the skillet and allow the chocolate to slowly melt. When the chocolate is almost melted, *turn the heat off*. Let the chocolate finish melting slowly, stirring gently from time to time. If the water becomes too cool, reheat it briefly. A small amount of chocolate will quickly melt, while larger amounts will take more time.

USING A DOUBLE BOILER: Fill the bottom of the double boiler with 1 to 2 inches of water. Alternatively, any pot can be used with a stainless steel or glass heat-proof bowl placed over it. The bowl should be wider than the pot and should not touch the water. Bring the water to a boil and then reduce it to a simmer. Place the chopped chocolate in the top portion of the double boiler or bowl and set it over the simmering water. When the chocolate is almost melted, turn the heat off and allow the chocolate to finish melting slowly. Stir occasionally and *gently* to be sure the chocolate melts evenly. Care should be taken to prevent steam from reaching the chocolate. Never cover chocolate during or after melting.

MICROWAVE METHOD: My recommendation for small amounts of chocolate is to melt the chocolate on the defrost setting. Using this low setting, the chocolate melts more evenly, with less risk of overheating. Place the chopped chocolate in an ovenproof glass bowl. Using a defrost setting, melt the chocolate for about 1 minute. Stir with a rubber scraper, then return the bowl to the microwave for another 30 seconds. For larger amounts, heat the chocolate for 1 minute on medium setting. Stir gently with a rubber scraper and return to the microwave, continuing the melting process in 15- to 20-second increments. The time will vary according to the amount of chocolate you are melting and the wattage of your microwave. The chocolate often retains its shape although it is melted, which can be deceiving, so keep a sharp eye on it. It is not necessary for the chocolate to melt completely; it will continue to melt as it stands at room temperature. If it hasn't melted entirely when you're ready to use it, return the chocolate to the microwave for a few seconds.

Melting Milk and White Chocolate

I recommend melting delicate milk and white chocolates using only the stovetop, water-bath method. These soft chocolates need less heat and less time to melt than dark chocolate. They must be watched carefully because they melt so quickly.

Start with milk or white chocolate cut into small pieces, $1/4$ to $1/2$ inch. Put the chocolate in a stainless steel bowl and place the bowl in a skillet filled with $1/2$ inch of *warm* water. Let the chocolate stand for a few seconds. Then gently stir with a rubber spatula until the chocolate is melted.

Shaving and Slivering Chocolate

At times, chocolate is shaved or slivered and added to dough or batter in an unmelted state. These shards or shavings of chocolate provide interesting contrast between the dark of the chocolate and the light of the dough or batter. Shaved chocolate is finer than slivered chocolate.

When cutting chocolate for slivers or

shavings, block or bulk chocolate works best, but 1-ounce squares of chocolate and small candy bars will do in a pinch. All chocolates should be very fresh, otherwise they are too brittle to shave or sliver. Begin with the chocolate placed on a cutting board and, using a chef's knife, cut the block starting at a corner. As the corner becomes wider, rotate the chocolate in another direction to find another corner.

Using a Water Bath

A water bath, also referred to as a *bain-marie*, can be used for both hot and cold mixtures. By surrounding the food with water, the heat is cushioned and protects and prevents the food from overcooking. In cookie baking, the hot-water method is used most commonly for melting chocolate. It takes two vessels to make a water bath, one large and the other smaller. For stovetop purposes, a small amount of hot water is placed in a shallow pan, such as a skillet, and heated to a simmer. Set a bowl holding the chocolate into the water. The level of the water should cover no more than one-fourth of the exterior of the inner bowl. Otherwise, the bowl may float or tip.

Working with Almond Paste

Since the consistency of almond paste is very dense, it is best to use it at room temperature and to break it into smaller pieces to smoothly blend it with other ingredients. Sometimes, the almond paste can be mixed in an electric mixer fitted with the paddle attachment. It can also be chopped in the food processor using the steel blade. Shred-

ding it with a box grater is another alternative. If the almond paste is dried out, it becomes very hard. You can try softening it briefly in a microwave. However, if it doesn't soften and it is a major ingredient in the cookie, I recommend discarding it.

Handling Nuts, Coconut, Seeds, and Fruits

Some adults and children do not like textured food, so at times nuts and seeds can be omitted from a recipe. However, a batter made without them might have an entirely different end result. As an example, because nuts and coconut provide bulk and also perform as "spacers," a brownie or bar cookie made without these ingredients will be more compact. To replace the volume of the ingredient that you are eliminating, you might try substituting ingredients, such as chocolate chips and other flavored varieties of chips. Fortunately, other than flavor, small seeds omitted from a recipe will have minimal effect on a batter or dough.

Toasting Nuts

Toasting nuts enlivens the oils, which greatly enhances their flavor, as well as adding extra crunchiness. I recommend toasting nuts before they are chopped and thoroughly cooling them before use. When I toast nuts, I like to toast a large batch at once and store them in a jar, refrigerated, ready for use. Toasted nuts must be cooled before use to allow the rich oils to be reabsorbed. If used when still warm, not only can they cause the butter to melt in a cookie dough or batter but if chopped, they can become pasty.

Nuts, which are high in fat, will burn easily, so they should always be toasted on a shallow, heavy-gauge, metal pan in a moderate to low oven, 300° to 325°. For even baking, they should be spread in a single layer to avoid crowding. Lining the pan with aluminum foil will save you a trip to the sink. The amount of nuts, their oil content, and their size are all determining factors in how long toasting will take. As an example, sliced almonds toast more quickly than whole almonds. When toasting large amounts of nuts, stir the nuts once or twice during baking for even browning.

To determine when nuts have reached their optimal toasting time, use color and fragrance as a guideline. The obvious sign on blanched or skinless nuts is a slight change in color. For unblanched nuts, fragrance is the best test. When the nuts are just beginning to release aroma, remove them from the oven. Overly roasted nuts are bitter and must be discarded. When toasting nuts, never mix different varieties on the same pan unless they have similar oil content. Pecans and almonds, for example, would not toast the same. Pignolis (pine nuts) are small, high in oil, and take the least amount of time, 3 to 5 minutes. High-fat nuts such as cashews and macadamias take 6 to 8 minutes, while walnuts and pecans take 8 to 10 minutes.

Although pistachios are small, they are somewhat soft, so toasting for 6 to 8 minutes is recommended. Hard nuts such as hazelnuts and almonds are less oily and require 12 to 15 minutes, or longer, to toast. Brazil nuts and peanuts are rarely toasted before using.

Chopping Nuts

Hand-chopping produces very uniform pieces with the least amount of oil lost, while nuts chopped in the food processor will be irregular in size and oilier. Because so many cookies use this important ingredient, I will address various ways for working with nuts.

Hand chopping can be used for all nuts; however, it is especially recommended for high-fat nuts like cashews and macadamias. These higher-fat nuts release more of the nut oil, making chopping more difficult. Brazil nuts, another high-fat nut, are difficult to chop because of their size. Before chopping, first cut them in two or three pieces with a paring knife.

BROKEN NUTS: Split nuts by hand into large, irregular pieces, about $3/8$ to $1/2$ inch. Applicable nuts are soft nuts such as walnuts and pecans.

COARSELY CHOPPED NUTS: Place nuts on a cutting board and chop with a chef's knife into the size of dried chickpeas, $^1/_4$- to $^3/_8$-inch pieces. Hand-chopping produces the most uniform size, with the least amount of oil loss.

MEDIUM CHOPPED NUTS: Chop nuts by hand into pieces slightly smaller than $^1/_4$ inch, much like the size of dried lentils or split peas.

FINELY CHOPPED NUTS: Chop nuts by hand into dried-barley-size pieces, about $^1/_8$ inch.

NUT MEAL: Grind or pulverize nuts to a meallike texture. The ideal home method for making nut meal is with a Mouli hand grater; this procedure produces the most powdery consistency, releasing the least amount of oil,

but it is a time-consuming process. Nut meals can be made in a food processor; however, a small amount of flour or sugar must be added to absorb the nut oils.

Using Fresh Berries

To wash berries, place the berries in a strainer or colander. Rinse under cool running water. Spread the berries evenly on a rimmed cookie sheet lined with a double layer of paper towels. Shimmy the pan back and forth a few times, then blot the berries dry with more paper towels. Note: Firm berries, such as blueberries, may be refrigerated after drying. Raspberries should be washed and dried immediately before using.

Using Mangoes

Mangoes range in size from 4 ounces to 5 pounds. Choose fruit that yields to the pressure of a gentle squeeze. A mango should be free of large bruises or blackening and exude a sweet, rich aroma. Note that the skin on mangoes, especially when unripe, contains a chemical substance which can cause severe allergic skin reactions in some people. When you eat a fresh mango, *always* remove the peel first.

Mangoes can be successfully ripened at home by leaving them at room temperature. Once ripe, they should be eaten within 2 to 3 days or they will quickly soften. Never refrigerate mangoes. The chilling robs the fruit of its lush tropical flavors.

The mango has a large, somewhat flat pit that does not separate naturally from the fruit. The flesh located on each side of the pit is referred to as the "cheek." To remove the cheeks, use a chef's knife and remove a thin slice from the bottom of the mango. Hold the fruit upright. With the chef's knife, cut into the mango from the top to bottom, positioning the knife slightly off-center and parallel to the flatter side of the fruit. Slice downward, cutting as close to the pit as possible. Repeat on the opposite side. Trim any large pieces of fruit that are still attached to the pit.

TO SLICE: Peel the cheeks with a paring knife, removing as little of the flesh as possible. Lay the fruit, flat side down, and cut on the diagonal into $1/4$-inch slices.

TO DICE: Using the tip of a sharp knife, score the flesh of the unpeeled cheeks into $3/4$-inch squares. Be careful not to cut through the skin. Press the cheek, on the skin side, to push the flesh out, forming a "porcupine" of mango chunks. Remove the cubes with a paring knife, cutting as close as possible to the skin.

Using Dried Fruits

Raisins, currants, prunes, dates, figs, and apricots are the familiar dried fruits. In recent years the selection has increased vastly, largely owing to the emphasis on healthier eating.

I cannot stress enough how important high-quality dried fruits are to baked goods. Seek out soft, moist fruits and be sure to read the labels thoroughly before you buy. Try to purchase only those fruits that are grown in places where pesticides and herbicides are monitored, and that have a minimum of chemical additives. I make an exception with fruits treated with sulphur dioxide, which is added to preserve color, freshness, and flavor. Oddly, I have found that fruits treated with sulphur dioxide cook into a softer puree than dried fruits without this additive. Avoid precut, smaller pieces of dried fruits because they can quickly lose their flavor. If you are purchasing fruit from bulk containers, taste a piece to be sure the flavor and moisture content indicate quality and freshness. If your supermarket does not stock the variety you are looking for, check out The Baker's Catalogue and order by mail (see page 381).

After opening dried fruit, reseal the package tightly, expelling as much air as possible, and cover with plastic wrap or place in plastic air-tight bags. Bulk fruit should be stored in a tightly sealed glass jar. If you will not be using the fruit within two or three weeks, put it in the refrigerator, where it will keep for up to three months.

PLUMPING DRIED FRUITS: To plump or reconstitute dried fruit, empty it into a heat-proof bowl and cover with boiling water to 1 inch above the level of the fruit. The recipe will specify the appropriate length of standing time; however, the freshness of the fruit will be a determining factor. Older fruit is harder and drier, and can take longer to soften. Smaller pieces of fruit, such as raisins, will plump in a minute or two while larger pieces, such as apricots or prunes, will take longer. When the fruit is ready, empty it into a strainer and rinse briefly with cool water to stop the heating process. Spread the fruit on doubled paper towels. Cover with another layer of doubled paper towels and blot dry. Use as directed in the recipe.

Separating Eggs

Always separate eggs (removing the white from the yolk) when eggs are cold. For recipes using whipped egg whites, select older eggs. As eggs age, the proteins strengthen and when whipped they form a stronger network.

All eggs should be separated using 3 bowls: one for the initial cracking in case the yolk breaks, the second bowl to hold the separated yolk, and the third to hold the separated white.

The method that I prefer for separating eggs is the following: take a cold egg in your hand and hold it over the first bowl. With a sharp knife, give a firm tap across the shell. Turn the egg so that the widest part is held in the palm of your hand. The shell forms a cup to hold the yolk. Now the white should flow freely into the bowl. Holding the empty shell in the opposite hand, alternate the yolk, placing it from shell to shell until all the white is removed.

Place the yolk into the second separate bowl. Pour the white into the third bowl. It is crucial that *not one drop of yolk* become mixed with the whites. When beating egg whites, the presence of yolk or fat, no matter how small, will reduce the volume.

Defeathering is the process of removing the two twisted strands of white, known as the chalazae, that are attached to the yolk. These strands of white or protein become hardened when heated either in the oven or on top of the stove. Its rubbery texture in such smooth mixtures as meringues or cooked fillings would be undesirable. While smaller strands are less significant in the finished product, larger pieces should be removed.

Clarifying Butter

Clarified, or drawn, butter is commonly used for such baking purposes as making pastries with phyllo. It is easy to prepare and can be stored for months in the refrigerator or freezer. When butter is clarified, it first must be heated until it separates into layers; a heavy-bottomed saucepan is essential. The foamy top layer contains whey proteins, or milk solids; this must be removed and discarded. This leaves a center layer of clear, golden liquid that is 100 perfect fat and is free of impurities. The remaining, bottom layer is a watery substance of milk proteins and salts, which should also be discarded. The melted butterfat can either be poured off or allowed to cook until the water evaporates, leaving behind a brown sediment. Butter cooked to this point has a stronger, more pronounced flavor.

Keep in mind that the volume of the butter you clarify will be reduced by 20 to 25 percent. For this reason, clarify a full pound of butter at a time. What isn't used immediately can be stored for later use.

STOVETOP METHOD: Cook 1 pound of unsalted butter over very low heat in a medium heavy-bottomed saucepan until white foam (the milk solids) accumulates on the surface. Carefully remove the foam with a skimmer or large spoon, repeating the process until no more foam appears. Keep cooking the butter over very low heat until the butterfat is clear and the milk proteins have settled at the bottom on the saucepan. For a full pound of butter, this could take 30 to 40 minutes. Cool until tepid. Allow the butterfat to remain undisturbed in the saucepan. Then place a fine-mesh strainer over a jar or bowl. Pour butterfat through the strainer, taking care to keep any of the sediment from slipping through into the clear fat.

Working with Pie Dough

I've relied on my years of teaching to do every-thing possible to take the guesswork out of making pies. So whether you're a novice or experienced baker, get your hands in some flour and learn all about working with pie pastry.

Lining a Pie Plate with Pastry

A little practice makes perfect, and these steps will ensure a tear-free dough.

1. Thoroughly butter the bottom, sides, and rim of an oven-proof glass pie plate.

2. Roll out the pastry to a 13-inch circle. To do so, imagine the pastry disk is the face of a clock. Start from the center and roll toward 12 o'clock. Then roll in the opposite direction to 6 o'clock, then to 3 o'clock, and finally to 9 o'clock. *Each time you roll, the starting position of the rolling pin should be from the center.*

3. Position the rolling pin 4 inches from the *top* of the pastry. Lift the dough over the top of the rolling pin and gently roll the dough away from you.

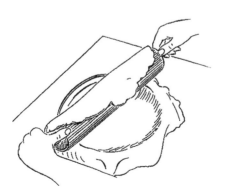

4. Lift the pastry up. Be sure to keep a finger pressed against the barrel of the rolling pin to keep it from slipping. Position the pastry over a 9-inch pie plate, leaving about 2 inches of dough hanging over the edge of the pan on the side closest to you. Then unroll the pastry over the pie plate, moving the pin away from you.

5. Drape the dough loosely into the pan, molding it into the crease. To do this, place your fingers against the side of the pan, and gently push the dough down toward the crease. Do this around the entire pan. *Be careful not to stretch the dough.*

6. Trim the edge with scissors, leaving a ¹/₄- to 1-inch overhang. The size is determined by the type of finished edge you plan to use.

Note: If the pie shell is to be filled before baking, be sure to leave some additional dough around the edge because the weight of the filling will cause the dough to "draw in" or contract.

Baking an Empty Pie Shell

After testing dozens of recipes for my books, I came to the conclusion that a fully baked pastry shell is the way to go. My reasoning is this: when a filling, be it fruit or custard, is placed in a fully baked shell, the uncooked filling becomes the insulator, keeping the crust cool enough to prevent overbaking. By the time the filling is baked, both the crust and the filling are properly done.

1. After the pastry is fitted into the pan, *lightly* prick the bottom and side with a fork at $1/2$- to 1-inch intervals. Do not pierce too deeply or the filling may seep through the crust. Place the pie plate on a half-sheet or jelly roll pan and refrigerate for at least 15 minutes.

2. Tear an 18-inch square of heavy-duty aluminum foil. Make a buttered circle in the center of the foil 2 inches larger than the size of the pan. Place the foil buttered side down, centering it into the baking pan. Using your hands, press the foil completely flush against the side. Fill with enough ordinary dried beans (any kind or size will do) or baking nuggets to *just* cover the surface of the pan.

3. Bake the crust on the lower rack of a 425°F oven for 15 to 18 minutes, or until the sides begin to brown. Let stand for 30 seconds, then gently remove the foil and beans.

4. Reduce the oven temperature to 375°F. Continue to bake for 3 to 5 minutes, or until golden brown.

Weaving a Traditional Lattice Top

A lattice-topped pie or tart is not as intimidating to make as you might think. While you can make a lattice top on a tart, these crusts work the best on pies because the baking dish has a rim that secures the crust. To make the most of a lattice topping, use it to show off a colorful fruit filling. Use lattice for pre-cooked fruit fillings or for fruit fillings that will not shrink too much during baking. I do not recommend a lattice on apple pies made with raw fruit or for other fruits where the filling is piled high above the rim of the pan. The fruit will shrink during baking, and the beautiful lattice work will be for naught.

1. Roll the second half of your pastry into a 13-inch circle. Using a fluted or straight-edge pastry wheel, cut twelve $3/4$-inch strips.

2. Start with the two longest strips of pastry. Place them slightly off center on top of the pie, leaving a $3/4$-inch space between each strip.

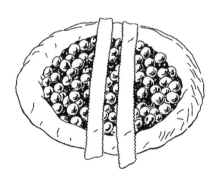

3. Take two more strips of dough, graduating the sizes, and place one on either side of the first two strips, again leaving a ³/₄-inch space between the strips.

4. Take two of the smaller strips, and place them on either side of the last two strips. You should have six graduated strips.

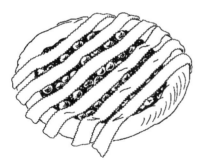

5. To weave the dough, fold strips 2, 4, and 6 back slightly more than halfway. Starting with the largest remaining strip of dough, place it slightly off center on top of the pie filling. Carefully return the folded strips to the edge of the pie.

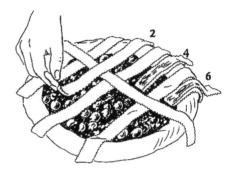

6. Now fold strips 1, 3, and 5 back. Use the next graduated strip of dough, and place it on top of the pie, leaving a ³/₄-inch space between it and the preceding row. Then return the strips to the edge. Repeat with a smallest strip, folding strips 2, 4, and 6 back. One side of the pie should now be woven.

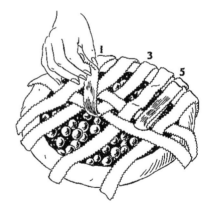

7. Turn the pie around. Weave the opposite side of the pie as you did the first side using the remaining three strips of pastry.

8. Trim the pastry strips, leaving a 1-inch overhang around the pie. Fold the pastry strips under the bottom pastry. Press the two layers together, forming a wall. Use the selvage to build up the thinner parts of the edge, then flute. Proceed with the baking directions in your recipe.

Making a Diagonal Lattice Top

A diagonal lattice top adds an extra-special touch to many fruit pies

1. Follow the directions for the traditional lattice top through step 4. Weaving is optional.

2. Turn the pie slightly, about one-eighth of a turn. Position the first lattice strip on the top of strip 1 and extend it to the bottom of strip 6.

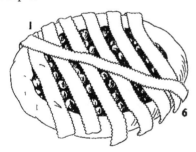

3. Continue with the remaining 5 strips, keeping them parallel and at equal distances. Repeat until all the pieces of pastry have been used. When you are done, the holes should be diamond shaped.

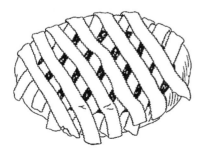

4. Continue with step 8 of traditional lattice top on page 362.

Making Decorative Edges

When I make a pie crust, my first concern is that it be tender and flaky, and have good flavor. Pictures of pies with beautiful, sculptured edges are pretty to look at, but they often aren't worth the trouble. A flavorful pie crust must contain an adequate amount of butter and vegetable shortening. Fat makes crusts tender and taste good, but at the same time it makes them lose their shape and easily crumble. The richer the dough, the more fragile it will be.

If you want a fancy edge, the quality of the pastry will have to be sacrificed. More flour and liquid have to be added to reduce the percentage of fat. This makes the dough stronger. While it will hold its shape better, it will be tough and tasteless.

To help decide what style of edge to make, keep in mind the type of filling you plan to use. For a double-crust fruit pie, choose an edge that seals well, so there is less risk of the juices leaking. (A lattice crust does not require a sealed edge because so much filling is exposed. The juices evaporate readily, so overflow is not as great a problem.) When making a single crust, use a "built-up" fluted edge. A high wall can hold more filling and also guard against spillage with more fluid mixtures.

Since pies are less-formal desserts, keep it simple. Forget about the braids—a homemade look is just fine. Here are some good choices for attractive edges that are easy to make.

The spacing measurements below are approximate and may vary with your finger size.

ANGLED FLUTE

Using one hand, pinch the dough at a 45-degree angle between your thumb and forefinger while twisting slightly outward. Repeat at 1-inch intervals.

POINTED FLUTE

Pinch the dough between your thumb and forefinger. With your opposite hand, using your forefinger in a bent position, push into the dough to form a point. Repeat at 1-inch intervals. *Note:* Fingertips can be used in lieu of a bent forefinger.

SCALLOPED

Spread thumb and forefinger 1 inch apart and place on the inner edge of the crust. With the other forefinger, pull the dough toward the outer edge to form a scallop. Repeat at regular intervals.

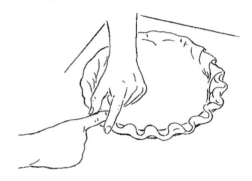

POLKA-DOT SCALLOP

Repeat above procedure for a scalloped edge. Make 24 pea-size balls from scraps of dough. Moisten the bottom of the balls with egg wash and press into the scallops.

DECORATIVE SCALLOP

Repeat the above procedure for a scalloped edge. When complete, press into the scallops with a floured, four-prong fork.

FORKED EDGE

Press a floured, four-pronged fork into the dough at regular intervals. With each movement of the fork, support the dough with the forefinger of the opposite hand.

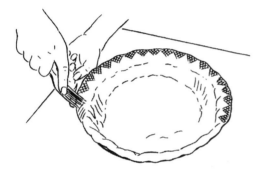

CROSSHATCH

Press a floured, four-pronged fork into the dough at a 45-degree angle. Then repeat, reversing the angle of the fork. With each movement of the fork, support the dough with the forefinger of the opposite hand.

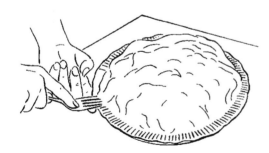

There are far fewer choices for finishing the edge of a tart than there are for a pie. The straight-sided, thin-edged metal pans that tarts are usually baked in do not lend themselves

to a decorative edge. As a rule, tarts have only a bottom crust, leaving less pastry to work with. Because the surface of a tart is usually decorative, the fancy edge is not missed.

Many tarts with a shallow filling require no edge at all. For these, the rolling pin is run over the surface of the pan to cut the dough, leaving a clean, flush edge. Tarts that require deeper shells have edges that are built up. The pastry has a $\frac{1}{2}$-inch overhang that is folded over to the inside edge of the pan, leaving a double thickness of dough. The pastry is pressed against the side, which pushes it upward—about $\frac{1}{4}$ inch higher than the edge of the pan. The dough can either be left plain, pinched with a pastry crimper, or notched with the tip of a knife, as illustrated below.

CRIMPED EDGE

Starting with built-up edge, press a floured pastry crimper into the dough at a 45-degree angle. Repeat, inserting the crimper into the impression left by the previous crimp. Each time you crimp, support the inner edge of the dough with the fingertips of your opposite hand.

NOTCHED EDGE

Starting with a built-up edge, press into the dough with the tip of closed scissors or the dull side of a table knife at each scallop of the tart pan.

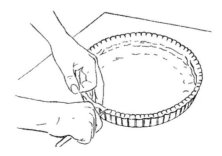

Spreading Batters and Doughs

Thin batters, which are poured into the pan, should be spread evenly into the pan's corners with the bottom of an oversized tablespoon. Thick doughs should be dropped in mounds from the tip of a spoon, spacing them equally in the pan. Spread them as evenly as possible with a small, offset spatula, distributing them evenly into the corners, as well. For a square pan, I make four mounds, for an oblong pan, I make six mounds, and for a jelly roll pan I make eight mounds. For doughs that are unusually thick, I flour my hands and form the dough into balls, arranging them evenly in the pan. For these dense doughs, I increase the number of balls per pan—about nine for a square pan, 12 to 15 for an oblong pan. This makes the dough easier to spread.

To spread dense doughs such as you find with bar cookies, flour the heel of your hand and pat the dough to flatten it, working it into the corners of the pan. Lay a strip of plastic wrap or wax paper over the surface of the dough and gently pat it with the bottom of a glass until it is even. Using a metal dough scraper, the straight side of a plastic bowl scraper, or the blade of a square metal spatula, neaten the edges by inserting the tool between the dough and the edge of the pan. This creates an even edge on the finished bar cookie and facilitates cutting.

Splitting Round and Other Cakes

Splitting a cake into thin disks is called "torting." There are many gadgets available that help perform this job, but it is a good idea to learn to do it by hand. As with most techniques, practice makes perfect, and if your first attempts are not exactly even, it really won't matter as a little extra frosting spread between the layers will help level the cake.

These directions are written for a round cake; if you are splitting a square cake, the procedure is the same. If you wish to cut a loaf cake, position the cake with the long side in front of you. Insert the knife on the right side of the cake and cut across. Since the cake is narrow, there is no need to rotate it while cutting.

1. First mark off each disk by inserting toothpicks into the sides at 12, 3, 6, and 9 o'clock. If you are slicing a layer into two disks, insert the toothpicks halfway up the side of the layer. If you are making three disks, insert two rows of toothpicks around the layer, $1/3$ and $2/3$ of the way up the side. If you wish, use a ruler held upright to make sure the toothpicks are evenly spaced.

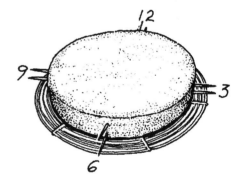

2. Choose a serrated knife with a blade long enough to reach across the entire cake.

Holding the knife at 3 o'clock if you are right-handed and 9 o'clock if you are left-handed, saw across the first layer using a gentle back-and-forth motion as you rotate the cake in a complete 360° circle. Just the cake is turned, not the knife. Use the toothpicks as your guide and keep your eyes only on the side of the cake you are cutting.

3. After you have cut completely through the cake, remove the first thin layer and place it on a piece of waxed paper. Continue with the next layer(s).

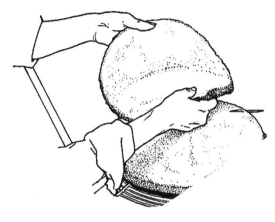

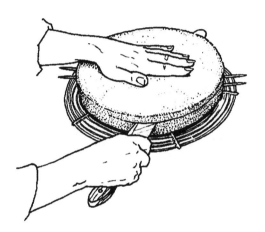

clear shiny glaze

MAKES ¼ CUP, ENOUGH FOR THREE 8- X 3 ¾- X 2 ½-INCH OR TWO 8 ½- X 4 ½- X 2 ¾-INCH LOAVES, OR 12 TO 14 PASTRIES

If you want to give a professional finish to your pastry, use this glaze. While it adds a touch of sweetness and a beautiful sheen, it has no color. Not only does it bring out the natural color of the pastry, it is also handy for securing nuts to the top of the pastry.

3 tablespoons sugar

3 tablespoons water

1½ teaspoons corn syrup

Combine the sugar, water, and corn syrup in a small saucepan. Bring to a boil over medium heat. Cook for 2 to 3 minutes. Keep warm.

vanilla glaze

MAKES ABOUT ⅔ CUP; ENOUGH FOR 4 DOZEN 2-INCH COOKIES

Making this glaze with milk gives a thicker covering, while water makes a more translucent finish. Use less liquid when piping.

2 cups strained confectioners' sugar, spooned in and leveled

2–3 tablespoons hot milk or water, plus additional as needed

1 tablespoon light corn syrup

½ teaspoon pure vanilla extract

Pinch of salt

Place the confectioners' sugar in a large bowl and add the remaining ingredients. Stir with a small whisk or spoon until very smooth. The glaze should pour from a spoon in a steady stream. Use additional liquid sparingly. A little bit goes a long way.

STORAGE: Store the glaze tightly covered in the refrigerator for up to 3 days.

⬤ Lemon or Lime Glaze

Substitute hot, fresh lemon or lime juice for the milk. Omit the vanilla extract.

⬤ Orange Glaze

Substitute hot, fresh orange juice for the milk and add ¼ teaspoon orange oil (see page 351). Omit the vanilla extract.

quick chocolate glaze

MAKES ABOUT ½ CUP (SMALL CAKE RECIPE) OR ¾ CUP (LARGE CAKE RECIPE)

This chocolate glaze has been a favorite of mine for years. It has wonderful flavor, is quick to whip up, and holds its gloss under refrigeration. It also freezes well. This recipe includes amounts for both small and large cakes.

SMALL RECIPE	LARGE RECIPE
1 ounce unsweetened chocolate, coarsely chopped	1½ ounces unsweetened chocolate, coarsely chopped
1 ounce semisweet chocolate, coarsely chopped	1½ ounces semisweet chocolate, coarsely chopped
2 teaspoons unsalted butter	1 tablespoon unsalted butter
⅔ cup strained confectioners' sugar	1 cup strained confectioners' sugar
2 tablespoons boiling water (about)	3 tablespoons boiling water (about)
2 teaspoons light corn syrup	1 tablespoon light corn syrup
½ teaspoon vanilla extract	¾ teaspoon vanilla extract
2 teaspoons dark Jamaican rum (optional)	1 tablespoon dark Jamaican rum (optional)

1. Place the chocolates and the butter in a small glass bowl. Set the bowl in a pan filled with 1 inch of hot water and stir until the ingredients are melted and smooth, or melt in a microwave. Off the heat, stir in the sugar and water alternately, beating well. Blend in the corn syrup, then the vanilla. Stir in the rum.

2. At this point the glaze should be glossy and pourable. If it is too thick, beat in drops of hot water to thin.

midnight chocolate glaze

MAKES ENOUGH FOR ONE 10-INCH BUNDT CAKE, A 9- X 13- X 2-INCH COFFEE CAKE, OR 16 TO 18 MUFFINS

Here is a glaze that has a beautiful, glossy shine and wonderful, rich chocolate flavor. While I think the best results are achieved if the glaze is applied when it is made, it can be made ahead and either refrigerated or frozen. The glaze will keep its sheen for up to eight hours, depending on room temperature and weather conditions. When I tested the recipe, it was impossible not to lick my fingers when scraping the pot clean.

$^1/_2$ cup water

$^1/_4$ cup granulated sugar

2 tablespoons light corn syrup

4 ounces fine-quality bittersweet chocolate, such as Lindt, finely chopped

$^1/_4$ cup strained powdered sugar

1 tablespoon Dutch-process cocoa powder

1 teaspoon pure vanilla extract

$^1/_4$ teaspoon lemon juice

Pinch of salt

1 tablespoon unsalted butter, soft

1. Place the water in a 3-quart heavy-bottomed saucepan. Add the granulated sugar and corn syrup, but *do not stir*. Cover and bring to a slow boil on medium-low heat. After 1 minute, check to see if any sugar crystals remain. If so, *gently* stir the mixture. Continue to cook the syrup uncovered for 3 to 4 minutes. (Large bubbles will form on the surface.)

2. Remove the pan from the heat and sprinkle the chopped chocolate over the syrup. Push the chocolate gently into the syrup, but *do not stir*. Let stand for 2 to 3 minutes, until the chocolate is melted, then stir gently with a small whisk.

3. When smooth, stir in the powdered sugar and cocoa powder, then blend in the vanilla, lemon juice, and salt. Stir gently with the whisk until smooth, then blend in the butter. If the glaze is not pourable, add 3 to 4 teaspoons of very hot water until the desired consistency is reached. *Note:* This glaze is best used immediately.

STORAGE: Leftover glaze can be refrigerated for several weeks. This glaze may be frozen. To use, reheat, adding very hot water to thin the glaze as needed.

chocolate candy glaze

MAKES ENOUGH FOR 4 DOZEN COOKIES

Nothing can be faster than melting a candy bar for a glaze.

8 ounces high-quality bittersweet or
    semisweet chocolate, such as Lindt
    Bittersweet or Classic Swiss White

1 tablespoon vegetable oil

Slowly melt the chocolate and vegetable oil together over hot water (see page 000). When the mixture is smooth, remove from the water. Cool briefly.

ganache glaze

MAKES 1 GENEROUS CUP

The versatility of ganache is a gift to a sweet kitchen. It makes a mirrorlike glaze when pourable. When chilled, it thickens to a consistency suitable for filling cookies, or it can be piped into rosettes, lines, or other beautiful ornamentations.

6 ounces fine-quality semisweet or
    bittersweet chocolate, such as Lindt
    Bittersweet, cut into 1-inch chunks

$^3/_4$ cup heavy cream

1 tablespoon light corn syrup

$^3/_4$ teaspoon vanilla extract

$^1/_2$ to 1 teaspoon hot water, if needed

1. Place the chocolate in the work bowl of a food processor fitted with the steel blade and process until finely chopped.

2. In a small saucepan, over low heat, heat the heavy cream and corn syrup together until it comes to a simmer. *Immediately* pour the hot cream over the chocolate in the processor bowl. Let stand for 1 minute so that the chocolate begins to melt. Pulse three or four times, then let rest 1 additional minute. Add the vanilla and pulse three or four more times.

3. Empty into a container. If the ganache's surface appears oily, add the hot water, a few drops at a time, stirring well after each addition. The ganache will thicken as it stands, but should remain pourable. If the sauce fails to thicken, refrigerate it for 4 or 5 minutes.

STORAGE: Ganache may be left at room temperature for several hours, but should be reheated over low heat if being used as a glaze. When ganache is used as a filling for a drop or sandwich cookie, it is best chilled to spreading consistency. It may also be made ahead and stored in the refrigerator in an airtight container for up to 2 weeks or frozen for up to 9 months. To thaw frozen ganache, heat slowly in a water bath or a double boiler or place entire container in a pan of hot water.

applejack glaze

MAKES ENOUGH TO GLAZE ONE 9- X 13- X 2-INCH OBLONG CAKE, A 10-INCH ROUND CAKE, OR 16 TO 18 MUFFINS

Use this snappy glaze for cakes and muffins featuring apples or other spice cakes.

1 cup strained powdered sugar, spooned in and leveled

1 tablespoon boiling water

2 teaspoons applejack, Calvados brandy, or rum

2 teaspoons light corn syrup

Pinch of salt

Combine the powdered sugar, boiling water, liqueur, corn syrup, and salt in a medium bowl. Stir until smooth. (*Note:* If the glaze is made ahead of time, you will have to thin it with a few drops of boiling water. Use the water sparingly; a little goes a long way.)

sugar syrup

MAKES 1 CUP, ENOUGH FOR ONE 10-INCH LAYER, SPLIT INTO 3 DISKS

1 cup water

1/4 cup sugar

2 tablespoons dark rum or orange-flavored liqueur

Place the water and sugar in a small heavy saucepan. Bring to a slow boil and simmer 5 minutes. Off the heat, add the liqueur. Allow to cool slightly before applying to the cake. This may be made in advance. *Rewarm before using.*

quick buttercream frosting

MAKES ABOUT 3 CUPS, ENOUGH TO FILL AND FROST TWO 9-INCH LAYERS; THREE 8-INCH LAYERS; THE TOP AND SIDES OF A 9- X 13- X 2-INCH OBLONG CAKE; OR A 10-INCH TUBE CAKE

I came upon this wonderful buttercream through my friend, Sherry Nashmy, whose grandmother made it for all special family occasions. It is a quick and delicious alternative to a classic buttercream. The consistency is not as refined as that of a traditional buttercream, but is light and fluffy, making it seem less rich.

3 tablespoons all-purpose flour

1 cup milk

1 cup (2 sticks) unsalted butter

1 cup superfine or strained sugar

$1^1/_2$ teaspoons vanilla extract

1. Place the flour in a small saucepan. Whisk in the milk slowly, until the mixture is smooth and free of lumps. Over low heat, stir constantly until mixture comes to a boil and thickens to a thick white sauce.

2. Remove the saucepan from the heat and continue to whisk until the sauce is very smooth. Set aside to cool to tepid, about 5 to 10 minutes. The sauce should not be too warm when it is added to the butter, or the butter will melt. However, do not allow the sauce to become too cold or it will not blend smoothly into the butter/sugar mixture.

3. While the custard is cooling, cut the butter into 1-inch pieces and place it in the large bowl of an electric mixer fitted with the beaters or whip attachment. Soften on low speed, then increase the speed to medium-high and cream until light and smooth, about $1^1/_2$ to 2 minutes.

4. Reduce mixer speed to medium. Gradually add the sugar, 1 tablespoon at a time over 3 minutes. Then add the sauce 1 tablespoon at a time over 30 seconds. Blend in the vanilla and continue to beat for about 20 to 30 seconds or until the frosting is somewhat fluffy.

Quick Chocolate Buttercream Frosting

In a small heatproof container, slowly melt 2 ounces of bittersweet or semisweet chocolate. Cool to tepid. Add to the buttercream just before the vanilla extract in Step 4.

shiny fudge frosting

ENOUGH TO FILL AND FROST TOP AND SIDES OF TWO OR THREE 9-INCH LAYERS

$^1\!/_2$ cup sugar	3 tablespoons unsalted butter, softened
$^1\!/_4$ cup water	2 cups strained confectioners' sugar
2 tablespoons light corn syrup	2 tablespoons very hot water
4 ounces unsweetened chocolate, coarsely chopped	1 teaspoon vanilla extract

1. Combine the sugar, water, and corn syrup in a medium-sized saucepan. Stir briefly, cover, and bring to a slow boil. Brush sides of saucepan occasionally with clear water to prevent crystals from forming. When sugar is completely dissolved, simmer syrup about 3 minutes.

2. Remove the sugar syrup from the heat and add the chocolate all at once, stirring continuously with a metal spoon until the chocolate is dissolved. Beat the butter into the chocolate *mixture, then add the sugar alternately with the hot water, dividing the sugar into two parts and the water into two parts. Blend in the vanilla and beat again until smooth and shiny.*

3. *Set the pan in a shallow saucepan filled with inch to 1 inch hot tap water until ready to use. This frosting tightens quickly, so it must not be prepared too far in advance, and then should be* kept slightly warm to keep it pourable. If icing is still too thick, add a bit more hot water. Do not let the icing become excessively hot, or it will be too fluid.

cream cheese frosting

MAKES ENOUGH FOR ONE 8-INCH SQUARE OR 9- X 5- X 2$^3\!/_4$-INCH LOAF, OR 12 TO 14 MUFFINS (SMALL RECIPE); OR ONE 9-INCH SQUARE OR TWO 8$^1\!/_2$- X 4$^1\!/_2$- X 2$^3\!/_4$-INCH LOAVES, OR 20 MUFFINS (LARGE RECIPE)

This recipe for a classic cream cheese frosting will surely bring back childhood memories. It pairs beautifully with cakes, muffins, and quick breads made with fruits and spices. Use it often and enjoy!

SMALL RECIPE (SCANT 1 CUP)	**LARGE RECIPE** (1$^1\!/_3$ CUPS)
4 ounces cream cheese, cold	6 ounces cream cheese, cold
4 tablespoons unsalted butter, soft	6 tablespoons unsalted butter, soft
1 cup strained powdered sugar	1$^1\!/_2$ cups strained powdered sugar
$^3\!/_4$ teaspoon pure vanilla extract	1 teaspoon pure vanilla extract
$^1\!/_4$ (generous) teaspoon freshly grated navel orange zest	$^1\!/_2$ (generous) teaspoon freshly grated navel orange zest

Combine all the ingredients in the work bowl of a food processor fitted with the steel blade. Pulse 3 to 4 times, then process for 3 to 4 seconds. Stop the processor, scrape down the side of the bowl, and empty into a small bowl. Cover with plastic wrap and refrigerate until ready to use.

STORAGE: Store in the refrigerator for up to 3 days, or freeze in a plastic container for up to 3 months.

warm fudge sauce

MAKES 1½ CUPS

This sauce is a chocolate lover's dream. It is thick and shiny, with a flavor that promises to please.

4 ounces bittersweet chocolate, coarsely chopped

1 ounce unsweetened chocolate, coarsely chopped

³⁄₄ cup heavy cream

1½ teaspoons vanilla extract

½ cup sugar

¼ cup light corn syrup

2 tablespoons unsalted butter

1 teaspoon espresso powder (optional)

1. Place all the ingredients in a medium, heavy saucepan. Bring to a boil over low heat.

2. Reduce the heat and simmer for 8 to 10 minutes, or until the sauce has thickened and is smooth and shiny. This sauce will thicken further as it cools.

STORAGE: Store in the refrigerator in a tightly sealed glass jar. This sauce will keep for 4 to 6 weeks. Reheat before serving.

butterscotch sauce

MAKES 1½ CUPS

The flavor of butterscotch complements most fruit pies and tarts, as well as those made with nuts. If superfine sugar is unavailable, grind granulated sugar in the blender or food processor. This will keep the caramel from being grainy.

¾ cup superfine sugar

3 tablespoons water

3 tablespoons light corn syrup

1½ cups plus 2 tablespoon heavy cream

6 tablespoons unsalted butter

1½ teaspoons vanilla extract

1. Place the sugar, water, and corn syrup in a small, heavy saucepan. Stir gently to combine. Cover the saucepan and bring to a boil over medium-low heat. Check the sugar syrup occasionally to be sure that the sugar on the bottom of the pot has dissolved. If not, gently stir again.

2. When the syrup comes to a boil, uncover the saucepan. Reduce the heat and simmer until the mixture turns golden brown. This can take from 8 to 10 minutes or longer, depending on the weight of the pan. While the sugar syrup is boiling, *brush the side of the pot frequently with cold water* to remove small particles of sugar that may be clinging. Because the syrup burns easily, watch carefully.

3. When the syrup becomes a golden-brown caramel, immediately remove it from the heat and add 1½ cups heavy cream. *Be careful;* the mixture will bubble up when the cream is added. The caramel will immediately harden.

4. Return to low heat and cook, stirring constantly, until the caramel melts and the mixture is smooth. Add the butter and continue to cook for 10 to 20 minutes.

5. When the surface of the sauce has very large bubbles and the mixture thickens, remove the saucepan from the heat and place it in an ice-water bath. Stir occasionally. When the sauce is cool, beat in the remaining 2 tablespoons cream and vanilla.

STORAGE: Store in the refrigerator in a tightly sealed glass jar. This sauce will keep for 4 to 6 weeks. Reheat before serving.

clear lemon filling

MAKES ABOUT 1½ CUPS, ENOUGH TO COVER A 9- OR 10-INCH LAYER OR TWO 8-INCH LAYERS

One of my favorite cake fillings, this is marvelous between layers of plain yellow or white butter cake.

³/₄ cup plus 2 tablespoons sugar

3 tablespoons cornstarch

3 tablespoons unbleached all-purpose flour

³/₄ cup water

¹/₂ cup fresh orange juice

¹/₄ cup fresh lemon juice

2 large egg yolks

1 to 2 tablespoons soft, unsalted butter

1 teaspoon grated lemon rind

1. In a 1½-quart saucepan, combine the sugar, cornstarch, and flour. Using a whisk, stir until thoroughly blended.

2. In a small bowl, combine the water, orange juice, and lemon juice. Gradually add the liquids to the dry ingredients, whisking until smooth. Bring to a gentle boil over low heat, stirring constantly with a wooden spoon. The mixture will be very thick. Simmer on *very low* heat 1 to 2 minutes longer, stirring gently.

3. Place the egg yolks in a small bowl and whisk lightly to blend. Gradually add ¹/₄ of the sauce to yolks, stirring, to temper them. Then whisk the yolk mixture into the saucepan. Cook over low heat until filling comes to a second boil. Be sure to stir into the edges of the saucepan with a wooden spoon to reach any sauce that might cling.

4. Off the heat, blend in the butter and lemon rind. Transfer the filling to a bowl, then butter a small piece of waxed paper and place it greased side down onto the surface of the filling to keep it from filming. Put the filling in the refrigerator for at least ¹/₂ hour or until completely cool. Stir briefly to smooth out before using.

STORAGE: This filling is at its best when used the day it is made.

vanilla pastry cream filling

MAKES ABOUT 1⅓ CUPS, ENOUGH TO COVER A 9- OR 10-INCH LAYER OR TWO 8-INCH LAYERS

This basic vanilla cream filling is lightened with whipped cream. Since it requires refrigeration, it is best used with sponge-style cakes.

1 cup milk	2 tablespoons cornstarch
1(2-inch) piece vanilla bean	1 tablespoon flour
3 large egg yolks	⅓ cup heavy cream
¼ cup sugar	1 teaspoon vanilla extract

1. Put the milk and vanilla bean in a 2-quart saucepan. Over *low* heat, bring to just below the boiling point. Set aside.

2. Place the egg yolks in a small mixing bowl. Gradually add the sugar, whisking until the mixture lightens in color. Blend in the cornstarch and flour.

3. Remove the vanilla bean from the milk and slit it lengthwise with the tip of a paring knife. Scrape the small black beans from inside the pod into the milk. Discard the pod.

4. Whisk ¼ of the milk into the yolk mixture, mixing until smooth. Then add the yolk mixture to the remaining milk. Place over low heat, and continue to stir constantly around the sides of the saucepan with a wooden spoon, until the mixture comes to a gentle boil and is quite thick.

5. Using the whisk, stir the filling briefly just until lumps are removed and the mixture is smooth. Simmer on low heat for 1 minute, stirring occasionally with a wooden spoon. Be sure to scrape the sides. Place the saucepan in a bowl of ice filled with a small amount of water, and cool until *just tepid*. This will only take a few minutes.

6. While the filling is cooling, whip the cream to the soft peak stage. Fold the cream and vanilla extract into the tepid custard, incorporating until smooth.

STORAGE: Cover with a piece of buttered waxed paper or parchment and refrigerate for at least ½ hour. This filling is at its best when used the day it is made.

Praline Cream Filling

Substitute 2 tablespoons praline (see page 380) for the vanilla bean in Step 1, whisking it into the heated milk until smooth. If the praline paste does not readily dissolve, press it frequently against the sides of the saucepan with a spoon to soften. Strain the milk before adding to the yolk mixture to remove lumps. Proceed with the recipe, reducing the vanilla extract to ½ teaspoon.

almond crunch streusel

MAKES ENOUGH FOR ONE 10-INCH ROUND OR 9- X 13- X 2-INCH COFFEE CAKE, OR 12 TO 14 MUFFINS

This crunchy streusel is laced with a sweet, toasted almond crunch—making it absolutely perfect for those who crave nuts in their crumb toppings. In the variation of my Favorite Vanilla Muffins (page 126), it not only crowns the top of the muffin, but enlivens the batter. It can also be used with fruit muffins and coffee cakes.

ALMOND CRUNCH

1 large egg white

1 tablespoon sugar

³/₄ cup unblanched, sliced almonds

STREUSEL

¹/₃ cup (²/₃ stick) unsalted butter

¹/₂ cup all-purpose flour, spooned in and leveled

6 tablespoons sugar

¹/₂ teaspoon ground cinnamon

¹/₂ teaspoon ground cardamom

¹/₄ teaspoon baking powder

¹/₄ teaspoon salt

¹/₄ teaspoon almond extract

MAKE THE ALMOND CRUNCH

1. Position the rack in the lower third of the oven. Heat the oven to 325°. Line a baking sheet with Silpat or Release nonstick aluminum foil. Set aside.

2. Beat the egg white in a small bowl until foamy. Add the sugar and almonds and toss to coat. Spread the almonds on the prepared pan and bake for 10 minutes. Remove from the oven, and using a spatula, turn the almonds over and break up the large pieces as best you can. Bake for another 8 minutes, or until crisp and golden brown. When cool enough to handle, break the nuts into smaller pieces.

MAKE THE ALMOND CRUNCH STREUSEL

3. Place the butter in a heavy-bottomed, 2-quart saucepan and heat until almost melted. Remove from the heat and cool to tepid.

4. Place half of the almond crunch in the work bowl of a food processor fitted with the steel blade. Add the flour, sugar, cinnamon, cardamom, baking powder, salt, and almond extract. Process until the almonds are finely ground and the mixture resembles fine meal. Add to the tepid butter and stir with a fork to combine.

5. Place the remaining almond crunch in a plastic freezer bag, release the air, and secure the top. Break up the nuts into smaller pieces by hitting them 10 times with a rolling pin, or the bottom of a small saucepan. Stir into the streusel.

praline

Praline is not as difficult to make as you may think. It contains two ingredients, sugar and nuts. When sugar is heated, it melts and turns into syrup; the syrup is heated through various stages from the thread stage at 215° to the blackjack stage at 415°. Hundreds of confectionery items are made at different points in between.

This is a classic recipe for praline, in which skinned hazelnuts are added to the sugar syrup at the hard crack stage, a temperature of 300° to 310°. The mixture is quickly turned onto buttered parchment. After it cools, it becomes a brittle candy. You may also use skinned almonds or pecans, but I prefer the distinctive flavor of hazelnuts.

1 cup (4½ ounces) hazelnuts	⅔ cup sugar

1. Toast the hazelnuts in a 300° oven for 12 to 15 minutes or until the skins begin to pop. Remove the nuts from the oven and turn them onto a clean dish towel or several layers of paper toweling. While they are still hot, rub them briskly back and forth to remove their skins. It's OK if a small amount of skin remains.

2. Line a jelly roll pan with parchment and lightly butter the parchment.

3. Put the sugar in a heavy, 10-inch skillet. Heat on a low flame for about 10 to 20 minutes, or until sugar begins to melt around the edges. Sugar heated in a thin, metal skillet will melt faster, but slower cooking in a heavy pan will prevent scorching and ensure better flavor. *Do not stir the sugar.* Swirl the pan as necessary to keep the melted sugar from burning. Brush the sides of the pan with water to remove any sugar crystals. If the sugar in the center of the skillet does not dissolve, stir *briefly.*

4. When the sugar is completely melted and caramel in color, remove the skillet from the heat. Stir in the nuts with a wooden spoon and separate the clusters. Return to low heat and stir to coat the nuts on all sides. Cook until the mixture starts to bubble. Take care when working with the syrup at this point, as it is dangerously hot.

5. Turn the mixture into the parchment-lined jelly roll pan, spreading evenly as best you can. As it cools, it will harden into a brittle.

6. Break the candied nuts into pieces and place them in the container of a food processor. Pulse to a medium-fine crunch. (You can also process until the brittle turns into a powder as a flavoring for desserts, pastries, fillings, and frostings. If you wish to make a nut paste, process for several minutes.)

STORAGE: Store in an airtight container in a cool dry place completely free of humidity. Do not refrigerate.

Sources

A Cook's Wares
211 37th Street
Beaver Falls, PA 15010
www.cookswares.com
800-915-9788
Gourmet foods, such as honey, Lyle's Golden Syrup, pure maple syrup, Nielsen-Massey vanilla, high-quality chocolate, and spices. Baking equipment includes spatulas (straight and offset), Nordic Ware and All-Clad bakeware, springform pans, brioche molds, pastry blenders, cookie sheets, Microplane graters, measuring equipment, and bowls. Catalog available.

Arrowhead Mills
110 South Lawton Avenue
Hereford, TX 79045
www.arrowheadmills.com
806-364-0730
Distributes an extensive line of grain and specialty flours, including whole wheat pastry flour.

Ateco
August Thomsen Corporation
36 Sea Cliff Avenue
Glen Clove, NY 11542
www.atecousa.com
800-645-7170
Carole Walter's personally designed heavy-weight pastry cloth with rolling pin cover, and 12-inch-barrel, solid rock maple, ball-bearing rolling pin.

The Baker's Catalogue
58 Billings Farm Road
White River Junction, VT 05001
www.prm0.net/bakerscatalogue
800-827-6836
High-quality flours, including nut flours, sparkling white sugar and decorating sugar, nuts, dried and candied fruits, crystallized ginger, Key lime juice, pure maple syrup, Nielsen-Massey vanilla, extracts, and oils. High-quality chocolate. Wide range of baking equipment, including cookie cutters, cookie sheets, half and quarter sheet pans, cooking racks, cookie jars, cookie presses, biscotti pans, teaspoon and tablespoon scoops, pastry boards. Silpat mats, measuring equipment, and chocolate dipping fork.

Bridge Kitchenware
563C Eagle Rock Avenue
Roseland, NJ 07068
www.bridgekitchenware.com
973-240-7364
As a chef and restaurant supplier open to the public, Bridge offers a complete line of domestic and imported cookware and bakeware, including decorating equipment, baking accessories, and baking parchment (packaged in sheets) sold in bulk. The company also sells high-quality strainers, Springerle and Speculaas molds, heavy-duty cookie sheets, and rolling pins.

Broadway Panhandler
65 East 8th Street
New York, NY 10003
www.broadwaypanhandler.com
866-266-5927
Varied line of domestic and imported cook- and bakeware, baking accessories, giftware, linens, and serving pieces. No catalog available.

Chef's Catalog
5070 Centennial Boulevard
Colorado Springs, CO 80919
www.chefscatalog.com
800-338-3232
Mail-order catalog that offers "Professional Restaurant Equipment for the Home Chef."

Clay City Pottery
510 East 14th Street
PO Box 79
Clay City, IN 47841
www.claycitypottery.com
800-776-2596
Fifth- and sixth-generation family pottery
business offering traditional stoneware that's
durable and safe for the dishwasher, oven,
and microwave.

Cooktique
9 West Railroad Avenue
Tenafly, New Jersey 07670
www.cooktique.com
201-568-7990
Broad selection of baking pans and baking
accessories, gadgets, cookbooks, cake decorating equipment, quality chocolate and flavorings, praline paste, unusual china, glass and
hand-crafted cake plates, domed cake covers,
and cake service gifts. Catalog available.

Cookware & More
2586 Industry Lane
Trooper, PA 19403
www.cookwarenmore.com
800-272-2170
Discount source for upscale cookware, Kaiser
and Chicago Metallic bakeware, and Wusthof
knives. Brochure available.

Cuisinart
150 Milford Road
East Windsor, NJ 08520
www.cuisinart.com
800-211-9604

Dean & DeLuca
560 Broadway
New York, NY 10012
www.deandeluca.com
800-221-7714
Select baking equipment, praline paste,

premium flavorings, high-quality dried fruits
and nuts, unusual jams and jellies, cocoas
and chocolates. Catalog available.

Ghirardelli Chocolate Manufacturing
1111 139th Avenue
San Leandro, CA 94578
www.ghirardelli.com
800-877-9338
Good-quality domestic chocolates. Catalog
available.

The House on the Hill
650 West Grand Avenue, Unit 110
Elmhurst, IL 60126
www.houseonthehill.net
877-279-4455 (US only)
630-279-4455
Cookie molds, including historic and Springerle and Speculaas molds and cookie cutters.

J.B. Prince and Company
36 East 31st Street
New York, NY 10016
www.jbprince.com
212-683-3553
Sells primarily to the professional trade.
Complete line of imported and domestic
bakeware, tart and tartlet pans, flan rings,
extensive selection of baking accessories and
decorating equipment. Catalog available.

KitchenAid
PO Box 218
St. Joseph, MI 49085
www.kitchenaid.com
800-541-6390

La Cuisine
323 Cameron Street
Alexandria, VA 22314
www.lacuisineus.com
800-521-1176
Offers an extensive line of high-quality
baking equipment, maple pastry boards,

rolling pins, imported wooden spoons and spatulas, cookie presses, decorating equipment and baking accessories, including Springerle and Speculaas molds, extensive line of cookie cutters. Imported and domestic cookie sheets, jelly roll pans, Silpat mats. Catalog available.

Lindt Chocolate
www.lindtusa.com
877-695-4638
Premium chocolate for baking.

Maison Glass, Inc.
PO Box 317-H
Scarsdale, NY 10583
www.maisonglass.com
800-822-5564
Professional-quality baking supplies, including premium dried and glace fruits (available year-round), nuts, high-quality nut pastes, and bulk chocolate. Catalog available.

The Nestlé Co, Inc.
383 Main Avenue
Norwalk, CT 06851
www.nestle.com
203-750-7230
Excellent-quality domestic chocolates, Burgundy dark chocolate especially recommended. Sold in bulk. No catalog.

New York Cake and Baking Distributors
56 West 22nd Street
New York, NY 10010
www.nycake.com
800-942-2539
212-675-2253
Specialty baking pans, cookie packaging supplies, cookie sheets, large selection of cookie and canape cutters, cake boxes, and cake rounds, as well as an extensive line of decorating equipment. Rolling pins, Silpat

mats, dipping forks, small cupcake liners. Stocks bulk chocolate. Catalog available.

Salmon Falls Stoneware
Box 452
Dover, NH 03820
www.salmonfalls.com
800-621-2030
Traditional salt-glazed pottery specializing in bakeware that's safe for the dishwasher, oven, and microwave.

Sur La Table
84 Pine Street
Seattle, WA 98101
www.surlatable.com
800-243-0852
An upscale kitchen shop with a complete line of specialty baking pans and accessories, as well as rolling pins, cookie sheets, cookie presses, Springerle molds, cookie cutters, decorating equipment, cookware, kitchen gadgets, small appliances, candy-making supplies, and gift items. Catalog available.

White Lily Flour Company
218 East Depot Avenue
Knoxville, TN 37917
www.whitelily.com
865-546-7736
High-quality flours for baking.

Williams-Sonoma
Corporate Headquarters
3250 Van Hess Ave
San Francisco, CA 94109
www.williams-sonoma.com
800-541-2233
"A Catalog for Cooks" features upscale, cutting-edge equipment, baking accessories, and giftware. Cookie sheets, cookie cutters, cookie presses, decorating sugars, icing pens, candy cups, novelty gift boxes, and custom-

ized paper for packaging cookies. Also a good source for Nielsen-Massey vanilla and premium chocolate for baking. Many items are available through the catalog only.

Zabar's
249 West 80th Street
New York, NY 10024
www.zabars.com
800-697-6301
Large selection of baking pans and accessories, small appliances, coffee beans, high-quality specialty foods. Catalog available.

Credits

Illustrations by Laura Hartman Maestro (pages 271, 334, 366, and 367); Meredith Hamilton (pages 191, 195, and 205); and Rodica Prato (pages 155, 360, 361, 362, 363, 364, and 365)

Pie Photographs by Gentyl & Hyers (page 153)

Recipe Photographs by Mitch Mandel/ Rodale Images:
Banana Cream Pie with Pecan Brittle (page 174); Blueberry Crumb Pie with Warm Blueberry Sauce (page 156); Boston Cream Pie (page 320); Carole's Best Brownies (page 36); Carrot Honey Cake (page 234); Chocolate Marble Cheesecake (page 342); Coconut Layer Cake (page 312); Double-Header Pear Cobbler (page 148); Fluted Cream Cheese Flan with Fresh Berries (page 178); French Jelly Roll (page 296); Fruit and Nut Applesauce Cake (page 232); Jeweled Almond Biscotti (page 120); Lemon Meringue Pie (page 170); Majestic Mandarin Cake (page 328); Manhattan Cheesecake (page 332); Peppermint Cloud (page 308); Pignoli Lemon Cake (page 260); Pineapple Upside-Down Cake (page 280); Shaved Chocolate and Pistachio Biscotti (page 122); Snow-Capped Chocolate Cream Cake (page 258); Southern Pecan Pie (page 168); Sticky Buns (page 200); Three Berry Crisp with Butter-Nut Crumb Topping (page 142); and Zucchini Loaf with Apricots and Dates (page 244)

Recipe Photographs by Duane Winfield:
Almondates (page 16); Broken and Chopped Nuts (pages 256-257); Carole's Really Great Chocolate Chip Cookies (page 2); Chocolate Shortbread Nuggets (page 92); Chocolate Snowcaps (page 17); Classic Sour Cream Cinnamon and Nut Coffee Cake (page 222); Coconut Lemon-Lime Tassies (page 89); Coconut-Crusted Key Lime Napoleons (page 60); Crackly Cinnamon Wafers (page 28); Crispy Gingersnaps (page 24); Crumb Buns (page 186); Favorite Lemon Squares (page 58); Favorite Vanilla Muffins (page 126); Florentines (page 62); French Lace What-Nots (page 84); Grandma Jennie's Date and Nut Bread (page 240); Jeff's Chocolate-Glazed Midnight Muffins (page 136); Lemon Poppy Seed Shortbread (page 94); Minna's Apricot Squares (page 56); Old-Fashioned Buttermilk Biscuits (page 98); Peanut Butter Balls (page 15); Poppy Seed Thumbprints (page 30); Rocky Road Garganchewas (page 4); Rustic Cinnamon Walnut Horns (page 194); Scalloped Chocolate Pecan Strip (page 198); Sesame Coins (page 29); Sour Cream Marble Cake (page 228); Ultra-Rich Corn Muffins (page 130); Zach's Blueberry Buttermilk Muffins with Streusel Topping (page 138); and Zach's Chocolate Coconut Devils (page 18)

Index

Underscored page references indicate boxed text. An asterisk (*) indicates recipe photos are shown in the color inserts.

L

Lemons
Clear Lemon Filling, 377
Coconut Lemon-Lime Tassies,*
89
Favorite Lemon Squares,*
58–59
Glazed Lemon–Pine Nut
Biscotti, 124–25
Golden Citrus Chiffon Cake,
300–301
Holiday Stollen, 192–93
Lemon Cream Cheese Pound
Cake, 218–19
Lemon Glaze, 368
Lemon Meringue Pie,* 170–71
Lemon Poppy Seed Short-
bread,* 94–95
Lemon Roulade, 294–95
Pignoli Lemon Cake,* 260–61
Poppy Seed Lemon Cream
Cheese Pound Cake, 219
Starmount Sponge Cake,
288–89
Limes
Coconut-Crusted Key Lime
Napoleons,* 60–61
Coconut Lemon-Lime Tassies,*
89
Lime Glaze, 368
Liqueurs, 351
Lyle's Golden Syrup, 351–52

M

Macadamia nuts
Crystallized Ginger and Maca-
damia Wafers, 25
Stephen Schmidt's White
Chocolate Macadamia Bars,
40–41
White Chocolate Chunk Maca-
damia Cookies, 10
Mangoes
Black and Blue Mango Pie,
160–61
choosing, 357

cutting, slicing, and dicing,
357–58
ripening, 357
Maple syrup
Candied Maple Walnut Pancake
Loaf, 246–47
Maple Pecan Apple Crisp, 143
Maple Walnut Cake, 264–65
Rustic Maple Pecan Cookies,
32
Rustic Maple Pecan Date Cook-
ies, 32
Marshmallows
Rocky Road Garganchewas,*
4–5
Meringue, preparing, 171
Mint
Black-Bottom Mint Cheesecake,
344–45
Peppermint Cloud,* 308
Triple Chocolate Peppermint
Bars, 46–47
Molasses
Golden Apple Upside-Down
Gingerbread Cake, 236–37
Joanna Pruess's Molasses Spice
Cookies, 22
Muffins
Almond Crunch Muffins,
127
Blueberry Corn Muffins, 131
Cape Cod Cranberry Muffins,
128
Chocolate Chunk Vanilla Muf-
fins, 127
Favorite Vanilla Muffins,*
126–27
Jeff's Chocolate-Glazed Mid-
night Muffins,* 136–37
muffin batter, refrigerating,
137
Oatmeal Raisin Muffins, 129
Peanut Butter Banana Muffins,
134–35
Raspberry Buttermilk Muffins
with Streusel Topping, 139
Sam's Oodles of Apple Muffins
with Country Crumb Top-
ping, 132–33

Ultra-Rich Corn Muffins,* 130
Zach's Blueberry Buttermilk
Muffins with Streusel Top-
ping,* 138–39

N

Nectarines
Nectarine Cake, 277
Nuts. *See also* Almonds; Peanuts;
Pecans; Walnuts
chopping, 356–57
Crystallized Ginger and Maca-
damia Wafers, 25
Fruity Viennese Linzer Tart,
176–77
Glazed Lemon–Pine Nut
Biscotti, 124–25
Hazelnut Blitz Torte with Pra-
line Cream Filling, 325–27
Nut Brittle, 175
Pignoli Lemon Cake,* 260–61
Praline, 379
Praline Cream Filling, 378
Praline Crunch Cake, 262–63
Sally's Deep 'n Dark Frosted
Brownies, 38–39
Shaved Chocolate and Pistachio
Biscotti,* 122–23
Stephen Schmidt's White
Chocolate Macadamia Bars,
40–41
toasting, 356
White Chocolate Chunk Maca-
damia Cookies, 10

O

Oats
Autumn Fruit Crumble with
Oatmeal Crunch Topping,
150–51
Chock Full of Crunchies, 12
Chocolate Chip Oatmeal Cook-
ies, 6
Chocolate Chip Oatmeal
Crispies, 7